KT-466-339

Jancis Robinson's wine course

JANCIS
ROBINSON'S
WINE COURSE

TED SMART

Published by BBC Worldwide Ltd, Woodlands, 80 Wood Lane, London W12 0TT

This edition produced for
The Book People Ltd, Hall Wood Avenue, Haydock, St Helens WA11 9UL

First published in 1995
Reprinted 1995 (six times), 1996, 1997 (twice)
Second edition (paperback) published in 1999
This third edition published 2003

© Jancis Robinson 1995, 1999, 2003

The moral right of the author has been asserted. All rights reserved. No part of this
book may be reproduced in any form or by any means without permission in writing
from the publisher, except by a reviewer, who may quote brief passages in a review.

ISBN 0 563 48796 9

Designer: Judith Robertson
Cartographer: Eugene Fleury
Illustrators: Neil Tully and Alicia Durdos
Picture researcher: Nadine Bazar and Claire Parker
Production controller: Christopher Tinker

Set in Goudy
Printed and bound in Singapore by Tien Wah Press
Colour separations by Radstock Reproductions Ltd, Midsomer Norton

CAPTIONS

PAGE 2 Verdicchio dei Castelli de Jesi
vineyards in the Marche, Central Italy.

PAGE 3 Italian grapes being dried for Vin
Santo, Tuscany's sweet wine speciality.

PAGE 6 Top: Fermentation tanks at
Bulgaria's Sliven winery.

Bottom: Liquid gold from California,
made from botrytized Semillon grapes.

PAGE 7 The basics of winemaking are
taught in a nursery school in Umbria,
Central Italy.

PAGES 10–11 Tasting Chardonnays in
the Hunter Valley, New South Wales,
Australia.

PAGES 58–9 Bottles of pale pink sparkling
Saumur are upended to lose the all-
important yeast deposit.

PAGES 94–5 Cabernet Sauvignon grapes at
the Ornellaia estate in Tuscany.

PAGES 154–5 Spring mustard, a vineyard
cover crop, flowering in Carneros in
California.

For Julia and Rose
may they never lack confidence

This book was originally conceived as an accompaniment to the award-winning 1995 BBC television series of the same name but I have been delighted to see it develop its own identity.

I have been amazed by the number of people who have adopted it as their one book on wine, a complete introduction that combines solid, practical, accessible advice on how to taste, buy and store it with all the basics of how it is made and grown, and how and why different wines taste so different.

This is why there is a need for this completely new edition. The world of wine has been changing so extraordinarily fast. To bring this book up to date I have had to make changes to the great majority of pages and have also dramatically extended the World of Wine section at the back to include increased coverage of Italy, Spain, Portugal and most of the New World, as well as bringing the Vintage Guide and all those little details at the back of the book completely up to date.

Throughout the process of updating I have been helped enormously by Julia Zimmermann, Rachel Copus and Nicky Copeland of BBC Books, proofreader Steve Dobell and by designer Judith Robertson – as well as, as ever, by my literary agent Caradoc King.

I hope you will enjoy this book and that it will help you to enjoy the wonderful drink that is wine even more.

The people to whom I owe most of all are my ever more astounding
family, particularly William and, of course, Nick.

Contents

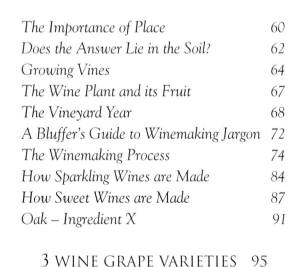

4 THE WORLD OF WINE 155

INTRODUCTION

The point of wine is to give pleasure, as much of it to as many people as possible. Anyone who suggests otherwise – that wine appreciation is a difficult business which only a very special élite are worthy and capable of, for example – should be treated with scorn. In my experience, anyone who claims to be a wine expert invariably has little to offer except prejudices.

Wine is emphatically not a serious subject. Wine is one of life's perks, an indulgence, a mood-lifter, a social mixer. It's just that understanding a bit more about it brings the confidence to relax and enjoy it.

Although wine is clearly much more than mere lubrication, to appreciate it, all you need is an interest and a sense of smell. This book explains that by taking you from the glass in your hand, back along the supply line, making sense of tasting, serving, choosing and buying wine (Getting the Most Out of Wine pages 11–57), to How Wine is Made (pages 59–93) before embarking on two important and parallel guides to help make sense out of the thousands of wines available: Wine Grape Varieties on pages 95–153 and The World of Wine on pages 155–336.

From the outside, the world of wine looks horribly complicated. Wine's great attribute, its variety, is also one of its drawbacks. Wine lists in restaurants and rows of bottles on a shelf can seem like an impenetrable jungle of proper names in foreign languages.

But help is at hand. Learning about wine has become a great deal easier over the last few years as more and more wine producers are putting the names of the main grapes from which their wines are made on labels, either the main label or an explanatory one on the back of the bottle. Classicists deplore this trend, arguing that wine should be an expression of place

---

A FEW INSIDER TIPS TO SET YOU ON YOUR WAY:

Wine amateurs may say...	**But professional winos say...**
Opener	Corkscrew
Crate (of wine)	Case (= 12 bottles)
Drink (active verb)	Taste
Champagne (for all fizzy wine)	Sparkling wine (for all fizzy wine except that made in the Champagne region in north east France)

Wine amateurs may think:	**But professional winos know:**
Sediment in a bottle is a bad sign	It's a sign of a producer who worships quality above cosmetics
Claret is any old red	Claret is a word used in Britain exclusively for red bordeaux
Zinfandel is white	Zinfandel's a red grape that no one wanted so someone cleverly began to make a very commercial off dry white out of it in California in the 1980s

rather than grape variety and that only wines labelled geographically with no mention of grape varieties are 'real' wines.

With respect, as they say, I think this is rubbish. Of course the perfect wine is an expression of the exact slope of the vineyard, its latitude, altitude, soil texture (though not, as is commonly thought, soil composition) and so on, but that's the second stage in wine appreciation (and how many wines demonstrate their provenance so clearly that any experienced blind taster can immediately locate the village in which they were made?). The first stage, the main factor shaping the characteristics of most wines in commercial circulation, is the grape variety or varieties used. And the pathways through that supposedly impenetrable jungle are to a large extent the result of recognizing the relationships between, say, different Chardonnays from around the world – all of which in any case also carry some geographical clues that help us make up a picture of the world of wine and its influences on grape varieties so that eventually we reach the second stage by accumulating an impression of, for example, California's Alexander Valley or Meursault in Burgundy.

So the great thing is that to learn about wine today, you don't need to learn hundreds of different foreign place-names. All you need to begin with are about seven names, those of the main grape varieties from which a sizeable proportion of wines you are likely to come across are made: Chardonnay, Sauvignon Blanc and poor, undervalued Riesling for whites and Cabernet Sauvignon, Merlot, Pinot Noir and Syrah (or Shiraz) for reds.

Wine Grape Varieties provides a detailed guide to these seven varieties as well as a great deal of information about hundreds more varieties, those that are now mentioned more and more on labels as producers increasingly experiment, and become more conscious of consumers' needs in their labelling. Here and throughout the book I have tried to explain the most important thing – how wines are likely to taste.

The World of Wine takes you on a detailed tour of those corners of the globe where wine is produced, highlighting what makes them different and, of course, which grape varieties are grown there, and explaining not just how things are but giving the real explanation (not necessarily the same as the public relations pitch) of why they are that way.

As a subject for study, wine happens to come with an amazing amount of baggage, which we can choose to revel in or ignore. Its history stretches back past the Bronze Age, to at least 5500 years ago. Its geography encompasses all of the world's temperate zones (and quite a few of the tropical ones too). The wine business is conducted in some of the most beautiful corners of the world, and its personalities are some of the most colourful in any field of commercial activity. Wine is rich in religious symbolism, and has the unusual attribute of being able to last and evolve for centuries, providing a direct, tastable link with past generations. Yet today, wine production is a scientifically sophisticated business that is unusually open about what in many other businesses would be its secrets.

This book, which has been a seriously exciting project for me, aims to give you an insider's view of the world of wine. As I became involved in planning and then began writing, I realized not just how rapidly the world of wine is changing, but how much less ignorant (I would certainly not say more knowledgeable) I am now – partly thanks to editing *The Oxford Companion to Wine* – and how much more insider information and advice I want to communicate. My hope is that in some small way this book will help its readers to get even more pleasure out of wine.

1
GETTING THE MOST OUT OF WINE

THE TRUE SENSE OF TASTE

As far as I'm concerned, the enjoyment of wine has to begin with the glass in your hand. Swotting up on wine geography and vintage ratings is an optional extra and comes a very long way down the line from working out how every single drop of wine can give as much pleasure as possible.

I often wonder what proportion of all the wine that is consumed in the world today actually manages to deliver all the messages it is capable of, and how much is just thrown down the gullet without a thought or even a sniff. It is very difficult to over-estimate the sensitivity of the nose as a tasting instrument, and if I could give just one piece of advice to any newcomer to wine, it would be: *don't forget your sense of smell*.

You have only to think of how food, even quite strongly flavoured food, tastes dull when you have a nose blocked by a head cold to realize what an important role the sense of smell plays in what we call taste. Tasting something involves persuading it to release molecules which stimulate special nerve cells in the mouth or the much more discriminating ones in the nose. In fact we can sense flavour only as an aroma because our flavour-sensitive nerve cells are concentrated in a small, postage-stamp-sized area at the top of the nose

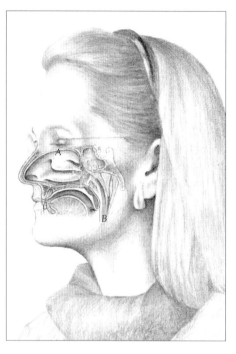

We each have an olfactory area (A) at the top of our noses where millions of nerve cells react to volatile molecules bearing flavour messages to the brain. These messages are merged and sorted into patterns which may be recognized and identified by the brain. Vapour also reaches the olfactory area from the back of the mouth up the retro-nasal passage (B).

called the olfactory area, which transmits specific messages to the brain, and the only way of getting molecules up there is as a vapour given off by a liquid. (This is why hot food always seems to be so much more smelly than cold food – the vapour that it gives off transports flavour-packed molecules up the nose.)

To be able to experience the flavour of a liquid such as wine to the full, therefore, molecules should be encouraged to escape the wine's surface by swirling the wine around before the taster takes a deliberate sniff. Doing this before each mouthful of wine may feel rather pretentious at first, but makes simple good sense. If wine has anything to offer other than the alcohol you can find in vodka or beer, it is the extraordinary range of flavours available not just in a single bottle, but in individual glasses of wine as they change under the influence of oxygen. Since man and nature went to so much trouble to put them there, it really does make sense to smell a wine every time before you taste it. This ensures not only that you get maximum value out of every wine you buy, but also slows down the consumption rate – which is useful for both body and bank balance.

At this point many wine drinkers may be puzzled. They will reckon they already have a pretty good grasp of wine flavours, without ever having consciously sniffed (or 'nosed', as professional wine-tasting parlance has it) a glass in their lives. This is partly because wine naturally vaporizes quite easily, and some wines such as those made from Sauvignon Blanc and Riesling grapes are inherently quite aromatic so their molecules need very little encouragement to float up the nose of the drinker. It is also, however, because of the retro-nasal passage (see B on the diagram opposite) which allows some flavour molecules to reach the olfactory area directly from the back of the mouth, without any conscious effort.

This is how most foods are 'tasted'. Food is chewed in the mouth, transforming it into a liquid from which flavour molecules ecape up the retro-nasal passage to reach the olfactory area – although many food professionals take just as much trouble to smell different ingredients and dishes before consuming them as wine tasters do.

But what of all those nerve cells in the mouth? These also have an important, but quite different role to play in the business of tasting, and are what we call taste buds – about 10 000 of them distributed all over the tongue and, to a much lesser extent, the inside of the mouth, with a few at the back of the throat. Rather than distinguishing between thousands of different flavours the way that the olfactory nerve cells can, taste buds are sensitive to nothing more sophisticated than the basic 'tastes': sourness or acidity, sweetness,

HUMAN VARIATION

Almost anyone can be a wine taster; all it takes is a will and a nose. We vary from person to person not just in terms of the compounds we're particularly sensitive to, and the strength of those sensitivities, but also in our physical make-up. A small minority, sometimes called anosmics, have a poor, defective or damaged sense of smell – either from birth, or as the result of hormonal upsets, head injury, radiation therapy or, most commonly, advancing years. Smell and taste nerve cells may be the only cells in the nervous system that are replaced when they become old or damaged, but the human sense of smell still tends to be most accurate between the ages of 30 (when we have sufficient understanding and experience to interpret what our nerve cells tell us) and 60 (when the messages tend to start to become fainter). Different animals have different smelling and tasting abilities; whereas the human has quite a small part of the brain devoted to interpreting messages from the nose area, a dogfish has a very large one.
Dogfish would make great wine tasters.

bitterness, and saltiness (some posit a fifth taste, umami). We all vary enormously in the distribution and concentration of our taste buds and as a result there is a certain amount of disagreement about exactly how they function but, in very general terms, the taste buds around the tip of the tongue are most likely to be sensitive to sweetness; those on the upper edges of the tongue may well tingle most obviously at sourness; the flat back of the tongue is usually most sensitive to bitterness; and the front edges are most often particularly susceptible to saltiness.

Wine contains three more components that can also have an effect on the inside of the mouth. Tannin (see page 73) is a red wine preservative that comes from the grape skins, pips and (sometimes) stems, and has the same effect (tanning, as in leather) on the inside of the cheeks as it does when encountered in very well-stewed tea. Some tannins can also be bitter to taste. Alcohol (see page 72), quite apart from giving an impression of sweetness, has its own, often delightful, effect on our nervous system, but wines that are particularly high in alcohol can leave a 'hot' sensation on the palate after they have been swallowed. And many wines contain a perceptible amount of gassy carbon dioxide (see page 72), which has a physical effect that can vary from a gentle prickle in the mouth to an uncomfortably overwhelming froth.

HOW TO TASTE WINE

All you need is a glass (see pages 26–7) and a moment's attention. A lot of unnecessary fuss is made about extraneous smells (taking that argument to its logical conclusion we'd never serve food with wine) and about the condition of the palate. The handful of seriously distracting foods is considered on page 34, but a mouthful of water or neutral food such as bread is enough to neutralize the palate after all but the fiercest chilli. A more serious enemy to wine is toothpaste; many's the glass of champagne that has been wasted because of toothbrushing immediately before drinking it. Non-minty mouthwashes can freshen the palate without immobilizing it.

Step 1 Looking at a wine is the least important (and least pleasurable) part of wine tasting – although it can be immensely useful to someone trying to guess the identity of a mystery wine.

Tilting the glass away from you, preferably against a white background, exposes the different shades of colour (the more the better), especially at the rim where the age of a wine tends to show. The browner a wine the older it usually is. Red wines tend to go from deep purple to pale tawny, while whites go from pale greenish yellow to deep gold (see photographs on page 43). The best wines usually have a luscious sheen to them, while commercial, heavily treated ones can look dull and monochrome.

Some wine professionals hold the glass by the base, but using the stem is much easier and keeps wine equally unaffected by body heat.

Step 2 The importance of smelling the wine is outlined on pages 12–13. Since a wine's flavour molecules are given off only on the liquid's surface, they can be seriously encouraged by maximizing the wine's surface area, by swirling the wine round in a glass, ideally one with a stem so that a graceful movement which has no effect on the wine's temperature can be achieved, and preferably no more than half-full so that no wine is spilt. The ideal wine glass goes in towards the rim so that swirled wine tends to stay in the glass and so does the heady vapour above it. Just one short sniff while you concen-

trate is enough. Notice whether the smell is clean and attractive (if not, either reject the wine as on page 54, or deliberately avoid smelling it!); how intense the smell is; and what the smell reminds you of. Grapes contain thousands of compounds, many of which are also found in other familiar substances. Furthermore, the processes of fermentation and maturation can add their own layers of flavour as different compounds react with each other. It is not surprising, therefore, that words are poor describers of something as subtle, subjective and private as smell perceptions. The best we can do to describe the smell, or flavour, of a wine is list those things of which it reminds us (see page 17), but there may be many thousands of other substances in wine which have no direct counterpart elsewhere, or which are too obscure to have their own name. Flavour compounds – the monoterpenes found in florally aromatic grapes and the grassy methoxypyrazine found in

Sauvignon Blanc and Cabernet Sauvignon, for example – are being energetically researched by the wine industry and may even eventually be created artificially and added to cheaper wines.

Step 3 Take a mouthful of wine and try to ensure that all of the palate, or at least all of the tongue, is exposed to the liquid, the better to gauge the dimensions that can be sensed in the mouth. Notice how sweet, sour/acid, bitter, tannic/astringent, alcoholic and gassy the wine is, as explained on pages 12–13. Try to gauge the **body** of the wine (see page 16) i.e. how unlike water it is. It also helps draw vapour up the retro-nasal passage if you take a little air into the mouth at the same time (which is the reason why all professional wine tasters sound so disgusting).

Try also to note a wine's overall impact on the inside of the mouth. Some people use the term 'mouth feel' for sensations of varying intensity which may be rasping, gripping or satin smooth. Then comes the great divide between tasting for work or play: workers (who may taste 100 wines a day) spit, while players swallow.

Step 4 Now is the moment to assess the wine as a whole. Were the dimensions of sweetness, acidity, alcohol and the possible elements of bitterness, tannin and gassiness in **balance**, or was one of them obtrusive? In young red wines, for example, tannin often dominates, while young whites are often very acid. This lack of balance would be a fault in an older wine. Was the sweetness counterbalanced by acidity or did it taste sickly? The other great indicator of quality is **length** – how long did the impact of the wine last after you swallowed it? A mediocre wine may leave no trace on the palate or in the olfactory area at all, but a fine wine can still continue to reverberate for 30 seconds or more after it has been swallowed.

SOME TASTING EXERCISES

- *Put a clothes-peg or diving clip on your nose, and see whether you can tell black coffee from black tea. Blindfold as well, you probably couldn't tell milk chocolate from cheddar cheese. All of this demonstrates just how important the nose is in identifying flavour.*

- *To work out how your palate reacts to* **acidity**, *smell and then taste lemon juice or vinegar. It takes only a smell to make the sides of my tongue start to crinkle up, but different tasters react differently.*

- *To identify tannin in wine, rinse a mouthful of cold black tea round your palate and notice which* parts of your mouth react most dramatically. The insides of my cheeks pucker up. (Notice how you can't smell tannin, or sugar, however.)

- *To get some idea of body as it relates to wine, notice the difference in palate impact between a light bodied Mosel (German wine in a tall green bottle) with an alcohol content of less than 10 per cent and a full-bodied Chardonnay or white Rhône wine with an alcohol content of more than 13 per cent. Notice in particular how unlike water the latter is, and how it may leave a hot, sweet sensation on the palate (alcohol often tastes sweet).*

TASTING TERMS

The following list includes terms used, often with a delightful lack of precision, in connection with both the **dimensions** of wine and tasting itself. 'B' for 'Bad' indicates critical descriptive terms, 'G' for 'Good' is used in praise. See the aroma wheel opposite for terms used to describe actual **flavours**. See pages 72–3 for any technical terms missing from here.

Acetaldehyde, compound formed when alcohol is exposed to air. Marginally present in all wines but ideally noticeable only in flor sherries (see page 234).

Acetic, VOLATILE acid. Often found in cool-fermented whites, but a fault when excessive.

After-taste, strictly the flavour(s) left after the wine is swallowed. See FINISH.

Aroma describes a simple, often fruity smell or flavour present in young wine. See BOUQUET.

Astringent, critical term usually used for relatively TANNIC white wines. (B)

Balanced, a wine in which all dimensions – acidity, sweetness, tannins, alcohol – make a harmonious whole. (G)

Blind tasting, an attempt to identify and/or assess wines without knowing their identity. Bottles, not humans, are masked.

Body, important characteristic of a wine determined chiefly by its alcoholic strength (see pages 36–7) but also by its EXTRACT. The more body a wine has the less like water it tastes.

Bottle age, the mellowing effect of years spent inside a bottle.

Bouquet, the complex and multi-layered smells or flavours which develop as a result of ageing. See AROMA.

Chewy, some but not obtrusive tannins.

Closed, not very smelly, assumed because of its stage of maturity.

Concentrated, good EXTRACT and/or intense flavour(s). (G)

Corked, wine that has been spoilt and smells off-puttingly mouldy because the cork is tainted. See page 18. (very B)

Crisp, perceptible acidity. (G)

Dried out, old wine in which the initial FRUIT has faded diminishing flavour and EXTRACT. (B)

Dumb, not smelly.

Esters, compounds formed by acids and alcohols either during fermentation or ageing, often intensely aromatic (' polish remover smells strongly **esterified**).

Extract, an important dimension, the sum of a wine's solids, includes phenolics (see page 73), sugars, minerals and GLYCEROL; i.e. what would be left after boiling.

Finish, the sensory impact of a wine after it has been swallowed (or spat). Wines can be said to have a LONG or SHORT finish.

Firm, tannins perceptible. (G)

Flabby, too low in acid. (B)

Flavour, is really AROMA.

Forward, having aged more rapidly than expected.

Fresh, attractively acid. (G)

Fruit is the youthful combination of flavour (AROMA) and BODY coming from the grapes rather than winemaking or ageing.

Fruity is used either to describe wines with good FRUIT or, often in white wine marketing speak, as a euphemism for slightly sweet.

Full, or **Full-bodied,** wine with considerable BODY.

Glycerol, colourless, natural, sweet-tasting substance which can add to the impression of BODY.

Green, too acid. (B)

Hard, too TANNIC. (B)

Hollow, lacking FRUIT. (B)

Horizontal tasting, comparative tasting of different but related representatives of the same year.

Hot, too alcoholic. (B)

Lean, lacking FRUIT but not acid. (B)

Legs, see TEARS.

Length, persistence of the tasting experience in olfactory area and mouth after swallowing. Such a wine may be called **long**. (G)

Lift(ed), wine with perceptible but not excessive VOLATILITY.

Light, or **Light bodied,** with relatively little BODY.

Mature, probably aged to its full potential. (G)

Mellow, sometimes used for reds as a euphemism for sweet.

Middle palate, jargon for the over-all impact of a wine in the mouth, as in 'There's not much FRUIT on the middle palate'.

Mouth feel, the physical impact of a wine on the mouth, its texture. Tannins and BODY surely play a role here.

Nose, used as both noun and verb, as in 'It's a bit DUMB on the nose' and 'Have you **nosed** this one?'

Oxidized, harmfully exposed to oxygen. See page 73. (B)

Powerful, high level of alcohol or EXTRACT. (G in this competitive day and age.)

Rich, with some apparent sweetness; curiously, much more complimentary than 'sweet'. (G)

Round, good BODY and not too much tannin. (G)

Short, opposite of LONG. (B)

Soft, not much tannin.

Spritz(ig), slightly gassy.

Supple, not too TANNIC. (G)

Tannic, aggressive tannins (see page 73). All young red wines destined for ageing are expected to have some tannins, but these should ideally be counterbalanced by FRUIT. (B)

Tart, very acid. (B)

Tears, the colourless streams left on the inside of a glass after a relatively alcoholic wine has been swirled. They have nothing to do with GLYCEROL.

Vertical tasting, a comparative tasting of different vintages from the same provenance.

Volatile, a wine with such a high level of volatile, not particularly stable, acids that it smells almost vinegary. (B)

AROMA WHEEL

Everyone has their own battery of 'tastes like' terms for flavour (i.e. aroma) terms. The following is my own personal adaptation of a ground-breaking graphic which was devised by Professor Ann C. Noble and her colleagues at the University of California at Davis in an attempt to instil some rigour into the use of tasting terms. It may help develop your own tasting vocabulary.

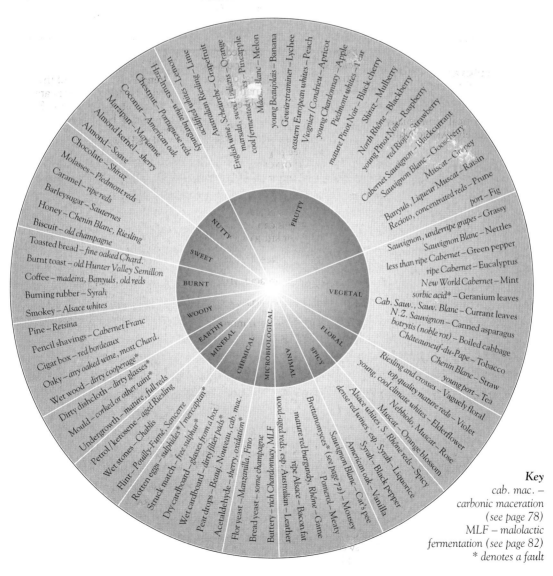

Key
*cab. mac. –
carbonic maceration
(see page 78)
MLF – malolactic
fermentation (see page 82)
* denotes a fault*

BECOMING A WINE TASTER

I believe that anyone with a sense of smell and an interest in wine can become a wine taster, and that it takes hardly any time at all. I am bolstered in this belief by years of listening to professionals trying to describe the same wines and doing it with completely different and even contradictory words. In practice, applying words to wine is a complete free-for-all.

No one other than you can ever know exactly how a wine strikes your senses. When it comes to wine tasting there are no absolutes. And so the opinion of the novice is every bit as valuable as that of the expert. The only difference is that the expert has been allowed to gain self-confidence, so we propound our theories rather more loudly than most newcomers.

In fact I often find that novice tasters are much better at coming up with the perfect word to describe a wine flavour than us professionals who used up our tasting vocabulary years ago. (Débutants can even be better at blind tasting than professionals, partly because they have tasted fewer confusing exceptions to the rule, and also because less is expected of them.)

Wine tasting is the definitive subjective sport. Once you have consciously tasted a few wines, you can build on that experience by starting to notice the common characteristics of the wines you like. Putting that together with the profiles of different grape varieties (in most cases the dominant factor in shaping how a wine tastes) in Section 3 and the chart on page 53 should help you pick out the sorts of wine that happen to appeal to your palate.

A FEW CLUES FROM TASTING

See the aroma wheel on page 17 for clues from specific flavours.

General
• Colourless streams after swirling – high alcohol and therefore very rich grapes which means either a hot climate or else an exceptionally hot summer in a cooler region).
• Slight fizz – could be a New World wine that is naturally slightly low in acidity and has been pepped up by retaining a bit of carbon dioxide in solution. If a supposedly still wine is visibly foaming at the edge this could be a second fermentation in bottle – a fault.

Reds
• Deep colour – warm summer, Cabernet, Syrah/Shiraz, Nebbiolo, or long maceration.
• Pale – cool climate, Beaujolais, Pinot Noir.
• Purple – young.
• Brick rim – old.

Whites
• Light body – cool climate or very high yields, German if aromatic to boot.
• Full body, pale colour – barrel fermentation?
• Brownish tinge – old, oxidized or barrel matured after protective winemaking.

And if the wine smells plain horrid…
• Wines that have been affected by a tainted cork smell off-puttingly mouldy and are described as **corked**. The longer the wine is exposed to the air, the stronger the smell gets, and the wine usually tastes rather nasty and unfruity too. The only thing worth doing with a corked wine is to return it to the supplier, who should provide a substitute. Cork moulds develop because cork processing plants, most of them in Portugal, are still relatively unsophisticated. The incidence of this sort of taint seems to have been increasing (perhaps partly because consumers are increasingly knowledgeable) and is currently put at between one bottle in 15 and one in 50. This wide disparity is because, as with all compounds, we vary in our sensitivity to corkiness. In a sense, those of us with a high corkiness threshold are the lucky ones.

SCORING WINE

Professional wine judges often give wines points out of 100, 20 or 10 because they are expected to come up with a ranking of how a group of wines showed on a given day. It might amuse you to keep written notes like (or probably neater than) the ones shown here and to append scores to them. For my own interest I certainly try to make a record of the state of maturity of each wine I taste, using arrows in different directions for their likely future.

Many wine critics and wine publications publish wine scores, which can be useful summaries of how the particular bottles seemed to that particular taster on the day of the tasting. Wine changes so unpredictably, however (and different casks and even bottles vary), and wine preferences are so subjective, that it is important not to be mesmerized by the apparent precision of these ratings. Find a wine critic whose taste you share and follow his or her recommendations, but not slavishly, please. And always remember that wine critics tend to taste scores of wine at a time, so the flashy ones get the highest scores. The saddest thing

I ever heard was when my most intelligent, wine-loving friend reported, crestfallen, about a wine tasted the previous evening, 'I really enjoyed it, but I looked it up in Parker [the powerful American wine critic] and he only gave it an 83.'

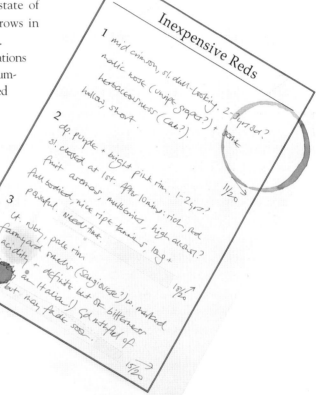

THE MECHANICS OF
SERVING WINE

I am almost certainly biased, but I think there are few social acts as hospitable, relaxing and inclusive as offering someone a glass of wine. Pouring wine into a couple of glasses is so much less of a performance than anything involving 'How much tonic/water do you like? Ice? Lemon?' And a modest glass of wine (which nowadays costs far less than most bottles of beer) can transform the simplest food into an occasion (quite apart from making the food taste better). But these, I happily admit, are the rantings of a confirmed wine addict.

If the occasion is an informal one, I see no shame or disrespect in pouring from an already opened bottle. See page 25 for reasons why the wine might actually taste better, and for advice on keeping opened bottles of wine.

More formal entertaining does call for a certain amount of planning, however. About the most disconcerting way of greeting your guests is with 'Just hang on a minute; I have to pop out and get something to drink.' Imagine substituting the word 'eat' at the end of this sentence... See pages 32–3 for specific suggestions about wine styles and quantities.

The thoughtful host is just that, working out how many bottles of any wine to be served may be needed and, most importantly, getting them ready in advance. If by any chance you're serving a wine with a sediment such as vintage or crusted port and most fine red wine more than about five years old, these bottles need to be stood upright for at least a day and preferably several to let the deposit fall to the bottom. (It is a good sign incidentally, if a wine has a sediment. It means that the winemaker didn't filter it too heavily, and left it with enough tiny particles to age and bond together to make a more interesting wine.) For most wines, however, the most important aspect to plan is the crucial question of serving temperature (see page 28).

Sparkling wines and light white wines can, conveniently, be put in the refrigerator the morning before the evening you plan to serve them. Full-bodied whites (see page 36) are usually better off given only an hour or two's chilling before your guests arrive. Most red wines will get to approximately the right temperature if left all day in the room in which they'll eventually be served – although lighter bodied styles (see page 37) may need half an hour's chilling before serving, or could be kept in cellar conditions (see pages 42–4) until just before serving. I tend to move bottles round the house according to their style. The top of the tumble drier (when it's switched off) is usefully cooler than our dining area, but one of these days a bottle of red burgundy will be spun off it into messy smithereens.

Big parties tend to put impossible stresses on most domestic refrigerators. I find the Great British winter can be a fine outdoor alternative to chilling bottles mechanically. A bucket, basin or even bath full of ice and water (a much more effective cooling agent than ice cubes alone, which inevitably touch only a fraction of a bottle's surface) is a viable solution, no matter what the outdoor temperature.

If you need to chill bottles in a hurry, an ice (and water) bucket is a most effective method. Microwaves can be used to warm bottles fast, but err on the side of caution when setting the timing. And remember that a glassful of too-cool wine can be warmed quite fast by being cupped in the human hand.

See pages 24–5 for advice on when to open bottles and decanting. One little question, however: should one wipe clean bottles which have painstakingly acquired cellar dust? Most hygienically minded people would answer with an unequivocal yes. I think they should know, however, that in the United States it is possible to buy artificial dust to spray on wine bottles.

OPENING THE BOTTLE

THE IDEAL STOPPER?

The world's wine producers spend a lot of time asking themselves and each other how to persuade more people to drink wine (fewer than one in every three Americans, for example, does so with any regularity). And yet they continue to sell one of the very few products left in the world which cannot even be opened, let alone consumed, without a special bit of equipment, great patience and dexterity, and acceptance of a considerable failure rate. The continuing use of cork, a cylinder of tree bark, to stopper wine bottles is in many ways extraordinary – especially since a growing body of scientific research suggests that a crown cap or screwcap would do the job just as well (provided bottle tops are redesigned to accommodate them).

But many producers are unwilling to switch to easier, more reliable stoppers because all research suggests that con-sumers are wedded to corks and corkscrews as part of the wine-drinking experience. Plastic corks are therefore encroaching.

I too love the 'pop' sound of a cork being pulled (and, especially, the popping of a champagne cork, which, restaurateurs report, can have an instant effect on other diners), and I love the idea that cork is an ecologically sound material. But I feel even more passionately about how difficult some corks are to extract (especially from Italy's narrow bottle-necks), how they can eventually crumble and fatally let in air, and how frequently they are affected by cork taint and result in completely spoilt 'corked' wines (see page 18).

Cork is a unique material in that it is light, elastic, inert (i.e. does not normally react with the wine), and shouldn't let liquids out or air, wine's enemy, in. Once it is lodged in a bottle-neck and absorbs wine it should offer an airtight seal. Crystals on the bottom of a cork are not sinister, just harmless tartrates deposited by wine's naturally high level of

(Continued on page 24)

1 This cork is one of the cheaper, shorter varieties. The cheapest of all are even shorter and made of tiny fragments of low-quality cork glued together.

2 The flashiest, most expensive corks can be up to 6 cm long. This cork has become narrower after spending a decade in the bottleneck.

3 Synthetic cork made from a by-product of the petro-chemical industry. These are widely used because they are free of cork taint, but signs are they start to let in air after a year or two.

4 The screwcap: effective and already widely used, particularly for unoaked whites.

5 Crown caps: used for the first stage of sparkling wine maturation and capable of keeping any wine in good condition for decades.

6 A champagne cork before it is hammered into a bottleneck. It is too wide to be punched out of a single thickness of bark so it is made up of discs of cork stuck together.

7 The same cork (as 6), with its metal capsule, after several years in a bottleneck.

CORKSCREWS

1 *Regular corkscrew with a perfect hollow, pointed helix.*

2 *Butterfly, twin levered model (usually all metal). This model requires less strength because of its twin levers but has a potentially problematic solid helix.*

3 *This wooden model employs an inner screw and therefore needs less effort than some, but has the disadvantage of concealing where the action is.*

4 *Screwpull broke new ground in corkscrew design by introducing Teflon coating of the screw and adapting advanced engineering to minimize the human effort in cork extraction. This Lever model, however, is Screwpull's most magical offering by far, screwing corks out of the bottle and off the screw with two easy movements. Its cost, about the same as two bottles of expensive bordeaux, makes it a viable proposition only for the rich or seriously wine-demented, however.*

5 *This twin-pronged (for insertion either side of a cork) model, called a 'Butler's friend' for its ability to remove corks without marking them and thereby facilitating their reinsertion, is particularly popular with American wine drinkers. It depends on wrist-twisting but may end up pushing in particularly loose corks.*

6 *The 'waiter's friend' incorporates a penknife for cutting foils and allows corks to be levered out against the rim of the bottle. It also requires considerable dexterity and strength, however, and might not be such a friend to the average waitress.*

7 *The Screwpull foil cutter costs about as much as a bottle of Muscadet and, once it has been used, becomes an essential wine serving tool. Clasp the foil over the bottle-neck between its two prongs, give it a quarter turn and its four tiny circular blades should neatly trim off the top of the foil, leaving a decent margin below the rim* (see page 24 for more details).

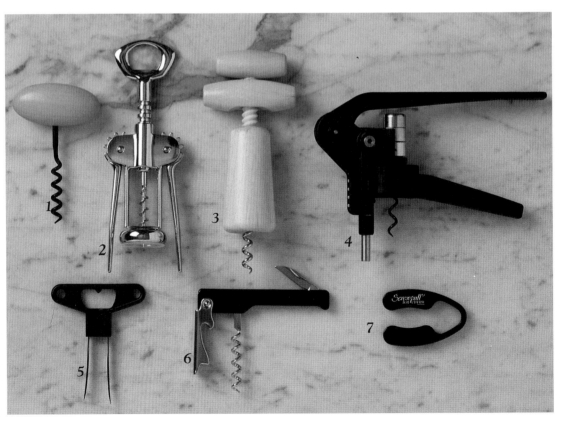

WINE PARAPHERNALIA

1 Ice buckets, either glass or metal, are much heavier and potentially messier than a vacuum bottle holder. The trick is to fill them as full as possible with a mixture of ice and water, not just ice, so that every bit of the bottle is in contact with a cooling agent.

2 Just one of many designs of bottle holder whose job is to keep a wine at the temperature it was when inserted. It works on much the same principle as a vacuum flask, is easy to clean and can be just as useful for keeping red wines from heating up in very high temperatures as for keeping white wines chilled.

3 and **4** Decanters tend to come in single-(**4**) or double-bottled (magnum) size. Antique ones can be unearthed from junk shops for relatively little money, especially since you don't strictly need a stopper for a decanter used only for serving. Spirits and madeira can be kept in a (stoppered) decanter virtually for ever, but port and even sherry tends to deteriorate after a week or so. And most table wines deteriorate after just 24 hours – although some tannic monsters may improve.

5 The Vacuvin works by pumping out air from an opened bottle and trying to create a vacuum therein. It is better than nothing but is not very effective over more than a day or two.

6 This sparkling wine stopper will keep the bubbles in an opened bottle in the fridge for several days.

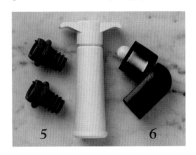

tartaric acid (see page 73). Some mould on the top of a cork is not necessarily a bad thing either, as it is probably the result of the cellar rather than the wine (I still remember the glory of a Château d'Yquem 1945 from under a cork that was so mouldy it was visibly moving). If a cork is very damp at both ends, it may have allowed some wine out and, more dangerously, some air in. If you notice that a bottle is leaking, or a cork fits so loosely in a bottle-neck that it can be moved, extract the cork and replace it with a tighter one as soon as possible, after checking that the wine has not been oxidized (see page 73) by taking a small sample.

THE MECHANICS OF OPENING

Before wrestling with the cork, the wine drinker encounters another illogical barrier to wine enjoyment, the often impenetrable foil or capsule that covers the cork. An increasing number of wine bottles are allowed on to the market without this addition, once useful for protecting against cork weevils but now largely cosmetic, except for bottles kept in a wine rack where foils can be useful for identification. Although the practice was outlawed in 1993, lead was often used for foils, potentially leaving harmful deposits on the rim of the bottle (which is why it is sensible to get into the habit of wiping the rim of every wine bottle once the cork has been pulled). For the same reason professionals try to cut the foil in a straight line round the bottle-neck a few millimetres below the rim so that wine doesn't come into contact with the foil when it is poured. (The wine won't taste any different if you rip the entire foil off, as is sometimes inevitable, but it deprives you of one of the wine's distinguishing marks.) A sharp knife and a steady hand can achieve a neatly cut foil, but a specially designed foil cutter such as the one shown on page 22 does it with much less effort. A foil cutter is no good, however, for those few bottle-necks still dipped in wax which, in my experience, has to be painstakingly chipped off with a sharp knife and a chisel.

Once the foil has been removed, you have to hope that a corkscrew such as one of the best of those illustrated on page 22 will do the rest. Aim the screw down the centre of the cork. Ideally it should be a hollow, sharply pointed helix rather than a solid cone which can all too easily pierce a hole straight through the cork. It can help to stand the bottle on a flat surface, holding it steady, while inserting the screw, and to jam it between your knees while pulling. As with modern business, leverage is all.

If the cork crumbles under the impact of the corkscrew but won't come out, try inserting a corkscrew with a long narrow screw at an angle and/or into a different part of the cork. If that doesn't work, as with any intractable cork, you could try inserting the two prongs of a butler's friend type corkscrew down either side of the cork and pulling it out, or you may have to simply push the cork into the bottle using, for example, the handle of a wooden spoon (a little more wood contact won't harm the wine). Because the remains of the cork tend to float and block the bottle-neck (provided the wine is not some terribly fragile ancient liquid whose precious bouquet may be lost after a few minutes' exposure to air) it is worth continuing to push them down with your stick-like instrument while pouring the wine into a jug. You can then pour the wine, through a funnel lined with a clean coffee filter or muslin if necessary, into a clean bottle or decanter. I cannot tell you how useful I find a plastic funnel and muslins.

Another possible ploy which requires some cunning is to warm the bottle-neck without actually warming the cork. A cloth soaked in boiling water can be held round the bottle-neck using an oven glove.

If none of these ploys works, and it is feasible, take the bottle back to where you bought it and complain. (This is just one of the reasons why it can be a good idea to keep more wine in the house than you expect to consume.)

Plastic cylinders dyed and sometimes even mottled to look like corks are used increasingly to avoid the problem of cork taint while offering some of the 'cork experience'. I can't stand them. They have none of the ecological soundness of real cork. They look silly. Many of the ones I have come across are too inelastic to re-stopper an opened bottle. And, worst of all, they involve all the effort of trying to pull a fat cork out of a narrow bottle-neck.

LEFTOVERS

Too much air, or at least oxygen, turns wine into vinegar eventually, which is why it makes sense to store leftover wine in a *stoppered* bottle with as little head space as possible, i.e. in a bottle whose capacity is as close as possible to the volume of wine left over (clean half- and quarter-bottles can be very useful). All sorts of complex reactions (accelerated by heat) take place when wine is exposed to air, as happens when a wine is poured or sits in a glass, which is why a wine can taste quite different 10, 20 or 30 minutes after being poured.

BREATHING

Many wine drinkers deliberately open bottles an hour or so before pouring them because they like the wine to 'breathe'. Wine scientists point out that the surface area of wine in a bottle-neck is so small relative to its volume that very little is likely to be achieved by this except, in some rare cases, the dissipation of any 'bottle sickness' (see pages 39–41).

In that opening a bottle an hour or two ahead of time is unlikely to do any harm to all

OPENING A BOTTLE OF SPARKLING WINE

An eye doctor in the champagne town of Épernay treats up to 20 people a year who have been injured by wayward corks. The pressure in a bottle of sparkling wine is about three times that in the tyre of a double-decker bus, so champagne corks must be eased out of the bottle-neck with enormous care. Untwist the wire muzzle and keep a thumb over the top of the cork. Point the bottle away from you and away from anyone else or any precious object, at an angle to increase the surface area of the wine and decrease the pressure in the bottle-neck. Twist the bottle off the cork rather than vice versa (to avoid breaking the cork), all the while holding the cork into the bottle-neck with the thumb so that it is eased out producing 'the gentle sigh of a satisfied woman', as cricket commentator and wine writer John Arlott would have it. Pour the wine gently into each glass, possibly taking a lesson from pub staff by holding the glass at an angle to control the foam.

but the most fragile wine relics, however, there are practical reasons for getting this job out of the way before, for example, your guests arrive.

TO DECANT OR NOT

There are also strong practical reasons for separating a wine with sediment (see page 20) from that sediment, which can taste bitter and physically gets in the way of enjoyment. This traditionally involves standing the bottle upright for a day or two beforehand and pouring the wine into another clean glass container (glass is inert and if clear allows you to enjoy the colour of a wine, which can be a great pleasure) with a strong light source behind the bottom of the bottle-neck so that you can stop pouring when the sediment is about to slip into the neck. That light source could be a candle or any strong light such as a desklight or a table lamp without the shade.

I often decant full-bodied white wines which may have no sediment at all, simply because they look so gorgeously golden in a decanter. See page 23 for some classic decanter shapes, but a glass jug or clean bottle would do just as well.

Scientists say we should decant at the last possible moment so that no part of the wine's reaction with air be lost to us. As a host I confess I am prepared to sacrifice completeness for convenience with all but the most fragile old wines, say those over 25 years old, depending on their body and the style of the vintage.

GLASSES

Wine is drunk out of glasses rather than teacups or silver goblets because glass is inert, relatively thin and allows full appreciation of a wine's appearance. The perfect wine glass has a stem and a bowl that goes in towards the rim (see page 14). It is also made of clear glass so that the wine's colour, an important element in assessing and enjoying wine to the full, can be appreciated. Wine nuts also like to commune with their wine as physically closely as possible, which means that thin crystal is highly valued whereas patterned and cut glass are not.

There is no real need for glasses of different sizes except that we tend to need smaller servings of sweet wines and fortified wines. It has always seemed unfair to me that white wines are conventionally served in smaller glasses than red wines.

1 Tumblers may be used in earthy and aspiringly earthy Italian restaurants, but the thickness of the glass and the difficulty of swirling the wine makes them pleasure-killers for wine enthusiasts.

2 The 'Paris goblet' is one of the cheapest wine glasses available (four can be bought for the price of a bottle of the cheapest wine). It fulfils the criteria of having a stem and going in towards the rim, and is better than narrower 'tulip' shapes, but the glass is too thick to provide intimate or luxurious contact with the wine.

3 The ISO glass carefully designed in the 1970s by the International Standards Organization, advised by a panel of professional wine tasters, does the job extremely well without winning any prizes for glamour. Machine-made versions are available and each one costs no more than the cheapest bottle of wine.

4 and 5 Classic wine glass shapes on an attractively spindly stem. Eastern Europe, and the Czech Republic in particular, have a long history of providing good-value glassware.

6 The classic 'copita' used for serving sherry by those who really understand it – the people who make it. Like any wine, sherry is best appreciated in a glass only half to two-thirds full.

CARING FOR GLASSWARE

Glasses should be stored upright somewhere free from dust and strong smells. Aesthetically, glassware needs to be clean, and has the annoying habit of being extremely breakable and showing every speck and dribble. The important thing as far as the wine is concerned is that the glass smells of nothing – not washing up liquid (which can stop the formation of bubbles in fizzy wine), and certainly not dirty glass cloths.

Many smart wine glasses, including the Riedel range, are happy in a domestic dishwasher and benefit from the high temperatures there. Water has to be soft, however, and there is no need for detergent. Hand washing glasses achieves best results if glasses are washed in very hot water, rinsed in cold, and polished with linen tea towels reserved for the purpose – I'm told. In an ideal world we would all have unlimited supplies of new, fine crystal glasses.

1, 2 and *3* No one has done more work on wine glass design than Austrian Georg Riedel. Working on the principle that how the liquid hits the tongue affects how it will taste, he has evolved slightly different glass designs for dozens of wine types which include, for example, young as opposed to mature red bordeaux, both non-vintage and vintage champagne, and a glass for each of vintage port, tawny port, Chianti Classico and Brunello di Montalcino. To indulge freely in the Riedel way of life you would clearly need to build a special glass storage wing on to your house. The Gourmet glass (*1*) is his least expensive all-purpose model; the Chardonnay machine-made Vinum (*2*) is perhaps more elegant for the dinner table. Glasses in the beautiful,

similarly shaped but hand-blown Sommelier range (3) cost so much that I would not dare wash one.

4 The only non-standard glass shape you might think of investing in is a tall, thin glass for sparkling wines (often called a flûte), which allows minimal gas escape, lets you watch each bubble's journey and is a suitably glamorous shape in itself. Some champagne producers prefer a glass that has more of a bowl so that you have a better chance of smelling the wine's bouquet.

5 The old-fashioned coupe, supposedly modelled on the shape of Marie-Antoinette's breast, is easy to spill and encourages the precious carbon dioxide to escape as fast as possible.

TEMPERATURE – THE CRUCIAL ELEMENT

It is impossible to overestimate the effect of serving temperatures on how a wine will taste. Serving a wine at the most flattering temperature may seem absurdly high-falutin and precious as an activity, but it really can transform ink into velvet. Conversely, getting the temperature wrong turns zest into flab. (Unlike the wine itself, it need not cost anything either...)

The principles are delightfully simple:
1 The cooler the wine the less it will smell.
2 The warmer the wine the more it will smell.
3 Low temperatures will emphasize acidity and tannin.
4 High temperatures will minimize them.

The result of rule 1 is that if you find yourself with a wine that tastes (i.e. smells) truly horrid, but you have to serve or drink it, then chill it to pieces. (If it's a full-bodied red such as those listed on the bottom half of page 37 it could be difficult to pull this off – you'll just have to boil off the flavour and serve it, with added spice and sugar, as mulled wine. See page 56.)

Rule 1 also means that the more naturally aromatic a wine is (Riesling, Sauvignon Blanc, Cabernet Franc, Gamay for example), the cooler you can afford to serve it – a useful observation if you need the refreshment of a cool drink. Sparkling wines also suit low temperatures, which slow down the release of carbon dioxide.

Rule 2 means that full-bodied wines (whites too), those which appear towards the bottom of the charts on page 36–7 and whose flavour molecules struggle to escape to deliver messages to the olfactory area, can be served much warmer than lighter wines. The limit to this rule is reached above 20°C (68°F) when some compounds may be literally boiled off.

Rule 3 means that you can make a flabby wine taste infinitely better by chilling it a little. Thus, all but the most perfectly balanced sweet wine benefits from being chilled, as do many red burgundies and soft red wines such as Beaujolais, which could do with a bit of artificially encouraged structure.

Rule 4 is particularly useful because it means that young red wines, and those listed on the right hand side of page 37, which would seem almost hideously tough when served slightly cool, can be immeasurably improved by serving them on the warm side.

The chart gives a rough guide as to suitable serving temperatures. See also pages 36–7 for guidance on which wines are light/full-bodied, which sweet or dry, and likely tannin levels.

Wine style	Ideal serving temperature, °C (°F)	Practical advice: refrigerator for (hrs)
Light, sweet whites	5–10 (41–50)	4+
Sparkling whites	6–10 (43–50)	4
Light (aromatic), dry whites	8–12 (46–54)	2
Sparkling reds	10–12 (50–54)	1.5
Medium-bodied, dry whites	10–12 (50–54)	1.5
Full, sweet whites	8–12 (46–54)	2
Light reds	10–12 (50–54)	1.5
Full, dry whites	12–16 (54–61)	1
Medium reds	14–17 (57–63)	–
Full or tannic reds	15–18 (59–64)	–

NB Throughout, rosés behave as slightly fuller bodied equivalent whites.

28

SERVING THE RIGHT BOTTLE

For me, choosing the right wine to serve on a particular occasion is almost as thrilling as drinking the wine itself, perverse as that may seem. It gives me real pleasure to feel that the bottle, or bottles, have been just right for the circumstances, the people, the time, and any food that's served with the wine. Slowly, as I have learnt more about wine, I have learnt a little more about this aspect of wine appreciation, which is by no means a modern phenomenon. In the first century BC the Latin poet Horace wrote extensively about the art of matching wine to guest and occasion. And it is an art.

It is by no means the single most important thing about wine. It is hardly catastrophic to serve a wine that jars with your main course, or your guests' tastes or expectations, but a few simple considerations can ensure that you maximize your own and your friends' enjoyment, and that the money you spend on wine is spent most effectively.

It is usually a waste, and entirely inappropriate, for example, to think that the more you spend on wine, the more it will please. Typically, the most expensive bottles in a wine shop are tough little babies in terms of their evolution: mute, scrunched-up bundles of ingredients that have many years' bottle maturation ahead of them before they will begin to prove, in mellow middle age, why they were worth paying through the nose for. (See pages 39–41 for more about this magical process.)

And there is a place and a time for everything – even the fanciest bottle of wine. I shall never forget that the first time I ever tasted the fabulous Château Cheval Blanc 1947 was at an outdoor lunch in a sunny Suffolk garden where the breeze playfully wafted into the hot, blue sky every nuance of its subtle bouquet. A well-chilled, flavourful dry rosé would probably have been just the thing for this outdoor lunch, and yet it would probably taste extremely dreary at an urban dinner party in midwinter.

Other examples of the right bottles in the wrong place (for a wide variety of reasons) include: Mosel Riesling with hearty stews; New Zealand Sauvignon served to any but the most cosmopolitan native of Sancerre; heavy Chardonnay at lunchtime; tough, tannic young reds served to wine débutants; Châteauneuf-du-Pape drunk in midsummer in Châteauneuf-du-Pape (or indeed most full-bodied, alcoholic reds in the heat of the summer that is responsible for that alcohol).

HOW TO CHOOSE

It is worth trying to match a wine's

quality level
style
flavour
geographical origins

to:

people – take account of an individual's likes, dislikes, prejudices, and capacities for alcohol.

occasion – whether it's the most casual encounter or a formal celebration may influence the most appropriate price level.

weather – the ambient temperature and humidity level can have an enormous effect on what sorts of wine taste best. In hot weather we crave cool drinks, which means choosing wines that taste good when chilled. On muggy days it can be difficult to persuade the flavour molecules out of the glass, so choose an aromatic wine.

time of day – may be a significant factor as far as alcohol intake is concerned.

place – inside or outside? Is more than one wine appropriate, or feasible?

food – see pages 34–7 for full details of the extent to which food and wine matching matters; and see pages 32–3 for ideas on wines to be served without food as an aperitif and those that come into their own after a meal.

BRINGING A BOTTLE

Some people think that because of their age or status, it is somehow not 'done' to bring a bottle of wine, whereas others would never dream of crossing a friend's threshold without a bottle of wine in hand. I can't see why anyone would resent the gift of a bottle thoughtfully chosen; although anyone who expects every guest to bring a bottle and gets upset if they don't, is probably wise to spell this out in advance.

One of the touchier questions of modern etiquette is whether you have to open a bottle that someone brings, or can you keep it and savour it on another occasion? I would say that if someone brings a bottle of white or sparkling wine ready-chilled or, as has frequently happened to me, a red wine already decanted, then this should be taken as a pretty strong hint that its donor expects the wine to be drunk there and then. If, however, your guest arrives and puts a bottle on one side without comment, then you are not duty-bound to open it – although the perfect host would probably unwrap it at some point, express thanks, and ask whether the guest would like to taste it ('taste' being such a useful euphemism for 'drink').

Two useful rules are never to take a bottle that you would not be happy to drink yourself, and, if you really want to drink it, hand it over personally and explain how keen you are to 'taste' it.

Bottles to blush about
• Branded wines e.g. Piat d'Or, Mateus or Lancers Rosé, Blue Nun or any Liebfraumilch.
• Any really inexpensive table wine.
• Wines in funny, asymmetrical bottles.

More respectable than people think
• Supermarket own-label wines: although few look good enough to present to design gurus, some taste quite good enough for the rest of us.
• Mineral water: perhaps it's just my friends, but some hosts are much better at providing booze than the water needed to stop the dehydration effect.

Smart bottles
• Champagne: almost always appreciated. Bollinger and Louis Roederer (or Krug if you can afford it) are gold chip presents; Deutz, Gosset, Alfred Gratien, Charles Heidsieck, Laurent Perrier, Moët & Chandon, Bruno Paillard, Perrier-Jouët, Pol Roger, Pommery, Renaudin, Ruinart, Taittinger and Veuve Clicquot are all reliable; Billecart-Salmon Rosé would show that you really know your stuff; as would a bottle from one of the best growers such as Château de Boursault, Gimonnet or Vilmart. Vintage-dated is a treat.
• Obscure wines: either a small, unknown producer of a well-known wine such as Beaujolais or California Chardonnay, or something new (a weird new grape variety or curiosity from Latin America or the Far East), or something not in general commercial distribution (such as Château Latour's basic Pauillac, effectively its 'third wine', for example). A good independent wine merchant can be invaluable here, or a bottle brought back from abroad.
• Sweet wines: good Sauternes, Vouvray, Monbazillac, Jurançon and Late Harvest Riesling are all stylishly unusual, and usually appreciated even in half-bottles.
• Olive oil: estate bottled oils are what wine pros take to each other's houses.

The ultimate bottle party, the annual Paulée de Meursault, a marathon lunch held in the village of Meursault on the day after the annual Hospices de Beaune auction. Guests from all over the world converge on particularly good bottles brought by Burgundy's wine producers.

ENTERTAINING WITH WINE

QUANTITIES

A tricky one, this. Individuals' capacity for alcohol varies enormously, as you have doubtless observed yourself. No one could possibly accuse a host who provided his or her guests with the equivalent of a bottle of wine a head over the course of an evening of meanness. And yet there are some occasions, a weekday lunch, for example, at which it would be extremely sophisticated to provide one stunning bottle (of champagne or white burgundy perhaps) for six people, allowing them each one generous glassful of luxury but minimizing the dangerous snooze factor of a bibulous lunch.

As a general rule, an average of between half and a bottle a head consumed over several hours at a table makes for a very jolly occasion. If there are many drivers in the party then the lower limit would be more sensible.

Wine served without a meal is potentially much more potent, especially before lunch when most bodies contain little food to buffer alcohol's effect. A quarter of a bottle a head, or two small glasses, could well be enough if there is a significant proportion of abstainers in the group, although for a long daytime reception such as a wedding it would be safer to allow up to half a bottle a head (and as much as a bottle for an all-evening event).

Like many hosts, I frequently overlook the non-alcoholic drinks in my concern to serve just the right wine(s). Try to serve as much water as wine at the table, and to provide a reasonably sophisticated non-alcoholic alternative at parties such as fizzy mineral water with fresh orange juice or a drop of elderflower syrup, or spiced tomato juice cocktails before lunch.

Serving something to eat cuts down quite dramatically on the intoxication rate of an alcoholic aperitif. Eating olives out of doors (the only time I encourage my children to throw stones) can seem just right, though they can seem distractingly mediterranean and strongly flavoured for a northern wine like champagne.

Radishes, celery, pistachio nuts and quail's eggs are less intrusive, but most of these involve some potentially inconvenient debris (although halves of quail's egg on a dollop of mayonnaise on toasted rounds of French bread are easy to eat and look glamorous). Little cheesy biscuits such as the Dutch Roka brand complement most wines, as do Italian breadsticks or *grissini*, even with prosciutto wound round them.

SOME SPECIFIC SUGGESTIONS

Pre-meal drinks party

Wine (plus a non-alcoholic alternative) is much easier to serve than lots of different mixed drinks. People with carpets tend to prefer to serve white wine, and it is true that most reds are too full-bodied and tannic to be at their best without food. Sparkling wine seems special and (in some cases *but*) goes to the head quicker; a good champagne can be the greatest treat of all, but perfectly well-made, more economical alternatives can be found from Saumur, Limoux, Alsace, California, Australia, New Zealand and even England (a cool, or cooled, climate is vital). Still white wines that fit the bill of being light enough but not too acid to drink without food include many not-too-expensive examples from Alsace; Kabinett and Spätlese wines from Germany (Mosel especially); light Chardonnay and Sauvignon Blanc such as a Vin de Pays d'Oc, Chablis and unoaked examples from the southern hemisphere; well-made Pinot Blanc/Bianco and Pinot Gris/Grigio which manage to combine the softness of Pinot with an appetizing tang.

All-evening informal party

The wines listed above could certainly be served all evening, but after a while your guests may start to crave something more substantial. Red wines that can happily be sipped at with no substantial food to break their fall on the palate tend to be light bodied and low in tannin (those in the top left hand quarter of page 37). Beaujolais and other Gamays; red Loire and other Cabernet Franc wines; simpler Merlots; young

Pinot Noir (except for most red burgundy); the new generation of juicy young reds from Spain and Portugal; Dolcetto; light Zinfandel; many eastern European reds; and of course practically any rosé can fit the bill here. And if you really are fonder of your carpets than of humouring your guests, you could always switch to a fuller bodied, oaked white such as a Chardonnay or Semillon when you start to serve the food.

Extended lunch party

A similar range of wines as for an evening party could be served here, but in smaller quantities perhaps. Warmer weather may require the addition of some examples from the following.

Outdoor wines

It is usually a waste to serve too fine a wine out of doors, especially in hot weather when the bouquet is lost all too easily to the sun and breeze. Barbecued food, however, calls for its own brand of earthy, robust flavours and, perhaps not too surprisingly, hot climate wines come into their own here, including wines from Australia, the southern Rhône, dry rosés and reds from Provence, practically anything produced on the shores of the Mediterranean, even retsina from Greece.

Before a meal

Any of the wines suggested for a pre-meal drinks party make fine aperitifs, as drinks designed to stimulate the appetite are called. The classic aperitif is dry sherry, probably too strong and too misunderstood for general consumption, but one of the wine world's great, undervalued treasures. In warm weather a freshly opened bottle of Fino or Manzanilla can give even more concentrated pleasure than a fine white wine (and is the perfect foil for green olives and salted almonds), while a dry, nutty Amontillado is the perfect antidote to cold weather and an incipient cold. Sercial Madeira can also be beguilingly tingly. The most classical unfortified wines to serve as aperitifs are champagne, Mosel and lighter Alsace wines.

Dinner party

I usually serve an aperitif (see above), one or two (related) first course wines, usually two and sometimes even three different main course wines (moving from lighter to fuller bodied and from young to old), one of which may continue with the cheese, and sometimes a strong, sweet wine at the end. The whites might be two Californian Chardonnays or white burgundies from different producers, the reds could follow a geographical, varietal or even vintage theme. But then I want to show off, and this is wildly in excess of what is necessary or even sensible, which is probably an aperitif, a white and a red (to cater for those who just can't handle one or other colour). All I would say in my defence is that you learn so much more when comparing similar wines than when drinking them in isolation. Also see Wine and Food on page 34.

After a meal

To my mind and palate, sweet wines taste much more delicious drunk on their own (or with cheese) than they do with most sweet food. Any reasonably sweet wine can be delicious after a meal, and those with a fair degree of acidity such as Germans, Austrians, Loire or Jurançon can refresh as well. This is also the time to serve sweet fortified wines (port, sherry, madeira, marsala, malaga, Liqueur Muscat, southern French and indeed all rich Muscats, and so on) as well as wine in its strongest, i.e. distilled, form: cognac, armagnac and other brandies. The spirit that finds most favour with wine fanatics other than brandy is Chartreuse which, like wine but unlike any other spirit, has an uncanny way of developing in the bottle.

Daytime drinking

I may be a killjoy, but low alcohol (see page 49) seems the crucial element when sipping between meals. Mosel comes into its own here, as does Italy's panoply of lightly fizzing Moscato, the wrongly reviled Asti included. Buying an example other than the cheapest is the key to enjoyable grapey froth instead of a headache.

WINE AND FOOD

With its relatively low alcoholic strength, appetizing acidity and lack of sickly artificial flavours, wine is the perfect accompaniment to food. Am I kidding myself that a well-chosen wine makes food taste better? Surely not...

The most important rule about food and wine matching is that there are no rules. You can drink any wine at all with any food – even red wine with fish! – and the world will continue to revolve. Anyone who thinks worse of you for serving the 'wrong' wine is stuffy, prejudiced and probably ill-informed.

There are, however, some very simple guide-lines for getting the most out of particular foods and bottles.

• The single most important aspect of a wine for food matching is not colour but body (which corresponds closely with alcoholic strength).

• The second most important aspect is tannins for reds and sweetness for whites.

See the charts on pages 36–7 for help in assessing these vital statistics.

• Try to match a wine's body to the power of the strongest ingredient in the food (some examples are given between the white and red wine charts but the list is very far from exhaustive). Serve delicate-flavoured foods such as simple white fish or poached chicken with lighter bodied wines (on the top half of pages 36 and 37) and stronger, more robust foods such as grilled tuna with spiced lentils or osso buco with full-bodied wines (on the bottom half). It should be clear from the charts that many white wines will do jobs which are conventionally regarded as red wine jobs, and vice versa.

• A tannic wine such as those on the far right of the chart on page 37 can taste softer when served with chewy foods, notably unsauced red meat. (Sauces are often more powerful than what they are saucing and are usually a better guide to the ideal wine accompaniment.)

• All wines taste horribly acid if served with sweet food, unless they are sweeter than the food itself – which seriously limits the choice of wines to be served with most sweet courses to those on the very far right of the white wine chart on page 36 and the asterisked reds on page 37. It also makes wine purists wary of sweet relishes such as chutneys, jellies and fruit sauces. (But sweetish wines can go surprisingly well with savoury food – a Vouvray demi-sec can taste gorgeous with a savoury creamy sauce, for example – while sweet wines can go well with cheeses on the sweet and salt principle, as in melon and prosciutto.)

• Very acid foods such as citrus fruits and vinegar can do funny things to seriously fine, perfectly balanced wine, but can flatter a slightly acid wine (from a particularly cool climate or year) by making it taste less sour.

• Similarly, freshly ground black pepper might distort our impression of a complex, venerable wine but acts as a sensitizing agent on most palates and flatters young, light wines (in the top half of the chart) by making them taste fuller and richer.

DIFFICULT FOODS FOR WINE

There are very few foods that destroy wine, but very hot spices tend to stun the taste buds so that you could still smell a wine but would find it impossible to experience its dimensions because the sensory equipment in the palate is ablaze.

Globe artichokes and, to a lesser extent, asparagus can make wine taste oddly metallic, and most chocolate is so sweet and mouth-coating that it tends to annihilate all but the sweetest, strongest wines.

And don't forget how wine styles can be manipulated by care with serving temperatures (see page 28).

*The increasing importance of vegetables and salads has had its own sunny
influence on food and wine matching. Their direct flavours can seem better suited to New World
wines than the dusty complexity of many an Old World classic.*

CHARTING WINE AND FOOD

To match food and wine, try to assess the power of the food by its similarity in terms of impact on the palate to the sample foods listed, in increasing powerfulness, on the outside edges of the charts below. Then choose a wine type at about the same height on the page, but remember the guide-lines about sweetness (page 36) and tannin (page 37) offered on page 34, which mean that special conditions may apply to wines on the far right hand side of each chart

Food	% Alc	BONE DRY	DRY	MED. DRY	MED. SWEET	VERY SWEET
	8	Mosel trocken	Mosel Kabinett			Moscato Spumante
				Mosel Spätlese		
			English wine			Moscato d'Asti
					Mosel Auslese	
				Liebfraumilch / QbA		
	9	Gros Plant				Mosel BA/TBA
		Colombard	Swiss wine			
		Rhine trocken	Rhine Kabinett	Mateus Rosé		Asti
			vin de table	Rhine Spätlese		
		Ugni Blanc / Trebbiano				
	10			**Riesling**		
oysters		Muscadet	S. African Chenin Blanc		Rhine Auslese	
unadorned white fish		Vinho Verde	Vin de Pays		Rosé d'Anjou	
				Cal. Chenin Blanc		Rhine BA/TBA
			Soave			
	11		Pinots Grigio & Bianco			
fish tartare		Rhine Spätlese trocken	Loire Chenin Blanc			
spring rolls		**Aligoté**	Vouvray	Vouvray demi sec	Vouvray moelleux	
prawns		Sancerre / Pouilly-Fumé	European whites			
		Albariño	Alsace Riesling			
salmon	12	**Sauvignon Blanc**				
goats cheese			Entre-Deux-Mers / AC Bordeaux / Bergerac			
		Chablis Champagne				
risotto		Vino de mesa			Jurançon moelleux	
fish cakes			Vernaccia	**Grüner Veltliner**		
savoury soufflés		**Chardonnay**	Graves			
garlic mashed potatoes			Frascati	S. Aus. Riesling		
		Washington & Chile whites			Blush wines	
Thai flavours		**Semillon Viognier**			White Zinfandel	
		Bourgogne Mâcon	S. African Chardonnay		Ste-Croix-du-Mont	
		Cal. Sauvignon Blanc Pinot Blanc				
battered fish					Monbazillac	
sweetbreads			Pouilly-Fuissé dry Muscat			
tapenade	13	Provence rosé	Portuguese & Spanish whites			
		Village Burgundy				
			Côtes-du-Rhône			
crab		Premier Cru Burgundy			Loupiac	
red mullet			Aus. & Cal. Chardonnay		Alsace Vendange Tardive	
tuna / ham		Retsina				
curry sauce		Pinot Gris d'Alsace			Alsace SGN	
		Châteauneuf-du-Pape		**Gewürztraminer**		
			Aus. Semillon			
					Barsac	
	13.5	Grand Cru Burgundy	Hermitage	Tavel rosé	Tokay 5 puttonyos	
			Mediterranean whites		Sauternes	
olives	15	Manzanilla		Vin Santo		
chorizo	17	Fino			S. French Muscats	
nuts			Dry Amontillado Sercial		Marsala	
				Amontillado		
		Dry Oloroso				
				Bual Oloroso		Malaga
					Pale Cream	
						Malmsey Cream Sherry
	18					Moscatel PX

and asterisked reds (which are sweet). Of course there is wide variation between different examples of the same wine type. Warmer climates and years produce fuller bodied wines and vice versa. Tannin levels drop dramatically with age (see pages 39–41) and can vary according to the year's weather and wine-making techniques. Variation is particularly marked between different regions' renditions of a single grape variety, although I have marked an average spot for varietal (see page 48) examples of the main ones in bold.

Soft	Medium Tannins	Hard	Tough as Old Boots	%Alc	Red
Sangria*				9	
vin de table					
Nouveau					baked / scrambled eggs
German reds	Alsace reds				
Gamay	Lambrusco*	cheap Italian reds		10	
	vino de mesa				
AC Beaujolais					
	Bardolino				poached chicken
	cru Beaujolais				plain pasta
	vin de pays Valpolicella				
Eastern European reds				11	
	AC Bourgogne				cold cuts / charcuterie
red Loire	**Cabernet Franc**	Portuguese reds			carpaccio
		AC Bordeaux			
	Sangiovese				
	Pinot Noir **Barbera**				
	village Burgundy Chianti Classico			12	roast chicken
	Merlot				pizza
	Navarre Languedoc ACs	**Cabernet Sauvignon**			bresaola
Dolcetto	Premier Cru Burgundy Cahors **Syrah**				turkey and trimmings
		Madiran			
Oregon Pinot Noir	Côtes-du-Rhône Provence				duck
	Chile & Washington reds	Médoc			roast lamb
Cal. Pinot Noir	Rioja St-Émilion	Graves			aïoli
		Cal. Cabernet Sauvignon			sauce bolognese
	Grand Cru Burgundy Pomerol				lamb shanks
	Pinotage Aus. Cabernet Sauvignon Supertuscans				lentils
	Ribera del Duero				roast beef
	Côte Rôtie				teriyaki
	Zinfandel Douro red			13	steak
	Hermitage				boeuf bourguignonne
	Mediterranean reds **Nebbiolo**				venison
	Vino Nobile di Montepulciano				game
	Shiraz				osso buco
	Southern Italian reds Brunello di Montalcino				
Châteauneuf-du-Pape					sausages
	Barbaresco				jugged hare
	Malbec				chops
	Barolo			14	roast meat
	North African reds				
	Amarone			16	
	Banyuls*				
ruby port*	Recioto*			18	strong cheese
tawny port*					
	vintage port*			20	

This chart is my personal adaptation of a graphic cleverly devised by Michael Broadbent MW in his classic handbook *Wine Tasting*.

Key
BA/TBA – *Beerenauslese/Trockenbeerenauslese*
QbA – *Qualitätswein bestimmter Anbaugebiet*
PX – *Pedro Ximénez*
Cal. – *California Aus. – Australian*
AC – *Appellation Contrôlée, i.e. generic version*
SGN – *Sélection de Grains Nobles*
* *indicates sweet red*
Grape varieties are in bold

WINE AND HEALTH

Wine contains alcohol, which is just one of the many reasons I like it so much. A glass of wine can lift the spirits and make the world seem a very much more attractive place. But alcohol has the power to change our behaviour, and in particular to make us less careful, which is why I try never to drink without thinking of the consequences. I try to limit my wine drinking to times, places and circumstances in which the effects of alcohol are minimized or easy to cope with – with food, in the evening, relaxing either at home or somewhere I won't have to drive from, for example.

Wine's alcohol content is also my most serious occupational hazard. Conventionally the palate is thought to be most suited to professional wine tasting in the morning, so many is the day on which I've tasted 80 wines before lunchtime. Like all professional wine tasters I carefully spit out every mouthful, but some alcohol always enters the system, either as dribbles of liquid or as vapour, so it takes enormous control and determination to feel stone cold sober after a wine tasting (which may be one of the reasons why everyone in the wine trade seems so frightfully nice).

In the days before proper sanitation, wine was regarded as a much healthier drink than water, because the alcohol and particular acid it contains kill off almost all bacteria that are harmful to man. Wine was regularly prescribed by doctors well into the twentieth century but for many decades we wine drinkers have received less encouraging messages.

Drinking too much alcohol can lead to alcohol dependency, accidents, liver damage and dementia. Connections have been made between heavy drinking and cancer of the mouth, strokes, raised blood pressure, increased infertility. A host of other unwelcome conditions have also been reported, which for much of the 1980s cast a shadow over even light social drinking. And in the United States women have been persuaded that any alcohol consumption during pregnancy 'may lead to birth defects', a message printed on every bottle of wine in commercial circulation.

The more recent news that there may be some positive health benefits from light to moderate drinking is therefore particularly welcome. Any sensible person can imagine how alcohol can relieve stress, but it has taken some rigorous research to demonstrate that drinking one or two glasses of red wine a day may help to reduce the risk of heart disease, the most common killer in Western society. It seems that the phenolics (see page 73) that distinguish red wine from white reduce the amount of cholesterol deposited in the arteries, making heart attacks less likely.

British medical authorities' 'safe limits' for average drinkers are 21 'units' of alcohol a week for women and 28 for men (women's body tissue being more prone to alcohol-related damage). A 'unit' of alcohol is one-ninth of an average bottle of wine whose alcoholic strength is 12 per cent (see pages 36–7). To some drinkers these limits seem very conservative. I drink between a third and half of a bottle of wine most evenings and am consoled by the fact that safe limits are based on people's own reporting of how much they drink. When you gross up any representative survey of how much Britons say they drink, you find it is almost exactly half as much as HM Customs *know* they consume.

Which neatly brings us to hangovers. Self-inflicted injury is by far the worst sort. Drinking at least as much water as wine can help enormously, as does a good painkiller, particularly one that contains ibuprofen, after real party nights. Milk thistle is a homeopathic aid to healthy liver function.

See also page 57 for information on wine allergies etc.

WHETHER TO STORE WINE

It is difficult to devote 20 years of your life to commenting on wine without developing some bees in your bonnet. One of my most treasured bees concerns wine and time, and the way that so many wine producers and retailers leave their customers completely in the dark about how long to keep individual bottles, especially that minority of bottles that actually needs keeping.

Most wine made today should be drunk as young as possible, while its youthful fruit can be enjoyed. But the myth that all wine improves with age lingers on and the reality is that *far more wine is drunk too late than too early.*

Wine, like any fresh food, changes with time. But whereas most consumables deteriorate from the moment we buy them, wine is one of the very few things we buy regularly that has the capacity to change for the better. Perhaps the top 10 per cent of all reds and five per cent of all whites (and those are generous estimates) will be more pleasurable and more interesting to drink when they are five years old than at one year old. The top one per cent of all wine made has the ability to improve for a decade or two or, in some cases, even more. The great majority of all wine, however, will actually start to lose the fruitiness that gives it youthful appeal within six months of being bottled. But how is the poor old consumer to identify which bottles to store lovingly and which to consume as fast as he or she possibly can?

The supermarkets, to give them credit, have responded quite well to

this problem in recent years. Many back labels on their own bottlings give specific advice on when to open them (typically 'within six months to a year of purchase'). But it can be extremely difficult to get reliable advice on when to open finer wines. How many people realize, for example, that the most expensive bottles of red wine in a store are probably those least likely to give pleasure that evening – because they are the ones with a long life expectancy which have been stacked full of mouth-puckering, inky tannin and are generally commercially available only in their youth?

The most obvious candidates for long-term ageing in bottle are the reds on the right hand side of page 37, botrytized sweet wines (see pages 87–9), Loire wines made from the Chenin Blanc grape (see pages 182–4), most wines made from the Riesling grape (see pages 120–1), and grand cru white burgundy (see pages 166–9).

Much is made of a wine's need to 'settle down' after a journey and certainly any wine

Just one corner of Baroness Philippine de Rothschild's cellar under Château Mouton-Rothschild – only a dream for most of us.

with a sediment (i.e. no wine younger than five years old) will need to be stood upright for a day or two simply to allow the deposit to fall. But it is difficult to see what would be particularly traumatic for a bottle about its journey from shelf to household. The most traumatic operation a wine is ever likely to be subjected to is bottling, and many commercial bottling lines shake up the wine so much, and expose it to so much oxygen, that it can take some weeks afterwards to recover from 'bottle sickness', before all its ingredients have fully reacted with the oxygen that has dissolved in the wine. More sophisticated bottling lines treat wine more gently by using inert gas. Some wines, particularly slightly sweet, very cheap ones, may be pasteurized before bottling so that they are incapable of any change in bottle. But how is the consumer to know how long ago a wine was bottled and in what way? The best advice I can give is to relax. Unless a wine has sediment, or is extremely expensive, it can usually be opened as soon as you like.

WHAT HAPPENS WHEN WINE AGES

The more fruit, acid and phenolics (see page 73) that go into a bottle of wine at the beginning, the more complex interactions there can be between all these compounds and the more rewarding it can be to age that bottle. This means that the less water there is in the grape

DOES WINE 'TRAVEL'?

Many people who bring wine back from foreign parts are disappointed with the results and blame this on wine's supposed inability to travel. It is difficult to see what is different for a bottle of wine about a ride in a private vehicle or as hand luggage as opposed to one on the back of a container truck (the most common commercial means of transport for wine).

What this difference in perceptions illustrates is not some particular shortcoming in the wine, but the general fact that wine tasting is extremely subjective, and we tend to be in a much more receptive, forgiving mood when travelling abroad than in our own homes. Wine can and indeed does travel all the time. The only serious hazards it can be exposed to are excessive heat and sharp temperature swings which can literally boil off some of the flavour (see pages 28 and 42–3). Wines that have not been heavily filtered are particularly vulnerable to sharp swings in temperature and are often deliberately shipped only in cooler weather.

(and therefore the thicker the grape variety's skins, the drier the growing season, the less irrigation used, and the lower the yields), the more likely it is that the resulting wine will repay cellaring. Tannins and colouring matter known as anthocyans are the most obvious types of phenolics and they are what preserves red wine as these interactions occur. These and other compounds continue to interact, forming bigger and bigger complex compounds which, after a few years, are too big to remain in solution and are precipitated as sediment. So as good quality, concentrated red wine ages it becomes paler and softer to taste, while gaining considerably in the range of flavours it presents (which by now constitute a bouquet [see page 16] rather than simple aromas). Any red wine with visible sediment is likely to be relatively mature.

Even less is known about how white wine ages, although acidity is thought to be the preservative white counterpart to tannin. Undoubtedly, the longest-lived white wines are those with good extract (see page 16) but good acidity too. The fact that white wines have far fewer phenolics explains why fewer of them can last as long in bottle (although botrytis, the 'noble rot' described on pages 87–9, can preserve sweet white wines for decades). Very few rosé wines improve with age, presumably because they tend to have less acidity than white wines and far fewer phenolics than reds.

For more information see page 42.

WINES TO DRINK AS YOUNG AS POSSIBLE

It follows from the previous section that the majority of wines, made to be easy to appreciate in youth, are not worth giving 'bottle age', the jargon for what happens when wine is kept for years in sealed bottles. The economics of producing a wine selling for less than about £5 or $7 a bottle mean that there is unlikely to be a sufficient concentration of ageable ingredients in that bottle. All of the following should usually be drunk within a year of bottling, and ideally sooner when their youthful fruit is most obvious.

Table wine (Europe)

Jug wine (US)

Wine in boxes or cans

Most inexpensive varietals (with the possible exceptions of some Cabernet Sauvignon)

Most vins de pays

Nouveau/primeur/novello wines

Branded wines (with the exception of better vintages of branded red bordeaux)

Germany's QbA wines

Rosé and blush wines

Asti and Moscato Spumante

Vermouth, basic port, most sherry, all spirits, sweet Muscats

The most common examples of the white wines in the top left hand corner of the chart on page 36 and those down the left hand side of the red wine chart on page 37.

WINES THAT REPAY KEEPING

In very general terms, the more expensive a bottle, the more it will repay bottle ageing. One simple clue to how long to keep a bottle is (yet again) the principal grape variety from which it was made. Below are some rough guide-lines with an approximate number of years in bottle in brackets (although there is considerable variation between wine regions and different vintage conditions). Remember that storage conditions can affect the rate at which wine ages. See page 42.

Red wines

Aglianico of Taurasi (4–15)

Baga of Barraida (4–8)

Cabernet Sauvignon (4–20)

Kadarka of Hungary (3–7)

Melnik of Bulgaria (3–7)

Merlot (2–10)

Nebbiolo (4–20)

Pinot Noir (2–8)

Plavac Mali of Croatia (4–8)

Raboso of Piave (4–8)

Sangiovese (2–8)

Saperavi of Russia (3–10)

Syrah/Shiraz (4–16)

Tannat of Madiran (4–12)

Tempranillo of Spain (2–8)

Xynomavro of Greece (4–10)

Zinfandel (2–6)

White wines

Botrytized wines (5–25)

Chardonnay (2–6)

Furmint of Hungary (3–25)

Hunter Valley Semillon (6–15)

Loire Chenin Blanc (4–30)

Petit Manseng of Jurançon (3–10)

Riesling (2–30)

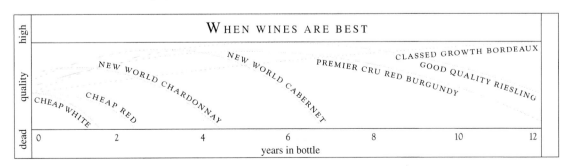

HOW TO STORE WINE

IDEAL STORAGE CONDITIONS

Once it is firmly stoppered in a bottle, wine should be protected from its greatest enemy, the oxygen in the air (see page 73). If, however, the cork dries out and eventually shrinks so that it no longer acts as an airtight seal, it may start to allow oxygen into the wine, which will spoil it. For this reason, wine bottles have traditionally been stored on their sides, so that the wine keeps the cork thoroughly damp and swollen to fill the bottle-neck.

There is a revolutionary new school of thought, however, which suggests that it may be

better for wine to store bottles at an angle, which ensures that both wine and the air bubble are in contact with the cork. This will keep the cork damp but allow any expansion and contraction of the air bubble due to temperature variation to result in air, and not wine, passing through the cork. When bottles are stored horizontally the distance of the air bubble from the cork means that when higher temperatures cause it to expand, wine may be forced out between the cork and bottle-neck (the sugary deposits round the neck of many sweet wines are cited as evidence for this). Then when the temperature drops, the air bubble contracts to form a vacuum and oxygen may be drawn into the bottle. That amount of oxygen may reach harmful levels if temperatures fluctuate dramatically.

For the moment, almost all wine racks in commercial circulation are blithely ignorant of this new theory, however, so if you want to store wine in a place in which the temperature can vary by more than 10°C (18°F) it might be wise to put a wedge underneath the front of the rack so as to tilt the whole thing at the (newly) approved angle.

For the reasons outlined previously, **temperature fluctuation** is the most serious hazard for wine storage, although the cooler wine is kept, the slower, and very possibly more interestingly, it will develop. The warmer it is stored, the faster it will mature (because heat inevitably speeds up all reactions and vice versa).

A London basement in which the most common problem of all – a central heating boiler in the most suitable wine storage space – has been completely solved, by boxing in the boiler with foam-insulated, silvered panels like the one propped up on the right (used to block out sunlight in high summer).

Red wines become browner (and less blue) with time but they lose colour and become paler as tannins and colouring agents, or anthocyans, are precipitated as sediment. The one-year-old fine red bordeaux on the left will taste tough and inky, while many of the tannins have fallen out of its 12-year-old counterpart on the right, leaving a mellow, much more interesting liquid.

The left hand white wine is one year old, while that on the right has had 20 years to deepen and turn browner, as various components oxidize.

The actual **temperature** at which wine is stored is also important. Care should be taken that it never falls below –4°C (25°F), the temperature at which the lightest wines freeze, which can fatally force corks out of bottle-necks. On the other hand, there is a temperature, about 25°C (77°F), above which a wine's more volatile compounds may be boiled off forever. In very general terms the ideal wine storage temperature is probably between 10 and 15°C (40–59°F), but no great harm will come to wine stored between 15 and 20°C (59–68°F) – so long as the temperature does not fluctuate dramatically. Maximum and minimum thermometers can be very useful for monitoring potential places to store wine.

Wine dislikes **light** as well as heat. Strong light can adversely affect the taste of wine, particularly sparkling wine, and particularly if the bottles are made from clear or pale glass. (This is why wine is sold increasingly in almost black bottles, and why champagne is often wrapped in tissue paper or a special light-proof cellophane.)

Humidity is also quite important. If wine is stored in too dry an atmosphere for several years, the corks can dry out and stop being an effective seal. Damp storage places are good for the condition of the wine but can rapidly damage labels. (The Japanese will apparently pay a premium for old wine with perfect labels, whereas some British wine connoisseurs are wary of this combination.)

Lack of **vibration** is useful for wines with a sediment, although this widespread belief is based more on hunch than hard evidence, and an absence of strong **smells** is absolutely vital (no old cans of paint or garden chemicals). In practice, **security** has to be weighed against **ease of retrieval**, with the relative importance of these two factors dependent on things like your income and willpower.

THE IDEAL CELLAR

It follows from all of the above that the ideal place for wine storage is a nice, dark, roomy, slightly dank cellar with a single discreet entrance to which only you have the key. It is lined with wine racks but has masses of room to walk around and to stack wine in its original cases, as well as a little tasting corner and a large desk for keeping cellar records up to date. For most of us, alas, this cellar belongs in the realm of fantasy.

THE REALITIES OF STORING WINE AT HOME

Most modern dwellings have a shortage of storage space of any kind, let alone somewhere cool, dark, quiet, slightly damp and roomy enough for a cache of bottles. Garden sheds and all but the most protected outbuildings are unsuitable in the British climate because of the danger of the temperature's dropping below −4°C (25°F). The main problem with most possible indoor places, on the other hand, is that they are too warm. Central heating boilers tend to be put wherever there is spare storage space, which rules out storing wine there – unless the boiler can be insulated, as in the photograph on page 42. Insulation of this sort is generally the key to establishing some decent permanent territory for a large wine collection, whether of a basement, an attic, or a slice of a room which becomes a walk-in wine cellar. Many people will be unwilling to make this much commitment, however, and are really looking for somewhere to store a dozen or two bottles. They could be kept in an attic, basement or corner of a spare room under an insulation blanket, or even in an old fireplace or possibly under the stairs. It is useful if possible to keep a bowlful of water on the ground near the wine to keep the humidity level up.

Bottles can be stored in wooden wine cases, or those made from the strongest cardboard, so long as the corks are kept damp. A proper wine rack will last longer and can be made to any shape required. Double depth models are useful.

The worst place to store wine (a fact unbeknown to most kitchen designers) is by a cooker or on top of a fridge where there are frequent blasts of hot air.

If you are serious about wine there are several relatively expensive 'artificial cellars' you could buy. It is quite possible to buy a large, humidity-controlled cabinet like a refrigerator which keeps reds and whites at desirable temperatures in different parts of it, but such things can usually store only a few dozen bottles. It is also possible to buy a spiral cellar which can be sunk into a specially excavated hole under ground level, but the installation can be very messy.

TRUSTING YOUR WINE TO SOMEONE ELSE

Much the easiest option in some ways, particularly if you have a large quantity of young wine, is to have it stored by professionals, either under the auspices of the merchant(s) you bought it from or directly with one of the specialists in wine warehousing. This will cost a few pounds per year per 'case' (the standard box containing a dozen bottles) and should ensure that the wine is stored in ideal conditions, but it rules out the spontaneity of picking bottles at random from your wine collection.

GETTING SERIOUS ABOUT COLLECTING WINE

Wine sometimes gets to otherwise sane people. They are smitten with the desire to exchange large sums of money for a collection of bottles that will mature over their lifetime. They scramble for smart or rare wines offered *en primeur*, as futures, paying for it (from a respectable merchant, please) long before it's delivered. They may also fill gaps in their collections by buying older wines at auction, notably from Christie's or Sotheby's. It is a mistake to buy wine solely as an investment. Wine prices go down as well as up. But, like all forms of collecting, it can bring a great deal of pleasure (and costs much less than collecting, say, works of art). Reasonably good record-keeping is needed to ensure that wines don't languish past their drink-by dates. And some wine collectors need to be reminded every so often that *wine is for drinking!*

CLUES FROM THE PACKAGE

A wine shop is a terrifying place, with rows and rows of virtually identical packages labelled in a dizzying range of languages with hundreds of unfamiliar proper names. However is the poor consumer to pick up the clues available? Happily, the proportion of wine stores staffed by people who know one end of a bottle from the other is slowly increasing. (See pages 342–43 for some specific recommendations.) Self-service stores are also getting better at putting useful information on back labels and on the shelves themselves, but it can be difficult to get answers to the most basic questions of all, which is what I try to provide below.

BOTTLE SHAPES AND COLOUR

The bottle is the standard wine container because, supposedly, its capacity, usually 75 cl (27 fl oz), is about one lungful of air, an important consideration when all bottles were individually blown. Straight-sided bottles developed to make storage easier, and the diameter of the bottle-neck may well have evolved because this is roughly the thickness of the strips of bark peeled off cork trees every nine years or so to provide suitable stoppers for bottles (see page 21).

There are two basic red wine bottle shapes, the narrow, high-shouldered 'bordeaux bottle' and the wider, sloping-shouldered 'burgundy bottle' (see photographs overleaf). In very general terms wines sold in bordeaux bottles are either from the greater Bordeaux area (south west France) or are made in the image of red bordeaux, whether from Cabernet and Merlot grapes, or simply sharing red bordeaux's characteristics of being relatively tannic (i.e. slightly tough and possibly worth ageing) and not very full-bodied (such as most reds from the Languedoc, Central Italy and Portugal). Red wines in burgundy bottles are typically from greater Burgundy (including Beaujolais and Mâcon), or

from the Rhône valley, or are made from Pinot Noir grapes, or are meant to taste softer and perhaps more full-bodied than average. Rioja producers, for example, quite often produce wines in these two different styles, bottled in the two different shapes.

Red bordeaux producers (and those making other long-lived wines such as Barolo, Barbaresco and vintage port) have been putting their wines into darker and darker glass because of the threat of damage by strong light (see page 42) to these wines designed for the long term. Burgundy has traditionally been put into pale green glass, possibly acknowledging that red burgundy does not usually need to be kept as long as red bordeaux.

There are three different basic white wine shapes: the bordeaux and burgundy shapes plus a taller, slimmer shape, which is used for more aromatic wines such as those from Germany and Alsace, and from Riesling and Riesling-like grapes generally. Green glass is used for Mosel, Alsace and lighter bodied wines, while brown glass often signifies a heavier wine or one from Germany's Rhine regions.

The bordeaux shape is used for white bordeaux, in clear glass for most sweet wines and green glass for dry wines (although clear glass is used for some dry wines too). It is also used for a wide range of sweet wines and dry wines from the Bordeaux grapes Sauvignon Blanc and Semillon and for a wide variety of lightish dry whites. The high alcoholic strength and extract of sweet wines means that most can withstand the exposure to light they get from clear glass quite well, but a producer has usually to be confident of a fast turnover to put a light dry white into clear glass.

The standard white burgundy bottle is made of pale greenish-yellow (*feuille morte* or 'dead leaf') glass and is widely used for all sorts of white wines, especially those which, like white burgundy, are dry, full-bodied and, often, aged in oak. This includes not just a wide range of Chardonnays but also many a Sauvignon, Semillon, and – so popular is this wine style – almost any white grape variety you can imagine.

In very general terms, therefore, *the wider the bottle, the more body it is likely to have.*

Top quality bottles are made from thick glass and often have large indentations in the base called 'punts'. Most champagne bottles (which are made of particularly heavy glass to withstand the pressure inside) have these and they enable you to pour even this bottle with one hand, the thumb anchored in the punt. A producer can save a significant amount per case by packaging wine in thin glass stoppered with a short, agglomerate cork.

Different regions and even different producers have developed their own special bottles. These can often add slightly to the cost of the wine and, especially in the case of those strange deformed assymetrical ones, add nothing whatever to its quality.

BOTTLE SIZES

You are usually charged a premium for any bottle size other than the standard one, partly because the bottling technology costs more. Half-bottles are extremely useful but wine producers hate the special bottling lines they

demand and wine scientists argue that the relatively high ratio of air to wine in a half-bottle accelerates the ageing process, sometimes to the detriment of the wine. (This problem can be even more acute for quarter-bottles.) Bottles containing 50 cl are becoming increasingly popular with health-conscious consumers.

Purists argue that magnums, containing 1.5 l or the equivalent of two standard bottles, provide the perfect size for stately wine maturation, but you are usually asked to pay a little extra for this, unless the wine is particularly cheap and cheerful. Larger sizes still are available, particularly for red bordeaux, but need buyers with a very long-term view. Larger sizes of champagne are a better idea for exhibitionists than wine lovers (see page 86).

CONTAINERS OTHER THAN BOTTLES

Today wine is sold in boxes, cartons, cans, pouches, plastic bottles and all manner of materials other than glass. Few of the materials used are as inert as glass and none has so far proved itself suitable for keeping wine for more than a few months. Wine boxes can be extremely useful for big parties and for those who want to keep on drawing off quantities smaller than a bottle at a time over a week or two, but the wine can deteriorate quite rapidly once the seal has been broken.

THE BACK LABEL

The role of the back label is conventionally to give the consumer additional information not accommodated on the front label. As con-

Typical bottles for (from left to right) white bordeaux, Semillon, Sauvignon Blanc; red bordeaux, Cabernet Sauvignon, Merlot; white burgundy, Chardonnay; red burgundy, Rhône, Loire, Pinot Noir; Rhine wines (Mosels are green glass), Rieslings; half bottle of champagne.

These two pairs of wines show just how powerful packaging is. On the left, a red bordeaux and burgundy bottled and labelled following their respective regional conventions. On the right, how the same wines would look if the bordeaux were dressed up like a burgundy and vice versa. It would take very careful study to work out that, for instance, the bottle on the far right is not bordeaux.

sumers have become more knowledgeable, the proportion of genuinely informative back labels, often giving useful production details, has risen substantially. The standard back label typically used to claim that the wine was 'made from the finest grapes, grown on the best sites, picked at the optimum moment and vinified with the greatest care'. If the wine was white it would invariably be suggested that it was drunk with fish and white meats, while red meats and cheese were routinely suggested for red wines.

THE FRONT LABEL

This is by far the most important clue to how a wine is likely to taste, although there is annoyingly little uniformity about naming wines.

The label is also effectively the wine's travel permit, which means that it has to give certain information. (Artistically minded producers sometimes put this mandatory information on something clearly meant to be a back label but pretend to officialdom that this back label is in fact the principal label rather than the technically illegal creation on the other side of the bottle. See Cloudy Bay labels on page 50.)

WHAT'S THE WINE CALLED?

It can be extremely difficult to work out which of the many rows of type on the label is actually meant to be the crucial name of the wine, although technically it should be the letters in the biggest type.

Some wines, and almost all of those made in the less traditional wine-producing countries, are named after the grape variety (or varieties) from which they are made. These are the so-called **varietal** wines called after the grape varieties detailed in Section Three (Chardonnay, Cabernet Sauvignon, etc.). This sort of naming gives the consumer a very clear idea of the sort of flavours and style he or she is likely to encounter in the bottle, which is probably why varietal labelling has become so popular.

The other, and more sophisticated, way of naming wine, that embraced by France and many other European countries, is to name it **geographically**, after the region where it was produced (such as Chablis, Bordeaux, Valpolicella, Rioja, etc.). It is much more difficult than most wine retailers realize, however, for newcomers to remember whether it's Chablis or Chardonnay that is the grape and which of them is the place.

There are thousands of wine place-names but probably no more than a score of important grape varieties. (This is just one of the reasons why I believe that knowing one's way round the major grape varieties [see Section Three] is such a useful starting-point to learning about wine.)

Branded wines tend to be named with a heavily promoted invented name such as Blue Nun or Mateus Rosé.

QUALITY DESIGNATIONS – OFTEN USEFUL

If a wine is labelled geographically, the label usually carries not just the name of the region but also the name of one of the carefully regulated quality designations listed in the table below. Division One comprises, in theory at least, the crack corps of that country's wines, whereas Division Two is the middle ranks. Division Three is included for completeness. In fact wines which qualify for these lowly titles are not usually allowed to claim any geographical provenance; they simply belong to Europe's soft underbelly of, often surplus, wine production.

The quality designations listed under Division One lay down very strict regulations about the exact land included, permitted grape varieties, yields, minimum ripeness levels and vine-growing and winemaking techniques allowed. Many New World producers are thrilled that they do not have these constraints and can plant anything they like where they like, but an increasing number of them are seeing the virtues of developing awareness of their own region (which cannot be duplicated elsewhere) and geographical labelling is generally on the increase, often supplementing varietal labelling (as in, for example, Sonoma Chardonnay, Coonawarra Cabernet Sauvignon and Casablanca Sauvignon Blanc).

OFFICIAL CATEGORIES OF WINE			
COUNTRY	DIVISION ONE	DIVISION TWO	DIVISION THREE
FRANCE (see page 157)	Appellation Contrôlée[a] (AC or AOC)	Vin de Pays	Vin de Table
ITALY (see page 207)	Denominazione di Origine Controllata (DOC) DOCG (like DOC but 'Garantita' too)	Indicazione Geografica Tipica (IGT)	Vino da Tavola
GERMANY (see page 261)	Qualitätswein mit Prädikat (QmP)	Qualitätswein bestimmter Anbaugebiete (QbA)	Deutscher Tafelwein
SPAIN (see page 234)	Denominacíon de Origen (DO)	Vino de la Tierra	Vino de Mesa

[a] There is also a small category called Vin Délimité de Qualité Supérieure (VDQS) which is basically an Appellation Contrôlée-in-waiting.

WHO MADE IT?

The name of the producer, or at least the bottler, should be on every wine label. In most cases this is the single most important bit of information. There can be a world of difference between a lacklustre bottler's Chablis blended to meet a price and one from a seriously quality-conscious individual with a reputation to lose. It is at this point that wine knowledge becomes complicated, but see Section Four for hundreds of names of recommended producers.

ALCOHOLIC STRENGTH

This is one of the most useful vital statistics about a wine which should be on the label of almost all wines in commercial circulation. A guide to the approximate alcoholic strength (expressed as a percentage of pure alcohol by volume) of the main types of wine is given on pages 36–7. Generally speaking, less alcoholic wines come from the coolest climates and vice versa, sunshine being converted directly into sugar in grapes, most of which is fermented into alcohol (see page 74). Although one might think that the drinker would hardly notice the difference between a 12 per cent wine and a 13 per cent one, I find that a higher alcohol wine can really catch me out the morning after, whereas most German wine is so light it can be gulped with abandon.

OTHER INFORMATION

Almost all wines in Divisions One and Two should be vintage dated. See pages 306–9 for details of specific **vintages** in specific regions. Division Three wines are not usually allowed to specify a year but are almost invariably made from the produce of the most recent vintage or, in crossover periods, a blend of the two most recent. Table wine is held in store, often lightly refrigerated, until an order is received.

Most labels should give some **bottling information**, ideally stating the wine was bottled by its producer (Estate Bottled, Gutsabfüllung, or Mis en Bouteille à ... etc). This may refer simply to a mobile bottling line which visits the property and in some cases professional contract bottlers may do a better job. I am always slightly wary of wines bottled a long way from their source as it can expose the wine to more risk from temperature variation and oxygen. It can also save considerably on its cost, however, as in some of the wines shipped in bulk from Australia (where bottling costs are exceptionally high) to use up spare bottling capacity closer to their eventual consumers.

Many more precise, geographically specific clues to quality may appear on wine labels: expressions such as premier cru, cru classé, vieilles vignes, Villages, Classico, Kabinett, etc. See Section Four for more details.

WORDS FOR SWEETNESS LEVELS				
	FRENCH	ITALIAN	GERMAN	SPANISH
BONE DRY	brut	–	–	–
DRY	sec	secco	trocken	seco
MEDIUM DRY	demi-sec	abboccato	halbtrocken	semi-seco
MEDIUM SWEET	doux	amabile	mild	–
SWEET	moelleux	dolce	lieblich	dulce
VERY SWEET	liquoreux	–	süss	–
WORDS FOR FIZZINESS				
GENTLY SPARKLING	perlant	frizzante	spritzig	–
FULLY SPARKLING	mousseux	spumante	Sekt	espumoso

DECIPHERING THE LABEL

VARIETAL WINES

A pair of varietal labels from the southern hemisphere. Cloudy Bay's 'front label' is purely cosmetic, although it shows all the information vital to the consumer. (Its design is based on a photograph taken by the winemaker.) The narrower label on the back of the bottle has all the information vital to the regulators, however, and is therefore officially the main label.

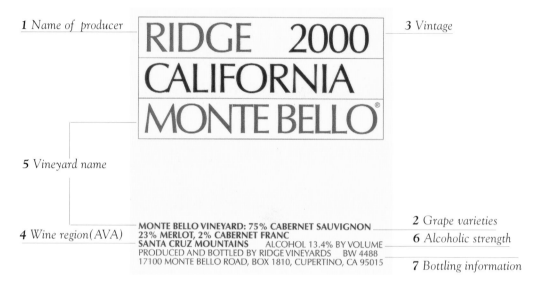

1 Name of producer

3 Vintage

5 Vineyard name

4 Wine region (AVA)

2 Grape varieties

6 Alcoholic strength

7 Bottling information

MONTE BELLO VINEYARD: 75% CABERNET SAUVIGNON
23% MERLOT, 2% CABERNET FRANC
SANTA CRUZ MOUNTAINS   ALCOHOL 13.4% BY VOLUME
PRODUCED AND BOTTLED BY RIDGE VINEYARDS   BW 4488
17100 MONTE BELLO ROAD, BOX 1810, CUPERTINO, CA 95015

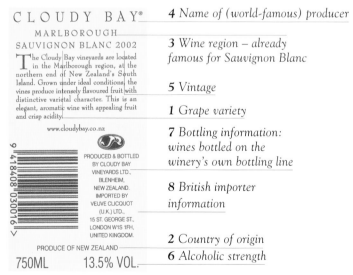

4 Name of (world-famous) producer

3 Wine region – already famous for Sauvignon Blanc

5 Vintage

1 Grape variety

7 Bottling information: wines bottled on the winery's own bottling line

8 British importer information

2 Country of origin

6 Alcoholic strength

Explanations are numbered in the order I would examine the label. Grape type is usually the most important aspect of a varietal wine followed by country of origin and then producer and any more specific geographical information in an order determined by the maturity of the wine-producing country and the extent to which its wine regions have managed to establish a meaningful identity. Vintage and any other information are usually of less vital importance than in the most marginal wine regions.

GEOGRAPHICALLY NAMED WINES

A fine white and red from complex Burgundy. Note the two forms of showing the name of the controlled appellation. Also, how the Meursault is obviously a 'domaine bottled' wine, produced and bottled at the same small wine *domaine*, while the Chambolle-Musigny, perhaps a blend from different producers, is bottled by a large merchant, or négociant.

2 *Quality designation or appellation (Charmes is a Premier Cru vineyard within the village of Meursault)*

5 *Bottling information (bottled at the cellar)*

4 *Vintage – extremely important in Burgundy, excellent for white burgundy (see pages 307)*

6 *Alcoholic strength*

3 *Name of (irreproachable) producer*

1 *Country of origin*

3 *Name of producer, an extremely reputable négociant who also owns vineyards (whose produce would be described on the label as mis en bouteille à la propriété or au domaine)*

4 *Bottling information for a wine made from bought-in grapes (or wine)*

2 *Quality designation of appellation (this 'village burgundy' can contain wine made anywhere within the village of Chambolle-Musigny)*

1 *Country of origin*

Explanations are numbered in the order I would examine the label. If a wine is French, then the name of the appellation is paramount, and should give a fine clue as to the likely taste of the wine. The name of the producer is almost as important, though – especially in Burgundy, and in Bordeaux where the producer is usually Château Something. Vintage is generally much more important in northern Europe than elsewhere and Drouhin puts its vintages on neck labels.

HOW TO BUY THE RIGHT BOTTLE

How, faced with the array of bottles in a wine store, do you pick the right one off the shelf? Here are a few random but specific suggestions.

• Decide on a price bracket and stick to it, but it can be worth spending at the top of the bracket. Bear in mind that in Britain, where excise duty alone is more than £1 a bottle, the price of the wine inside a bottle selling at £2.99 is roughly 60p, whereas there is about £1.50 worth of wine in a bottle selling at £4.99 and more than £4 worth in a bottle priced at £9.99.

• Take special offers very seriously. In the competitive market-place of today, heavily scrutinized by a bevy of wine critics, these bargains are almost certainly there to lure you into the shop rather than to offload rubbish.

• If possible, pick a bottle that has been lying on its side, and has not obviously been kept in a place where the temperature may have varied considerably. Avoid bottles which have been standing upright in strong light (although the better stores have a policy of constantly changing the one representative bottle with another from a horizontal lot).

Be wary of bottles which have 'wept' around the cork or have a relatively low fill level as both of these are signs of temperature variation (see page 42).

SOME PARTICULARLY CONFUSING NAMES:

*Pouilly-Fuissé (pronounced 'Pwee-Fwee-say') is the most concentrated white wine of the Mâconnais between Beaujolais and Burgundy proper and is a broad, full-bodied wine made from Chardonnay grapes. **Pouilly-Fumé**, on the other hand, is very like Sancerre, a piercingly aromatic Loire relatively light, tart, dry white made from Sauvignon Blanc grapes.*

*Muscadet is a bone dry, somewhat neutral white from the mouth of the Loire while **Muscat** is the name of a particularly fruity grape variety usually made into very sweet, strong wines, also sold under the name **Moscato** and **Moscatel**.*

*Semillon is a grape variety which makes full-bodied white wines, notably in Bordeaux and Australia. **St-Émilion**, on the other hand, is the name of a pretty town in the Bordeaux region, and the deep-coloured, plummy red wines made around it.*

• Try to grasp the names at least, and ideally the characteristics, of the major grape varieties (see Section Three).

• If, once you have become relatively familiar with the most common wine names, you spot a bottle with an unrecognizable pedigree, give it a try. It is probably there only because someone passionately believes in its inherent quality; wine buyers generally err on the side of caution.

• On the subject of familiar names, the well-known international wine brands such as Mateus Rosé, Blue Nun, Jacob's Creek, Gallo, Turning Leaf and Mouton Cadet can offer a reliable minimum quality level in a strange place with a very limited selection but are usually relatively expensive (all that advertising has to be paid for).

• Be wary of wines designed for early consumption (see pages 39–41) that are more than two years old.

• Bear in mind that wines (especially reds) that are extremely expensive and carry vintage dates less than three or four years old are almost certainly years from being fun to drink.

• Try to remember to make a note of any wine that you particularly like so that you can use the chart opposite as a way to discover new wines with a similar style.

SOME RELATIVELY UNDERPRICED WINES

The market changes all the time according to the weather (e.g. crop reduction caused by frost damage), fashion and supply, but the following wines were better bargains than most at the time of writing.

Whites

The best Corbières, Minervois and Coteaux du Languedoc, from individual estates
Chilean Sauvignon and Chardonnay
Hungarian varietals
South African Colombard and Chenin
Vins de Pays des Côtes de Gascogne
Better AC Bordeaux and Entre-Deux-Mers
Alsace Pinot Blanc
Menetou Salon, Quincy and Reuilly
Mature fine German wines
Australian traditional method sparkling wines

Reds

Spanish Monastrell (Mourvèdre)
The best Corbières, Minervois and Coteaux du Languedoc, from individual estates
Chilean Cabernet, Merlot, Carmenère, and some Pinot Noir
Hungarian varietals
Montepulciano d'Abruzzo
Valdepeñas
Ribatejo and Alentejo from Portugal
AC Bordeaux
Premières Côtes de Bordeaux
Vins de Pays

HOW TO TRY A NEW WINE

Here are some possible routes from some of the most popular wines to less familiar names offering better value and/or a slight variation on the taste.

Whites

Chardonnay		Sancerre/Pouilly-Fumé	Liebfraumilch
LIGHT, CRISP	FULL, OAKY	New Zealand Sauvignon Blanc	German Spätlese
Chablis	Semillon Chardonnay	Chilean Sauvignon	Riesling Kabinett
Pinot Blanc	Semillon	Fumé Blanc from anywhere	Alsace Riesling
Chardonnay, Vin de Pays d'Oc	Bordeaux blanc (oaked)	Slovenian whites	any Alsace white
Limoux	Graves	Friuli whites	any Gewürztraminer or
New Zealand Chardonnay	White Châteauneuf-du-	Riesling!	Traminer
Sauvignon Blanc	Pape		any Pinot Gris
Jurançon Sec	Fino sherry or Manzanilla		Argentine Torrontes
			Albariño/Alvarinho
			Viognier
			Condrieu

Reds

Cabernet Sauvignon

LIGHT, AROMATIC	CRISP, CRUNCHY	OAKY, TANNIC	MELLOW, ROUND
Cabernet Franc	Teroldego	Syrah	Merlot
Anjou-Villages	Tempranillo	Hermitage	Bordeaux
Bourgueil	Sangiovese	Nebbiolo	St-Émilion
Chinon	Chianti Classico	Barbaresco	Pomerol
Cru Beaujolais	Brunello	Barolo	NewWorld Pinot
Old World Pinot Noir	Supertuscans	Douro reds	Argentine Malbec
Burgundy			
Overdraft			

CHOOSING WINE IN A RESTAURANT

Thanks to the advent of self-service in wine retailing, about the only time we have to make a public statement about wine and our wine preferences is when ordering in a restaurant, pub or bar. In fact for most consumers this is probably the only time that they have actually to pronounce wine names, and it is certainly the time that they pay most for the pleasure of drinking wine.

HOW MUCH TO PAY

It is standard practice in restaurants with high overheads to calculate prices on the wine list by doubling, trebling and sometimes even quadrupling the basic wholesale prices. It is naive to expect a restaurateur to sell wine at exactly the same price as a wine retailer. He or she has all sorts of extra bills to pay, not to mention the cost of building up a cellar. But you can ensure that the premium you pay for drinking wine in a restaurant is kept to a minimum: wherever a straight percentage mark-up is applied it is pure folly to go for one of the seriously grand wines and *it makes sound financial sense to order one of the cheapest bottles on the wine list*.

A benevolent minority of restaurateurs add something closer to a standard cash mark-up to all bottles, no matter what the price, in order to encourage customers to buy something special to go with what one hopes is a superior standard of cooking. Unfortunately, however, you need to know quite a lot about wine and wine prices to take advantage of this sensible approach.

SOME SAFE CHOICES

The following have been chosen because they are relatively inexpensive, go with a wide range of foods, and poorly made examples are relatively rare. See also previous page.

Whites
• South African Sauvignon Blanc (cheap but can be thin).
• Alsace whites, especially please-all Pinot Blanc.
• Many Chardonnays, especially St-Véran and other Mâconnais whites and good bottlings from California and Australia.

Reds
• Corbières, Minervois and Coteaux de Languedoc with a Château or Domaine name.
• Beaujolais-Villages or cru Beaujolais (i.e. Morgon, Moulin-à-Vent, Juliénas, Chénas, Regnié, Brouilly, Côte-de-Brouilly, Fleurie, St-Amour and Chiroubles).
• Estate bottled Côtes-du-Rhône and Gigondas Bourgueil, Chinon, Anjou-Villages.
• Zinfandel (restaurateurs don't usually list the dross).

THE GREAT TASTING RITUAL

The joke about this often embarrassing restaurant practice is that few of those who offer or taste the initial sample from the bottle ordered have a clue why they are doing it. The great wine-tasting ritual has its origins in a time when the wine was much less reliably stable and healthy than it has become.

The customer is meant to be checking the temperature and that the wine is not out of condition (corked, oxidized, refermenting, hazy). To check this, all you need do is look to see that the wine is clear and still (unless it is meant to be sparkling) and then smell it to ensure it smells clean and not musty or mouldy. *This tasting has nothing to do with whether you like the wine or not*. You can send the wine back only if it has one of the faults listed above, in which case the restaurateur can return it to the supplier and get

a refund or replacement. Because I am paranoid about seeing a fussy wine bore, I probably err on the side of caution, but I have sent wine back only three or four times in 20 years of tasting wine and dining out, by saying 'I think this wine is corked/oxidized/refermenting/hazy'. The wine should be presented, by the way, to whoever ordered it. It is then up to them to suggest someone else tastes it if they'd rather. Despite the ceremony of some wine waiters, or 'sommeliers', sniffing the cork is no reliable guide to the condition of the wine.

Wine with bits of cork floating in it, by the way is not 'corked'. These are harmless cork fragments which may be the result of an inefficient corkscrew. They should simply be scooped out with a spoon (although many waiters have the annoying habit of whisking away the entire glass – of wine you have paid for – and pouring a new one).

A wine that complements your mood and meal certainly need not be the most expensive.

WINE BY THE GLASS

This is a fantastically good idea, imaginatively executed by most American restaurants and completely ruined in most British pubs. Now that wine is such a democratic drink (and usually well made), and it is so easy to preserve wine leftovers (see pages 23–5), there is no excuse for serving out-of-condition filth by the glass.

SOME COMMONLY MISPRONOUNCED NAMES		
	CORRECT	INCORRECT
Riesling	Reece-ling	Rize-ling
Moët	Mow-it	Mo-way
Montrachet	Mon-rashay	Mont-rashay

SOME SPECIAL WINES

REDUCED ALCOHOL WINES

Some wines are naturally low in alcohol, either because they are produced somewhere far from the equator such as the Mosel valley with limited amounts of sunshine to produce fermentable sugar in the grapes or because, like Asti, the fermentation is deliberately stopped half-way through to produce a sweet, low alcohol wine.

As we have become more aware of our alcohol intake, however, all sorts of semi-industrial low-alcohol and no-alcohol wine-like products have been concocted. Most of them taste decidedly unlike wine. The Lambrusco producers willing to offer a Lambrusco Light (and White, and Pink) are not exactly among the noble Italian region's most respected. There are dealcoholized products from California and from the Australian wine giant Southcorp which are more convincing than most, but they do strike me as quintessentially substitute products, just like nut cutlets. Why fashion something without ingredient X in the mould of those things that contain X? A really good soft drink (see page 32) or a spritzer (see below) usually gives me more pleasure.

COMMERCIAL WINE MIXES AND COOLERS

Commercial bottled blends of fruit juices and wine sell in relatively vast quantities. The development of artificial essences of peach, apricot, raspberry and so on have helped this trade enormously. When it comes down to it, some of the best are duplications of the most successful fresh mixes of wine and fruit juice – orange juice and sparkling wine (Buck's Fizz) and peach juice and sparkling wine (Bellini). The commercial brands can taste a bit artificial, however, and are invariably very sweet.

WINE MIXES TO MAKE AT HOME

Buck's Fizz, a blend of dry sparkling white wine with one to two times as much fresh orange juice, makes a great Sunday morning refresher. It's useful for a short party but a bit wearing after two glasses (and fresh juice can make washing up the glasses tricky). A **Bellini** is a Venetian version in which peach juice is substituted for orange juice. It is best made with jars of Italian peach juice which is incredibly thick. To allow the bubbles to escape with more abandon, dilute the juice with some water. The Irish mix Guinness stout with dry fizz to produce the powerful **Black Velvet**. Drink with caution.

Perhaps the simplest mix, and the most refreshing aperitif in hot weather, is a **Spritzer**, made up of roughly equal parts of white wine and sparkling water.

Another way of livening up a glass of dull or neutral dry white is to add enough blackcurrant cordial or the alcoholic version from Burgundy, crème de cassis (about half a teaspoonful), to make a pale pink, fruity **Kir** or **vin blanc cassis**. Served with sparkling wine it becomes a **Kir Royale**, with red wine a **Cardinale**. You can substitute other strong fruit cordials.

Any red wine, even the cheapest and nastiest, can provide a base for the spicy, warming brew known as **Glühwein** or **mulled wine**. Gently heat three to five bottles of red wine with an orange studded with cloves, a cinnamon stick and white sugar, and possibly a little lemon juice. The alcohol is boiled off unless you are careful about how the mixture is heated. Once warmed, it is best left on a low heat as the first duty of mulled wine is to be hot.

LOW-CALORIE WINE?

Wine is not slimming. The two components which contribute to its calorific value are alcohol and sugar, so the most fattening wines are those in the bottom right hand corner of page 36 and the asterisked examples in the lower half of page 37. The least calorific are those in the top left hand corner of page 36 and those along the top of page 37. It is by no means the case that white wine is less fattening than red, nor that dry wines are necessarily low in calories (all the wines in the bottom half of page 37 are relatively high in calories).

WINES FOR SPECIAL MEDICAL CONDITIONS

Diabetics should take care to choose bone dry wines, which means any wine down the left hand side of page 36 and any red wine except the ones asterisked on page 37. Wines sold specifically as Diabetic are usually low in both sugar and alcohol.

Many people find that their bodies react badly to either white or red wines. Since red wines contain a much wider range of components than white, the second of these reactions is easier to understand and some think it may reflect red wine's histamine content. Perhaps the white wines which have caused an allergic reaction are rather higher than most in sulphur (see page 73) and some asthmatics react particularly badly to this common food preservative.

Much more research is needed in this area, but the wine trade is generally composed of people who react extremely well to wine and there has therefore been little enthusiasm for this research.

Some wine drinkers report that they feel much better after drinking organic wines (see page 65) rather than those produced using agrochemicals.

Since some finings (see page 72) contain animal products (egg whites, fish bladders and casein from milk), some wine producers deliberately use other finings so that they can offer their produce as vegan wines. It should be noted, however, that finings are not designed to remain in the finished wine.

NOUVEAU, NOVELLO AND ALL THAT

The Beaujolais producers once had such enormous success with their Beaujolais Nouveau released in November that a flood of similar infant wine has flowed onto the market. These wines are generally light in body and alcohol and are fermented and stabilized at top speed so that they can be sold just a few weeks after the harvest. Very good for the cash flow. The Gamay grape of Beaujolais does lend itself to this somewhat brutal treatment and versions from the Loire valley, notably Gamay de Touraine, have been quite successful. The craze spread downriver to the Muscadet region for a white version. Some of these French wines are labelled Primeur rather than Nouveau. Italy has its own riposte in various wines labelled Novello, while the New World has also tried its hand. None of these wines is desperately exciting, and they rarely improve in bottle, but they don't decline quite as rapidly as some authorities would have us believe. I have drunk a five-year-old Beaujolais Nouveau and lived.

COOKING WITH WINE

There is a school of thought that any wine used in cooking should be top quality and/or of the same region as the dish. I find this hard to accept, particularly as so little research has been done on exactly what happens to wine when you cook with it. I am sure that if the wine in the dish (as in steeped strawberries, for example) is never heated, then it is worth choosing one that tastes as delicious as you can afford. If you want to reduce a sauce using wine, however, I would have thought you wanted one with as much body as possible – and that the wine's components may go through so many transformations that the initial flavour could not possibly be preserved. More research, please! Meanwhile, in our household we will continue to see cooking as a particularly satisfying way of using up wine leftovers.

2
HOW WINE IS MADE

THE IMPORTANCE OF PLACE

There is a saying in the restaurant business that the three factors which determine whether an establishment will be a success are location, location and location. In wine production place is not quite that important. The vineyard's location is just one of four main factors determining how a wine tastes. The others, in roughly decreasing order of how powerfully they can shape a wine's character, are the vine variety or varieties used (see pages 100–153), how the wine is made (see pages 74–93), and how the vines are grown (see pages 64–71). The most obvious reason why a vineyard's location is important is because it determines its weather and climate, but it has many other, more subtle but potentially crucial effects on the wine produced from it (see pages 62–3).

WEATHER AND CLIMATE

The weather that makes up the climate of a wine region, the so-called **macroclimate**, defines whether grape-growing is an activity that is (a) feasible and (b) commercially sensible. So long as there is enough warmth to ripen grapes every year, and winters are cool enough to give vines a restorative winter break, vine-growing can be a profitable agricultural activity.

The map opposite, showing the distribution of the world's wine regions, indicates how vine-growing, or viticulture, is essentially confined to two temperate bands around the globe, with local exceptional conditions resulting in a bit of manipulation here and there. Many of Argentina's best vineyards, for example, are so high that their altitude compensates for their relatively low latitude. England's vineyards, on the other hand, may be further from the equator than any others but warm ocean currents help to moderate the climate, so that vines need no special protection in winter, unlike many of their counterparts in Canada and Russia.

Dangerously cold winters apart, the main problem for vine-growers in cool climates is that in some years the grapes may not reach full ripeness, so that the sugar content of the juice needs additional help to ferment into the sort of alcohol levels we expect from wine (see chaptalization, page 72). Unreliable weather during the vine flowering in late spring can also cause havoc to vine-growing economics by severely affecting the number of flowers that are fertilized and therefore the number of grapes produced (see page 69).

Regions with high rainfall, however hot or cold they are, bring their own problems to vine-growing: fungal diseases such as various rots and mildews which flourish in damp conditions and usually demand frequent and expensive spraying to keep them at bay. Vine pests are becoming increasingly tolerant to many of these chemical preparations however, and every growing season sees more and more converts to some form of organic viticulture (see page 65).

Many very dry climates are quite capable of producing reasonably good wine, provided enough water is available for irrigation. Many of the vineyards of Chile and, especially, Argentina depend for their existence on irrigation channels dug, often a century ago, to direct the melting snows of the Andes into the land beneath them. Irrigation is not necessarily an evil thing designed to produce huge crops of dilute wine, although because it can be (and because northern Europe has quite enough water from the sky without recourse to ditches, sprinklers, or drip systems) the practice is regarded with deep suspicion by European law-makers. In much of the New World, irrigation is an economic necessity. Without it a very substantial proportion of the vineyards of, for example, the United States and Australia simply could not exist as wine production centres. Almost all new vineyards in climates with an average minimum annual rainfall of less than about 500 mm (20 in), or 700 mm (28 in) in hotter climates, are automatically designed to incorporate irrigation systems. Many of these systems are sophisticated enough to apply doses of water carefully determined by precise measurements of the amount of water in the soil at various times during the growing season.

Because in general terms the flavour elements in a grape need as long as possible to develop, and so the longer it takes for grapes to ripen the better, it is difficult to produce good quality wine too close to the equator. Problems also occur in such areas partly because tropical rains can result in galloping fungal disease (a problem in Japan and parts of China), and partly because where there is no winter the vine keeps on producing not-particularly-ripe fruit. In Brazil and Kenya, for example, vines may produce two or three crops a year, in 'seasons' artificially manipulated by careful timing of pruning and irrigation.

In some of the world's warmer wine regions some really determined vine-growers may also combat nature by using chemicals which encourage buds to burst or persuade the vine to stop growing.

Specific hazards of weather (as opposed to more general climate disadvantages) are described on pages 68–71, the vineyard year.

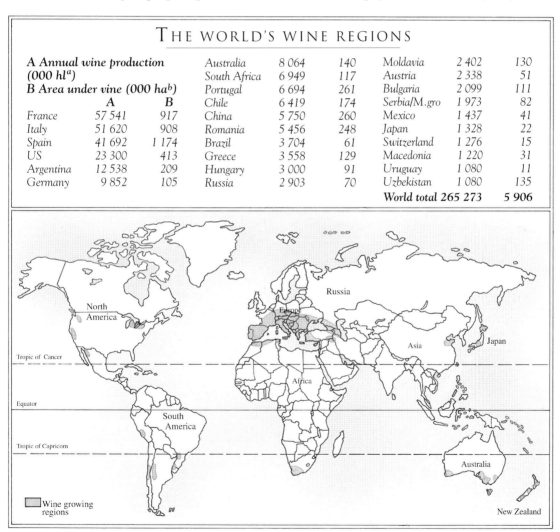

THE WORLD'S WINE REGIONS

A Annual wine production (000 hl[a])
B Area under vine (000 ha[b])

	A	B		A	B		A	B
France	57 541	917	Australia	8 064	140	Moldavia	2 402	130
Italy	51 620	908	South Africa	6 949	117	Austria	2 338	51
Spain	41 692	1 174	Portugal	6 694	261	Bulgaria	2 099	111
US	23 300	413	Chile	6 419	174	Serbia/M.gro	1 973	82
Argentina	12 538	209	China	5 750	260	Mexico	1 437	41
Germany	9 852	105	Romania	5 456	248	Japan	1 328	22
			Brazil	3 704	61	Switzerland	1 276	15
			Greece	3 558	129	Macedonia	1 220	31
			Hungary	3 000	91	Uruguay	1 080	11
			Russia	2 903	70	Uzbekistan	1 080	135
						World total	**265 273**	**5 906**

[a] hectolitres (100 litres) – approx. 133 bottles [b] hectares (2.5 acres) Office International du Vin's 2000 figures for the most significant wine-producing countries. At least another 35 countries, including New Zealand and the UK, produced less than a million hl of wine.

DOES THE ANSWER LIE IN THE SOIL?

While the macroclimate of a wine region may govern whether it is capable of producing ripe wine grapes at all, the subtle characteristics of a much smaller area – a particular vineyard, or even part of a vineyard – may determine the sort of wine that can be produced from that area. These characteristics include the climate of that smaller area, its **mesoclimate** (for long called its 'microclimate', but see page 66 for more up-to-date usage); its soil; the lie of the land, or its topography; and the effects each of these three elements have on each other. Any gardener, or even garden observer such as myself, can see at a glance (on a frosty morning, for example) how each part of the garden is heavily influenced by all these characteristics.

The French, typically, have one elegant word for this long list of natural characteristics: **terroir**. Indeed they have based their entire wine industry on the premise that a wine's characteristics are uniquely determined by the terroir, the natural environment, of the place in which the grapes were grown (see pages 48–9 and 157 for a description of the famous appellation contrôlée system). One has only to look at the complicated, hierarchical patchwork of different vineyards and appellations in Burgundy's Côte d'Or (see pages 166–8) to see how fundamental is this principle in grading and pricing fine burgundy. The produce of one vineyard separated only by a narrow track from another, lowlier one may fetch three or four times as much. To the outsider this seems like hocus pocus, and the argument would certainly be a lot more convincing if all wine experts could immediately identify which vineyard a wine comes from when blind tasting. But there is no denying that an individual producer's wine from a humble Bourgogne Blanc vineyard is always discernibly less concentrated than his or her smart Premier Cru white burgundy, which

itself rarely develops the grandeur of a Grand Cru. (One producer's Bourgogne Blanc may be better than another's Grand Cru, but that is another story.)

Because in very well-established wine regions such as Bordeaux and Burgundy it was possible to map wine quality, and therefore to rank individual vineyards, for long it was thought that it was the individual chemical composition of the soil of each vineyard that uniquely determined the sort and quality of wine it could produce. Much human effort over the years has gone into studying the individual geology of specific sites and there was a time when it seemed impossible to be a real wine expert without detailed knowledge of Quaternary deposits and Bathonian oolitic limestone. No one could have been more delighted than me to discover that more recent research suggests the chemical composition of a vineyard's soil, subsoil and underlying rock is very much less important than their physical characteristics, the most important factors that contribute to wine quality being that the soil is not too fertile, and is well drained but can store water within reach of vine roots so that the vine always has a steady but not excessive supply of water. The gravels of the Médoc, the clays of Pomerol, the marly limestone of the best Côte d'Or vineyards all fit these conditions and put the natural energy provided by sunlight into ripening fruit rather than producing too many leaves. Too much water means too much foliage at the expense of fruit.

Man can manipulate terroir by irrigation, or by persuading vines to grow in particular shapes (see page 64), but in the classical Old World wine regions terroir has been very much left to dictate what sort of wine is produced from a given site. Since sites for New World vineyards tend to be chosen because of pragmatic reasons

(the grower happens to own the land, for example, or the plot happens to be for sale), then the argument that terroir is all-important becomes far less attractive. Some French in particular have also left wine producers in the New World with the vague but implicit notion that because terroir is a French word, and because only the French have fully mapped their vineyards, only French

Just a glance at these vineyards demonstrates how their precise angle and altitude affects, for example, how much sunshine they receive, how sheltered they are from the wind, and how much soil erosion is likely.

vineyards have terroir! All spots on the globe have their own terroir of course, and there is no reason to suppose that the French, or indeed Europeans, have any kind of monopoly on suitable terroirs for fine wine production – it's just that the New World is a few hundred years behind most Europeans in finding them (and its vine-growers are more accustomed to manipulating them).

63

GROWING VINES

Only a few, ground-breaking vine-growers have a choice about the location of their vineyard, but they all have many **viticultural** choices about exactly how to grow the vines they plant there. For many Old World vine-growers, those choices are never consciously made; they probably live in an area which has evolved a way of growing vines that is perfectly adapted to their local conditions, their terroir (see page 62). On the poor, pebbly soils of the Médoc in Bordeaux, for example, vines are densely planted in low, neat, hedges in vine-yards that are as carefully drained as finances allow. (The first thing the Mentzelopoulos family did when they acquired Château Margaux in 1978 was to dig miles of drainage ditches to avoid their precious first growth vines' ever being waterlogged and becoming lazy about ripening fruit.)

Any tourist travelling around the wine regions of the world will notice some very obvious differences between how vineyards look, but because so many of the world's vine-growers simply do what their neighbours do or predecessors did, they are not always able to describe *why* their vineyards look as they do with the vines trained in a variety of ways.

The average Spanish peasant, for example, would probably be amazed by the difference in **vine density** between his vineyards and those of northern France – about 1400 and 10 000 vines per hectare respectively (560 and 4050 per acre). A tiny area of the relatively infertile soils of wet northern France can support one vine and good quality fruit, whereas a vine planted on the arid plains of La Mancha needs to draw on a large area of soil moisture to survive at all.

Vine density is also a function of **row spacing**, which can vary considerably. Old World vineyards tend to have just enough space between rows of vines for people or horses to move easily, and the advent of mechanization has simply meant that vineyard machinery is designed to straddle the relatively low, neat vine rows. Many New World vineyards were designed to be worked by tractor right from the start and rows can be as much as 3 m (9 ft) apart, needing much less investment in young plants, but with what look like wastefully wide margins to allow machines to turn at either end.

There are many different theories about **row orientation**, whether vine rows should go north–south or east–west to maximize exposure to the sun and/or protect vines from the wind, and whether they should follow contours or go directly uphill. Following contours minimizes soil erosion, particularly when special terraces are built, and makes the vineyard much easier for humans and machines to work. In places where vine rows go directly uphill and down dale, such as the Mosel and Côte Rôtie, individual vines may be trained on stakes instead of along restrictive wires so that the vineyard workers don't have to combine mountaineering with vineyard maintenance and picking.

One particularly obvious viticultural divide is between old-fashioned, relatively arid vineyards in which vines grow unsupported like wild bushes, and vines that are deliberately trained on stakes or along wires to control the leafiness, or **vigour**, of the vine. This helps prevent the spread of vine diseases and can also force the vine into the particular shapes deemed suitable for various combinations of vine variety, terroir and mesoclimate. In fertile soils a vine's natural tendency is to produce a luxuriant growth of leaves, or **canopy**, that can thoroughly distract from the process of yielding grapes, and can even hide the grapes from the sunlight that is so vital to ripening them. Excess irrigation and high rainfall exacerbate this pro-vegetation, anti-fruit situation. **Canopy management** is all about sculpting the vine into the most efficient grape factory. The precise climate of the leafy

ORGANIC AND OTHER VINES

One of the major reasons why average yields (usually measured in volume of wine per unit of land) have increased dramatically since the 1960s is the widespread use of chemicals, both as fertilizers and sprays, to combat the spread of rot and other fungal diseases of the vine (see page 96). Crops which were once decimated by a humid spell during ripening could be saved by a spraying or three, or sometimes as many as 10 or 12.

As in so many other forms of agriculture, and horticulture, an increasing number of growers have begun to wonder whether the sustained use of agrochemicals is such a good idea. Some of them are motivated by concern for the environment and possible pollution from chemical residues; some want to minimize the risk of any residues in the wine; some are inspired by the obvious deterioration in the quality of the soil after years of repeated applications of the same chemicals; while others, more hard-nosed perhaps, are simply exasperated by vine pests' increasing tolerance to the conventional preparations.

Whatever the reasons, there is a perceptible shift in viticultural philosophy world-wide towards more 'natural' methods of growing vines. 'Organic viticulture' encompasses a wide range of such practices.

Like most evangelical organizations, those governing organic viticulture tend to be locked in conflict with each other, but the basic principles are that no synthetic chemicals should be added to the vineyard, that the health of the soil is of paramount importance (compost, manure and bugs are highly valued), and that **cover crops**, other crops between the vines, even weeds, can substantially improve the quality and all-important texture of the soil. Growing grasses, barley or vetch between rows can, for example, make a real difference as to whether a tractor can make progress in a vineyard during the wet winter and spring seasons, or whether it risks being completely mired. These crops can also reduce vine vigour (the leafiness of the vines) by providing competition for the soil's nutrients and water and, sometimes, can distract predatory insects, which is particularly important if insecticides are not used.

The most extreme philosophy is the Steiner-inspired system called **biodynamism** or **biodynamics** whereby the soil is nurtured, often by minute, homeopathic doses of such substances as ground nettles and camomile, according to the phases of the moon. It sounds crazy, but the demonstrable health of the vines and wines produced by such adherents as Lalou Bize-Leroy of Burgundy, Michel Chapoutier of the Rhône, Nicolas Joly of Savennières and Didier Dageneau of Pouilly-Fumé, even in vintages that were disastrous for other, more conventional vine-growers, suggests that this may be a very successful recipe for those pursuing quality above all else.

It should be said, however, that it is much easier to practise organic viticulture in a dry climate than in a damp one where fungal diseases are a perennial threat. A winter cold enough to kill off harmful bugs also helps.

A rigorous system of winemaking which might be described as organic is much less common than using vaguely organic methods to grow vines. Only tiny amounts of sulphur dioxide are used and minimal fining and filtration are allowed, so the wines can be relatively unstable. As in the vineyard, there is a perceptible trend thoughout the world to use fewer and fewer additives and to reduce the level of sulphur additions to a practicable minimum. Some of the official organic organizations, however, have rules apparently dictated more by fanaticism than wine quality.

Can the experienced taster distinguish an 'organic wine' from a conventional one? The many indifferent organic wines made by less-than-inspirational winemakers do their best to cloud the issue, but it can be revealing to compare the 'organic' offerings from a single producer such as Robert Mondavi of California or Penfolds of Australia with the rest of their range. There does seem to be an intensity and sometimes even wildness of flavour, perhaps partly because yields are lower.

part of a vine is known by professionals as the **canopy microclimate.**

Some wine tourists are intrigued by the variation in colour of leaves between different patches of vines. A patch of summertime yellow in the middle of mainly green-leaved vines is usually caused by an iron deficiency in the vine. As grapes ripen the natural differences in leaf colour between

This Beaujolais vineyard looks mouth-wateringly beautiful, but the variation in colour may be a sign that some of the vines are suffering from viral diseases.

different vine varieties are accentuated, but many of the reds and oranges that make vineyards so beautiful in autumn are the result of vine virus diseases, some of which can inconveniently delay the ripening process. Leafroll virus is the most common example. Growers now try to plant vines which nurserymen guarantee as virus-free, but this is still a serious problem in many areas.

THE WINE PLANT AND ITS FRUIT

For all its heady symbolism and the beauty of its foliage, the vine is basically a fruit tree, which happens to produce a fruit, the grape, whose juice is particularly good when fermented. Any sweet liquid can be fermented into an alcoholic one (see page 74), whether it be a starchy mash into beer, pear juice into perry, or apple juice into cider. Grape juice is special, however. It has a naturally high sugar content, and so can be fermented into a relatively alcoholic liquid. But it is also unusually high in a particular acid, tartaric acid (in fact the cooking additive cream of tartar is made from the scrapings off the inside of old wine vats). This acid can fight off the sort of bacteria that attack most other foods and drink far better than, for example, the dominant acids in milk, citric fruit and apples (lactic, citric and malic acid respectively). Consequently fermented grape juice can last and, even better, evolve for much longer than most ferments. And the fact that there are thousands of distinct varieties of vine, and therefore grape, means that the flavours of wine, real grape wine, can be far more varied and rewarding than the fermented juice of other fruits.

The professional vine-grower's annual job is to ripen a commercially viable quantity of grapes in which the grape sugars, produced from sunlight and water by the photosynthesis that makes all plants grow, are balanced by a suitable level of acidity. The major component in grape juice is water, up to 85 per cent. The proportion of other components such as sugars and acids,

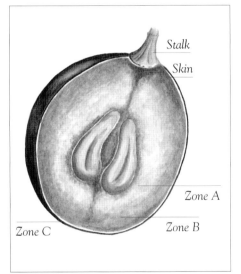

Cross-section through a grape.

however, varies considerably according to how ripe the grape is and how heavily it is pressed, as the illustration suggests. As the sugars in the grape increase so do all the exciting flavour elements and astringent preservatives such as pigments and tannins, which are to be found in highest concentrations just under the skin in Zone C. Some bitter tannins are also to be found in Zone A just round the pips. The least astringent juice is therefore that in Zone B, which also happens to be the first juice to be pressed from a mass of crushed grapes, known as the **free-run juice.** This is highly valued for making many delicate white wines which would be spoilt by being astringent.

Although a vine's yield is strongly influenced by both pruning and annual weather conditions, the quality and quantity of grapes produced by a vine also vary considerably according to its age. Most vines produce a crop of commercially interesting size only in their third year and reach a plateau of productivity between the ages of about six and 20 years. After this, quantity starts to decline but, as a direct result, quality often increases, which is why so many labels boast of *vieilles vignes*, or old vines (although 'old' can mean anything, from under 10 to 100 years). Many producers uproot vines in their twenties because they produce too little (or because they want to plant a more attractive variety or clone).

See pages 100–153 in Section Three for full details of the vine family and hundreds of different grape varieties.

THE VINEYARD YEAR

One of the greatest miracles of nature, it has always seemed to me, is the annual transformation of the barren, black-stumped midwinter vineyard into the luxuriant, juicy, green jungle that is a field of vines in high summer. Here's how it is done, and what humans need to do to shape the quality of wine produced as a result.

I have deliberately not mentioned specific months as these vary according to the hemisphere of course. In very general terms the grape harvest takes place in September and October in the northern hemisphere and from February to April in the southern hemisphere.

WINTER

Dormancy is the key word here – both in the vineyard and in the winery. The vine enjoys a prolonged period of inactivity after the rigours of carrying and ripening a crop and the canopy to support it. In extremely cool climates, however, frozen grapes may be picked for Eiswein/Ice wine (see page 89), sometimes as late as January in Germany.

In wine regions with particularly cold winters, such as Canada and Russia, vines may be routinely banked up so that they survive hard winter frosts.

Pruning is the most important, indeed the only, almost universal vineyard job to be done during the winter, although there is no rule about its precise timing. Pruning is extremely

FLYING WINEMAKERS

Because September's a quiet month for Australian (and New Zealand) winemakers, hundreds of them migrate each year to make wine in the northern hemisphere. This trend started in the early 1980s and has now spawned a phenomenon known as 'flying winemakers' whereby an increasing proportion of wine is made by itinerants. Although the result has been a dramatic increase in technically well-made wines, flying winemakers are not necessarily the perfect people to accentuate regional character and local identity. Incomers tend to upgrade technique, leaving the locals to apply it to their own special grape varieties and conditions. Most young producers in the Old World now also gain valuable experience by working abroad.

important, particularly in cooler climates where the amount of warmth and sunlight available to ripen grapes is more limited, because it is the chief way a vine-grower can impose his policy on **yield**, the quantity of wine produced, usually measured in Europe as hectolitres of wine per hectare of vineyard and in the US as tons of grapes per acre. (Although the conversion of weight of grapes to volume of wine depends on the characteristics of the grapes, what sort of wine is made and how hard the grapes are pressed, 1 ton/acre is equivalent to about 17.5 hl/ha.) Yields can vary from less than 20 hl/ha (1.1 ton/acre) in the case of extremely old, harshly pruned and non-irrigated grapes grown in a dry season to 200 hl/ha (11 ton/acre) from generously pruned and heavily irrigated vines. The association between low yields and high-quality wine is accepted so unquestioningly in Europe that maximum yields are laid down for each sort of wine by most European wine regulations (see page 48). Some New World producers, however, are unconvinced that a small quantity necessarily means high quality, arguing that many of Bordeaux's finest wines were produced in some of the highest-yielding vintages. In some circumstances climatic conditions can have a greater effect on quality than yield alone.

With a few careful snips of the secateurs (often in icy winds) the vine-grower can determine both the number of bunches each vine is likely to produce (by leaving only a certain number of buds on the vine) and the shape of the vine during the growing season. Pruning is a much more skilled job than, say, picking grapes and can therefore be one of the more expensive vineyard operations, but it is in the throes of being mechanized.

Some vine-growers in warmer climates, notably in Australia, have been experimenting with **minimal pruning**, a much more casual method, leaving vines unpruned so that they look like giant thorn bushes. As with wild vines, the fruit grows on the outside where the light can help ripen it. The argument is that the vine will itself find the correct balance between grapes and leaves, but in cooler regions it would be difficult to ripen all the bunches produced by an unpruned vine.

Cuttings for new plantings are usually taken in winter before the sap rises.

SPRING

Apparently miraculously, tiny green shoots emerge from the buds left on the vine after winter pruning at some point in early spring depending on the weather, the variety of vine, when it was pruned, and the amount of energy it managed to store during the previous growing season. This is the most important time for the growth of shoots, leaves and, beginning slightly later, roots.

Frost danger is the chief preoccupation of most vine-growers in early to mid-spring when vines, particularly varieties which bud early such as Chardonnay, are most vulnerable.

Heaters, wind machines and sprinkler systems can all help to protect tender young vine growth (and the subsequent crop, the commercial *raison d'être* of vine-growing). Heaters help to raise temperatures at vine height above –1°C (30°F) which is cold enough to cause damage. Wind machines act like a giant mixer of the cold, dense air at ground level with the warmer air above. Sprinklers (which in some

areas may double as irrigation systems) protect young vine leaves and shoots by coating them in ice, and warm the soil to boot. Vines are damaged only at temperatures below –5°C (23°F), but the ice coating keeps them at 0°C (32°F), so long as they are sprayed as soon as the temperature reaches zero.

The single most important event in the springtime vineyard, however, is **flowering**, a one- to two-week period anything from six to 12 weeks after the first buds appear, during which the potential size of the crop is pre-ordained. Tiny vine flowers appear from each bud and, depending on the weather, a proportion of them are fertilized to become berries, or baby grapes. Strong winds can blow off these delicate little plant fragments, which reduces the size of the potential crop, as does cold, wet weather, which discourages healthy growth and causes many individual baby stems to shrivel, a crop-diminishing phenomenon called **coulure**. Certain varieties such as Grenache and some clones of Merlot are especially prone to coulure.

The weather during the flowering period has an effect not just on the size of the current year's crop but also on the following year's, since this year's miniature buds on the vine will become next year's shoots.

SUMMER

During the summer it is essentially nature rather than man that does the work, although humidity may encourage vine diseases, which most growers combat with assiduous spraying.

In years when the vines are too heavily loaded with grapes, as a result of a particularly successful flowering for example, some producers may practise **crop thinning**, also known as summer pruning, *vendange verte* or *éclaircissage*. This highly skilled process involves cutting off individual bunches by hand so that the available energy will ripen the remaining bunches more successfully.

The canopy, the green parts of the vine, grows rapidly in early summer and will continue

to do so unless it is trimmed or there is shortage of water and the vines are subjected to **water stress**, a little of which may be good.

The berries or grapes meanwhile grow from hard, green little pellets to large, juicy fruits in which the acidity continues to diminish while the sugar increases. The most obviously decisive stage in this continuous process is called, in English as well as French, **veraison**, when the grapes begin to soften and change colour, those on the outside of the bunch first. Immediately after veraison, six to seven weeks after the completion of flowering, the grape ripening process goes into top gear, especially in warm, sunny, dry weather. If the water stress is too severe, however, the **ripening** process comes to a halt.

At about the same time as veraison, the shoots start to turn from green and springy to brown and hard. The vine is starting to store energy for the winter and the following year.

AUTUMN

All of the above operations have been directed towards the great event of the vine-growing and winemaking year, the **harvest**. The vine-grower's most crucial decision is when to pick and depends on whether the vine is an early, mid or late ripening variety; the health and characteristics of the grapes; the weather forecast; and what sort of wine is being made. Early ripening varieties (such as Chardonnay and Pinot

Grapes may be picked skilfully, expensively and picturesquely by hand, or automatically, economically and fast by machine.

As labour costs and bureaucracy increase, the machine (which does not require a three-course lunch) is winning, although hand picking is the rule for many top European estates.

Noir) that are destined for sparkling wine may be picked several weeks ahead of late ripening varieties such as Cabernet Sauvignon, whose deep colour and tannins are highly desirable, and even months ahead of some grapes destined for late harvest sweet wines.

As the grapes ripen they are analysed with increasing frequency to check levels of the acidity that keeps wine refreshing and the sugar that can be fermented into alcohol. In hot climates the aim is to keep the former as high as possible while having grapes that have accumulated enough flavour, while in cool climates, especially after a poor summer, the main aim can often be simply to reach a legal or self-imposed minimum sugar level before autumn rains set in or rot spreads.

As autumn progresses the leaves turn colour and fall off, notably after the first frost of the season.

A BLUFFER'S GUIDE TO WINEMAKING JARGON

Acidity is what gives wine, and most other drinks, its tang. Lemons have lots of it; potatoes very little. A wine's acidity comes from the **acids** (mainly MALIC and TARTARIC) in grape juice, which diminish as grapes ripen. A hot summer may reduce acids to such an extent that some have to be added from a sack. This is called **acidification**.

Alcohol is the potent mood-changer that differentiates wine from grape juice. A wine's **alcoholic strength** is its concentration of alcohol (see page 49).

Anthocyans, PHENOLICS which most strongly influence a red wine's colour, which is directly affected by its PH.

Ascorbic acid, or Vitamin C, is often added to MUST during winemaking since it prevents OXIDATION, usually together with SULPHUR DIOXIDE to keep white wines fresh.

Barrel, the winemaker's most fashionable tool. See pages 91–3 for more information about **barrel fermentation, barrel maturation**, etc.

Bâtonnage, French for LEES STIRRING.

Baumé, measure of sugar concentration in grape juice (and therefore grape ripeness) or MUST common in Australia.

Botrytis, fungus affecting grapes benevolently (as in the 'noble rot' responsible for great sweet wines, see page 88) or simply spoiling them with 'grey rot' or mould, depending on conditions.

Brettanomyces, wine fault so fashionable in the US that it is sometimes just called Brett. Wines affected by this spoilage YEAST smell off-puttingly mousey.

Brix, measure of sugar concentration common in the US. See BAUMÉ.

Cap, layer of skins floating on red wine in the fermentation vat.

Carbon dioxide is the harmless gas given off during fermentation that is responsible for the bubbles in all fizzy drinks, including wine.

Carbonic maceration, special way of making fruity, early maturing red wines, most notably Beaujolais, by fermenting them in a sealed vat filled with CARBON DIOXIDE. See page 78.

Chaptalization, common cool climate winemaking procedure which compensates for underripe grapes by adding sugar to the fermentation vat to produce a more alcoholic wine.

Clarification, umbrella term for processes designed to ensure wine is crystal clear, including FINING, FILTRATION and refrigeration.

Concentration, new technique for concentrating flavour (and ACID and TANNIN) in less ripe vintages.

Élevage, French term with no direct English equivalent for the wine-maturing processes involved between fermentation and bottling.

Enology, US spelling of OENOLOGY.

Ethyl alcohol, or **ethanol**, is the sort of ALCOHOL found in alcoholic drinks such as wine.

Fermentation, see pages 74–5.

Filtration, controversial CLARIFICATION process of pumping wine through various different sorts of filter to remove suspended solids. It can also strip out flavour.

Fining, CLARIFICATION technique involving adding a **fining agent** (such as egg whites or bentonite) which attracts solids to fall out of suspension (see page 83).

Flavour compounds, complex, still underexplored maze of compounds, many of them PHENOLICS, responsible for wine flavour.

Free-run is the juice or wine which flows without PRESSING.

Inert gas, one such as nitrogen which does not react with wine. May fill the head space of a container to prevent OXIDATION.

Lees are the solids left at the bottom of a fermentation vat after fermentation. Relatively neutral-tasting white wines are often deliberately given prolonged **lees contact** and even **lees stirring** to generate more flavour and make them more stable.

Malic acid, the sharp, appley acid most notable in grapes from cool years.

Malolactic fermentation (MLF or 'le malo'), increasingly common second fermentation in which harsh MALIC ACID is converted to softer, lactic (milky) acid softening the resulting wine.

Mercaptans, wine fault popular with Australian tasters. A skunky smell results from YEAST reacting with the LEES. It can be cured by careful RACKING.

Must, useful word for the pulpy mass at any stage between grape juice and wine.

Oak, see pages 91–3.

Oechsle, measure of sugar concentration common in Germany. See BAUMÉ.

Oenology is the science of wine-making, practised by a (usually qualified) **oenologist**.

Organic winemaking, avoidance of chemical additives and, often, of certain fining agents. See page 65.

Oxidation, potentially serious calamity that can strike grapes, grape juice and wine if they are over-exposed to OXYGEN, making them go brown (like a cut apple) and taste flat. Wines suffering from oxidation, often from a less-than-airtight stopper, are **oxidized**.

Oxygen, both good and bad fairy in the winemaking process. A small amount during barrel maturation deepens colour, smooths flavour and makes the wine more stable. But too much oxygen causes OXIDATION and may eventually turn the wine to vinegar. Winemaking may be deliberately **oxidative** or PROTECTIVE.

pH, one of the wine bore's buzz words. pH is a measure of the concentration of ACIDITY in a liquid but higher readings mean lower acid. Water, for example, has a pH of 7, while most wines have a pH of between 3 and 4, with very acidic wines having a pH of less than 3. pH and colour are also closely related: the lower the pH, the brighter the red wine.

Phenolics, varied group of compounds found mainly in skins, stems and seeds in the case of grapes. They include ANTHOCYANS, TANNINS and some FLAVOUR COMPOUNDS. Precipitated, they form an important part of wine's sediment and play a considerable role in wine ageing. Red wines are much higher in phenolics than white, which is why red wine is better at protecting against heart disease.

Pressing, important winemaking operation involving pressing the juice (white wines) or astringent **press wine** out of the skins. The quality of the resulting juice depends on how hard the grapes are pressed (as explained on page 67).

Protective winemaking involves protecting the grapes, juice, MUST and wine from OXYGEN, typically by using sealed containers, low temperatures, SULPHUR DIOXIDE and sometimes ASCORBIC ACID.

Pumping over the juice, alternative to PUNCHING DOWN.

Punching down, winemaking process whereby the CAP of skins is physically immersed in the MUST so that more PHENOLICS are leeched into the resulting wine.

Racking is the operation of transferring wine from one container (typically a barrel) to another, leaving behind the LEES. It can usefully expose the wine to oxygen and avoid REDUCTION.

Reducing conditions are those which favour **reduction**, or losing OXYGEN, the opposite of OXIDATION. In excess, where a (usually red) wine is starved of oxygen, they can result in off-putting MERCAPTAN or SULPHIDE smells.

Residual sugar (RS), the amount of unfermented SUGAR left in a wine after fermentation is complete, usually measured in grams per litre (g/l) or per cent. A residual sugar level of less than 2 g/l (0.02 per cent) is imperceptible to most palates. Although ACIDITY counterbalances residual sugar, most wines with 25 g/l (2.5 per cent) residual sugar taste distinctly sweet.

Skin contact, deliberate policy of trying to extract from the grape skins as many FLAVOUR COMPOUNDS, and ANTHOCYANS into red juice, as possible.

Sorbic acid, additive widely used in the food and drink industries to stun YEASTS and moulds. Sometimes used for inexpensive sweet wines, it smells of crushed geranium leaves, excessively to some particularly sensitive humans.

Stabilization, umbrella term for all the winemaking operations (e.g. FILTRATION, chilling to precipitate TARTRATES, adding ASCORBIC ACID) designed to stop wines developing a fault in bottle such as a haze, cloud or fizz, no matter what the storage conditions. It is practised most brutally on everyday wines.

Sulphides, off-smells reminiscent of bad eggs which can taint heavily REDUCED wine. Hydrogen sulphide (H_2S) is most common.

Sulphur dioxide, the most common and most useful winemaking additive used since Roman times, mainly as a preservative, disinfectant and to ward off OXIDATION. Its use has been declining as consumers have become less tolerant of the freshly-struck match smell associated with sulphur. Some asthmatics react badly to high doses of sulphur, which has led to some countries requiring the legend 'contains **sulfites/sulphites**' on wine labels. A tiny but increasing proportion of wines are made using no sulphur at all but they tend to be fragile. Sulphur reacts readily with many other wine ingredients to form **bound sulphur**; it is only **free sulphur** which can be detected, although individual sensitivities vary considerably.

Sugar is built up in the pulp as grapes ripen, and is transformed into ALCOHOL during fermentation.

Sur lie, French for a wine treated to LEES CONTACT.

Tannins, preservative PHENOLICS found mainly in red wine and derived chiefly from dark grape skins as well as seeds and stems. Tannin management is one of the red winemaker's most important jobs. See pages 16–17, 40 and 79.

Tartaric acid, the most common and distinctive wine ACID (see page 67) and a particularly good preservative. A lot of the acid is precipitated as crusty deposits called **tartrates**, usually seen as harmless white crystals in white wine, and dyed deep red in red wines.

Topping up, the regular filling of barrels to avoid oxidation.

Whole bunch pressing and fermentation. See page 78.

Yeast, see page 74.

THE WINEMAKING PROCESS

It is a healthy sign that more and more wine-makers are admitting that 'Wine is made in the vineyard not the cellar'. Some of them are even getting their boots dirty nowadays. But presumably modern winemaking man has been skulking in the winery all this time because, as we have seen on pages 60–71, he has so much less power over nature in the vineyard.

Turning grapes into some sort of wine is a relatively easy process (it's only making a wine that tastes thrilling and will last for-ever that is difficult). Ripe grapes contain sugar which can, under the influence of minute organisms called yeasts, be converted into alcohol and carbon dioxide gas. (Much the same thing happens when jam starts to ferment: it starts to bubble and taste headier and less sweet.)

Those who share my enthusiasm for neat expla-nations in the form of equa-tions may find comfort in the following:

Trucked grapes may get crushed and start to ferment, so increasingly they are transported in shallow plastic boxes.

$$C_6H_{12}O_6 \longrightarrow 2C_2H_5OH + 2CO_2$$
sugar   alcohol   carbon dioxide

Those who hated chemistry should ignore this bit, and those wary of such scientific precision are quite right. This is a gross simplification of the horrifyingly complex sequence of opera-tions that is alcoholic fermentation. All sorts of other things happen, but a detailed grasp of them does little to enhance our enjoyment of the resulting liquid.

To set the fermentation process in motion, all that is needed is to put the sugar present inside ripe grapes in contact with the millions of invisible yeasts that are present in the atmos-phere of any wine region by splitting the skins, which means crushing the grapes. This explains why wine (unlike spirits) could be made so many thousands of years ago – no special skill or equip-ment was needed other than a container in which to keep the resulting alco-holic liquid. But if wine is exposed to air it will turn, sooner or later, into vinegar (as anyone clearing up the morning after a particularly good dinner will know). In fact the very word vinegar derives from *vin aigre*, which is French for sour wine. Until the development of stoppered containers such as amphorae, the ancients knew wine almost exclu-sively as a nouveau (see page 57) or a weak liquid that was heavily disguised with herbs, honey, lead or even sea water.

Modern consumers are more demanding, however, and modern wine-makers like to be in control, so winemaking today is a much less hazardous process.

The following are some of the more impor-tant decisions modern winemakers have to make and how they influence the resulting wine – although all co-operative wineries and many wine producers, especially in the New World, have their work cut out to control some of the first operations described below since they buy in, rather than grow, most of their grapes.

Winemakers' decisions appear in roughly the order in which they have to make them, although that order depends on the very first decision of all. Consult the bluffer's guide on pages 72–3 for a fast track to understanding the technical terms, and the diagram on pages 76–7 for the basic steps in winemaking.

WHAT SORT OF WINE TO MAKE

Grape colour and quality determine to a certain extent what sort of wine can be made. Red wines can be made only from dark-skinned grapes as all grape juice is the same dull grey and will be tinted red only if anthocyans can be leeched out of the skins into the must. This means that red wines have to be made from skins as well as pulp. Grape skins, though, are high in other phenolics which make them astringent. This may be a good quality in a tannic young red wine but is unattractive in a light white. Juice alone is also much easier to work with than a mixture of skins and juice, so the juice is separated from the skins before white wine fermentation. The principal difference between red and white winemaking is whether the grapes are pressed before or after fermentation.

Dark-skinned grapes are needed to make Léoville-Barton this colour – the warmer the summer the deeper the pigment.

White wines can be made from dark-skinned grapes (many sparkling white wines are) provided the juice is separated from the skins carefully and early enough. See pages 84–6 for details of sparkling winemaking. Rosés, or pink wines, are made just like white wines, except that the juice is lightly tinted from short contact with dark skins before fermentation. Very ripe grapes can be used to make sweet wines (see pages 87–8) or fortified wines.

WHEN TO PICK

Until very recently grapes were picked by numbers: as soon as sugars reached an acceptable level in cool climates, and in warmer regions just before acids fell dangerously low (and pH rose dangerously high). Today more and more wine producers understand that numbers alone may not be sufficient indicators of real, sometimes called 'physiological', ripeness. Visible ripening of the grapes' skin and stem (including the ease with which a grape can be pulled off it) is one of the indicators that quality-conscious producers now use to decide the optimum picking time. They are especially interested in fully ripe, or sometimes even overripe phenolics, particularly for red wines, because the tannins will be much riper and the wines more welcoming. Some growers even deliberately pick a mixture of slightly under-ripe, ripe and slightly over-ripe grapes to give a wine complexity, notably with slightly anodyne grape varieties such as Semillon or Sauvignon Blanc.

HOW TO PICK – MAN OR MACHINE

Hand picking may be the only option in some places – either particularly steep or inconveniently designed vineyards for example – and for certain sorts of wines such as sweet wines which involve selection on the vine or those made using whole bunches (including stems), such as some burgundies and sparkling wines. Vineyard labour is generally becoming scarcer and more expensive, however, and only the very top estates and domaines of France can afford to boast that they will never, ever use mechanical harvesters. Machines can harvest much more

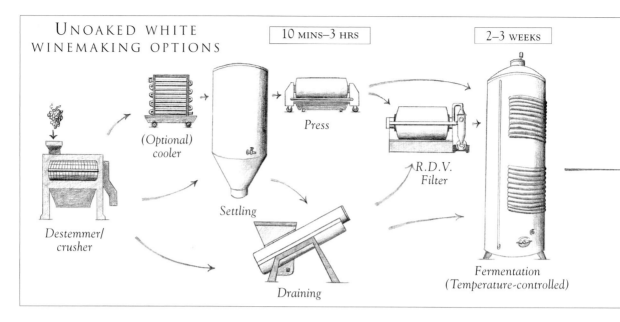

UNOAKED WHITE WINEMAKING OPTIONS

10 MINS–3 HRS

2–3 WEEKS

(Optional) cooler

Press

Settling

R.D.V. Filter

Destemmer/ crusher

Draining

Fermentation (Temperature-controlled)

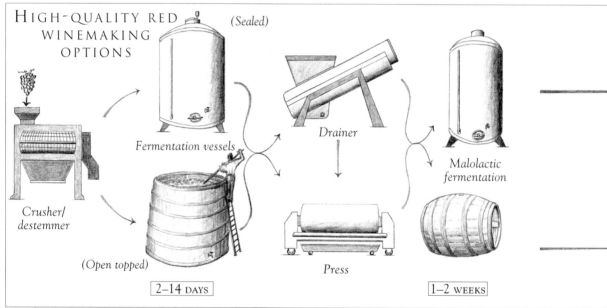

HIGH-QUALITY RED WINEMAKING OPTIONS

(Sealed)

Fermentation vessels

Drainer

Malolactic fermentation

Crusher/ destemmer

(Open topped)

Press

2–14 DAYS

1–2 WEEKS

cheaply and quickly than humans, but they do give the vines a terrible shake every year, are unable to discriminate between healthy and unhealthy grapes, tend to harvest not a few leaves and vine fragments too, and like mud even less than humans. Machine harvesters are particularly useful in hot climates where they can be used at night to deliver grapes at naturally low temperatures, which can save refrigeration costs and the use of sulphur dioxide in some cases.

HOW (AND WHETHER) TO TRANSPORT GRAPES TO THE WINERY

The longer grapes sit around between the vine and the winery, the more likely they are to be crushed by their own weight, to oxidize and to lose their fresh, fruity flavours (which matters particularly for light white wines). Adding sulphur dioxide can help but the early 1990s saw two important developments in grape harvesting: using shallower and shallower containers for transport to the winery and a

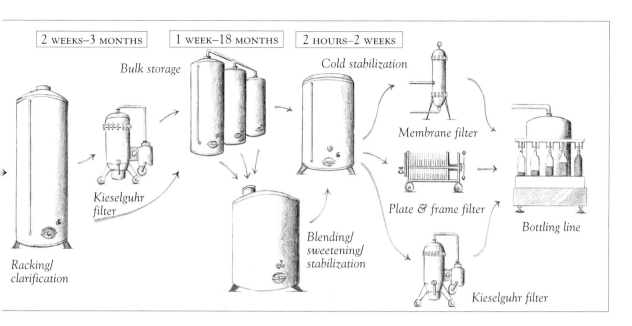

2 WEEKS–3 MONTHS   1 WEEK–18 MONTHS   2 HOURS–2 WEEKS

Bulk storage

Cold stabilization

Membrane filter

Kieselguhr filter

Plate & frame filter

Bottling line

Racking/clarification

Blending/sweetening/stabilization

Kieselguhr filter

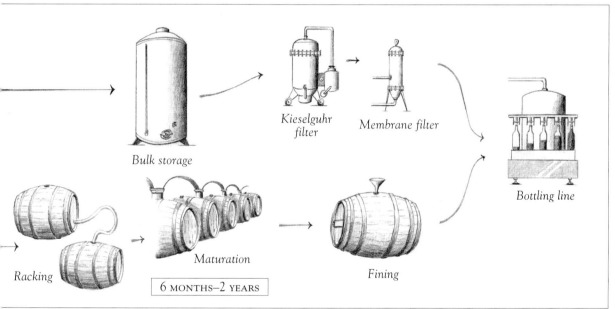

Bulk storage

Kieselguhr filter

Membrane filter

Bottling line

Racking

Maturation

6 MONTHS–2 YEARS

Fining

perceptible move towards building crushing (and destemming) centres immediately beside vineyards so that what is transported in the midday sun is not fragile, freshly-picked grapes but carefully treated and protected pulp or juice. Heat speeds up all reactions, so picking in the cool of the night can also help.

WHETHER TO SORT

A multitude of Bordeaux and Burgundy producers installed sorting tables, or *tables de tri(age)*,

for the rain-sodden vintages of the early 1990s when there was wide variation in the health and quality of the grapes coming into the winery. A slowly moving belt between trailer and crusher allows sorters to discard any rotten or unripe grapes as well as 'MOG' (material other than grapes).

WHETHER TO CHILL GRAPES OR MUST

Chilling helps to preserve fresh, primary aromas and inhibits yeast, harmful bacteria and oxidation, allowing winemakers in hot climates to delay fermentation until the must is in a fit state for this complex process. Some producers store juice at low temperatures for months before fermentation in order to cut down the amount of fermentation capacity and winemaker attention needed at the busiest time of year. In warmer wine regions and for white winemaking in all but the chilliest extremities of the wine world, refrigeration is an important winemaking tool. Cooling grapes, must or wine preserves the fruity primary aromas and gives winemakers breathing space.

The equipment above, at Undurraga in Chile, is just part of what's needed to keep temperatures low enough to make fresh fruity wines.
Below is a typical destemmer. Stems are separated from grapes in the perforated rotating cylinder.

PROTECTIVE OR OXIDATIVE JUICE HANDLING?

Many winemakers actively protect grapes and juice against oxidation by using sulphur dioxide and/or tank presses which are completely enclosed (see picture opposite). This effort is particularly important for white grapes because as soon as they are crushed the juice starts to brown as a result of reactions between oxygen and phenolics in the juice. Some producers, however, deliberately expose white juice to oxygen in order to exclude these 'heavy' phenolics from the resulting wine, and with them the risk of browning the wine prematurely in bottle.

WHETHER TO DESTEM AND CRUSH

Practically all grapes are deliberately fed into a crusher before fermentation in order to put the sugar in contact with the yeast, and most are automatically destemmed (increasingly before rather than after crushing) to eliminate the harsh flavours and astringent characters that stems can impart.

The main exceptions to this are wines such as most Beaujolais, and the Languedoc-Roussillon's Carignan, which are fermented using some form of carbonic maceration. This bathes whole berries in carbon dioxide and depends on a particularly fruity sort of yeast-free fermentation taking place inside each berry (although the grapes at the bottom of the vat are crushed anyway of course and tend to ferment in the normal way). The resulting wines are bright red, soft and have a distinctive smell of pear drops.

Other wines made using whole bunches of grapes include some ambitious still white wines (especially botrytized sweet wines) and most top quality sparkling wines which are very gently pressed using the stems as conduits for the resulting juice.

A number of top quality red wine producers, notably in Burgundy, pour whole bunches into their fermentation vats (which must be open to allow the cap to be broken up). If the grapes (and therefore stems) are anything less than very ripe, however, or are a highly tannic variety such as Cabernet Sauvignon, the inclusion of stems can result in unpleasantly tough wines.

DURATION OF SKIN CONTACT

The incidence and timing of this pre-pressing operation is different for red and white wines (see diagram on pages 76–7). Red wines are red precisely because of skin contact before, during and sometimes after fermentation. In cooler regions winemakers tend to try to extract every last ounce of colour and phenolics from the floating cap of skins by maximizing the contact between them and the juice. They typically manage this either by pumping juice over the cap, by punching it down once or twice a day or submerging it beneath some form of perforated headboard. Many European producers also deliberately leave the new wine in the fermentation vat for a week or two after fermentation has finished in order to extract more colour, tannins and flavour from the skins. This is particularly effective since alcohol is a good solvent. In warmer regions, however, where grapes tend to be too deeply coloured, the result of such a policy can be a bitterly tannic wine and some producers even separate the juice from the skins before fermentation is over, finishing it off in small barrels (see pages 90–3).

For white wines, skin contact has to work its magic before fermentation, but the exact nature of this magic is much less clear-cut. A few hours' skin contact for relatively bland varieties such as Sauvignon Blanc and Semillon can add extra flavour but in this case the grapes must be perfectly healthy and protected from oxidation.

Rosé is the result of applying the technique described above to dark-skinned grapes.

Two of the many sorts of press: a modern tank press (above) completely protected from the air, and an old-fashioned basket press (below), treasured by many traditionalists.

PRESSING THE GRAPES OR PULP

Juice is pressed out of white grapes after the free-run juice has been run off but before fermentation. In red winemaking the job is to extract as much usable wine as possible from the solids left in the fermentation vat after the free-run wine has been run off. The gentler the pressure, the less coarse the wine or juice, which is why presses are designed to be ever gentler.

The typical modern horizontal press consists of an inflatable airbag inside a perforated rotating cylinder through which juice falls to a tray below (see diagrams on pages 76–7). If the whole thing is enclosed from the harmful effects of oxygen it is called a tank press.

Alternative highly regarded presses include the vertical 'basket press', of which variants are used in Champagne and Sauternes, and for some full-bodied red wines. Whereas most horizontal presses can be worked (if not cleaned) mechanically, the basket press uses up both time and manpower, but similarly squeezes juice gently through slats into a tray below.

Inexpensive wines are frequently made using much harsher continuous presses which don't need expensive human supervision of individual batches.

An important decision in winemaking is what to do with the press juice or wine. Almost all top quality white wines are made exclusively from free-run juice. The best of what's left in the press may be recovered using a rotary drum vacuum (R.D.V.) filter. The character of each vintage may determine how much red press wine is included in the final blend. A very dry year may produce very tannic wines which would not be flattered by adding the even more tannic press wine. Different labels provide homes for the rejects.

AMBIENT OR CULTURED YEASTS?

This, with filtration, is one of the hottest issues in winemaking. Traditional winemakers in traditional regions simply rely on the local, varied population of yeasts in the air which have built up over the years and seem perfectly trained to do the job in hand. Modernists are perturbed by this practice, which can sometimes mean waiting a few days for fermentation to start, increases the danger of the harmful effects of 'wild yeasts' which may not be as well disciplined as wine yeasts, and may occasionally result in a 'stuck' fermentation. The debate began because winemakers in new wine regions had to import their own, single strains of specially cultured yeasts (themselves originally selected from ambient yeasts) which tend to be much more predictable. Some producers in newer wine regions have experimented successfully with ambient yeasts, showing that it does not take too long to build up a useful local wine yeast population. They argue that ambient yeasts may result in wines with a wider range of flavours than a single strain of cultured yeast, but the genetic complexity of the yeast world has acted as a brake on conclusive research.

WHAT SORT OF CONTAINER FOR FERMENTATION?

Size, shape, material and design of a container can all have a tastable effect on any wine fer-

mented in it, and certainly have enormous practical ramifications for the winemaker. The larger the fermentation vat the more difficult it can be to control the vast amounts of heat generated by the fermentation process, and the more likely it can be that certain flavour compounds are 'boiled off', unless careful refrigeration is used. Whereas white wine can be made in a very tall, relatively narrow, space-saving tank, makers of red wine generally prefer wider vessels which maximize the area of the cap, putting as much liquid as possible in contact with the skins so as to extract lots of colour and flavour. And if they want to punch down the cap regularly, either with special long-handled tools, or, even better, feet, the vessel will have to have an open top, or at least a board over the top that can be lifted off. Pumping over also requires an opening at the top, and submerged caps require specially designed tanks with movable headboards.

White, rosé and many red wines are made in fermentation vats with closed tops to avoid oxidation, although they must have some valve to allow the carbon dioxide given off during fermentation to escape. A winery during vintage is heady with the smell of carbon dioxide, grape solids and, increasingly, alcohol. Because carbon dioxide reduces the available amount of oxygen, it can be very dangerous to spend too long in an enclosed space in which must is fermenting; cellar work can occasionally be fatal.

Although some fermentation vats are made of stone, ceramic, concrete, and various forms of plastic, by far the most common material selected by modern winemakers is stainless steel. It is easy to clean and can easily be fitted with temperature control devices such as refrigerated jackets and special coils.

European traditionalists may well favour wooden vats, however (closed for whites and open for reds), as wood's capacity to retain heat can be useful for extracting colour. White wines fermented in large, old wooden vats include many top Alsace, Loire, German and Austrian wines, while white burgundy and ambitious dry white wines the world over are fermented in small, new oak barrels. (See pages 91–3 for more details.)

WHICH ADDITIONS TO MAKE

As explained on page 73, a little sulphur dioxide is added to the raw ingredients of almost all wines, especially those made from slightly rotten grapes, but perfectly healthy, ripe grapes may need no further additions.

Cool summers may result in underripe grapes whose natural sugars would ferment into a liquid that the winemaker, or local regulation, reckons is not quite alcoholic enough. Chaptalization is therefore regularly practised throughout northern Europe, in Canada, in the wineries of China and Japan, and in the far south of New Zealand and Chile. It is banned (i.e. formally deemed unnecessary) in South Africa and Australia but some very southerly producers on the Cape coast and Tasmania would dearly love dispensation to chaptalize, particularly in less successful vintages. In Europe winemakers are rarely allowed to add more than 2 per cent to the final alcoholic strength of the wine as a result of chaptalization (although English winemakers regularly need more). In Bordeaux and Burgundy chaptalization is almost routine in some cellars, however, as these regions often lack sufficient sun to ripen the grapes enough to provide the sort of alcohol levels the producers like. This seems crazy in an age when alcohol and additives are popularly regarded as demons, but many oenologists argue that the extra alcohol is needed to 'support' the flavour.

The routine addition in warmer wine regions, on the other hand, is acid, most commonly in the form of added tartaric acid. Winemakers would rather harvest grapes a little late but with all the additional flavour compounds that develop late in the ripening process and then compensate for the reduced natural acidity level.

In official recognition of a succession of hot summers in the 1980s, many Europeans are now allowed to acidify too, although acidifying and chaptalizing the same vat is officially deemed too much of a good thing. After particularly cold summers, in northern Germany for example, seriously underripe grapes may need to be deacidified (commonly by adding chalk or a similar soother) as well as chaptalized.

DOES THE FERMENTATION NEED A KICKSTART?

Fermentations that are slow to start because of underripe or unhealthy grapes can be encouraged by adding special nitrogen-based yeast nutrients. Many New World winemakers routinely add nutrients to make the fermentation efficient and predictable (when Australian-trained flying winemakers introduced this trick to eastern Europe in the early 1990s they were regarded as wizards by the locals). If air temperatures are particularly low, the fermentation vat may have to be heated to begin with.

A WARM OR COOL FERMENT?

Once underway, fermentation generates huge quantities of heat and one of the main refinements of modern winemaking has been to install methods of cooling fermentation vats so that the winemaker can control the temperature of the must throughout fermentation. This means that not only is the danger of boiling off flavour compounds avoided, but also the winemakers gain potential control over the extraction of all sorts of soluble elements, particularly different tannins and other phenolics, since they all dissolve at different temperatures. Many modern wineries have sophisticated control panels which can monitor and control the temperature of each vat with the flick of a switch. Low-tech enterprises may still employ the early twentieth-century Bordeaux technique of using ice blocks.

The winemaker can dictate the flavours and character of a wine by controlling the fermentation temperature. Whites, which depend more on primary fruit aromas and have no need to encourage extraction, are almost invariably fermented cooler than most reds. Those fermented at the low end of the normal New

World white wine fermentation temperature range of 12–17°C (54–63°F) tend to smell of tropical fruits (particularly pineapple) and their own varietal flavour. This suits highly aromatic varieties but Europeans tend to ferment Chardonnay in the 18–20°C (64–8°F) range or even warmer so that they can benefit from some of the more complex aromas associated with warmer fermentations. Reds, being less delicate, withstand higher fermentation temperatures and in cooler regions may need them to encourage the extraction of colour, flavour and tannin. (Red wines fermented cool are generally higher in these primary fruit aromas and can often taste skinnier than their more complex counterparts that are fermented at higher temperatures.)

Again, Europeans tend to be less wary of high fermentation temperatures, allowing some vats to reach 30°C (85°F) or even more – although to go much higher risks stunning the yeast into total inactivity and the fermentation may be fatally flawed.

MALOLACTIC FERMENTATION?

Virtually all red wines and an increasing proportion of whites undergo this second, 'softening' fermentation which, under the influence of heat and some special, 'lactic' bacteria, takes place usually after the main alcoholic one. As well as making a wine more stable, this process helps to make it taste softer, fuller and

Shiny stainless steel tanks are so much easier to clean than the barrels involved in the traditional Burgundian method of lees stirring, or bâtonnage, now practised all over the world.

more complex, but can add a rather obvious buttery flavour if overdone. The winemaker can encourage the 'malo' by keeping the new wine at relatively high temperatures and/or by deliberately introducing lactic bacteria. This method is expressly avoided, however, in simple, warm-climate white wines in which every ounce of acid is needed to keep them lively.

LEES CONTACT AND STIRRING?

Red wines usually sit on the lees – the deposit left after fermentation – as a matter of course if the winemaker believes in a post-fermentation steeping period.

For white wines, leaving new wine in contact with the lees involves a conscious decision. Some winemakers, particularly those fermenting white burgundy and its Chardonnay counterparts in small barrels, deliberately stir up the lees every week or so to stop sulphides and mercaptans developing and to encourage extra flavour from the lees themselves. Stirring lees also has the effect of minimizing the wine's absorption of harsh tannins and flavour from the wood and tends to result in pale wine with a smooth texture.

MATURATION CONTAINER AND DURATION

The major decision here is oak or not (see pages 91–3). Basically, the longer the producer can afford to leave the new wine to settle, the fewer clarifying treatments detailed below are needed. Time (and oak) is a great alternative to additives.

Nouveaux may be 'matured' for no more than the few weeks needed to clarify and stabilize the liquid (see below), while some full-bodied reds may be kept in cask for years before being bottled. In very general terms, most high-acid white wines and commercial wines of any hue are matured in inert containers and bottled during the spring following the vintage, while serious red wines are usually bottled during the second spring or summer after fermentation.

HOW MUCH AIR?

Oxygen can easily harm delicate white wines but full-bodied red wines can benefit from a little exposure to air, particularly because it encourages many of the reactions involved in barrel maturation (see pages 91–3) and avoids reduction and the formation of sulphides and mercaptans. Because of this, many producers have a deliberate policy of regular racking from one barrel to another, which can introduce an ideal amount of oxygen. Others experiment with micro-oxygenation, introducing tiny amounts of oxygen to wine held in bulk over several months.

The purist's nightmare, a sheet filter (above). If the sheets are not clean, the wine may taste of wet cardboard. If there are too many of them, the wine may be tasteless. The wine writer's nightmare, a bottling line (below).

MAKING THE WINE LIMPID AND STABLE

Most wine drinkers, or at least wine retailers, prefer wines that are crystal clear and clear of crystals, even harmless ones such as tartrates. To this end commercial wines are routinely chilled (cold stabilization) before bottling to precipitate all these crystals and are rigorously filtered in order to remove any organisms that might cause nasty smells, hazes, cloudiness or an embarrassingly fizzy fermentation in bottle. Slower but cheaper and in some cases less brutal than using filters are various forms of fining. Beaten egg whites are regularly used as a fining agent in individual barrels at top estates in Europe, while sacks of bentonite, a useful American clay, are commonly added to tanks of wine (and juice) around the world. Fining agents do not remain in the wine; they merely serve to attract the larger solids (those that might discolour white wines or make red wines taste bitter) to fall to the bottom of the container so that clear wine can be racked off.

Wines that are designed for early consumption, particularly white wines which are more fragile, may well have preservatives added to them. The most common are ascorbic acid and sometimes sorbic acid for sweet wines, added together with sulphur dioxide to stop relatively delicate wines from oxidizing or refermenting in bottle. Time, settling and racking can, however, be an alternative to all this. Wines which have not been harshly filtered must be treated gently and kept cool so that no unwelcome reactions, refermentations or bacteria develop.

HOW SPARKLING WINES ARE MADE

This account should really be called 'how wines are made to sparkle', for the fundamental principle of making a sparkling wine is somehow to dissolve carbon dioxide in a given base wine and bottle it so that when the bottle is opened, the gas escapes in the form of bubbles.

CARBONATION, OR THE BICYCLE PUMP METHOD

The crudest way of doing this is to borrow a technique from the fizzy drinks industry and simply pump carbon dioxide into a tankful of wine and bottle it under pressure so that the gas cannot escape. Only the very cheapest, most basic sparkling wine will have been subjected to this process, however, which results in a dramatic, but short-lived explosion of large bubbles.

THE CHAMPAGNE OR TRADITIONAL METHOD

The most painstaking way of making a wine sparkle, and one which can give it a persistent stream of tiny bubbles which may still be fizzing slightly even the next morning in an open bottle, is the method used in Champagne. It may variously be described as the traditional or classic method, *méthode traditionnelle*, *méthode classique*, *metodo tradizionale/classico*, or in South Africa Méthode Cap Classique. Wines made this way may even be described on the label as 'fermented in this bottle', which is the essence of the technique.

But any serious maker of sparkling wine would agree that his job starts long before this curious bottle-as-fermentation-vat stage. The real key to making a fine sparkling wine lies in the particular character and qualities of the grapes used to make the still base wines. These base wines should emphatically not taste delicious in their still state. Fine sparkling wine demands relatively neutral, acid, light wines because the classic method of sparkling wine-making changes them so substantially, adding not just carbon dioxide, but alcohol and many layers of additional flavour.

Chardonnay, Pinot Noir and Pinot Meunier are the classic grape varieties for champagne and are widely used for top quality sparkling wine elsewhere, with local variations such as Pinot Blanc in California and Italy. The dark-skinned grapes especially have to be pressed with particular care and speed so that a minimum of pigments, and none of the harsh tannins, taint the juice.

This grey juice is then fermented in the normal way, with wines from different varieties and vineyards kept separate, so that over the winter the young wines can be tasted and assessed and, ideally, a perfectly matched blend of them, or **cuvée**, can be assembled. One of the major differences between blenders in Champagne and the New World has been that the former tend to have much more experience of how different components in a blend react with each other and with time, although the gap is narrowing.

By spring the base wines have been blended and are then bottled, in the extra-strong, semi-opaque bottles in which the wine will eventually be sold, along with a carefully measured dose of sugar and yeast. The point of this is to achieve a second fermentation in bottle which, like any fermentation, will give off just the right amount of carbon dioxide (see page 74). This gas is then trapped inside the bottle until it escapes as bubbles in the glass of the eventual consumer. This second fermentation also raises the alcohol content, typically from about 11 to 12.5 per cent, and, crucially, leaves a sediment of dead yeast lees.

Lees contact is increasingly used to make still wines (see page 82), but this sparkling winemaking technique is the only one which depends on the slow but myriad reactions between the dead yeast cells and the wine in a completely sealed container. Bottles are laid on their sides, ideally in dark, cool conditions with a constant temperature, and simply left to their own devices (sparkling wines are particularly sensitive to light). The longer this process is allowed to continue, the more complex the flavours to compensate for the naturally high acidity and neutrality of a young sparkling wine. Unfortunately, however, keeping thousands, and sometimes millions, of bottles on their sides for years at a time is extremely expensive, so truly fine sparkling wine is necessarily a luxury item. Those who have studied the ageing of sparkling wines in bottle claim that they need at least 18 months on the sediment to achieve any perceptible development.

Once the sparkling wine producer decides he or she can no longer stand the financial strain of maturing a particular lot of wine, the sediment has to be removed – not because it makes the wine taste nasty, but simply because consumers expect their wines to be crystal clear. The traditional way has been to literally shake the sediment off the belly of the bottle and into the bottle-neck by gradually moving the bottle from a horizontal to upended vertical position, simultaneously giving the sediment a quick, loosening shake. This process is called *remuage* in French, **riddling** in English.

The bottles are then moved, still upside down with the sediment just above the crown cap with which ageing champagne bottles are stoppered, to a bath of extremely cold brine which freezes the bottle-neck and its contents, allowing the sediment to escape as a frozen pellet when the bottle is sharply returned right way up and unstoppered. This process is called **disgorgement**, or *dégorgement*.

Before the proper champagne cork (a curious amalgam much wider than the usual wine cork) can be driven in, the bottle has to be topped up, usually with some more wine of the same sort blended with a predetermined amount of sugar known as the **dosage**. The driest sparkling wines are usually labelled Brut and contain an amount of sugar that would make most still wines taste distinctly sweetish, but the naturally high acidity of most sparkling wines means that the dosage is usually imperceptible (although many very cheap champagnes are betrayed by the amount of sugar added to compensate for their toe-curling acidity). Sec or Dry, Demi-Sec or Medium Dry, and Rich betray increasingly high dosages.

The cumbersome *remuage* operation, although concerned far more with cosmetics than inherent wine quality, has come to play a large part in what is viewed as the mystique of champagne and similar sparkling wines. It is very labour intensive, however, and during the 1970s when labour costs rose rapidly, the Spaniards developed an automated substitute, pictured overleaf.

There are even newer alternatives too, such as yeasts encapsulated in tiny alginate beads which look like shot, inside which the dead yeast cells are trapped, enabling the sediment simply to be poured out of the bottle before disgorgement. A special cartridge that can be inserted into the bottle-neck has also been developed and, like the beads, results in wines very similar to those made by the traditional method. Neither technique finds favour with traditionalists, however, nor with those concerned about unemployment.

THE MOST COMMON METHOD – IN TANK

This process, developed by an enterprising Bordeaux wine merchant early this century to transform his region's white wine surplus into something more commercially attractive, involves provoking the second fermentation in giant tanks rather than in bottle, so that the wine can simply be settled and the clear wine pumped off the lees to be bottled under pres-

The girasol, gyropalette in French, is a large metal cube-shaped crate into which bottles are packed parallel to each other and riddled by computer (which needs no sleep or weekends off). This results in bottle-necks like the ones below, and dramatic clunks and clicks at unexpected intervals in many of the more automated sparkling-wine cellars, including quite a number in Champagne.

sure. It takes months rather than years, and is very much less labour intensive, but the resulting wine has none of the interest and character generated by extended contact between maturing wine and the lees in a container as small as a bottle. That said, few grape varieties other than the Pinots and Chardonnay seem particularly well suited to the champagne method, and the tank method is a much more suitable process for grape varieties such as the Muscat used to produce Italy's light, fruity spumante (see page 89). The tank method is also known variously as the Charmat, Carstens, and cuve close process.

OTHER METHODS

Variations on the two principal methods outlined above have also been devised. The **transfer** method, for example, involves the rather cumbersome process of conducting the second fermentation in bottle and then either sucking out the deposit or emptying the contents of the bottles into a large tank, filtering it, and then rebottling the result under pressure.

Transversage is an occasional twist on the champagne method whereby, immediately following disgorgement, the contents of bottles of sparkling wine made by the champagne method are emptied into a pressure tank to which the dosage is added before the wine is bottled, typically in another (often small) size of bottle, under pressure. This is how many half-bottles, all airline 'splits' or quarter-bottles, and virtually all giant bottles of champagne are filled. For this reason champagne usually tastes best from a regular bottle or magnum.

HOW SWEET WINES ARE MADE

Why do strong men and women waste so much time and effort making top quality sweet wines? Because they taste so uniquely other-worldly, that's why. And why is it a waste of time and effort? Because so few consumers appreciate great sweet wines, the wine world's most hard-won treasures.

The extraordinary Botrytis cinerea fungus, or noble rot, which literally and systematically desiccates ripe grapes, increasing their sugar content and complexity – if the weather co-operates. If it attacks grapes that are less than fully ripe or if the weather is too wet, the grapes simply putrefy on the vine.

This is probably because so much bad quality sweet wine has been launched on the poor consumer. The more residual sugar a wine has, the greater the danger of some yeast acting on this sugar and starting a fermentation in bottle, giving off gas which will disturb both the wine and the consumer and may even break the bottle. Winemakers have therefore tended to add vast quantities of sulphur dioxide to ward off any possible yeast activity. This, together with the fact that in the days of 'Spanish Sauterne' (sic) far too many sweet wines lacked enough acidity to balance the residual sugar, must have put thousands if not millions of potential consumers off all sweet wines. Today, winemakers add much more conservative doses of sulphur, and tend to be much better at balancing sweetness with its natural antidote, acidity. A great sweet wine is so well balanced that it is quite possible to drink it throughout a meal, with all sorts of savoury dishes. I know because I've done it, with drools of pleasure.

BOTRYTIZED WINES

The *Botrytis cinerea* fungus can work magic on ripe grapes, making the skins thinner, encouraging evaporation of water and thereby concentration of the sugar and acidity, and adding all sorts of extra, still mysterious ingredients into the bargain that add extraordinary flavour and longevity. It will do this, however, only to grapes that are ripe and healthy, and only if the weather co-operates by alternating misty, moist mornings to encourage the fungus with warm, sunny afternoons to dry out the grapes and stop the mould spreading too rapidly. If the fungus attacks unripe grapes, or those whose skins have been broken (by hail for example), or if the weather is rainy or humid, then the fungus is an unremitting curse rather than a blessing and copious sprayings may be needed to combat rampant rot spreading through the vineyard, spoiling colour and flavour, especially in reds.

'Good botrytis' is called noble rot in English, *pourriture noble* in French, *Edelfäule* in German and *muffa* in Italian. Bad botrytis is called grey rot (or sometimes just rot). Sweet wines made from grapes affected by good botrytis are often called botrytized.

Making botrytized wines is particularly difficult because the juice is extremely viscous (and in very short supply, given the concentration effect of the fungus). The grapes have to be picked by hand, sometimes involving many forays through the vineyard to pick only grapes at the optimum point of (apparent) decay.

Botrytized wines, which have a distinctive sort of cabbagey smell in youth and seem almost immortal, include château-bottled Sauternes in suitable vintages, lesser sweet white bordeaux appellations and Monbazillac in exceptional vintages for Bordeaux sweet whites (see page 306), Loire wines labelled Moelleux in vintages such as 1989 and 1990, Alsace wines labelled Sélection de Grains Nobles, Germany's Trockenbeerenauslese and Beerenauslese rarities, Austria's much less rare counterparts (notably from Burgenland), Hungary's sweetest forms of Tokay, a few Italian specialities labelled Muffato, and a host of speciality bottlings from all over the world, among which botrytized Chardonnay and Sauvignon Blanc seem to work surprisingly well. Some producers, notably in California and some in Australia, pick grapes and then spray them with botrytis spores in the winery, replicating the ideal weather conditions artificially. The resulting wines often taste similar although it is too early to say whether they age as well.

LATE PICKED SWEETNESS

Some sweet wines are sweet simply because they are made with ultra-ripe grapes, unaffected by botrytis but sometimes almost raisined on the vine. Jurançon is made like this every year, as are cheaper Sauternes and other sweet whites from south west France, or grander ones in less successful vintages. Germany's Spätlese and Auslese wines also depend on this sort of natural ripeness for their sugar content.

SWEET WINES MADE FROM DRIED GRAPES

Another way of concentrating a grape's natural sweetness is to dry, or raisin, the grape, encouraging its moisture content to evaporate, typically by spreading whole bunches on trays, well aerated to avoid the danger of mould (or outside in the hot sunshine in very dry climates). This classical practice is most obviously – though by no means exclusively – continued in north east Italy where sweet wines made this way are often described as Recioto (dry ones as Amarone). France also makes some *vin de paille* from grapes dried traditionally on straw (a rare speciality of Hermitage).

EISWEIN AND ICE WINE

These fashionable wines are, for obvious reasons, the speciality of wine regions as cold as northern Germany and Canada. Ripe, healthy grapes are picked when actually frozen on the vine. When such grapes are pressed, water is eliminated in the form of crystals left in the press and the natural sugar content (and acidity) is thereby concentrated. An increasing proportion of grapes are devoted to making such wines, rather than botrytized wines, in suitable parts of the world, since low temperatures are usually more reliable than the coincidence of botrytis fungus with suitable weather conditions, and yet Eiswein and proper Ice wine (made as a result of natural rather than artificial freezing) sells for almost as high a price.

ADDING EXTRA ALCOHOL

One way of making a wine that is both sweet and stable is to add alcohol to it, to make a mixture in which yeast would be completely incapable. This is the classic recipe for sweet fortified wines. Port, madeira, malaga and marsala, indeed all of the world's sweet fortified wines are sweet and strong because fermentation is stopped half-way by the addition of enough spirit to stun the yeasts. The only exception to this is sweet sherry, which is sweetened by adding specially concentrated grape syrup. See pages 240–42 for full details of how port and madeira are made.

The technique is also applied to grape juice that has hardly started to ferment to make France's *vins doux naturels* such as Muscat de Beaumes-de-Venise and other Languedoc-Roussillon Muscats, and red and tawny Rasteau (in the southern Rhône) and Banyuls as well as Maury and Rivesaltes in Roussillon. These sweet, alcoholic, but slightly raw mixtures of alcohol and part-fermented grape juice may then be carefully matured, either in wood or glass, in varying degrees of heat and humidity.

France also produces a range of sweet, grape-based drinks made by adding neutral grape spirit to grape juice before it has even started to ferment. Pineau des Charentes is the most important of these, made in Cognac.

EVERYDAY SWEET WINES

Some commercial sweet white wines, notably in Bordeaux and the Loire, are still made by leaving high levels of sugar in the wine and then adding lots of sulphur, but much more common (and more attractive to taste) is to ferment all the grape sugar into alcohol to produce a dry wine and then to add sweetness in the form of unfermented grape juice, sometimes concentrated. The sweet mixture (which is of course a little less alcoholic than the original wine) is then heavily filtered to remove any possible yeasts and bottled carefully to produce a stable liquid that should be drunk as young as possible. This, for example, is how most commercial German wines (Liebfraumilch *et al.*) are made.

Then there is the north Italian way of making a wine that is both sweet and fizzy: stopping the fermentation part-way through so that the wine is low in alcohol, high in sugar and still contains some carbon dioxide given off by the fermentation. This results in wines such as Asti and Moscato Spumante.

Trees grow so slowly in the Tronçais forest in France's Allier département *that its oak (shown here during the all-important years of outdoor seasoning and being shaped into barrels) is tight-grained and highly sought-after.*

OAK – INGREDIENT X

There is no doubt whatsoever that the second most important plant in the late twentieth-century world of wine, after the vine, is the oak tree. Winemakers everywhere are seeking to add cachet, dimension and value to their products by making or ageing them in oak barrels. And whereas they may haggle with their customers over pennies when it comes to the price of the wine they sell, these same producers seem willing to pay the earth in order to acquire what is widely seen as the magic winemaking ingredient, a top quality barrel. French oak carries the highest reputation and price tag and, while France's wine producers have seen their exports shrink over the last decade, the country's coopers (*tonneliers* in French) have enjoyed unparalleled prosperity, exporting barrels to wine producers all over the globe.

At one time wooden barrels were used to transport and store practically every commodity. Today the cooperage industry is kept alive only by demand from wine and dark spirits producers. Much less than 10 per cent of all the wine produced in the world today is aged in small barrels, but these wines attract a disproportionate amount of attention because they are some of the world's most exciting.

WHY OAK?

Wood can have two possible sorts of effect on a wine held in it: it can impart flavour, colour and tannins from the wood itself; and it has the physical property of allowing the wine much more contact with air than an inert material such as stainless steel or lined cement. But different woods vary enormously in their suitability for wine containers. Chestnut, pine, redwood, acacia and various other woods have all been used for larger wine vats, but oak is ideal for small barrels because it is hard, strong, watertight yet supple, and its characteristics seem to have an affinity, however ill-understood, with those of wine. Fully understanding the complicated interactions between flavours and physical properties of different sorts of oak and wine will keep researchers busy well into this millennium. What is known, however, is that most of the oak's flavour is leeched into the first wine put into a barrel, and that ageing wine in a small oak barrel encourages it to become clear and stable in the most natural way.

WHAT WOODEN CONTAINERS ARE USED FOR

Many older wineries are equipped with large wooden storage and/or fermentation tanks which are so old that they can no longer

FAR LEFT Barrel remnants (top) are sometimes inserted, in a perforated container, in an old barrrel while the toasted oak chips (bottom) are suspended in the fermentation vat in a sort of teabag. LEFT Much finer oak chips (the bottom ones have been toasted and therefore have more flavour) are either suspended in a teabag or used as a flavoured fining agent.

impart anything directly to the wine (see below) but, so long as they have been kept scrupulously clean, they can still be useful for settling and clarifying wine.

Modern wineries actively choose to invest in wood for one of two purposes in most cases: either large fermentation vessels of any age, often open-topped, in which wood's physical properties can be useful (but stainless steel is much easier to cool and clean); or small, new barrels expected to impart the wood's own flavour as well as its physical characteristics to wine deliberately matured in them for many months (barrel maturation) and often, especially in the case of full-bodied white wines, fermented in them too (barrel fermentation).

OAK-RELATED FACTORS WHICH AFFECT HOW WINE TASTES

WHERE THE OAK COMES FROM

Winemakers tend to be punctilious in their choice of oak provenance. Many is the New World winery visitor who seeks or receives exact information on the percentage split between Vosges, Allier and Tronçais barrels in a particular blend. Some of those who have wandered through forests and timber yards are a little more wary of oak labelling.

Like the wine-producing vine family (see page 96), the wine-maturing oak family is most readily divided into its European and American members. The United States is the biggest commercial grower of oak (a business sustained by the regulation that requires bourbon to be matured in a new American oak barrel). American oak is in general more powerfully flavoured than European oak, often with a slightly sweet vanilla-like note, and is so dense that it remains watertight even after sawing. Its more obvious flavours mean that it has been used mainly for powerfully flavoured red wines, notably in the Americas, Spain (which for historical reasons has a tradition of importing American barrels) and Australia, but carefully seasoned American

oak can be used to quite subtle effect on other wines such as warm climate Chardonnays too.

France is by far the most important source of European oak, and its forests, which cover a quarter of the country, have been carefully managed for at least three centuries – an important consideration in a business where the ideal product should be at least 80 and ideally 100 years old. Coopers usually distinguish between 'tight-grained' oaks (the result of slow growth in close planted, dense forests) and more porous, more tannic, 'wide-grained' oaks, typically Limousin oak grown in western France, which are of more interest for brandy than for wine maturation. France's most revered oaks for winemaking come from central France (Allier and Nièvre/Nevers in the upper Loire) or from the hills west of Alsace as pale Vosges wood. Tronçais and Bertranges are specific forests within the respective *départements*, France's 'counties', of Allier and Nièvre.

Before the Russian revolution Baltic oaks were the most highly prized and trade in eastern European oaks is once more increasing, even though many forests have been poorly maintained. Slovenian oak is widely used in Italy.

HOW THE WOOD WAS SEASONED

Barrels are made from staves cut from long planks of wood left outside in a suitably unpolluted environment for two or more years so that the harsher elements are leeched out naturally. Drying in a special steam kiln is a way of artificially accelerating this process. It is increasingly obvious that the duration and quality of this 'seasoning' plays just as important a role as the provenance of the oak. One ancient tree typically provides fewer than two small wine barrels.

HOW THE BARREL IS MADE

Staves are fashioned as gently as possible from these planks and bent over small fires, secured by hoops and hammered into a barrel shape. The extent to which these fires are allowed to 'toast' or char the wood has become an important dimension in buying and selling barrels (again, partly because of the focus of the Mondavi experiments). Barrels given only a light toast are more likely to impart substantial oak flavour and tannins than one with a medium toast, although heavily toasted barrels, popular in Burgundy, can impart their own charred flavour to a wine matured in them.

SIZE OF CONTAINER

The larger the barrel the lower the ratio of surface area to volume and the less impact the wood is likely to have on the wine in either physical or flavour sense. However, barrels holding less than 190 l (50 gal) can overwhelm a wine with oak flavour and tannins, especially if they are new (see below). The most widely used barrels hold either 225 l (59 gal) like the Bordeaux barrique or 228 l (60 gal) like the Burgundian pièce, but hogsheads of 300 l (79 gal) are also used quite widely in the New World.

AGE OF CONTAINER

The newer a barrel the more oak flavour and tannin it has to be leeched into the wine. For this reason, brand new barrels are prized by most wine producers (except Piedmont traditionalists and those who make sherry, which is best matured in an old example of the traditional 600 l [158 gal] American oak 'butt'). In practice a new barrel is used once or possibly twice for a top-of-the-range wine, before being used once or twice for a medium-quality wine. After that it has almost no flavour to impart and will be used on lesser wines merely for its physical properties of helping to clarify the wine.

PERIOD IN CONTAINER

One crucial factor in determining how a wine will taste is whether it is fermented in a new oak barrel. An increasing proportion of fine wines are at least partly fermented in barrel, which leads naturally to the enriching process of lees contact (see page 82). The natural variation in temperature of such a small container can add complexity and the buffering effect of the lees can result in delicate, pale wines that have an extra-silky texture. (White wines put into small barrels after fermentation often turn brown in the bottle because they still contain heavy phenolics.)

Some red wines, particularly in warmer climates where grapes are deeply coloured enough without extended maceration on the skins after fermentation, are drawn off the skins and put into small barrels part-way through fermentation. Barrel fermentation of reds was initially most popular in Australia, where it can result in wines with a charred, 'sweet' aroma reminiscent of tomato ketchup and, combined with frequent rackings, can accelerate ageing.

The length of time a wine is matured in oak will strongly influence how it tastes. Even if it is only in the first few months that much oak flavour is imparted from a new barrel (and that depends on the toast and the extent to which any lees are stirred), the longer a wine stays in the lightly aerated atmosphere of a barrel, the more phenolic compounds will be precipitated and the faster it will age (see pages 39–41). This ageing process is accelerated by each racking because of exposure to oxygen.

CHEAPER ALTERNATIVES

The most common alternative to an expensive oak barrel is to add a sackful of small oak chips or shavings to the fermentation tank and rely on some oak flavour being leeched out by the heat and alcohol generated by fermentation. There will be none of wood's physical advantages, however, and the oak flavour may be shorter lived than in a barrel-aged wine. The labels on such wines may refer to 'oak ageing', 'oak influence' or 'oak maturation' but the B-word (barrel) should be obvious by omission. Another alternative is to suspend oak staves in an inert vat to impart oak flavour.

Chips and inner staves are not necessarily a bad thing; they provide consumers with the sort of flavours they seek for a fraction of the cost of a real oak barrel, but they cannot provide the physical properties of barrel fermentation and maturation.

3
WINE GRAPE VARIETIES

THE VINE FAMILY

The grapevine, the world's most important fruit crop, is a natural creeper, a distant relative of Virginia creeper in fact, as can be seen by inspecting closely this colourful plant that clings to many houses. All sorts of vine grow wild wherever plants thrive. Botanists call the family to which the vine belongs *Vitis* and have identified about 60 different species within it. The Far East has its own native vine species such as the *Vitis amurensis* of Mongolia, which has particularly good resistance to extreme cold. Europe and the Middle East has just one native vine species, the one from which almost all of the world's famous wines are made, called *Vitis vinifera*, often called simply **vinifera**. (The word does not exist in classical Latin but was dreamt up by a botanist to convey 'wine-grape bearing'.) Within each species, hundreds, often thousands, of different varieties have been identified. Cabernet Sauvignon and Chardonnay are two of the most famous varieties of vinifera.

As the early European colonists discovered to their initial delight (see page 264), North America has the greatest diversity of vine species, most of which look quite different from vinifera, having much flatter leaves and thinner shoots. Some of the most famous are called *Vitis labrusca*, *Vitis riparia* and *Vitis rupestris* and, in the south eastern states, *Vitis rotundifolia*, which has particularly round leaves with less marked indentations than most other vines. Wine made from many of these American vines, particularly *Vitis labrusca*, tastes quite different from wine made from vinifera vines. It has a strong smell reminiscent of musk or very strong artificial wild strawberry flavour which wine tasters often call 'foxy'. It can be quite attractive to palates brought up on such wine, but comes as a shock to those used to the flavours of 'European' varieties, by now widely disseminated all over the wine-producing world, including North and South America, Africa and Australasia.

The early American settlers, seeking familiar flavours in their wine, imported European vine cuttings and were puzzled as to why they refused to flourish in the new colonies. The explanation did not emerge for more than 200 years, at the end of the nineteenth century.

In the mid-nineteenth century the vineyards of France in general and Bordeaux in particular were ravaged by a fungal disease called *oïdium*, or **powdery mildew**. Eventually spraying vines with a preparation of copper sulphate (called Bordeaux mixture) was found to ward off this debilitating disease, but no sooner had the vines recovered from this, in the 1860s, than they started to suffer from another much less explicable condition, apparently slowly dying before horrified growers' eyes. This phenomenon spread throughout France and eventually to almost all parts of the wine-producing world. After decades of despair, trials and research, it was found to be the work of a tiny louse, called **phylloxera**, which loves nothing more than a nice juicy vinifera vine root. It munches its way through root after root, literally killing the plants above. The only vines which in the long term have demonstrated apparent immunity to phylloxera are certain native American species and vines growing in very dry and/or very sandy conditions.

It is now clear that the dreaded louse and the fungus responsible for powdery mildew (and that which causes another vine disease, **downy mildew**, which arrived in France soon after the first effects of phylloxera were noted, just to complicate an already traumatic situation) are native to North America. Most native American vines have therefore developed a good resistance to them, but when in the mid-nineteenth century Europeans began to travel and bring back across the Atlantic botanical specimens kept alive in special glass cases, the effects on the European vine were devastating, for they brought phylloxera, to which European vines had no resistance whatsoever, with them too.

Phylloxera literally threatened the entire world's wine industry and a long-term solution had to be found. Eventually, after all sorts of experimentation with chemicals and flooding, it was found that phylloxera could be combated by **grafting** vinifera vines on to American **rootstocks**, so that the part of the plant vulnerable to phylloxera became resistant to it. Since the late nineteenth century nurserymen have worked hard at breeding rootstocks designed for particular environments and goals. Today about 85 per cent of the world's wine-producing vines are European vinifera varieties grafted on to rootstocks containing a high proportion of American genes in order to minimize the risk of phylloxera damage. There are some particularly isolated, or very dry or very sandy wine regions where growers are prepared to take the risk of planting ungrafted vines. Chile, for example, has never suffered phylloxera damage. The vineyards of the French Camargue and Colares in Portugal are almost all seaside sand. South Australia (but not neighbouring Victoria) is unaffected by phylloxera and, so far, growers in New Zealand, Greece, the Pacific Northwest and England have been prepared to trade off the cost savings of planting ungrafted vines against the very obvious presence of phylloxera.

The most obvious effects of phylloxera were seen in the 1990s in Northern California where the great majority of vines were vinifera grafted on to a rootstock called AXR 1, a hybrid of the vinifera vine Aramon (see page 130) and a member of the *Vitis rupestris* species. (Crosses of members of different species are called **hybrids**, while those of members of the same species, such as Müller-Thurgau, for example, are called **crossings**.) California growers were encouraged to choose AXR 1 as their rootstock because it was usefully productive. Its acknowledged low resistance to phylloxera was thought to be unimportant; phylloxera had not affected Northern California since the late nineteenth century, when it had almost wiped out the local

wine industry. But as the 1980s came to an end it was clear that thousands of acres of vineyard had been fatally invaded by phylloxera. A dramatically comprehensive replanting programme, designed to match popular varieties to suitable sites and to establish modern vine-training systems, cost billions of dollars but resulted in a much more robust wine industry – although there is still widespread disagreement about which rootstocks are most suitable replacements for AXR 1.

For decades after phylloxera first devastated European vines, discussions raged about whether the wine produced 'pre-phylloxera' was better than the produce of vines grafted on to American rootstocks. Since so much was in flux at that time, we shall never know. Certainly I would never claim to be able to taste the difference between the produce of grafted and ungrafted vines.

It is interesting to note, however, that the most intelligent vine-growing consultants in Chile now realize that there are disadvantages to their famously ungrafted vines. Because there has never been a phylloxera epidemic (probably because the soils here are so dry), no one has any experience of vine rootstocks and there are strict quarantines, as elsewhere, on bringing in plant material. This means that it will be several years before it is legally possible to plant rootstocks on a commercial scale in Chile – and yet the right rootstock can be an extremely useful tool to a vine-grower who is plagued by over-vigorous (leafy) vines and soil pests called **nematodes**, as many Chileans are. Rootstocks are not necessarily a bad thing!

In the early twentieth century, in the wake of phylloxera and the two mildews, when quantity rather than quality was the abiding preoccupation of wine producers everywhere, vine breeders concentrated on developing an array of hybrids designed to resist all these scourges and produce lots of wine. The first generation of these so-called hybrid 'direct producers' (i.e. ungrafted vines) was bred from American vines. Concord, Catawba and Isabella are examples of **American**

hybrids still grown today in North America and humid climates such as that of Japan.

Wines made from such vines found little favour with Europeans, however, which led to a new generation of hybrids, the so-called **French hybrids**, bred from a mixture of American and European vines. These were extremely useful for a France in transition, because of their good disease resistance and lack of foxy flavour, but as the agrochemical industry obliged with preparations specially designed to fight mildew and rot, these French hybrids have gradually been replaced with vinifera vines in almost all wine regions. Baco, Chambourcin and Seyval Blanc are examples of French hybrids grown today in Gascony, New South Wales and England respectively, and none of them has the remotest hint of foxy flavour.

Vine-breeders more recently have worked on increasing yields and in Germany, where ripeness is revered, building up grape sugar fast.

Germany's vineyards have accordingly been invaded by a new generation of crossings such as Ortega, Optima, Kerner and Ehrenfelser.

The French way of doing things has been to develop particular **clones** of the important varieties with particular abilities, the most popular of which is often prolific yield. Burgundy's vineyards suffered considerably in the 1970s and early 1980s as too many growers chose Pinot Noir clones designed with quantity and/or rot resistance in mind rather than wine quality.

Different varieties of vine produce discernibly different grapes, which in turn produce discernibly different wines. The science of describing and identifying different vine varieties is called **ampelography**. It is nowadays considerably augmented by **DNA analysis** which has identified many fascinating relationships between different vines.

Some varieties are more prone to mutation than others – Pinot and Grenache, for example,

Northern California vines were burnt to rid the state of any traces of the phylloxera louse that still remained (left), while an ancient poster in Chinon in the Loire Valley (right) reminds today's vine-growers of the dangers of mildew in a damp climate such as France's.

both mutate easily and can therefore be found with all sorts of different colours of grape skin, from dark purple through red-pink and violet to gold and green. Red and pink wine need some pigment and therefore must be made from dark-skinned grapes, but white wine can be made from grapes of any colour. Many varieties called 'grey' (Pinot Gris, for example) have pink-skinned berries but naturally produce deep-coloured white wines. If dark-skinned berries are pressed very gently on the other hand, as Pinot Noir grapes are in Champagne, they will yield pale juice and white wine. The only grapes incapable of producing white wine are those very unusual ones whose flesh is not the usual grey-green common to 99 per cent of all wine grapes harvested but is actually tinted red. Such varieties are called Teinturiers in French, Tintoreras in Spanish – literally 'dyers'.

The wine grape varieties that follow are those the enthusiastic wine drinker is most likely to come across and are divided into pale-skinned (White Wine Varieties) and dark-skinned (Red Wine Varieties). There are thousands more, however, with particular concentrations in Portugal, Galicia, Greece and Central Europe. It would be very sad if we lost this diversity to Chardonnay- and Cabernet-mania.

WHITE WINE VARIETIES

Airén, the grape of the vast La Mancha region in central Spain and therefore the world's most planted wine grape, which produces crisp, fairly neutral wine, much of it being distilled into brandy.

Albana, Emilia-Romagna vine related to GRECO DI TUFO, making deep-coloured wines.

Albariño, the perfumed, elegant aristocrat of Rias Baixas in north west Spain. Sometimes VIOGNIER-like.

Albillo, Spanish variety producing quite neutral but full-bodied wine, mainly in Ribeiro but also used to perfume Ribera del Duero reds.

Aligoté, Burgundy's second white grape, making tartish wine for early consumption, best from Bouzeron. Also grown in Bulgaria, Romania and Russia.

Altesse, another name for Savoie's ROUSSETTE.

Alva, see ROUPEIRO.

Alvarinho, ALBARIÑO in Portugal's Vinho Verde region where it is also prized.

Amigne, Valais rarity making rich, heady wines.

Ansonica, Tuscan name for INZOLIA.

Arbois, minor Loire variety making soft wines in Touraine.

Arinto, Portuguese grape making high-acid, sometimes lemony wine in Bucelas, Ribatejo, Vinho Verde amongst others.

Arneis, floral-scented Piedmont speciality rescued from extinction. Has been fashionable. Drink young.

Arrufiac, Arrufiat, grainy traditional Gascon ingredient in Pacherenc du Vic-Bilh.

Arvine, Petite Arvine, AMIGNE's cousin.

Assyrtiko, from the Greek island of Santorini but valued increasingly widely on mainland Greece for its acidity, apple and lemon flavours, and ability to express terroir.

Auxerrois, slightly fuller, less acid version of PINOT BLANC, widely planted in Alsace and blended with it (although the blend is almost invariably called Pinot Blanc on the label). Treasured in Luxembourg for its low acid.

Avesso makes full-bodied, scented wine in Vinho Verde. May be JAEN.

Azal, Vinho Verde grape with usually high acids.

Bacchus, conveniently early ripening German crossing that can bring grape sugars but little else to a blend. Some currant varietals from Franken and England.

Baco Blanc, Baco 22A, French hybrid named after its creator in 1898. Good at being grafted but on the way out of Armagnac, once its stronghold. See also BACO NOIR.

Baiyu, Chinese name for RKATSITELI.

Baroque, full, nutty mainstay of Tursan from south west France.

Bergeron, local name for ROUSSANNE in the Savoie appellation of Chignin.

Bical, Bairrada's crisp speciality, which is useful for sparkling wines.

Blanc Fumé, SAUVIGNON BLANC in Pouilly-sur-Loire.

Boal, great rich varietal of Madeira, Anglicized to Bual.

Bombino Bianco, a widely planted vine in Apulia as well as further north up Italy's Adriatic coast. Extremely prolific but Valentini's 'Trebbiano d'Abruzzo' demonstrates what can be achieved.

Borrado das Moscas, BICAL in Dão (Portugal).

Bourboulenc, potentially fine Languedoc variety at its best in La Clape, where it can smell attractively of iodine.

Bouvier, lesser central European table grape, a crossing of Chardonnay and Zöldsilváni vines planted in Austria, Hungary and, as Ranina, in Slovenia.

Burger, once very important in California, now down to a minor role in the Central Valley.

Carignan Blanc, a white mutation of the widely planted CARIGNAN found particularly in Roussillon in France.

Catarratto, Sicily's most important grape after SANGIOVESE and therefore one of the world's most planted. It can be full and lemony but much of it ends up as grape concentrate or at the bottom of the European wine lake.

Cayetana, prolific producer for brandy de Jerez in Spain's south west.

Cerceal, Portuguese grape responsible for the driest, most elegant form of madeira, Sercial (see page 241). This late ripening vine, also grown on the mainland, provides grapes that are eye-tinglingly high in acidity and wines that can last for decades.

Cereza, basic pink-skinned Argentine.

Chardonnay, the most famous vine variety of all. So powerful is the C-word on a wine label that, like Cabernet Sauvignon, Chardonnay has virtually no synonyms – although in Styria in southern Austria some winemakers persist with the tradition of calling it Morillon.

In the 1980s something extremely important to the history of wine happened: 'Chardonnay' became a name more familiar to the world's wine buyers than any of the geographically named wines this vine variety had for centuries produced, such as Chablis, Montrachet or Corton-Charlemagne.

When the emerging New World wine industries introduced varietal labelling, calling wines by the name of their principal grape variety, it was Chardonnay that made the most friends. Wine drinkers find it flatteringly easy to enjoy, with its broad, exuberant charms, relatively high alcohol and low acidity, and lack of powerful scent. Vine-growers find it easy to grow productively and profitably (it can yield well, ripen usefully early, although buds rather too early for frost-free comfort in cool climates). And winemakers revel in the range of different

winemaking techniques to which Chardonnay readily submits: not just a wide range of dry white wines with more weight than most, but delicate sparkling wines and even a few extremely successful sweet white wines made with the benefit of 'noble rot' (see page 88).

All over the world, producing Chardonnay is seen as a rite of passage in new wine regions. Almost any wine producer with ambitions to belong to the great international club of wine grown-ups has to prove that he or she can make a Chardonnay with the best of them, preferably a Chardonnay fermented and matured in new-(ish) oak barrels the Burgundian way. The fact is that most of this sort of wine is far more a product made in the cellar than in the vineyard. Or, to put it another way, skilfully made barrel-fermented Chardonnays tend to taste much the same wherever they are made. Indeed when many people say they like the taste of Chardonnay, what they often mean is that they like the taste of oak, or at least the qualities of oak maturation.

So, although in terms of total area planted Chardonnay lags well behind such workhorse varieties as Spain's Airén and Italy's Trebbiano, it is more widely distributed than any other grape variety – probably even more widely than its red wine counterpart Cabernet Sauvignon, which needs more sunshine to ripen it than Chardonnay.

However, Chardonnay mania, of which French coopers have been the major beneficiaries, is a relatively recent phenomenon. In the early 1970s it was hardly grown outside its Burgundian homeland and Champagne. It accounted for only a tiny proportion of all vines grown in California and Australia, for example, whereas by the early 1990s it had become the most planted white wine grape in both.

At times demand for Chardonnay grapes from wine producers has been so much greater than supply (Australia in the mid-1990s springs to mind) that Chardonnay has been blended with one or two other varieties. Semillon-Chardonnay ('SemChard') and Chardonnay-Colombard blends became the pragmatic solution to an industry's problem.

The Chardonnay vine is nothing if not adaptable. Commercially acceptable Chardon-

nay can be produced in really quite hot wine regions such as the hot interiors of California, South Africa and Australia, where clever wine-making can give it tropical fruit flavours and even some suggestion of oakiness, often using oak chips. In cooler wine regions such as Chablis, Carneros and Tasmania, on the other hand, it can produce apple-crisp tingle juice which, in less ripe years can have rapier-like acidity. The best examples can benefit from five or even more years in bottle to soften that acidity and develop rounder flavours to balance it – although less concentrated examples produced in cool years may simply taste even leaner as the bloom of youth fades. Excluding premier cru and grand cru burgundy, Chardonnay does not make wines for long ageing.

Cooler regions are also particularly good sources of lively, relatively subtle Chardonnay fruit for makers of sparkling wine, who value acidity and an absence of obvious flavours.

Chardonnay is, for example, the second most important grape variety grown in Champagne (see page 172), and it was largely the dramatic expansion of the Champagne vineyard that propelled Chardonnay into first place among France's white grape varieties in the 1980s. Chardonnay can bring a floral or even steely character to a sparkling wine in its youth, which can age into toastiness after years in bottle.

Chardonnay's tendency to bud early means that in very northerly wine regions such as Chablis (left), frost is a perennial hazard against which fires have to be lit in the vineyard.
The Chardonnay grapes grown in New South Wales, Australia (right) have no such threats to their existence. Overripeness is the problem here.

The wines of Chablis, one of the coolest wine regions in France, have a very particular flavour. It reminds me of wet stones, with some suggestion of very green fruit, but without the strong aroma and lean build of a Sauvignon Blanc. Traditional, top quality examples designed for a long life can even taste slightly musty in middle age, as though those wet stones had sprouted some moss. And then after about eight years in bottle they can develop much more complicated, often deliciously honey-like, flavours.

In more temperate climates Chardonnay can yield some of the finest dry white wine in the world. The heartland of Burgundy, the Côte d'Or, is effectively the nerve centre of this style of wine: savoury and dense, the grape a transparent medium through which different vineyards (and winemakers) can communicate their own individual styles, often only after many years in bottle. Most of the wines are made with extensive use of small oak barrels, and many of them are simply too 'closed' (low in aroma and flavour) and dour to enjoy before their third birthday, depending on the vintage. Hazelnuts, liquorice, butter and spice are just a few of the many aromas that can be found in the heady perfume that can develop in these markedly full-bodied wines. Montrachet, Puligny-Montrachet, Chassagne-Montrachet, Meursault and Corton-Charlemagne are some of the most famous names. Typical Meursault tends to be butter-golden and a little heavier and earlier maturing than a typical wine from 'The Montrachets' (as the villages would doubtless be called in Britain), which has more lean, pure, nuanced character capable of developing for up to a decade in bottle, while Corton-Charlemagne can be nutty, almost almond-flavoured. But 'typical' burgundy hardly exists. Wines here are made with exasperatingly varied levels of skill, so that one winemaker's Bourgogne Blanc, the most basic appellation, may be better than another's Montrachet, even though it costs a fraction of the price.

The Mâconnais tends to produce a more New World style of Chardonnay: plump, open, user-friendly wines that can taste of melon, or apples warmed by the sun. Most of these wines, particularly Mâcon Blanc and St-Véran, are designed to be drunk within two or three years of the vintage, although the most ambitious producers in the region, notably in Pouilly-Fuissé, are making wines with Côte d'Or pretensions, but usually without Côte d'Or prices. Chardonnay grown between the Mâconnais and the Côte d'Or in the Côte Chalonnaise tends to taste somewhere between the two styles.

These are France's traditional Chardonnay vine strongholds, but the variety's influence has been spreading within France as elsewhere. Wine producers in the Loire valley have embraced this fashionable grape so enthusiastically that the laws explicitly ban more than 20 per cent of the variety in blends for sparkling Saumur and the dry whites of Anjou and Touraine in order to preserve the Loire's own traditional character. Some producers of Muscadet have also been experimenting with oaked Chardonnays. And several of France's more cosmopolitan producers in distinctly non-Chardonnay territory have quietly planted a row or two for their own interest.

Within the appellation system Chardonnay has invaded Limoux with the blessing of the authorities, to add finesse to the local sparkling Crémant de Limoux as well as producing rather fine, lemony barrel-fermented still wine.

Increasing amounts of Chardonnay are also grown on the lower, flatter vineyards of the Languedoc to produce Vin de Pays, usually Vin de Pays d'Oc. As one would expect in an area known as France's New World, the quality of these wines varies according to the position of the vineyard(s) (for many of them are blends) and the quality and style of the winemaking. Price offers a fairly good guide. The cheapest Languedoc Chardonnay is simply a relatively full-bodied dry white wine, while the very best, usually given full oak treatment in the winery, can offer some of the class of Burgundy.

Thanks to an extraordinary boom in plantings, Chardonnay has become synonymous with white wine in California (see page 268) and is responsible for a remarkably homogeneous ocean of off-dry, golden, quite alcoholic, easy-to-drink liquid. While the most commercial examples are usually deliberately slightly sweetened to give them wide appeal, the key to serious quality in a California Chardonnay is climate. Wherever coastal fogs reliably slow down the ripening process, extending the growing season of this early ripening variety, and yields are kept in check, then California can produce some very fine wines indeed, with considerable Burgundian savour to them, but without the Old World surliness in youth. Carneros, Santa Maria, and much of Sonoma, particularly Alexander Valley, have all produced some fine Chardonnay made very much in the mould of a good Meursault.

The variety is also grown almost everywhere in North America where it has even half a chance of thriving, including the cool wine areas of Canada and New York state (where Long Island has proved successful) as well as Washington and Oregon, which may respectively be better suited to Riesling and Pinot Gris.

Australia's strong suit is the reliable quality and varied character of her middle-range Chardonnays (see page 285). They have been hugely successful commercially with their obvious, simple fruitiness, perked up with (usually added) acid and, often, oak chips. Lindemans Bin 65 is now an international brand and quality has been staggeringly high, considering the volumes of it that gush forth from the company's vast plant at Karadoc in Australia's irrigated interior. More concentrated examples of this exuberant, user-friendly style are also produced, typically from warmish regions where yields are more restrained. Cowra in New South Wales, for example, has long been a source of golden Chardonnays that somehow taste as molten and lustrous as they look. Mudgee too has produced some fine Chardonnay from a rare clone of the variety that locals believe was imported in the nineteenth century, decades before Chardonnay mania hit Australia in the early 1980s.

Cooler areas of Australia can produce more subtle Chardonnay, more reminiscent of Côte d'Or wine in structure if not flavour. Tasmania makes the leanest examples, some so lean they are snapped up by Australia's bubbling sparkling wine industry. The Adelaide Hills, Yarra Valley and the southern vineyards of Western Australia have all proved themselves capable of making top quality Chardonnays, whose higher acidity levels can preserve them for several years in bottle (whereas most commercial Australian Chardonnay should be drunk as young as possible and ideally before its second birthday).

Australian producers may envy the high acid levels that their counterparts in New Zealand can hardly avoid, while New Zealanders would probably be happier with more reliable ripeness (see page 296). Despite New Zealand's reputation for Sauvignon Blanc, the country consistently produces more Chardonnay. Winemaking standards have been varied but those prepared to restrain yields and oak influence can produce subtle, sometimes exciting wines. Gisborne Chardonnay has long had its followers but there have been dramatic examples from wineries all over the North and South Islands.

Experimentation with the world's favourite grape variety in South Africa was severely hampered in the 1980s by the fact that the original official planting stock was seriously inferior, but quality is improving rapidly, even if a Cape style is yet to emerge. Blending with other varieties, Sauvignon Blanc and even Riesling, is common.

The vineyards of South America have also been invaded by Chardonnay only relatively recently. The vine has shown a certain amount of promise in Chile, where the produce of cool Casablanca can blend well with riper Maipo fruit. Argentina has, for the moment, only a tiny proportion of its extensive vineyards planted to Chardonnay, but almost exact reproductions of California Chardonnay have been produced under the Catena label and investors from a host of different countries have been establishing cooler, higher vineyards such as those at Tupungato.

In the Old World, Spain has relatively limited plantings of Chardonnay, for the variety tends to ripen too fast in many regions, and its affinity with the prevailing American oak has been less obvious (although Australians and Californians have provided some excellent examples). Portugal has some experimental plantings and may fare better, although its own array of native vine varieties is surely reason enough to resist the international invader.

Italy made some of the earliest varietal Chardonnays and pretty vapid they were too, but it is now possible to find some stunningly ambitious wines made with great care. Chardonnay has long been grown in the north east of the country and can be found, often in simpler, unoaked varietal versions in Friuli, Trentino and Alto Adige, although much of the fruit is siphoned off for the spumante industry.

Since the break-up of the Soviet bloc British wine consumers have been treated to an ocean of eastern European wines labelled Chardonnay, but relatively few have so far demonstrated much varietal character and the first wave of oak-aged examples were often oily and heavy. Keeping yields down to a level at which interesting flavours develop has been a serious problem but doubtless by the turn of the century Bulgaria, Hungary, Moldova, Romania and Slovenia will all be producing Chardonnays of truly international standard (Slovenia is already starting to).

Austria and Switzerland have proved they belong to the international fine winemaking club by producing some very fine, concentrated barrel-fermented Chardonnays. The variety is also responsible for some delicious botrytized sweet wines in Austria's Burgenland, sometimes blended with Welschriesling for additional acidity and aroma.

Other excellent sweet wines made from nobly rotten Chardonnay grapes have come from the Mâconnais in France, Romania, New Zealand and a host of other places, proving yet another of Chardonnay's attributes.

Chasan, increasingly common crossing of CHARDONNAY and LISTAN. Useful Languedoc varietals.

Chasselas, table grape that is especially widely planted in Switzerland, where it is known as Fendant, and is also an important if neutral ingredient in some of the light whites of Savoie. In Alsace it tends to play a subordinate role in cheaper blends and in Germany it is known as Gutedel. In its time it has also been cultivated throughout central Europe and even in New Zealand.

LEFT *Chasselas may not be a noble grape but it is widely grown in Switzerland and in rural France such as here in Quercy.*
RIGHT *In Bonnezeaux, Chenin Blanc grapes begin to submit to the dramatically ennobling process of botrytis mould (or noble rot) which, if the conditions are favourable, will leave the grapes looking like bundles of ash.*
See page 87.

Chenin Blanc, surely the most chameleon-like of vine varieties. Most wine drinkers encounter Chenin Blanc on the labels of very cheap, sometimes slightly sweetened, everyday varietals from California (usually Central Valley) or South Africa where, sometimes known as Steen, it is the most planted vine. In these relatively hot wine-producing environments, Chenin Blanc's ability to hang on to its natural grape acidity is highly prized, and stops these inexpensive, usually rather bland wines tasting flabby.

In its homeland in the middle Loire (see pages 182–4), Chenin Blanc is also marked by its high acid, which is not necessarily a virtue in cooler years, but gives dry and medium dry (Sec and Demi Sec) white wines from here a much longer life than most. Damp straw, flowers, something vaguely honeyed and (sometimes) the acrid sting of sulphur are the usual distinguishing features.

Chenin Blanc comes into its own, however, in exceptional Loire vintages when seriously high sugars develop in the grapes, particularly when they are concentrated by noble rot (see page 88). A Vouvray or Montlouis labelled Moelleux or Liquoreux, Bonnezeaux, Quarts de Chaume and the best Coteaux du Layon and Coteaux de l'Aubance can be an absolute marvel of honey, lime and toast which can continue to improve in bottle for decades.

An increasing number of producers in South Africa, New Zealand and California are taking Chenin Blanc seriously for it can also make attractively assertive, full-bodied dry wines if the site is right and yields are restricted. It is widely distributed and its reliable acid level is valued as an ingredient in sparkling wines such as Blanquette de Limoux and those of South America, notably Argentina.

Chevrier, occasional name for SEMILLON.

Clairette, widely distributed southern French variety producing full, often flabby whites which can oxidize easily. It is a common ingredient in many southern French whites, but generally needs UGNI BLANC and/or TERRET to make a wine with enough freshness to please modern palates. Clairette du Languedoc has its own somewhat historic appellation. Clairette de Die, the curious sparkling wine in the far eastern Rhône Valley, depends heavily on MUSCAT for flavour. Clairette is also widely planted in South Africa, where it is generally used for blending. It is also, confusingly, used as a synonym for other varieties, including Ugni Blanc and BOURBOULENC.

Clare Riesling, South Australian name for CROUCHEN.

Clevner, see KLEVNER.

Códega, Douro name for ROUPEIRO.

Colombard or **Columbar,** widely planted Cognac vine producing neutral, relatively crisp wine, particularly in California where, as vast tracts of French Colombard in the Central Valley, it was for some time the state's single most planted wine grape. It can make fruity, crisp, inexpensive white wine to be drunk straight off the bottling line from California, South Africa, Côtes de Gascogne and the Charentes in France. The vine is on the wane in France's damp south west, however, because it suffers from mildew.

Completer, strangely feral east Swiss speciality.

Cortese, speciality of south east Piedmont in general and Gavi in particular. Crisp and, with luck, fruity.

Criolla Grande is Argentina's most common vine (in both senses) and makes huge quantities of deep-coloured white or light pink wine which is rarely exported except as a very minor constituent in a blend.

Crouchen, vine which was difficult to grow in its native south west France but which has surfaced in Clare, South Australia and South Africa where it is known respectively as Clare Riesling and Cape/Paarl/South African Riesling. Its wine can, like real Riesling, develop well in bottle and, within South Africa itself, it has sometimes been labelled simply Riesling.

Debina, a sprightly grape used to make the lightly sparkling white wines of Zitsa in Epirus, north west Greece.

Dimiat, Bulgaria's most planted native white vine, which makes vaguely perfumed everyday whites.

Dinka, very ordinary but widely planted white grape variety in Hungary and over the border in ex-Yugoslavia.

Doradillo, productive, undistinguished vine still grown in South Australia's Riverland.

Drupeggio, the white-berried form of CANAIOLO that adds interest to Orvieto.

Ehrenfelser, one of Germany's better Riesling-based crossings, found mainly in Pfalz and Rheinhessen. Fussier about site than KERNER.

Elbling, an historic German vine that is still planted in the Mosel valley where it produces extremely tart, lean wine which is sometimes made into Sekt.

Emerald Riesling, bumptious and quite floral California crossing of MUSCADELLE × RIESLING, which is designed for hot climates such as in South Africa.

Encruzado, useful ingredient in Dão.

Erbaluce, north Piedmont speciality which can make sweet golden wines round Caluso.

Ermitage, see HERMITAGE.

Esgana and **Esgana Cão,** mainland Portuguese names for CERCEAL.

Ezerjo, Hungarian rarity associated with a sweet style from Mór.

Faber or **Faberrebe,** early ripening Weissburgunder (PINOT BLANC) × MÜLLER-THURGAU crossing which can reach high ripeness levels while retaining acid, but is better at blending than ageing.

Favorita, pear-flavoured varietal from Piedmont whose wines can age better than ARNEIS.

Fendant, CHASSELAS in the Valais (Switzerland).

Fernão Pires, widely planted Portuguese grape whose wines can smell rank to outsiders but which have good assertive build. Popular in Ribatejo and, as Maria Gomes, in Bairrada. Some is grown in South Africa.

Feteasca, Fetiaska, Feteaska, scented Romanian speciality also found in Hungary as Leányka.

Its wines tend to be full and peachy and rarely bone dry. **Fetească Albă,** with GRASA, spawned the widely planted 1930s crossing **Fetească Regală,** known in Hungary as Királeányka.

Fiano, ancient vine of Campania in Italy. Strong wines. Also grown in Sicily.

Fie, middle Loire speciality which is related to SAUVIGNON BLANC.

Flora, rare but quite elegant GEWÜRZTRAMINER × SEMILLON crossing bred in California.

Folle Blanche, once important brandy grape making tart wine in south west France.

Franken Riesling, SYLVANER.

Freisamer, Freiburger, German SILVANER × PINOT GRIS crossing still grown in Baden and eastern Switzerland, where it makes some full, sweet wines.

French Colombard, see COLOMBARD.

Frontignac, Frontignan, synonyms for MUSCAT BLANC À PETITS GRAINS.

Frühroter Veltliner, Früher Roter Veltliner, early ripening red-skinned, flabbier version of GRÜNER VELTLINER.

Fumé Blanc, developed as a more glamorous name for SAUVIGNON BLANC by Robert Mondavi of California in the 1970s, it is now used all over the world, typically but by no means reliably to denote an oak-aged style of Sauvignon.

Furmint, famous in Hungary's sweet Tokaji (see page 257). Grapes succumb well to noble rot, producing fiery, heady wine with good acid and ageing potential.

Garganega, Veneto vine capable of making fine, lemon and almond-scented wines, notably but not exclusively from low-yielding vines in Soave, also Gambellara, Bianco di Custoza and so on.

Garnacha Blanca, Spanish name for GRENACHE BLANC.

Gewürztraminer, important vine grown all over the world to produce deep-coloured (from its pink skins), full-bodied whites with the characteristic and distinctive smell of lychees, veering towards bacon fat in very ripe examples. For many wine drinkers this (or SAUVIGNON BLANC) is the first varietal they learn to identify. It invariably ripens to a very high alcohol level and can lose acidity dangerously. Malolactic fermentation (see page 72) is therefore almost invariably avoided. Although there is probably a great deal of confusion, especially in newer wine regions, strictly speaking Gewürztraminer is the aromatic or *musqué* version of TRAMINER, and certainly the Italians distinguish between Traminer and Traminer Aromatico.

Alsace is Gewürztraminer's stronghold and here it can produce late harvest wines more reliably than any of the other three noble grape varieties. Winemakers of all nationalities like to play with it, however, and fine examples can be found in Washington, Oregon, northern California, New Zealand and northern Italy. In Iberia it is grown to a limited extent in the High Penedès. If ripened too fast it can be oily or even bitter.

Godello, the tangy grape of Valdeorras, north west Spain.

Goldburger, crossing of Welschriesling and Orangetraube grown in Burgenland (in Austria)

without any great distinction.

Gordo, See MUSCAT OF ALEXANDRIA.

Gouais Blanc, neutral medieval French vine which, with PINOT NOIR, is a parent of such varieties as CHARDONNAY, MELON, GAMAY and all the PINOTS.

Gouveio, Douro name for VERDELHO.

Grasă, Romanian speciality responsible for the once-famous sweet wines of Cotnari.

Graševina, the name the Croatians use for WELSCHRIESLING.

Grauburgunder, German name for PINOT GRIS, when made into a dry and crisp wine, in contrast to full, rich RULÄNDER.

Gray Riesling, California producer of off-dry wine, probably TROUSSEAU Gris.

Grecanico, increasingly planted Sicilian vine. Late-ripening and tangy.

Grechetto makes characterful, full-bodied wines in Umbria (Italy).

Greco, like the above two varieties, presumed

The pink skins of Gewürztraminer grapes (left) result in deeply coloured golden wines. 'Gewürz' is a speciality of Alsace in general and the Schlossberg vineyard above the village of Kaysersberg in particular (right).

originally a Greek vine which makes the sturdy Greco di Tufo in Campania and the extraordinary Greco di Bianco in Calabria.

Green Hungarian, diminishing and undistinguished California variety.

Grenache Blanc, light-berried Grenache which is planted all over southern France, producing full, scented, sometimes flabby wines which can oxidize easily, although careful winemaking can make attractive wines for early drinking.

Grillo, often astringent, earthy Sicilian variety.

Grolleau Gris, minor middle Loire variety used mainly for Vin de Pays du Jardin de la France.

Gros Manseng, the lesser sort of Manseng which usually makes drier forms of Jurançon.

Grüner Veltliner, Austria's grape speciality making crisp, peppery wines with real spark.

Gutedel, German synonym for CHASSELAS.

Gutenborner, MÜLLER-THURGAU × CHASSELAS crossing, more successful in England than Germany.

Hanepoot, South African name for MUSCAT OF ALEXANDRIA, the Cape's most common Muscat.

Hárslevelü, FURMINT's traditional blending partner in Tokaji, named after the lime leaf its wines can smell of.

Hermitage, occasional synonym for MARSANNE.

Humagne, Valais rarity, even richer than AMIGNE and ARVINE.

Huxelrebe, German crossing (also popular in England) which can produce full-bodied sweet wine if the yield is checked.

Inzolia, western Sicilian speciality with promising nuttiness.

Irsai Oliver, relatively recent crossing, a Hungarian table grape which can also produce rather fat, vaguely MUSCAT-like varietal wine.

Italian Riesling/Rizling, synonym for WELSCHRIESLING.

Jacquère, common Savoie vine.

Jaen, a rather ordinary central Spanish grape grown as AVESSO in Portugal. (See red grapes too.)

Johannisberg, Swiss name for SYLVANER.

Johannisberg Riesling, sometimes abbreviated to JR, a synonym for RIESLING in California.

Juhfark, very rare Hungarian vine associated with SOMLÓ.

Kéknyelü, Hungarian 'blue stalked' variety grown in the Badacsony region on Lake Balaton, producing heady, smokey wine.

Kerner, bred as recently as 1969 and one of Germany's most successful crossings, yielding wine of real RIESLING-like substance and ageing potential, yet ripening in a wider range of sites than EHRENFELSER. Can smell of blackcurrants.

Kevedinka, Kövidinka, see DINKA.

Királeányka, Hungarian name for the FETEASCA REGALA of Romania.

Kişmiş, Turkish name for SULTANA.

Klevner, occasional Alsace synonym for PINOT BLANC and local variants.

Lairén, synonym for AIRÉN.

Laski Rizling, Slovenian name for WELSCHRIESLING.

Leányka, Hungarian name for Romania's FETEASCA.

Len de l'El, Len de l'Elh, traditional vine of south west France which makes strongly flavoured but sometimes slightly flabby wine in Gaillac, usually blended with MAUZAC.

Lexia, see MUSCAT OF ALEXANDRIA.

Listan, French name for the PALOMINO of Spain's sherry vineyards.

Loureiro, fine Vinho Verde grape grown increasingly across the border in Spanish Galicia as **Loureira**. It is often found blended with TREIXADURA but sometimes it is sold as a varietal wine.

Macabeo, very common grape in northern Spain and, as **Maccabéo** or **Maccabeu,** in the Languedoc and Roussillon. It is known as Viura in Rioja, where it is very much the dominant variety for white wines. Its vaguely floral character develops at full ripeness but it is often picked earlier to retain acidity. As Macabeo it is an important ingredient in Cava.

Madeleine Angevine, table grape that produces some attractive wine in England.

Malagousia, Malagoussia, vine capable of making elegant, almost too aromatic Greek whites, saved from extinction and now at work at Domaine Carras in the north.

Malvasia, widely and sometimes loosely used name for a range of usually relatively ancient grape varieties, the most famous of which inspires the richest style of madeira (see page 241). The word is derived from the Greek port Monemvasia, through which so many rich, dessert wines passed en route for western and northern Europe in the Middle Ages. **Malvasia di Candia** (of Crete) is one common subvariety. In modern Italy there are at least 10 distinctive forms of Malvasia, planted all over the country. **Malvasia Toscana** is commonly blended with much more TREBBIANO in a wide range of Tuscan and Central Italian whites. **Malvasia Puntinata** is small-berried and superior. White Malvasia tends to be a deeply coloured, quite alcoholic wine which can oxidize easily but has an intensely nutty character, sometimes with notes of orange peel and dried fruits. Malvasia is also grown in Spain and is the richest of the Madeira grapes, its name having been Anglicized to Malmsey, and can be an interesting diversion (from the ubiquitous Chardonnay) in California.

Malvoisie, a name as confusing in France as Malvasia is in Italy. A wide range of often unrelated varieties are called Malvoisie, although most are light berried and make full-bodied, aromatic white wines. Perhaps it is most commonly encountered, in the Loire, Savoie and Switzerland, as a synonym for PINOT GRIS. The Languedoc's BOURBOULENC and MACCABÉO, Roussillon's TORBATO and Corsica's VERMENTINO have all been called Malvoisie in their time, however.

Manseng, see both GROS MANSENG and PETIT MANSENG.

Maria Gomes, see FERNÃO PIRES.

Marsanne, fashionable vine thanks to its origins as most common variety in the white wines of the Northern Rhône. (ROUSSANNE is declining, mainly because it is more difficult to grow.) Its wines tend to full-bodied, veering to heavy with flavours reminiscent of glue and marzipan. Marsanne is a permitted ingredient in many of the Languedoc's whites and is increasingly sold as a varietal Vin de Pays. The Australian state of Victoria has some of the world's oldest Marsanne vineyards, which produce sturdy examples, and California is also catching on.

Mauzac, or **Mauzac Blanc,** is the chief grape of Gaillac Blanc (in which it is blended with LEN DE L'EL) and sparkling Blanquette de Limoux (in which it is softened with CHENIN BLANC and CHARDONNAY). It has a particularly distinctive smell that is reminiscent of dried apple peel. Its late budding and ripening meant that it was traditionally fermented long and slowly, still bubbling in the spring. Hence its association with wines of varying levels of fizz and sweetness.

Melon, Melon de Bourgogne, the Muscadet grape, so successful in this region because it withstands cold well and is quite prolific. So popular is it in the Muscadet region that, unusually, plantings have been increasing. The wine it produces is neither very acid nor strongly flavoured, but rather a neutral base on which to embroider terroir and *sur lie* (lees contact, see page 82) characteristics. Some of California's 'Pinot Blanc' may be Melon.

Merseguera, bland Spanish variety that is grown widely in Alicante, Jumilla and Valencia.

Misket, Bulgarian crossing of DIMIAT with RIESLING, producing vaguely grapey wines.

Molette, relatively neutral Savoie grape improved by blending in ROUSSETTE.

Morillon, rare synonym for CHARDONNAY, still used in Styria.

Morio-Muskat, German SILVANER × WEISSBURGUNDER (PINOT BLANC) crossing which has not a single Muscat gene, yet manages to taste almost obscenely Muscat-like with its heady grapiness. Varietal Morio-Muskat can easily be overpowering, but the variety is widely used by

German bottlers to add a 'Germanic' note to an otherwise neutral blend, notably destined to be sold as Liebfraumilch. To ripen properly, however, it needs a good site, and can rot all too easily, so the variety is giving way to BACCHUS in some areas.

Moscadello, MOSCATO speciality of Montalcino.

Moscatel, Spanish Muscat, usually MUSCAT OF ALEXANDRIA.

Moscato, Italian Muscat, usually MUSCAT BLANC À PETITS GRAINS.

Moscophilero, deep pink-skinned grape variety which can make strongly perfumed white wine on Greece's high plateau of Mantinia in the Peloponnese.

Müller-Thurgau, Dr Hermann Müller's 1882 crossing has allowed the reputation of German wine to plummet. Taken up with enthusiasm by German growers after the Second World War, the vine has the practical advantages (in the cool German climate) of ripening extremely early, before the arrival of autumn rain in most years, and (unlike Riesling and Silvaner) yielding reliably on almost any site. The grape's disadvantage is that the wine, especially if produced from high yields, has little character and can be dangerously short of acid. It is almost invariably the major ingredient in Liebfraumilch and Germany's other cheap QbA blends (see pages 244–5). The crossing was either RIESLING × Riesling or SILVANER with some Riesling genes in there too. Unfortunately, they cannot be tasted. The more recent crossings EHRENFELSER, FABER, KERNER and well-ripened SCHEUREBE can produce much racier wine and there are signs that Müller-Thurgau, Germany's most popular grape variety for much of the 1970s and 1980s, is in decline.

Strangely, the variety seems to have a much higher strike rate outside Germany (although in Austria, where it is widely planted, it rarely achieves anything like as much interest as the native GRÜNER VELTLINER). Some of Washington's Müller-Thurgau, as well as Slovenia and Luxembourg's Rivaner and New Zealand and Switzerland's rather naughtily labelled Riesling-Sylvaner, and even Rizlingszilvani in Hungary,

can demonstrate aroma and crispness, and some of the better producers of Alto Adige and Friuli (most notably Pojer & Sandri) can make really quite exciting, even sought-after, wine from it. The variety also serves as a bolster to the English wine industry.

Muscadelle, with both SEMILLON and SAUVIGNON BLANC, the third grape of Sauternes, and other sweet whites in Bordeaux and Bergerac. The variety is in decline, but there is still a lot of it in Entre-Deux-Mers and it can plump out

ABOVE *Sherry grapes (these are probably Pedro Ximénez) were once routinely dried to concentrate their sugars to provide sweetening material for the nobler wines made from Palomino grapes.*
RIGHT *Muscat Blanc à Petits Grains grapes make a sweet wine in Beaumes-de-Venise because alcohol is added before fermentation is over.*

the two more famous varieties with youthful fruitiness (a bit like PINOT MEUNIER in champagne blends). It can be good in Monbazillac.

It has also been identified as the variety responsible for the rich, dark fortified wines of north eastern Victoria called by Australians Liqueur Tokay.

Muscat, great and ramified family of vine varieties, unusually producing wines that actually smell and taste of grapes. Muscat vines tend to thrive in hot climates and to come in many colours of grape skin, from greenish yellow through pink to dark brown, but almost all of them produce wine that was white at least in its youth (although see the dark-skinned Black Muscat or MUSCAT HAMBURG). They have historically made rich, heady dessert wines, but are increasingly being made into dry(ish) table wines in the style of Muscat d'Alsace.

Muscat Blanc à Petits Grains, the finest, most ancient sort of Muscat vine is small berried and usually light skinned. Its berries are round rather than the oval shape of the other, almost as widely planted MUSCAT, OF ALEXANDRIA, so the variety is sometimes also known as **Muscat à Petits Grains Ronds**.

This is the vine responsible for France's most distinguished vins doux naturels, Muscat de Beaumes-de-Venise, Muscat de St-Jean-de-Minervois, Muscat de Frontignan, Muscat de Lunel, the more obscure Muscat de Mireval, and supplies the best Muscat of Roussillon. Its wines often hint at orange flowers and spice. Other names for this widely planted variety include **Muscat of Frontignan, Frontignac, Muscat Blanc, Muscat d'Alsace, Muskateller, Moscato Bianco, Moscato d'Asti, Moscato di Canelli, Moscatel de Grano Menudo, Moscatel de Frontignan, Muscatel Branco, White Muscat, Muscat Canelli** and **Muskadel** (in South Africa).

It is grown all over central and eastern Europe and is the variety responsible, for example, for the extraordinarily rich Muscats of the Crimean Massandra winery. In Russian it may be known as Tamyanka, in Romanian as Tămâîoasă. This is the Muscat responsible for all of Greece's rich tradition of Muscats and,

as Moscato, for north west Italy's important spumante industry. An unusual dark-berried form known locally as **Brown Muscat** is responsible for Australia's Liqueur Muscats, although Muscat of Alexandria is by far the more common form of Muscat in Australia. Any Muscat with the words Alexandria, Gordo, Romain, Hamburg or Ottonel in its name is *not* this superior variety.

Muscat of Alexandria makes much less distinguished wine than MUSCAT BLANC À PETITS GRAINS (although Portugal's Moscatel of Setúbal and its dry counterpart João Pires can be interesting) but it can reach very high ripeness levels in hot climates and can be usefully productive. It produces more vaguely grapey wine, in which the sweetness often overpowers even its notes of geranium or, sometimes, tomcat. Marmalade rather than orange blossom is a useful shorthand. Californians use their Muscat of Alexandria for raisins, Chileans use theirs for the local spirit pisco, and the substantial harvest of 'Lexia' or 'Gordo' in Australia's irrigated wine regions alternates between the wine and raisin industries according to demand. Carefully vinified, it can provide useful blending material, particularly for medium dry blends. It is known as **Muscat Romain** in Roussillon, where it is the dominant Muscat for Muscat of Rivesaltes, **Hanepoot** in South Africa and **Zibibbo** in southern Italy. Any Spanish wine labelled simply Moscatel is likely to be made from this variety called, variously, **Moscatel de España, Moscatel Gordo (Blanco)**, and **Moscatel de Málaga**. Scholtz Hermanos of Málaga have shown that careful wood ageing can turn this Muscat into an exciting dark nectar.

Muscat Ottonel is a Muscat bred in the nineteenth century for the cooler climates of central Europe but has much less grapey flavours and substance. It makes lightish, usually dry wines and is widely grown in Alsace, but its finest incarnations may be late harvested sweet wines such as the Muscat grown round Austria's Neusiedlersee, Tămâîoasă Ottonel of Romania and the Muskotaly of Hungary. The variety is sometimes known elsewhere as **Hungarian Muscat**.

Muskateller, German synonym for various MUSCATS.

Muskat-Silvaner, telling German synonym for SAUVIGNON BLANC.

Muskotaly, Muskotalyos, MUSCAT OTTONEL grown in Hungary's Tokaj region, sometimes sold as a dry varietal.

Musqué, not the name of a grape variety, but if a grape variety is described as *musqué* it usually denotes a particularly aromatic grapey version of it, as in Chardonnay Musqué.

Neuburger, popular Austrian crossing of PINOT BLANC and SYLVANER making full-bodied whites.

Niagara, American hybrid making foxy wines in New York state.

Nuragus, basic Sardinian.

Olaszrizling, Hungarian name for WELSCHRIESLING.

Ondenc, declining variety in Gaillac, which is also known in Australia.

Optima, German crossing designed to notch up high must weights by ripening very early indeed. For this reason it is popular in England.

Orémus, Hungarian crossing of FURMINT and BOUVIER, occasionally sold as a dry varietal.

Ortega, another blowsy German crossing which can ripen spectacularly and is useful in cool years. Varietal examples exist but can lack acid, except in England.

Palomino, or **Palomino Fino** to distinguish it from the coarser Palomino Basto it has replaced, is the sherry grape, grown around Jerez in southern Spain. It can withstand drought well and produces a reliable crop of slightly low-acid, low-sugar grapes whose wine may oxidize easily – in short, perfect raw material for sherry. Outside sherry country, as in France where it is of declining importance, it is often known as Listan, or Listan de Jerez. It is known as **Perrum** in Portugal's Alentejo. It is grown to a limited extent in California's Central Valley and in Australia and South America, but Palomino is very widely planted in South Africa, where most of the wine is used for distilling or basic blends. It was planted in Galicia once.

Pansa Blanca, north east Spain's XAREL-LO.

Pardillo, Pardina, undistinguished vine widely planted in western Spain.

Parellada, the finest white grape of Catalonia used, with MACABEO and XAREL-LO, for Cava and also treasured as a blending ingredient in many still dry whites of the Penedès region. Fine acidity.

Pederna, ARINTO in Vinho Verde.

Pedro, Pedro Jiménez, Pedro Ximénez, known also as 'PX', is grown in the sherry region to produce dark, sweetening wines, sometimes after drying these thin-skinned grapes (see page 115). Some varietal fortified wines of this nature are produced, presumably to the dismay of dentists everywhere. It is grown all over southern Spain, particularly in the Montilla-Moriles region, where it is more important than PALOMINO. In Australia 'Pedro' has been known to produce delicious, long-lasting botrytized sweet wines in the irrigated vineyards of Griffith, New South Wales. Argentina grows substantial quantities of **Pedro Gimenez,** which may be a distinct variety.

Perle, aromatic German crossing grown in Franken.

Petit Courbu, south west French variety often blended with the MANSENGS and/or ARRUFIAC.

Petit Manseng, smaller berried than GROS MANSENG, is responsible for the shrivelled berries needed to make top quality sweet Jurançon and Pacherenc du Vic-Bilh Moelleux in south west France. Thanks to its thick skins, Petit Manseng is low yielding and perhaps that is why the resulting wine can seem so packed with tangy, verdant flavours. Like TANNAT, the variety was taken to Uruguay by Basques in the nineteenth century. It is acquiring a cult following among the more varietally aware wine producers from Languedoc to California.

Picolit, sweet white Friuli varietal revered by Italians and extremely expensive. At its best (not stretched with the blander VERDUZZO) Picolit smells of apricots.

The perilously steep vineyards of Urziger Würzgarten in the Mosel valley. Only Riesling is worth the difficulty and danger of working such steep slopes, warmed by sunlight re-radiated by the local slate.

Picpoul, Piquepoul, a many-hued traditional Languedoc variety that makes high-acid, full-bodied, lemony wines of which the best known is the Coteaux du Languedoc Picpoul de Pinet made around the village of Pinet.

Pigato, ancient Ligurian with heady aromas.

Pineau de la Loire, a synonym for CHENIN BLANC.

Pinot Beurot, Burgundian name for PINOT GRIS.

Pinot Blanc, a white-berried mutation of PINOT GRIS and therefore related to PINOT NOIR. It is widely planted in Alsace, northern Italy (as **Pinot Bianco**), and in Germany and Austria (as Weissburgunder). In Alsace it provides a basic, broad-flavoured, full-bodied dry white – often good value for money. It may be blended with AUX-ERROIS and is sometimes called Clevner or Klevner. In Italy it was worshipped as CHARDONNAY for years and continues to be made in that vaguely round-but-crisp style, as well as being used extensively for making sparkling wine. The Germans, who have few Chardonnay vines planted, tend increasingly to make dry white Weissburgunder using all the Chardonnay tricks of barrel fermentation and the like, sometimes with great success. In Austria's Burgenland, however, Weissburgunder can produce quite superb botrytized sweet wines, up to TBA levels (see page 245). The variety is also grown widely, sometimes called **Beli Pinot**, throughout central Europe and is also increasingly treasured as an alternative to Chardonnay in California. In general Pinot Blanc offers the body of Chardonnay with more smoke and less fruit and nut characters.

Typically blue-tinged Riesling grapes in Germany's Rheingau region.

Pinot Chardonnay, rare synonym for Chardonnay which acknowledges its membership of the Pinot family.

Pinot Gris, increasingly popular member of the Pinot family, a pink-skinned version of PINOT NOIR which can make deep-coloured, full-bodied, soft, gently aromatic white wines with lots of extract (see page 72), although Italians, who grow far more of it, as **Pinot Grigio**, than Pinot Bianco, have a habit of picking it before it can develop these characteristics. In Alsace it is, unlike PINOT BLANC, revered as a noble grape and can produce some commandingly rich wines from almost bone dry through Vendange Tardive to SGN levels of ripeness (see page 179). The drier of these wines are some of the finest whites to drink with rich savoury food. In the Loire and Switzerland it is known as Malvoisie and its innate smokey flavours survive.

The variety is more common in Germany than Alsace, however, where it is usually called Ruländer if it is sweet and Grau-burgunder if dry. In Germany, it is mainly grown in Baden and, to a lesser extent, Pfalz. In Hungary it is known as Szürkebarát and it is grown widely throughout central Europe. Admired in Luxembourg, the variety has shown real form in Oregon and is currently increasingly popular in California.

Plavai, late ripening Moldovan vine planted all over central Europe.

Prinç, Moravian name for TRAMINER.

Prosecco, Friuli's sparkling varietal with varying

degrees of residual sugar, although some dry, still examples are known. The wine is made fizzy by the tank method (see pages 85–6).

PX, see PEDRO XIMÉNEZ.

Ranina, see BOUVIER.

Räuschling, ancient German variety still grown in eastern Switzerland.

Regner, Oechsle-boosting German crossing.

Reichensteiner, German crossing which usefully resists rot and ripens well. It is popular in England.

Rheinriesling, Rhine Riesling, both synonyms for RIESLING.

Ribolla, light, floral, very crisp varietal made in Friuli and, as **Rebula,** across the border in Slovenia. It is almost certainly the ROBOLA of Greece.

Rieslaner, German SILVANER X RIESLING crossing which can make lovely wines with race and curranty fruit in Franken and occasionally in Pfalz.

Riesling ('Reece-ling') must be the world's most misunderstood, and mispronounced, grape variety. Acknowledged king of German vineyards, this variety happens to share a name with so many much more ordinary grapes and wines (more commercial examples of Cape Riesling, CLARE RIESLING, EMERALD RIESLING, GRAY RIESLING, RIESLING ITALICO, LASKI RIZLING, OLASZRIZLING and WELSCHRIESLING, for example) that its image has become tarnished. And, it must be said, the Germans themselves make some pretty awful Rieslings at the bottom end of the market that have done nothing for the reputation of their greatest asset.

Wine made from Riesling is quite unlike any other. It is light in alcohol, refreshingly high in fruity acidity (quite different from the harshness of added acid – see acidification on page 72), has the ability to transmit the character of a place through its extract (see page 72) and unique aroma and, unlike CHARDONNAY, is capable of ageing for decades in bottle. Very unlike Chardonnay, but similar to top quality CHENIN BLANC, it performs best if fermented cool and bottled early without any malolactic fermentation or wood influence. Riesling is a star and, as you may discern, one of my great wine heroes.

Relative to most other internationally known varieties, Riesling ripens quite early, so when planted in a hot climate its juice can be overripe and flabby long before any interesting flavours have developed in the grapes. In a very cool climate such as that of the Mosel valley in northern Germany, on the other hand, it is regarded as a late ripening relative to the host of precocious varieties that have been specially bred for these short summers. This means that, whereas MÜLLER-THURGAU will ripen just about anywhere, Riesling stands a chance of ripening fully only on the most favoured sites, those tilted most firmly towards direct and reflected sunlight, which is where it is planted so that it stays on the vine well into autumn, developing all sorts of subtle and ageworthy characteristics. Riesling from the Mosel and its even cooler tributaries the Saar and Ruwer is one of the wine world's most distinctive, least imitable wine styles: light, crisp, racy, refreshing as a mountain stream and somehow tasting of the slate which, by reradiating warmth overnight, helps ripen so many Riesling vines. This is the wine to drink while writing or reading; it refreshes the palate and sharpens the brain (or at least that's what it feels like).

A third of all Germany's Riesling grows in the Mosel, but the Pfalz region also grows a substantial quantity, making much richer but no less entrancing wine which can often taste exotically fruity (and can reach as much as 13 per cent alcohol if fermented out to dryness). Riesling is also *the* classic grape of the Rheingau, where it perhaps best reflects – in a steely, lemony, sometimes mineral-scented way – the differences between even neighbouring vineyards. The best estates belong to the VDP group, dedicated to making great dry Rheingau Riesling – although in warm years the Rheingau can also be the source of many excellent BA and TBA sweet wines (page 245). Riesling is an extremely fine candidate for botrytized sweet wines, although this noble rot tends to blur geographical differences and result in thick, almost raisiny, deep golden wines. Württemberg is also an important grower of earthy Riesling which rarely escapes the region. Crackling Rieslings are also made in the Nahe.

Riesling is also the noblest variety of the most Germanic region of France – Alsace – where the best of its tingly-dry, steely wines such as Trimbach's Clos Ste-Hune can age for a decade or two in bottle. There is a slight talcum powder aroma about the least concentrated examples of Alsace Riesling but these are great wines to drink as aperitifs (as indeed is all but the sweetest Riesling made anywhere). The Wachau in Austria rivals Alsace and the Mosel for the purity of its Rieslings, sometimes called **Rheinriesling** or **Weisser Riesling** here, except that these wonderfully characterful, bone dry, sculpted wines tend to have a bit more body. Much of central Europe, particularly Slovenia and Slovakia, has suitable spots for ripening Riesling, whose local name usually incorporates some variant on the the word Rhine (in Croatia it is known as **Rizling Rajinski**, for example). True Riesling (as opposed to Italian Riesling) is widely dispersed in Friuli, where it is called **Riesling Renano**, although few startling examples have so far emerged from the region. Riesling is also allegedly grown widely in the old Soviet Union, but much of this may in fact be Welschriesling.

Surprisingly, in view of its relatively warm climate, Australia grows an enormous amount of **Rhine Riesling**, which is often called colloquially simply 'Rhine'. Its perfect spots are in the cooler reaches of South Australia, notably but not exclusively Clare Valley and Eden Valley (see pages 288–91 for more details). New Zealand's Rieslings are developing and some fine sweet wines are made there, just as California had a long tradition of making rich, fairly fast-maturing late harvest **Johannisberg Riesling** or **White Riesling**. Washington and New York states can also produce some extremely delicate Rieslings, while Canada regularly produces stunning Ice wines from this variety.

Riesling Italico is how the Italians often style WELSCHRIESLING, much to the Germans' fury, whereas Germany's Riesling is called **Riesling Renano**.

Riesling-Sylvaner, a rather misleading name for MÜLLER-THURGAU used in New Zealand.

Rivaner, the Luxembourg name for MÜLLER-THURGAU.

Rizling, a term used at the insistence of Germans for WELSCHRIESLING, so that it can be distinguished from the RIESLING that is Germany's pride and joy.

Rkatsiteli, Russia's answer to Spain's AIRÉN – although the wine can have more character. It is also grown in Bulgaria, Romania and China (where it is known as Baiyu). It keeps its acidity well and is very good at withstanding cold. It has been grown in California.

Robola, a haunting, citrus-scented white grape variety grown on the Greek island of Cephanolia. Almost certainly Italy's RIBOLLA.

Roditis, fragile, light pink-berried Greek variety often used to add acid to the softer SAVATIANO, particularly for retsina.

Rolle, ancient Provençal variety known especially in Bellet but also planted in Roussillon. The French say it is the same as Sardinia's VERMENTINO. Some Italians say it is Liguria's **Rollo**, which is *not* Vermentino.

Romorantin, speciality of Cheverny.

Rotgipfler, with ZIERFANDLER, a variety that is responsible for Austria's full, spicy Gumpoldskirchner.

Roupeiro, basic variety of the Portuguese Alentejo. Also known as Códega in the Douro and sometimes as Alva in Alentejo.

Roussanne, red-berried North Rhône variety which yields irregularly and is therefore less popular with growers than MARSANNE. Its wine can be very fine, however, as witness varietals such as Château Beaucastel's oak-aged version (it, but not Marsanne, is allowed into white Châteauneuf-du-Pape). It can age better than Marsanne and smells of mountain herbs. In fact it shines in Savoie as Bergeron (in Chignin) and is also grown in Italy. Improved clones are available and it is increasingly planted in southern France and California.

Roussette, a fine Savoie speciality that produces lively, crisp but scented wines. Roussette de Savoie has its own appellation in four communes, most notably Frangy. If followed by the name of a commune on the label the wine will be made exclusively of Roussette; if not, Chardonnay may constitute up to 50 per cent of the wine.

Ruffiac, alternative name for ARRUFIAC.

Ruländer, main German name for PINOT GRIS, usually signalling a sweeter style. Also used in Romania.

Sacy, rather ordinary white grape grown in the greater Chablis area.

St-Émilion, Cognac name for UGNI BLANC.

Sämling 88, Austrian synonym for SCHEUREBE.

Sárfehér, vine traditionally grown on Hungary's Great Plain for sparkling wines and table grapes.

Sauvignon Blanc grapes at Domaine de Chevalier (above) are responsible for one of the longest-living Sauvignon-based wines of all. Just down the road, Sémillon grapes from old, thick-trunked vines make up the body weight of great Sauternes at Château Rayne-Vigneau (right).

Sauvignon Blanc, often called simply **Sauvignon** (whereas CABERNET SAUVIGNON is often called just Cabernet), extremely popular variety making crisp, dry, aromatic and extremely distinctive wines all over the world. The smell is sharp and piercing (unlike that of CHARDONNAY) and reminds different tasters variously of gooseberries, nettles, crushed blackcurrant leaves, and occasionally tomcats. With age, other aromas reminiscent of canned asparagus can develop. The smell of Sauvignon (which is most of its character) is relatively simple, so it is not surprising that it was one of the first to be explained in terms of its dominant flavour compounds, called methoxypyrazines (a name to drop at a professional wine tasting). Sauvignon also smells and tastes remarkably similar wherever it is planted so, like GEWÜRZTRAMINER, is a very good starting-point for learning to recognize different varieties.

Sauvignon Blanc's French stronghold is the upper Loire, and the twin appellations of Sancerre and Pouilly-Fumé in particular. Superior examples of these wines are drier, denser and longer-living than most New World Sauvignon Blanc, and the best genuinely express terroir with nuances dependent on the proportion of gravel and flint (*silex*) in the soil. Sauvignon is also grown widely downstream, notably to produce oceans of Sauvignon de Touraine which can, from the best producers, be good value – as can the Sancerre-like wines of less famous Menetou-Salon, Reuilly and Quincy.

Sauvignon is even more widely planted in Bordeaux and Bergerac, although it is much less important than the fatter SEMILLON with which it is commonly blended, as elsewhere in the world nowadays, to produce both dry (particularly in Pessac-Léognan, Graves and Entre-Deux-Mers) and (in Sauternes, Monbazillac and surrounds) sweet wines. Sauvignon traditionally supplies the aroma and acidity in the whites of greater Bordeaux, and the more expensive dry wines are often aged in small oak barrels. Sauvignon and oak can be an oily mixture unless managed with a deft hand.

Elsewhere in Europe, Sauvignon is a speciality of Rueda in Spain, Styria in Austria and Collio in north east Italy. Some German speakers refer to it as Muskat-Silvaner (which mixture of characters quite accurately describes how it actually tastes).

New Zealand has been so successful with its herbaceous style of Sauvignon Blanc, heady with the tropical fruit smells of a cool, prolonged fermentation, that winemakers throughout the New World, and especially in Chile, South Africa and the Languedoc, are now emulating it. In some vintages fruit is deliberately picked underripe, ripe and overripe to bring different characteristics to the final blend. Marlborough at the north end of the South Island is New Zealand's, possibly now the world's, Sauvignon capital, while the Casablanca Valley may have the potential to do the same job for Chile (being the only Chilean region to be planted substantially with Sauvignon Blanc rather than the less distinctive SAUVIGNON VERT). South Africa makes some delicious Sauvignon Blanc, perhaps partly because the vine has had so long to accustom itself to local conditions. Much of Australia, however, is too warm for the preservation of Sauvignon Blanc's characteristically 'green' (i.e. slightly underripe) aroma, but some fine examples have emerged from the Adelaide Hills.

California produces a distinct, full-bodied, often oak-aged version of Sauvignon Blanc, sometimes called Fumé Blanc and the variety has also sparkled in Texas and Washington. Some Sauvignon Blanc can last for several years in bottle but very little actually improves with age, for vibrant, young fruitiness and refreshment value, rather than subtlety, are Sauvignon's strong suit.

Sauvignon Gris, a darker-berried mutation of SAUVIGNON BLANC, producing a strong, smokey perfume.

Sauvignon Vert, variety distinct from SAUVIGNON BLANC also known as **Sauvignonasse,** or TOCAI FRIULANO.

Savagnin, characteristic, small-berried vine of the Jura that is responsible most notably for the sherry-like *vin jaune* (although it can theoretically make up some of the blend of any white Jura wine). Its apogee is Château-Chalon, and Savagnin wine is renowned for its aroma and ability to age. France's most eminent ampelographer (vine specialist) Pierre Galet maintains that TRAMINER is Savagnin Rosé.

Savatiano, widely planted Greek vine used to add bulk to retsina, though ASSYRTIKO and RHODITIS are often added for crispness.

Scheurebe, one of Germany's most successful crossings, a SILVANER X RIESLING that was the work of Dr Georg Scheu. If the site and weather are such that the grapes ripen fully the wine can taste most appetizingly of blackcurrants or even rich grapefruit. Some Pfalz producers are prouder of their 'Scheu' than their RIESLING. Acidity levels are very good, although the wines are unlikely to age as well as Riesling. Yields are not as high as most new crossings but the right site can yield BA and TBA wines (see pages 244–5) as often as nature obliges, and Spätlese trocken examples can also be very fine. Burgenland in Austria also produces some successful late picked examples from the variety, known here as Sämling 88.

Schönburger, pink-berried German crossing involving both PINOT NOIR and MUSCAT HAMBURG, but producing mellow white wine, notably in England but also in Germany.

Schwarzriesling, or 'black Riesling', German synonym for PINOT MEUNIER.

Semillon, in France **Sémillon,** is the great white grape of sweet white bordeaux, and also widely undervalued. As well as making many of the world's greatest sweet wines, it is responsible for Bordeaux's greatest dry whites and Australia's most distinctive white wine, Hunter Valley Semillon. Semillon is Bordeaux's most planted white grape variety, although the area devoted to its traditional blending partner there, SAUVIGNON BLANC, has been increasing. Semillon is the grape primarily responsible for Sauternes, the world's longest-living white wine, and it is sanctioned in most of the dry or sweet white wine appellations of south west France. It blends well with Sauvignon (traditionally four to one in Sauternes) because it lacks positive aroma (apart from the vague citrus, lanolin and beeswax of a young wine and the burnt toast of a mature Hunter) but makes up for Sauvignon's lack of body. If Semillon is picked before it

reaches full ripeness it can almost taste like Sauvignon. Semillon's thin skins make it prone to rot, which makes it an ideal producer of botrytized sweet wines, not just in Bordeaux and Monbazillac, but also in New South Wales and California. The wine can respond well to wood ageing, as in the great dry whites of Graves and Pessac-Léognan in Bordeaux.

Semillon is planted in virtually all of the world's wine regions but for the moment little is made of it. Australia perhaps has taken the most positive line on constructing varietals out of it, but it has also been used to stretch the available quantities of the fashionable Chardonnay while new plantings came on stream, initiating a category known as SemChard. Odd varietal versions have shone in Hungary and New Zealand, and Washington state clearly has potential. Semillon is also widely planted in Chile, although little evidence has yet been exported under that name.

Sercial, an Anglicized name for the CERCEAL of Madeira.

Seyval Blanc, French hybrid which withstands cold well and is grown in Canada, New York and England (where it is the most popular vine). It can be very crisp and fruity.

Siegerrebe, a relatively low-yielding German crossing famous for its high ripeness levels but not for the quality of its wine.

Silvaner, German spelling of the variety known as Sylvaner in Alsace and Austria. It is sometimes known as **Grüner Silvaner** in Germany. Probably of central European origin, Silvaner was Germany's most planted grape variety in the first half of the twentieth century. (It took over that position from ELBLING, then passed on the crown to the thoroughly undeserving MÜLLER-THURGAU.) The vine ripens earlier than Riesling but later than Müller-Thurgau and therefore needs rather better sites. The wines it produces are high in acidity and not particularly marked by flavour or longevity, but in the right spot, such as particular sites in Franken, it is capable of producing extremely racy, excitingly sleek wines.

Silvaner is cultivated over much of central Europe, where its local name generally incorpo-

rates the letters 'silvan' and in Switzerland it can shine, known as Johannisberg or Rhin, and tasting much fatter than the ubiquitous CHASSELAS. See also SYLVANER.

Smederevka, a common vine named after the town of Smederevo south of Belgrade and planted extensively in Serbia and Vojvodina in what was Yugoslavia. It produces good acidity and is often blended. Also found in southern Hungary.

Steen, South African name for CHENIN BLANC.

Sultana, variety commonly used for dried fruit but, when the market is buoyant in Australia

Vernaccia grapes in Tuscany (above) are almost exclusively used for full-bodied, characterful dry wines, whereas the Trebbiano and Malvasia grapes (opposite) are being dried to yield ultra-sweet Vin Santo, Tuscany's speciality, at the Selvapiana estate.

and California, some of its yield is often diverted into everyday white blends and the result is characterless wine produced from high-yielding vines.

Sylvaner, the Alsace and Austrian name for SILVANER. In Alsace Sylvaner can show the race and response to site that Riesling can, but it takes a very good vineyard and winemaker to extract much flavour from it. Most of Alsace's Sylvaner (and there is a great deal of it) is planted on the lower, less interesting vineyards of the Bas-Rhin and much of it is blended with slightly gentler wine to be sold as Edelzwicker.

126

Szürkebarát, Hungarian name for PINOT GRIS.

Talia, Thalia, Portuguese names for TREBBIANO/UGNI BLANC.

Tămaîioasă, a Romanian name used for various MUSCATS.

Tamyanka, a Russian name for MUSCAT BLANC À PETITS GRAINS.

Terret Gris, an ancient Languedoc variety that is widely planted and can make a full-bodied yet crisp varietal. **Terret Blanc** is less common and less distinguished. They are both allowed in to the white wines of Minervois, Corbières and, to a decreasing extent, Coteaux du Languedoc.

Thompson Seedless, SULTANA in California.

Tocai, Tocai Friulano, the most planted light grape in Friuli, which can make lively, crisp, aromatic wines to be drunk young. Most authorities agree that it is identical to Sauvignonasse or SAUVIGNON VERT (the Sauvignon that dominates Chile's vineyards). Some Italians argue it is related to the FURMINT of Tokaj. Some vines are grown in Argentina, where they are called Tocai Friulano.

Tokay d'Alsace, synonym for PINOT GRIS which the Hungarians are trying to outlaw.

Torbato, a smokey-flavoured Sardinian variety that is also known, in Roussillon, as **Tourbat** (and occasionally Malvoisie du Roussillon).

Torrontés is a Galician variety that is a speciality of Ribeiro, but is much more commonly grown in Argentina, where it produces full-bodied, crisp wines with a distinctive and confident aroma not unlike Muscat. It seems likely but is unproven that the vine was brought to Argentina by Galician immigrants. **Torrontés Riojano** is the most common Argentine subvariety, named after the northern province of La Rioja where, in Salta in particular, it is by far the most planted single vine variety. **Torrontés Sanjuanino** and the rarer, less aromatic **Torrontés Mendocino** are also grown. Chile has its own, similar **Torontel.**

Trajadura, Portuguese name for the aromatic Galician variety **Treixadura.**

Traminer, less aromatic progenitor of GEWÜRZTRAMINER, which is a *musqué* version of a pink-berried Traminer. It is named after the town of Tramin, or Terlano, in the Alto Adige, where a distinction is still made between Traminer and **Traminer Aromatico** (or *musqué*). Vines called variants of Traminer are planted throughout central Europe: **Tramini** in Hungary; **Traminac** in Slovenia; **Drumin, Pinat Cervena, Prinç** or **Liwora** in what was Czechoslovakia; occasionally just **Rusa** in Romania; and **Mala Dinka** in Bulgaria. It is also grown in Russia, Moldova and Ukraine, where it is sometimes used to perfume Soviet sparkling wine. Some of these vines may be the more aromatic Gewürztraminer but less than perfect winemaking has tended to obscure the aroma. Australians tend to use the term Traminer as shorthand for the rather more cumbersome Gewürztraminer.

Trebbiano, France's UGNI BLANC in its homeland, planted almost everywhere within Italy except for the far north, where it would not ripen reliably. Despite the fact that its wine is remarkably thin, tart and characterless, it is responsible for about a third of all DOC white wine production. Its many different local strains include **Trebbiano Toscano** (the most common, a possible ingredient in Chianti and chief inspiration for Galestro, the basic crisp mouthwash of the Tuscan hills), **Trebbiano Romagnolo** (making mainly vapid Trebbiano di Romagna), **Trebbiano d'Abruzzo** (of which the apparent master is Valentini, despite the fact that he uses BOMBINO BIANCO), yellow-berried **Trebbiano Giallo** and **Trebbiano di Soave.**

The variety is also planted, as Talia, in Portugal, and (where it is often called Ugni Blanc) in Bulgaria, Russia, Greece and extensively in South America. In California, too, occasional bottlings of wine made from old Trebbiano vines have shown extraordinary character and extract.

Tresallier, a rather undistinguished speciality of the Allier *département*, where St-Pourçain is produced.

Ugni Blanc, France's most planted white grape variety, widely grown as Ugni Blanc in South

America and, as TREBBIANO, ubiquitous in Italy too. As ST-ÉMILION it is the chief ingredient in Cognac and plays an important role in Armagnac too. The wine it produces is thin, light and tart. Hardly what the market wants nowadays. It is surprisingly common north of Bordeaux.

Veltliner, common name for Austria's GRÜNER VELTLINER.

Verdejo, characterfully nutty speciality of Rueda in Spain, often blended with SAUVIGNON BLANC.

Verdelho, Portuguese grape which inspires Madeira's second driest style but is most commonly found as a vibrant, lemony, full-bodied table wine from Western Australia. Grapes are small, hard and acid. This is probably the Douro's GOUVEIO and possibly Italy's **Verdello**.

Verdicchio, the grape of Italy's Marche, made famous by Verdicchio dei Castelli di Jesi in an amphora-shaped bottle – although Verdicchio di Matelica can be a more concentrated wine. Many are simply crisp and vaguely citric.

Verduzzo, north east Italian speciality which can make very appetizing honeyed sweet wines, some of which qualify for the Ramandolo DOC (see page 207). Dry wines can be astringently reminiscent of dried apple skins.

Vermentino, aromatic speciality of Sardinia and, to a lesser extent, Liguria, probably the same as ROLLE. It can make some of Sardinia's liveliest whites, with a slight prickle of gas.

Vernaccia, Tuscany's most characterful white wine grape, making deeply coloured, often nutty wines, particularly around the hilltop village of San Gimignano.

Vespaiola, Veneto vine which can make tangy, golden sweet wines. Named after the wasps attracted to its sugar-rich grapes.

Vidal, French hybrid which can make delicious Ice wine in Canada.

Vilana, relatively delicate speciality of Crete.

Villard Blanc, prolific French hybrid widely planted in France in the mid-twentieth century.

Viognier, extremely fashionable variety whose home is Condrieu in the Northern Rhône but which is now being energetically planted all over southern France, in California, in Australia and wherever a cosmopolitan wine producer lurks. The vine can yield poorly in cooler climates. Its full-bodied wines have a very distinctive scent of dried apricots and, almost, musk. The wine is usually best drunk young. Because of the strength of its aroma, it can withstand blending well. Best picked late.

Viura, Riojan name for MACABEO.

Weissburgunder, Weisserburgunder, Weisser Burgunder, German names for PINOT BLANC.

Weisser Riesling, alternative name for RIESLING.

Welschriesling, Wälschriesling, Welschrizling, just some of the many aliases under which The Other Riesling travels. This has nothing to do with the great German RIESLING, and its image was sullied for many years by poorly handled, sweetened-up liquids bearing names like Laski, Olasz and Pecs, but this central European vine can produce some good to very good wine – particularly in Austria's Burgenland, where it regularly makes superb sweet botrytized wines. It is planted widely in Friuli (Italy), Slovenia, Hungary, Romania, Albania and China. The vine ripens late to produce high-acid, gently aromatic wines.

White Riesling, occasional name for RIESLING, especially in California, where there have been Emerald, Gray and Hungarian Rieslings.

Xarel-lo, Catalonia's most characterful grape, producing wines which can smell of boiled cabbage to the uninitiated. Used widely in Cava. Known as Pansa Blanca in Alella.

Xynisteri, speciality of Cyprus.

Zalema, vine responsible for the heavier wines of Condado de Huelva in southern Spain.

Zibibbo, MUSCAT OF ALEXANDRIA in Sicily.

Zierfandler, nobler, fuller ingredient, with ROTGIPFLER, in Austria's Gumpoldskirchen. As **Cirfandli**, it is also grown in Hungary.

Zilavka, characterfully nutty variety grown mainly in Hercegovina, notably around Mostar in what was Yugoslavia.

RED WINE VARIETIES

Abouriou, minor variety in south west France.

Agiorgitiko, Nemea's St George, which can make substantial, very fruity Greek reds and some good rosé.

Aglianico, increasingly admired deep, dark, densely graphite-scented grape, most famously inspiring Taurasi of Campania and Aglianico del Vulture in Basilicata. Ripens very late.

Aleatico, Italian vine, making strangely grapey sweet reds. Also planted in New South Wales.

Alfrocheiro Preto, deep-coloured Portuguese grape useful in blends.

Alicante Bouschet, often just called **Alicante** (which is also a local Languedoc name for GRENACHE), red-fleshed grape once widely used to tint southern French table wine, especially Aramon. Now found in Corsica, Tuscany, Calabria in southern Italy, Yugoslavia, Israel, North Africa, California, Portugal and Spain, where it is known as Garnacha Tintorera. Vine-breeder Henri Bouschet crossed one of his father's crossings with Grenache, or Garnacha, to produce this early ripening variety in the late nineteenth century. Makes gutsy but short wine.

Aragonês, Portuguese name for TEMPRANILLO.

Aramon, extraordinarily high-yielding, low-quality variety that dominated the plains of the Languedoc in the late nineteenth and early twentieth centuries. Replaced by CARIGNAN in the 1960s.

Aspiran, historic Languedoc vine whose light, perfumed red wine may still be blended into Minervois.

Auxerrois, Cahors name for MALBEC.

Baco Noir, Baco 1, French hybrid planted in north eastern America to produce light reds untainted by foxy flavours.

Baga, Bairrada's speciality, thick-skinned, small grapes producing some very tannic, acid wines in northern Portugal.

Barbarossa, a lively grape of Emilia-Romagna, known as **Barberoux** in Provence.

Barbera, the most common grape in north west Italy, where for long it was responsible for light-ish, bitter cherry-flavoured wines with marked acidity. Produced at low yields and treated to barrel ageing it now makes extremely exciting wines with more than a hint of NEBBIOLO's serious scent. About 15 times as much Barbera is grown in Piedmont as Nebbiolo. It is also widely grown in Lombardy, often blended with BONARDA, as well as in California and Argentina.

Bastardo, undistinguished grape used in the Douro valley, port country.

Black Muscat, MUSCAT HAMBURG.

Blau, Blauer, German for blue and a common prefix of red wine grape varieties.

Blauburger, Austrian crossing of PORTUGIESER and BLAUFRÄNKISCH, making ordinary light reds.

Blauburgunder, Swiss German name for PINOT NOIR.

Blauer Spätburgunder, an Austrian name for PINOT NOIR.

Blaufränkisch, central European vine, producing lively, fruity, sometimes peppery reds with sufficient substance in the best Burgenland examples (see page 253) to be worth oak ageing, or blending with CABERNET and/or PINOT NOIR. It is called Limberger in Germany, Lemberger in Washington state, Franconia in Friuli, Gamé in Bulgaria (it was once confused with Gamay), Kékfrankos in Hungary and Frankovka in Slovakia and Vojvodina.

In the Langhe hills of Piedmont, Nebbiolo will ripen only on south-facing hillsides whereas Barbera is much less fussy about vineyard site. In autumn, the result is a patchwork of varieties at different stages of maturity.

Bobal, Spanish vine, making huge quantities of deeply coloured wine (and grape concentrate) on the Mediterranean coast. It makes slightly crisper, lighter wine than MONASTRELL, with which it is often grown. Probably Sardinia's Bovale.

Bonarda, an Italian variety or, more accurately, three different varieties by the same name. Most common is the Lombardy version, attractively juicy and the same as CROATINA. Argentina's most planted vine.

Bordo, the name for CABERNET FRANC in north east Italy.

Bouchet, name for CABERNET FRANC in St-Émilion and in Bordeaux's other right bank districts. It is known as **Bouchy** in Madiran.

Brachetto, north western Italian, making light, fizzy, strawberry-flavoured reds. Also known as **Braquet** in Provence, notably in Bellet.

Breton, the middle Loire name for CABERNET FRANC.

Brocol, Braucol, FER in Gaillac.

Brunello, SANGIOVESE clone developed in the Montalcino region of Tuscany.

Cabernet usually means CABERNET SAUVIGNON, although in north east Italy it can often mean CABERNET FRANC, since there is so much more of it.

Cabernet Franc, important variety famous for playing second fiddle to CABERNET SAUVIGNON, even though it has shown it can make some extremely fine wines (notably in St-Émilion and the middle Loire) in its own right. The vine looks very like Cabernet Sauvignon except that the leaves are much less indented, so it is probably an early mutation that is particularly well adapted to the Gironde right bank's cooler, damper climate where Cabernet Sauvignon can be difficult to ripen. Cabernet Franc buds and ripens earlier, which makes it more susceptible to coulure (see page 69) but it needs less heat to ripen fully. In left bank Bordeaux, on the other hand, it is seen, with Merlot, as a sort of insurance policy against a cool season. In very general terms, wine made from Cabernet Franc tends to be aromatically fruity, lighter and less tannic than Cabernet Sauvignon and, especially in the Loire, can smell appetizingly of pencil shavings. It is often rather herbaceous and can smell like unripe Cabernet Sauvignon. Cabernet Franc is an ingredient in most of the reds of south west France, and often the sole inspiration for the fine, silky reds of the Middle Loire such as Saumur-Champigny, Bourgueil, Chinon, and Anjou-Villages.

Cabernet Franc, sometimes called **Cabernet Frank,** is widely grown in north east Italy and some of its Friuli examples are ripe enough to be thrilling. The vine is also grown over the border in Slovenia, although Cabernet Sauvignon is far more common in the rest of central Europe. See also MENCÍA.

In the New World, in most of which Cabernet Sauvignon can easily be ripened, Cabernet Franc has been widely regarded as essential for respectability to make up the holy Bordeaux trio, along with Merlot (with which it has sometimes been confused in vine nurseries). Some varietal Cabernet Francs have emerged from Australia, South Africa and North America and shown just how appetizing this variety can be unblended – and how much more conveniently earlier maturing it is than Cabernet Sauvignon. Cabernet Franc may really shine in cooler regions, however, such as Long Island in New York state, parts of Washington state and New Zealand.

Cabernet Sauvignon, the world's most famous red wine grape signalled on labels all over the world. As the 'chocolate' to Chardonnay's 'vanilla', Cabernet is much more positively flavoured than Chardonnay, and ripens much later, so tends to be planted in rather warmer areas. The great distinction of the wine it produces is that it has a very powerful and recognizable aroma of blackcurrants wherever it is grown and, if matured in newish oak, can smell of cedar, cigar boxes and, sometimes, tobacco. Cabernet Sauvignon is also notable for being deep purple in youth and, although it is not especially alcoholic, it can be extremely long lived. This is because Cabernet Sauvignon's small, thick-skinned grapes have a very high ratio of solids rich in colouring matter and tannins to juice – although if the grapes are anything less than fully ripe the wine can smell of crushed green leaves, 'herbaceous', or more like its parent (with SAUVIGNON BLANC), CABERNET FRANC. All of this means that Cabernet can make great wine, but that it is not necessarily the best grape for wines to be drunk young, especially when it is grown in cooler climates.

While Chardonnay is a relatively recent globe trotter, Cabernet Sauvignon long ago strayed widely and successfully from its Bordeaux base. Contrary to popular belief Cabernet Sauvignon is not Bordeaux's most planted vine (see MERLOT). Because it is relatively late ripening, it needs a warmer, drier environment than most of Bordeaux can provide in order to stand a commercially interesting chance of ripening fully. In Bordeaux, therefore, it is grown in the Entre-Deux-Mers region as well as in the well-drained gravels of the Médoc and Graves where it is invariably the chief constituent, but always blended with Merlot, Cabernet Franc and sometimes with PETIT VERDOT, in the world-famous classed growths (see page 161). In the Médoc it is the main varietal component in St-Estèphes that are taut and austere in youth (although they are getting riper and more welcoming with every vintage); in the dense, mineral-scented Pauillacs; in many a lush, silky Margaux; and in the beautifully balanced yet long-lived St-Juliens. It brings crispness and long life to the wines of Graves and the suggestion of warm bricks common to several from Pessac-Léognan.

It is planted all round the greater Bordeaux region in those appellations grouped together as constituting south west France, out-tannined only by the Tannat of Madiran. Bergerac and Buzet are its chief strongholds.

Elsewhere in France there are growers who persist with it in the Loire (though Cabernet Franc is much easier to ripen), although most of the rest is in the south. In Provence it can blend beautifully with the spicier SYRAH to make ambitious, oak-aged wines for the long term. In the Languedoc it is all too often over-produced to yield rather lean, hollow Vins de Pays, although an increasing proportion of seriously fine wine is made.

Cabernet Sauvignon has been responsible for some extremely fine Italian wines, notably Supertuscans (see pages 214–17), in which it

seems happy blended with SANGIOVESE, but also bottlings from as far afield as Piedmont and Sicily. (Cabernet Sauvignon thrives in fairly hot regions as it retains its acidity well throughout its slow final ripening stage.) Bottles from north east Italy described simply as 'Cabernet', however, almost certainly contain more Cabernet Franc than Cabernet Sauvignon.

However, Cabernet Sauvignon is the dominant Cabernet planted widely and enthusiastically in central Europe. It clearly has great potential in Moldova and the Ukraine, although CABERNET SEVERNY's cold-resistance can make it more useful in Russia. Cabernet Sauvignon is extremely important to the wine industries of Bulgaria, Romania and what was Yugoslavia, and to a much lesser extent, Austria and Hungary. These Cabernets tend to be less refined than the Bordeaux prototypes, being intensely fruity, often recalling red fruits rather than black, and rarely showing any oak influence (other than occasionally that of heavy-handed oak chipping).

Cabernet is rare in Portugal and still relatively rare in Spain, although creeping internationalization of Spanish vineyards is resulting in more and more varietal examples and a dash of Cabernet in blends. In Navarre Cabernet Sauvignon has shown how well it blends with TEMPRANILLO (even though the two varieties have rather similar structures) and in Penedès has won considerable acclaim.

The variety performs well in the warmer Mediterranean regions, notably in Lebanon and Israel.

Many of South Africa's revered wines, and a few of her best, are Cabernets which already show some intensely satisfying regional variations. Cape winemakers, however, have tended to make 100 per cent Cabernets, unsoftened by Merlot or leavened by Cabernet Franc, as indeed was the initial effect of varietalism in California. California in general (see page 265), and particulary Northern California, has made some great, glossy, ultra-ripe Cabernets, some of them initially monstrous in their tannins (and occasionally acids) but nowadays made with great skill. Today there is growing understanding of the precise characteristics of various areas within Napa and Sonoma and how these are

In the red wine hall of fame, Cabernets
reign supreme – whether Cabernet Franc,
seen in the open fermentation vats of Chinon
(top) or the darker coloured, almost blue-black
Cabernet Sauvignon grapes of California's
Napa Valley (above).
Cabernet Sauvignon has a particular affinity
with the unusual, well-drained red terra rossa soils
of Coonawarra (right) in South Australia.

shown to best advantage. Much of the Napa Valley, other than the southern end, seems particularly well suited to Cabernet Sauvignon production and this will continue to be one of the world's most fruitful hunting grounds for lovers of Cabernet that has the ability to age (though not as long as Bordeaux). Many finer California Cabernets show a certain minty quality, others an earthiness. More and more of these wines are blends made according to the Bordeaux recipe and are often called Meritage here.

Washington's Merlot is generally more successful than its equally common Cabernet Sauvignon but there are some extremely appetizing exceptions. Cabernet may well have a future in Texas too, but has difficulty ripening in Oregon.

Cabernet cuttings were first taken to South America well over a century ago and indeed the Chilean wine industry was built on this very important variety. (In fact Chile's largest company Concha y Toro claims to be the world's most important owner of Cabernet Sauvignon vineyards.) Chilean Cabernet, most of it still ungrafted, has a very direct, fruity flavour, usually without the mintiness associated with parts of California and Australia.

Australia defined her perfect spot for Cabernet Sauvignon before consciously doing the same for any other variety: Coonawarra in the far south east of South Australia on a famous strip of terra rossa earth (see previous page). These wines tend to have a noticeably high level of acidity as well, often, as some notes of eucalyptus, sometimes so powerful that the wines can seem closer to cold remedies in youth. These wines can age superbly. Margaret River in Western Australia can also make great, refined Cabernet and there are other fine examples all over Victoria as well as in the Hunter Valley and elsewhere. Cabernet is sometimes blended with the country's much richer, fleshier SHIRAZ, and very complementary they can be too.

New Zealand's Cabernet Sauvignon can be too herbaceous and acid by half, but the best examples from Hawkes Bay and Waiheke are certainly crisp and lively. In many wine regions, however, the necessarily slow evolution of Cabernet is being re-evaluated, often to the benefit of other red varieties. It may be that in a decade or two, Cabernet will be more exclusively the preserve of the world's most ambitious winemakers.

Cabernet Severny, specially bred version of CABERNET SAUVIGNON designed to withstand Russia's harsh winters by incorporating Mongolian genes.

Cadarca, Romanian KADARKA.

Calabrese, another name for NERO D'AVOLA.

Caladoc, recent southern French crossing of GRENACHE and MALBEC.

Canaiolo, decreasingly popular ingredient in the original Chianti recipe.

Cannonau, Sardinian name for GRENACHE.

Carignan, Carignane in the USA, **Carignano** in Italy, and **Cariñena** in Spain, the most important but, sadly, by no means the most distinguished vine in France. It was chosen as replacement for the ARAMON which perished in the frosts of 1956 and 1963, because it is extremely productive and buds late, so rarely suffers frost damage. It also ripens quite late, however, so can only be grown in warm to hot climates, and produces tannic, quite acid wine, too often marked by a coarse, rustic smell of hot berries. To counter these characteristics, most Carignan in the Languedoc-Roussillon, where it dominates production even of appellation contrôlée wine, is vinified using some form of carbonic maceration (see page 78). Of all the thousands of acres of vines which have been ripped out in the Midi in an effort to curb Europe's wine surplus, Carignan is by far the major casualty. Carignan tends to be on low bushes that are unsuitable for mechanical harvesting. Very old vines in really warm climates can produce deep-coloured, warm, quite rich wine and there have been some quite creditable examples from California, and good Carignano del Sulcis in southern Sardinia. Carignan's origins are Spanish and it is still grown in Costers del Segre, Penedès, Tarragona and Terra Alta. In Rioja it plays a minor part as Mazuelo.

Carmenère, historic Bordeaux variety found widely today in Chile where it was long mistaken for Merlot. It is now forging its own more structured identity.

Carmenet, Médoc name for CABERNET FRANC.

Carnelian, 1936 California crossing of CARIGNAN and CABERNET SAUVIGNON with Grenache. Designed to be a hot climate Cabernet, it is grown to a limited extent in California's Central Valley and in Texas.

Castelão Frances, a versatile and characterful southern Portuguese variety known variously as Periquita, João de Santarém or Santarém, Mortágua and Trincadeira Preta. Wines are fruity, relatively fleshy, but can also be aged.

Catawba, deep pink-skinned American hybrid grown widely in New York state where it produces strongly flavoured deep pink to light reds.

Cencibel, La Mancha and Valdepeñas name for TEMPRANILLO.

Cesanese, Latium vine.

Chambourcin, French hybrid designed to thrive in damp climates. Popular in the Muscadet region and pioneered in a particularly hot, humid part of New South Wales by Cassegrain. The dark, aromatic wine shows no trace of any non-European vine parentage.

Chancellor, productive French hybrid grown in New York state.

Charbono, unusual California speciality produced as an occasional varietal in the Napa Valley. Some authorities claim it is DOLCETTO of Piedmont.

Chenin Noir, an alternative name for PINEAU D'AUNIS.

Chiavennasca, name used in Valtellina (northern Italy) for NEBBIOLO.

Ciliegiolo, cherry-flavoured grape planted in Central Italy.

Cinsaut, Cinsault, widely planted throughout southern France and Corsica (where it is now being ripped out at a great rate). With its lighter skins and soft perfume it is particularly suitable for rosés, although low yields are needed to eke out much flavour. It has the advantage over GRENACHE of being easy to pick by machine and there was a notable increase in plantings in the 1970s and 1980s in southern France, mainly in the Aude and Hérault *départements*. Cinsaut is used to add perfume and fruit to wines such as Minervois and Corbières. The variety withstands drought well and so has been important in North Africa, Lebanon, Israel and South Africa, where it is most famous as a parent of PINOTAGE. In southern Italy it is known as Ottavianello.

Colorino, now rare Tuscan colouring grape.

Concord, the 'foxiest' and most powerfully non-European-scented American vine planted extensively in New York state, and in Brazil.

Corvina, Corvina Veronese, the finest grape found in Valpolicella and Bardolino (see also RONDINELLA and MOLINARA), particularly good for dried grape wines such as Amarone.

Côt, Cot, alternative name for MALBEC.

Couderc Noir, French hybrid rapidly disappearing from the Languedoc, not before time.

Counoise, rare ingredient in red Châteauneuf-du-Pape. The wine can be peppery and usefully high in acid.

Criolla Chica, PAIS/MISSION in Argentina.

Croatina, a late ripening and high-yielding vine which makes juicy wines with bite. See also BONARDA.

Currant, a widely planted vine that is used almost exclusively for dried fruit, most common in Greece and Australia.

Delaware, dark pink-skinned American hybrid vine grown in New York state and, especially, Japan, where its habit of ripening early is useful. More European-flavoured than CONCORD.

Dolcetto, 'little sweet one', so named because it is naturally low in acidity. After Barbera, it is the most common red grape of Piedmont and, in youth, can be mouth-fillingly delicious. It is particularly useful to growers because it ripens much more easily than NEBBIOLO or even BARBERA, so tends to be planted on north-facing slopes. A little is grown in both North and South America.

Domina, modern German crossing useful for cooler sites but not particularly distinguished for its wine.

Dornfelder, the most successful red crossing in Germany, which makes juicy, deeply coloured red wines, especially in Pfalz and Rheinhessen. It is easier to grow and ripen than Spätburgunder (PINOT NOIR), PORTUGIESER or LIMBERGER, and can yield heavily. Understandably, it is becoming increasingly popular with German vine-growers.

Dunkelfelder, deep-coloured but otherwise undistinguished German vine.

Durif, southern French vine most famous for being closely related to California's PETITE SIRAH.

Early Burgundy, California vine identified as ABOURIOU.

Espadeiro, a productive vine in Galicia and Vinho Verde which makes generally rather thin wine.

Fer, Fer Servadou, wild speciality of Marcillac and encouraged elsewhere in south west France. Called Brocol in Gaillac and Pinenc in Madiran, it can add some rustic smokey flavours to the blend. It is also an important ingredient in the little-seen wines of Entraygues and Estaing, which are neighbours of Marcillac. Argentina also grows a Fer which is apparently a clone of MALBEC.

Franconia, BLAUFRÄNKISCH in Friuli.

Frankovka, see BLAUFRÄNKISCH.

Frappato, light, grapey Sicilian.

Freisa, Piedmont love-or-loathe variety making pale but quite tannic, tart wines, many of which are frothy and medium sweet.

Gaglioppo, Calabrian vine, making extremely alcoholic wines.

Gamay, the Beaujolais grape known in full as **Gamay Noir à Jus Blanc** to distinguish it from the host of red-fleshed **Gamays Teinturiers** which were once widely grown in France (and can still be found in eastern Europe). Everything about Gamay is hasty, in terms of both vine and wine, which means it can suffer frost damage but can ripen somewhere as cool as the Loire. Wines tend to be light coloured, often with a stong blue tinge and traditionally attract the vague adjectives 'fresh and fruity'. Rapid vinification using carbonic maceration (page 78), particularly to hasten Nouveau wines on to the market, can result in strong banana/peardrop/boiled candy/nail-polish remover aromas. Very

Gamay vines are cooled by autumn mists on the hills above Chiroubles in Beaujolais (left), while stereotypical Grenache grapes in Châteauneuf-du-Pape (right) are ripened by heat reflected from the large, pale stones known locally as galets.

little Gamay is designed to be aged; it is the red answer to Sauvignon Blanc. It can be extremely refreshing when served chilled, thanks to low tannins and high acidity. Gamay is grown in the Mâconnais to the north of Beaujolais, in the Touraine, and in outlying areas such as Châteaumeillant, Coteaux du Lyonnais, Coteaux du Giennois, Côtes d'Auvergne, Côtes du Forez, Côte Roannaise and St-Pourçain. In the Mâconnais and Switzerland Gamay is often blended with a bit of PINOT NOIR, to produce Bourgogne Passetoutgrains and Dôle respectively. Outside France only the Swiss are particularly keen on Gamay, although it can be found in parts of central Europe. It has often been confused with BLAUFRÄNKISCH.

Gamay Beaujolais, California name for what is thought to be a clone of PINOT NOIR.

Gamé, Bulgarian name for BLAUFRÄNKISCH.

Gamza, KADARKA in Bulgaria.

Garnacha, Garnacha Tinta, GRENACHE in its Spanish homeland. **Garnacha Tintorera,** the 'dyer' version of Garnacha, is the Spanish name for ALICANTE BOUSCHET and is widely planted, notably in Almansa.

Garrut, a Catalan speciality whose relatively tough wines can taste of liquorice.

Graciano, rare but fine and perfumed Rioja grape which is difficult to grow and has largely been abandoned. It is almost certainly identical to the equally rare MORRASTEL of the Languedoc, and very possibly an obscure variety known as **Xeres** in California. Argentina grows a variety called **Graciana.**

Grand Noir, Grand Noir de la Calmette, a vine that is, fortunately, fast disappearing from the Languedoc and Cognac. High yield and red flesh.

Grenache, Grenache Noir, the world's most widely planted dark-skinned grape variety because of its popularity in Spain and southern France. In the late Middle Ages the house of Aragon apparently took it far and wide around the Mediterranean – although Sardinians (who call it Cannonau) argue it was stolen from them. This archetypal hot climate vine, which has to be pruned very severely if it is not to produce too much bland wine, can produce slightly pale but quite alcoholic wine that can taste spicy and sweet. Like CINSAUT the grapes have relatively thin skins and musts tend to oxidize easily, but fine rosés can be made. Grenache is usually blended with other varieties higher in colour and tannin such as SYRAH and MOURVÈDRE, even in its perfect spot, Châteauneuf-du-Pape. Grenache inspires all the fine reds and rosés of the Southern Rhône, and is a permitted ingredient in most Languedoc-Roussillon AC wines. Its most distinctive produce is the vins doux naturels of Banyuls, Maury and Rivesaltes. GARNACHA TINTA is Spain's most important red grape and is grown extensively everywhere other than Andalucía. In Rioja it provides juicy ballast for the more structured Tempranillo. Priorato is Spain's finest incarnation of Garnacha Tinta (often incorporating some of the downier **Garnacha Peluda,** which is otherwise known as LLADONER PELUT).

Grenache is quantitatively very important in both California and Australia, but most of the vines are planted in hot, heavily irrigated vineyards where yields are too high to produce interesting wine. Dry-farmed, older vines are being sought out, however, as the market clamours for more and more Rhône-like wines. And in California the success of White Zinfandel spawned White Grenache. The variety is cultivated all round the Mediterranean.

Grignolino, a Piedmont speciality producing light bodied, herbal-scented aperitif wines, also grown to a very limited extent in California's Napa Valley.

Grolleau, Groslot, the middle Loire's basic, bland dark-skinned variety, used extensively with GAMAY for less distinguished pinks such as Rosé d'Anjou.

Gropello, Lombardy red.

Harriague, Uruguayan name for TANNAT.

Helfensteiner, German crossing and parent of the more exciting DORNFELDER.

Heroldrebe, another DORNFELDER parent, used for pink wine in Pfalz.

Isabella, widely planted *labrusca* vine (see page 96) grown mainly in South America, New York state and the ex-Soviet Union.

Jaen, very basic central Spanish grape. Also the name of a Dão variety in Portugal.

João de Santarém, CASTELÃO FRANCES in parts of Ribatejo.

Kadarka, Hungary's own red grape (even if its origins are Albanian) being replaced by the less rot-prone and earlier ripening KÉKFRANKOS and KÉKOPORTO. If yields are restrained it can make full, tannic wine such as supported the best Bull's Blood blends, but such wine is rare. It can also be found in Austria's Burgenland, in Vojvodina, as Cadarca in Romania and as Gamza in Bulgaria.

Kékfrankos, Kékoporto, Hungarian names for BLAUFRÄNKISCH and PORTUGIESER respectively, Kék being Hungarian for blue.

Lagrein, Trentino-Alto Adige speciality, making fullish everyday reds and rosés.

Lambrusco, very important and productive vine, making often sweet, usually fizzy red in Emilia-Romagna. About 60 subvarieties have been identified.

Lemberger, Limberger, see BLAUFRÄNKISCH.

Limnio, ancient Greek variety, making deep mineral-scented wines with good tannins.

Lladoner Pelut, Lledoner Pelut, downy-leaved, less rot-prone form of GRENACHE still grown in Languedoc-Roussillon and, as Garnacha Peluda, in north east Spain.

Magaratch Ruby, crossing of CABERNET SAUVIGNON and SAPERAVI.

Malbec, a black grape that is known as Côt in much of south west France and the Loire, Pressac in parts of Bordeaux (where it is still grown mainly in Bourg and Blaye), Auxerrois in Cahors (where it is the main grape variety) and occasionally **Malbeck** in Argentina, where it has also dominated red wine production. The vine is quite fragile in cooler climates, producing a wine that can taste rather rustically gamey, but in the best Cahors vineyards and, especially, the Luján de Cuyo region of Mendoza in Argentina it can create deep-coloured, intensely ripe and attractively velvety wines which are well worth ageing. Because it has been so widely grown in Argentina, the local producers tended to view it as distinctly third rate, but outsiders have managed to stop systematic replacement with Cabernet Sauvignon, which the whole world can supply. The vine is also grown in Chile, Australia, California and north east Italy.

Malvasia Nera, dark-skinned relative of light-berried MALVASIA, usually made as a sweet red, from Piedmont and Alto Adige to the islands of Sardinia, and Lipari off Sicily.

Mammolo, now rare, violet-scented ingredient in Chianti.

Mandelaria, grape of the Greek islands which yields dark, relatively light wines that are useful for blending.

Maréchal Foch, a very early ripening French hybrid grown in Canada, New York and the Loire at one time. The wines can show attractive strawberry fruit.

Marzemino produces a few lively wines in northern Italy.

Mataro, old-fashioned name used mainly in Australia and California for the fashionable MOURVÈDRE vine .

Mavro, Greek for black and the name of the most common dark grape on Cyprus.

Mavrodaphne, Greek variety made into a rich, port-like varietal around Patras.

Mavrud, Balkan vine with real potential to produce intensely rich yet dry and tannic wine, which is a speciality of Assenovgrad near Plovdiv in Bulgaria.

Mazuelo, CARIGNAN in Rioja.

Melnik, an abbreviation for Bulgaria's SHIROKA MELNISHKA LOSA.

Mencía, a variety that is grown widely in north west Spain, producing light, relatively fragrant reds and thought locally to be a strain of CABERNET FRANC. Others think it more like SYRAH.

Merlot grapes at Château Palmer in Bordeaux (left). With thinner skins than Cabernet Sauvignon, Merlot is particularly susceptible to fungal diseases, so may need constant spraying as in this St-Émilion vineyard (right).

Merlot, Merlot Noir, with CABERNET FRANC, famous as a blending partner for CABERNET SAUVIGNON, but possibly more widely planted in total than either. Merlot conventionally makes lush, plummy, velvety wine that can soften Cabernet's more austere frame and, usefully, matures much faster. Very much a wine of our times, it has enjoyed enormous popularity in the United States.

Merlot's homeland is Bordeaux, where it is the most planted vine variety and is the most important ingredient in most wines qualifying for the basic Bordeaux appellation. It makes its greatest wines on the right bank of the Gironde in Bordeaux, in Pomerol (where it is generally blended with minimal proportions of Cabernet Franc) and St-Émilion (where Cabernet Franc and sometimes Cabernet Sauvignon play a more important part). Despite Merlot's reputation as the user-friendly, early maturing wine, the best of these wines can continue to develop in bottle for decades, and I have been lucky enough to taste a mid-nineteenth-century Château Ausone at the château that was as lively as the châtelaine herself.

Merlot, like the Cabernets, is widely grown throughout south west France, notably in Bergerac and in Cahors, where it is the common blending partner of MALBEC. It is also very widely planted in the Languedoc, where it can make juicy, plump Vins de Pays (being generally more successful than Cabernet Sauvignon).

Just like Merlot the wine, Merlot the vine ripens earlier than Cabernet Sauvignon but is less resistant to rot and, if the weather is poor during flowering, can easily suffer from coulure (see page 69). It is conventionally, but by no means exclusively, associated with damp, clay soils.

Although almost two-thirds of the world's Merlot vines are grown in France, most of the rest until recently have been grown in north east Italy, particularly in Friuli, where the variety can make plumper wines than the prevailing Cabernet. Quality varies from basic light red varietals to rich, dense barrique-aged wines, which are often blended with Cabernet and/or Sangiovese. (This observation is also true of the Merlots that are produced in Switzerland's Italian Ticino.) Romania, Bulgaria and Moldova also grow significant quantities of Merlot, which can be difficult to distinguish in terms of wine quality from their Cabernet.

Today Merlot is being planted at a lick in both North and South America. It has a proven track record in Washington state, where its charms are attractively balanced by crisp acidity

and good colour. In California, its fruity charms are extremely popular when served up as a varietal wine and it is also a popular ingredient in Meritage blends. Its reputation has suffered, however, from the very ordinary quality of California Merlot at its most basic, as a sort of red Chardonnay.

Chile has already found its own perfect spot for Merlot, Apalta in Colchagua, and the best-made examples combine California gloss with even more obvious fruit (see CARMENÈRE). Argentina's Merlot has a less distinct identity – indeed almost all Argentine red already has inbuilt ripeness thanks to the climate, and so there is little need to augment this with a particularly ripe-tasting variety.

Although Merlot is grown as a blending partner for Cabernet in Australia and New Zealand, few varietal wines of real distinction have yet emerged, although they almost certainly will. South Africa has already shown just how gorgeous an oak-aged Merlot ripened in a relatively warm climate can be.

Meunier, see PINOT MEUNIER.

Mission, California's oldest but by no means most distinguished grape. It is rough stuff related to the PAIS of Chile and Criolla Chica of Argentina. See also MONICA.

Molinara, a variety that makes a tart contribution to Valpolicella.

Monastrell, Spain's name for MOURVÈDRE, known also as Mataro.

Mondeuse, spicy, sappy wine made from one of Savoie's most characterful varieties (see page 205). Many authorities think it is identical to Friuli's REFOSCO.

Monica, undistinguished Sardinian vine which *may* be related to MISSION.

Montepulciano, an Italian vine that will ripen only in the southern half of the country, producing good-value, full-bodied and characterful wines, especially in the Abruzzi.

Morellino, SANGIOVESE in western Tuscany.

Moreto, undistinguished vine grown mainly in Portugal's Alentejo.

Moristel, speciality of Spain's Somontano. The vine is frail and the wine oxidizes easily and may be best in blends.

Morrastel, rare Languedoc variety thought to be Rioja's GRACIANO. Also used in Spain as a synonym for Monastrell (the MOURVÈDRE of France). In North Africa the name Morrastel is used for both Graciano and Mourvèdre.

Mortágua, CASTELÃO FRANCES in the west of Portugal.

Mourisco Tinto, lesser port grape.

Mourvèdre, fashionable grape variety that is most obvious in Bandol but, as Monastrell, grown so widely in south east Spain that it is Spain's second most important red grape variety, but grown more patchily throughout southern France. For years it was called Mataro and dismissed as basic blending material in California and Australia, but now appears in much more highly priced Rhône-like blends. It needs a very warm site or summer to ripen it fully and the wine produced from it is deep coloured, alcoholic and almost aggressively gamey in flavour. It may be best suited to blending, notably with the more structured SYRAH.

Outside Spain, plantings are increasing all over the world.

Müllerrebe, German for PINOT MEUNIER.

Muscardin, lively but rare Châteauneuf grape.

Muscat Hamburg, common table grape which can even be ripened in England and produces light, grapey red throughout eastern Europe. It is also important to the developing wine industries of China and Japan and is also known as Black Muscat.

Napa Gamay, dwindling California speciality thought to be VALDIGUIÉ.

Nebbiolo, Italy's noblest vine and a speciality of Piedmont. Like PINOT NOIR, fussy about both soil and site and extremely expressive of it. It is grown, only in vineyards which stand a chance of ripening this late ripening variety, all over Piedmont, but reaches its high point in the hills of Barolo and Barbaresco, sometimes shrouded in autumn by fog, or *nebbia*, which may have inspired its name. It is also grown successfully, as Spanna, in the north of Piedmont to produce wines such as Gattinara and Ghemme and even, just over the border in Lombardy, in Valtellina, where it is known as Chiavennasca. In the alps of Valle d'Aosta and the far north west of Piedmont, where it is called Picutener, it makes Carema.

Wine made from Nebbiolo is markedly high in both acidity and, especially, tannin – which is why the grapes need to be sufficiently ripe to supply enough fruit to counterbalance all this astringency. Wines may be deeply coloured (although they can brown quite easily) and have a haunting smell that reminds many of tar, roses and sometimes violets. These wines are extremely serious and demand long ageing and attention. (DOLCETTO and BARBERA, however, are for earlier glugging.)

A little Nebbiolo is grown in California and Argentina.

Negramoll, see TINTA NEGRA MOLE.

Négrette, a Frontonnais speciality, producing supple, perfumed wine for early drinking.

Negroamaro ('black and bitter' in Italian), widely planted in Italy's deep south, especially on the heel of Italy in Apulia where it can make seductively heady, ageworthy reds such as Salice Salentino, Squinzano and Copertino. Some good rosés too.

Nerello, Nerello Mascalese, important Sicilian vine, lighter than NERO D'AVOLA but can be sweet and fragrant, especially for rosés.

Nero d'Avola, one of Sicily's most serious red wine grapes, also known as Calabrese. Very fruity though barrel maturation can work well.

Nielluccio, Corsica's answer to SANGIOVESE. Often blended with SCIACARELLO, which is more distinctive.

Noir, French for black and often a suffix of red wine grape varieties.

Ojo de Liebre, TEMPRANILLO in Penedès.

Ormeasco, Ligurian name for DOLCETTO.

Ottavianello, probably CINSAUT in southern Italy.

Pais, Chile's commonplace grape and descended from the Spanish conquistadores. It is identical to the MISSION of California and Mexico. Grown in southern regions for very ordinary wine.

Pamid, Bulgaria's common or garden red.

Periquita, the name for CASTELÃO FRANCES in Arrábida, Palmela and parts of Ribatejo.

Perricone, soft Sicilian.

Petite Sirah makes robust, tannic, earthy wines in both California and Mexico. It is less noble than, but probably related to, the true SYRAH and also to the obscure DURIF and its relatives.

Petit Verdot, a late ripening ingredient in the classic bordeaux blend to which, in warm years, it can bring an agreeable peppery spice. Some Californians have been planting it for Meritage blends (see CABERNET SAUVIGNON).

Piedirosso, Campanian speciality.

Pignolo, lively, dense Friuli vine that has real potential.

Pineau d'Aunis, a light, fruity middle Loire variety declining in favour of CABERNET FRANC.

Pinenc, FER in Madiran.

Pinot Meunier, the most commonly planted grape in Champagne, where its wine adds youthful fruit to CHARDONNAY and PINOT NOIR. It is called 'miller's' vine because its leaves are dusty white underneath. As Müllerrebe it is grown in Germany's Württemberg and some varietal still wines are also made in Victoria, Australia.

Pinot Noir, the red burgundy grape capable of producing divinely scented, gorgeously fruity expressions of place but often unwilling or unable to do so. In Burgundy Pinot Noir is merely the medium through which tiny environmental differences (terroir) express themselves (see pages 166–8). Flavours found in young red burgundies include raspberries, strawberries, cherries and violets; with time these evolve into a bouquet often reminiscent of game, liquorice and autumnal undergrowth. (There is an argument that red burgundy has to be very good indeed to be worth ageing more than about five years…)

This ancient eastern French vine is very prone to mutation (see PINOT GRIS, PINOT BLANC and GOUAIS BLANC) and enormous variation in wine quality between different clones. Planting the wrong clone in the wrong place is one of many reasons for the wide variation in quality between different red burgundies and different varietal Pinot Noirs from elsewhere. Pinot Noir is also very sensitive to the size of crop it is expected to produce, and many vapid examples exemplify an over-demanding yield. It ripens relatively early (Chardonnay and Pinot Noir are often harvested at the same time in Burgundy) so is not suitable for very warm regions where there would be no time to develop interesting flavours before acid levels plummeted. On the other hand, many of the cooler regions in which it thrives suffer autumn rains which can rot the thin-skinned berries of this variety, resulting in pale, tainted wines. The Pinot Noir grower's lot is not an easy one.

For years the received wisdom was that it was almost impossible to make decent Pinot Noir outside Burgundy but the 1990s definitively disproved this – and if the new wave of fine New World Pinot Noir for the moment lacks any great expression of place, it often provides considerably more pleasure per penny than the average bottle of burgundy.

RIGHT In Burgundy, Pinot Noir has acclimatized itself so successfully that adjoining vineyards produce wines with perceptibly different characters, such as in Gevrey-Chambertin. BELOW Pinot Noir grapes ripen so early that they can even be grown in England, as seen here at Denbies Estate.

Oregon in the American Pacific Northwest staked its wine reputation on Pinot Noir (presumably inspired by its distinctly Burgundian wet autumns) with considerable success. More unexpectedly, California has demonstrated that it too has no shortage of spots quite cool enough (thanks to ocean fog) to keep Pinot grapes on the vine as they develop welcoming fruity flavours and some texture to boot. Notable among these are Carneros, Russian River Valley and Sonoma Coast in Sonoma and the Central Coast, although Chalone and Calera wineries have proved that isolated Pinot greatness can also be found in the mountains south of San Francisco. Canada has made the odd hopeful Pinot and at the other end of the climatological spectrum even Chile has demonstrated a recent facility with this vine, in cooler corners, giving hope to Pinot Noir strugglers everywhere. Australians have identified Victoria (notably the Yarra Valley, Geelong and the Mornington Peninsula) and Tasmania as being cool enough for Pinot. New Zealand claims to make the best Pinot outside Burgundy and certainly Martinborough has also made some stunning examples. Most of South Africa is too warm for Pinot Noir, but the coolest coastal regions are promising.

Within Europe, Pinot Noir travels under a number of aliases. In Italy it is known as **Pinot Nero** and concentrated in the north east where average quality is increasing considerably. In Germany, as **Spätburgunder**, it is the most planted red wine grape and is increasingly inspiring, often thanks to top quality oak barrels, just as it is in eastern Switzerland as Blauburgunder and from the more serious winemakers of Austria (sometimes called Blauer Spätburgunder) and Alsace. (Pinot Noir from all these places has in the past tended to be pale, sweetish and not especially inspiring.) It is planted all over central Europe, called variously **Burgundac Crni** in what was Yugoslavia, **Nagyburgundi** in Hungary (although the name is also used for BLAUFRÄNKISCH) and **Burgund Mare** in Romania, where it makes very cheap, very lush, very atypical wine.

The French grow increasing quantities of Pinot Noir outside Burgundy, however, notably in Champagne, where it has proved itself the ideal black grape for a top quality sparkling wine (for which purpose it is widely used in Italy, California and Australia), in Alsace, all over eastern France such as in Sancerre, the Jura and Savoie, and even in the higher reaches of the Languedoc.

Plavac Mali, a Croatian speciality that makes dense, heady and tannic wines such as Postup and Dingač. Related to ZINFANDEL.

Portan, recent French crossing of GRENACHE and PORTUGAIS which ripens more reliably than Grenache. Sometimes in Vins de Pays d'Oc.

Portugieser, Blauer Portugieser, high-yielding, early ripening vine planted widely in Austria and Germany, producing rather ordinary, light wines with relatively low acid. Hungarians and Romanians know it as Kékoporto and Croatians as **Portugizac Crni,** or **Portugaljka.** A little is grown in France as **Portugais.**

Poulsard, Plousard, Jura rarity making perfumed, pale wine, usually blended with PINOT NOIR.

Pressac, MALBEC on Bordeaux's right bank.

Primitivo, most famous for being the southern Italian version of California's ZINFANDEL. Wines labelled Primitivo tend to be very alcoholic and deep coloured.

Prokupac, Serbian speciality reaching high grape sugar levels and often made into a dark rosé.

Prugnolo Gentile, SANGIOVESE in Montepulciano.

Raboso, a tough and sometimes tart, Veneto variety which can be too lean to sustain these attributes.

Ramisco, the astringent Colares vine.

Refosco, Refosco dal Peduncolo Rosso, historic, red-stemmed Friuli vine, making dense, lively wines with bite. Known as Terrano or Teran in Slovenia and Croatia. Possibly the same as MONDEUSE.

Rondinella, lesser Valpolicella grape (see CORVINA and MOLINARA).

Roriz, Tinta Roriz, common Portuguese name for TEMPRANILLO.

Rossese, a fine Ligurian vine, especially in Dolceacqua.

Rouchet, Ruchè, a scented, relatively tough Piedmont red. Rare.

Royalty, California red-fleshed French hybrid bred from TROUSSEAU.

Rubired, California red-fleshed French hybrid, bred from TINTA CÃO. Easier to grow and therefore more popular than ROYALTY. Used widely to add colour to less expensive blends.

Ruby Cabernet, once popular California crossing of CARIGNAN and CABERNET SAUVIGNON to combine Cabernet characteristics with Carignan productivity and tolerance of Central Valley heat. Also grown in South Africa and Australia.

Sagrantino, lively, spicy, often tough Umbrian red, a speciality of Montefalco.

St Laurent, an Austrian variety that can make lush, flattering, soft and rather PINOT NOIR-like wines. It is often blended with more internationally famous varieties and, if yields are limited, can be worth oak and bottle ageing. In Slovakia it is known as Vavrinecke.

Salvador, California red-fleshed French hybrid.

Samtrot, PINOT MEUNIER in Austria.

Sangiovese, Italy's most planted red wine vine and the underpinning of the majority of central Italian reds (notably Chianti, Brunello di Montalcino, Vino Nobile di Montepulciano – see pages 214–17 – as well as Rosso Conero and Rosso Piceno). It is known also as Brunello, Morellino and Prugnolo Gentile. There are many strains of varying quality, ranging from the lacklustre, over-produced vines responsible for the lightest Sangiovese di Romagna to the dense, long-lived Brunello. Late ripening Sangiovese makes well-structured, often high-acid wines with a certain farmyardy character, but a dense plumminess if fully ripe. Sangiovese has so far shown itself to be a much happier traveller than NEBBIOLO, turning out some quite

sumptuous (and some overpriced) examples in California – and some generally less inspiring examples in Argentina.

Santarém, the name for CASTELÃO FRANCES in parts of Ribatejo.

Saperavi, a Russian vine that produces deep-coloured wines (thanks to the pink flesh of its grapes) with good acidity. Wines respond well to ageing. **Saperavi Severny** is a hybrid designed to withstand very cold winters by incorporating Mongolian genes.

Savagnin Noir, Jura name for PINOT NOIR.

Schiava (pronounced 'Ski-arver'), Italian name for Alto Adige's common or garden variety (see page 213). The region's many German speakers also know it as Vernatsch and in Württemberg it is called TROLLINGER.

Schioppettino, speciality of Friuli whose characterful wines hint at violets and pepper.

Sciacarello, Sciaccarello (pronounced 'Shack-arello'), south western Corsican speciality that can make herb-scented reds and rosés but has been overtaken by Nielluccio.

Ségalin, recent French crossing of the obscure Jurançon Noir and PORTUGAIS, capable of producing well-structured wines.

Seibel, common name for many of the French hybrids, usually numbered to distinguish them.

Severny. Most vines with Severny in their name have been specially bred in Russia to withstand cold winters.

Shiraz, Australian and South African name for SYRAH, so any wine labelled Shiraz tends to taste richer, riper and more full-bodied than France's typical Syrah-based wines. Australia has regained her pride in Shiraz, the country's most planted wine grape variety, which can taste of baked pencils in the Hunter Valley, chocolate in Barossa Valley (arguably its spiritual home) and black pepper in cooler regions such as Macedon in Victoria. Very, very few Australian wine producers do not produce a Shiraz of some sort, and many make several qualities of Shiraz (including sparkling), as well as a range of

The Syrah grape in some of its finest
locations: (left) Shiraz grapes in a coolish
site in the state of Victoria in Australia; perhaps
the oldest Shiraz/Syrah vines in the world
(above) in Henschke's Hill of Grace
vineyard, South Australia; and terraces
of Syrah (right), trained up special stakes,
on the vertiginous slopes of Côte Rôtie
in the Northern Rhône.

Shiraz-Cabernet *and* Cabernet-Shiraz blends. Penfolds are arguably the past masters of Shiraz production, their Grange being Australia's very first serious 'collectable'. When it was first made, by the late Max Schubert after a trip to Bordeaux, it was dismissed as 'dry port tasting of crushed ants' by other Australian winemakers. In very general terms Shiraz tends to taste slightly sweet and can reach high alcohol levels. South African examples can taste rather earthy and hot.

Shiroka Melnishka Losa, means 'broad leaved vine of Melnik' in Bulgaria, close to the Greek border. This variety, oak aged, can produce spicy, powerful and ageworthy wine not unlike Châteauneuf-du-Pape, occasionally smelling of tobacco leaves. Usually sold as Melnik.

Sousão, Souzão, black grape which brings colour to port in the Douro valley and has been planted in California and Australia.

Spanna, NEBBIOLO around Gattinara.

Syrah, the great grape of the North Rhône responsible for the dense, burly, deep-coloured, long-lived wines of Hermitage and, slightly more seductively perfumed (traditionally thanks to some VIOGNIER in the blend) Côte Rôtie. Unlike many varieties, it demonstrates a strict relationship between how severely it is pruned and how good the eventual wine is. It can also lose its aroma and acidity quickly if left past optimal ripening stage (both of which explain why so many (though by no means all) French varietal Syrah Vins de Pays are so wishy-washy). Crozes-Hermitage is probably the best-value manifestation of Syrah around at the moment, although good St-Joseph exists and Cornas is becoming less obdurate. It can smell of black pepper or even burnt rubber.

During the 1980s Syrah was enthusiastically planted throughout southern France, where it is widely used as an ingredient in blends, notably to add structure and density to GRENACHE in Châteauneuf-du-Pape and other Southern Rhône wines, but also to spice up CABERNET SAUVIGNON in Provence. It is a much-valued ingredient in most Languedoc appellations, fast replacing Carignan even more decisively than Grenache, MOURVÈDRE and, to a lesser extent, CINSAUT. It can also make some fine wine in Italy and the sunnier spots in Switzerland's Valais.

In California it is being enthusiastically planted by the so-called Rhône Rangers, keen to demonstrate that Syrah may be even better suited to the climate of Northern California than Cabernet Sauvignon. Its influence is also increasing in Washington state, throughout South America and indeed virtually everywhere wine is produced and it's not too cold.

In South Africa and Australia, where it is extremely important, it is known as SHIRAZ.

Taminga, Australian crossing.

Tannat, distinctive, tough variety best known as the main ingredient in Madiran but grown in other regions of south west France and, as Harriague, in Uruguay where it was taken by Basque émigrés. Wine made from it is naturally very astringent because of the thickness of the berries' skins, but Madiran's best winemakers are learning how to tame this tannic monster.

Tarrango, Australian TOURIGA NACIONAL X SULTANA crossing which ripens very late and needs a hot climate. The ultra-fruity wine is relatively light bodied and markedly low in tannin.

Tempranillo, Spain's most widely planted top quality grape variety whose name comes from *temprano*, or early, which is when it ripens (although 'early' can be well into October in Rioja). Spain's answer to CABERNET SAUVIGNON, Tempranillo is similarly high in tannins and acidity but, unusually for Spain, is not necessarily very high in alcohol.

Wines based on Tempranillo are some of Spain's longest lasting. It provides the spine for Rioja (GARNACHA providing the flesh, see page 225) and is by far the main ingredient in Ribera del Duero, where it is so common it is simply known as Tinto Fino 'the fine dark one'. In Penedès it is important as Ull de Llebre and Ojo de Liebre, and in Valdepeñas, called Cencibel, it makes rather less concentrated wines (often lightened by blending in white grapes). It is also grown in La Mancha, Costers del Segre, Utiel-Requena and increasingly in Navarre and Somontano. It is grown, as (Tinta) Roriz in northern Portugal and may well be the variety known as **Valdepeñas** in California's Central Valley. Some **Tempranilla** is grown in Argentina.

Teran, Terrano, see REFOSCO.

Teroldego, Teroldego Rotaliano, lively, tooth-smacking varietal speciality of Trentino in northern Italy, usually drunk young.

Tibouren, Provençal rarity making earthy rosés with a genuine scent of the *garrigue*, the herby scrub of southern France.

Tinta, Tinto is Spanish for red.

Tinta Amarela, productive, rot-prone northern Portuguese vine.

Tinta Barroca, sturdy port grape also planted in South Africa where varietal table wines are also made from it.

Tinta Cão, fine port grape enjoying a revival in the Douro valley (see page 240).

Tinta Francisca, lightish port variety.

Tinta Negra Mole, the undistinguished but serviceable grape which steadily usurped Madeira's fine varieties in the early and mid-twentieth century. Spain's Negramoll may be identical.

Tinta Pinheira, basic Dão grape.

Tinto Fino, TEMPRANILLO in Ribera del Duero.

Touriga Francesa, perfumed, good quality port variety.

Touriga Nacional, the finest port variety grown also in the Dão region, and producing extremely concentrated, dark, tannic wines. Also grown in Australia.

Trincadeira Preta, an alternative name for CASTELÃO FRANCES.

Trollinger, German for SCHIAVA and its light, sweetish wines are a Württemberg speciality.

Trousseau, Jura vine, making robust wine but overtaken by PINOT NOIR.

Ull de Llebre, Catalan for TEMPRANILLO.

Uva di Troia, Apulian speciality.

Uva Rara, softener blended with NEBBIOLO in northern Piedmont.

Vaccarèse, rare, lightish Châteauneuf grape.

Valdiguié, prolific vine originally from south west France, now best known as NAPA GAMAY.

Vavrinecke, Czech for ST LAURENT.

Verdot, South American variety which *may* be related to PETIT VERDOT.

Vernatsch, see SCHIAVA and TROLLINGER.

Vespolina, Gattinara speciality often blended with NEBBIOLO.

Villard Noir, hybrid widely planted in France until the 1980s.

Vranac, a deep, dense speciality of Montenegro.

Wildbacher, Blauer Wildbacher, Styrian vine from which a deep, crisp, perfumed pink called Schilcher is made.

Xynomavro, 'acid black' Greek grape variety found in Naoussa. The wine ages well.

Zinfandel, California's most planted red wine grape, whose origins were for long a mystery, although DNA testing confirms the hypothesis that it is identical to the PRIMITIVO of southern Italy. The wine can be anything from a sweetened-up pale pink wine labelled White Zinfandel (an inspired 1980s solution to California's surplus of Zinfandel and shortage of white wine grapes) to a serious oak-aged, long-lived taut, spicy, dense, lively, full-bodied red. Berry flavours predominate. The vine has a tendency to produce too many grapes, which themselves tend to ripen unevenly, so the vine needs careful management to yield good wine, but there are pockets of very old vines all over California, and particularly in the Sierra Foothills. So high is Zinfandel's profile in California that it is planted in many other warmer wine regions in the USA as well as in South America, South Africa and Australia, all of which have a warm enough climate for it to ripen fully.

Zweigelt, Zweigeltrebe, Blauer Zweigelt, Austria's most planted red wine grape, bred locally from BLAUFRÄNKISCH and ST LAURENT to combine the bite of the former with the body of the latter. It yields prolifically and has been planted in Germany and England.

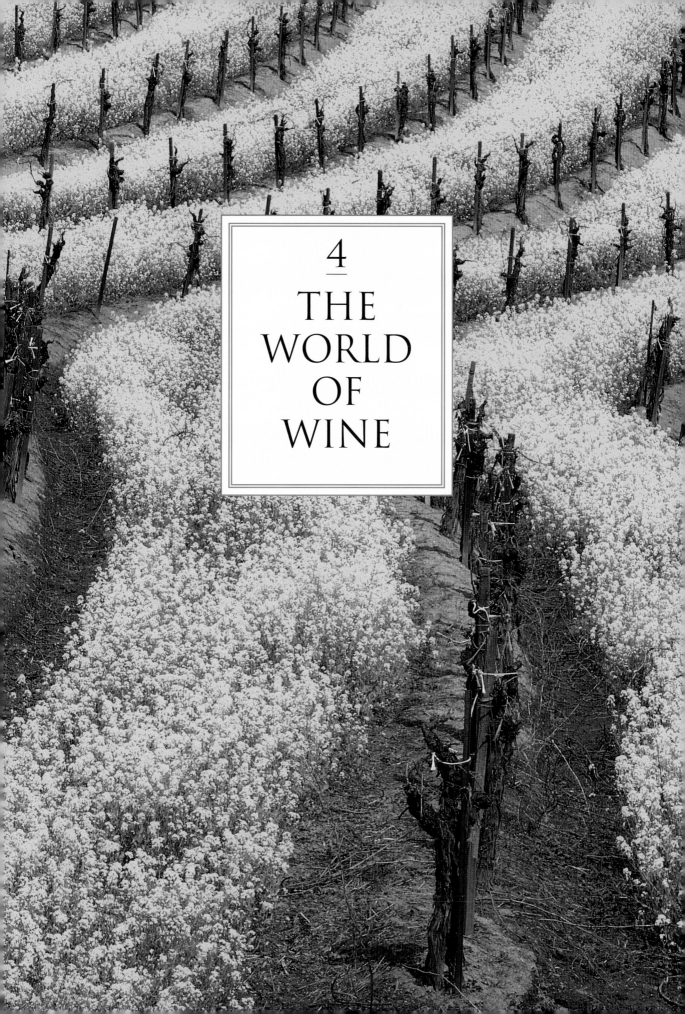

4
THE WORLD OF WINE

FRANCE

France has an extraordinary, and in many ways extremely difficult, position in the world of wine. To many of us, France *is* wine, and a certain sort of wine, not always the easiest to appreciate but often the most rewarding. France makes more wine than any other country except Italy (see page 61), which sometimes wins the race for quantity but only spottily comes near in terms of quality. France supplies the benchmarks by which almost all wines are judged. This perfectly temperate and varied climate and landscape can supply wines of virtually every style. Its finest red bordeaux sets a standard for the world's Cabernet Sauvignons. The millions and millions of Chardonnay vines planted around the globe owe their existence to white burgundy – just as their Pinot Noir equivalents depend on someone's memory of a great red burgundy. The produce of the Champagne region in the north east provides a model for every bottle of dry fizz, no matter where it is made. The Rhône valley supplies deep, rich reds while the Loire is better known for pinks and whites of all degrees of sweetness and fizziness. The vine dominates the Mediterranean hinterland in a swathe of vineyards across southern France which are capable of producing almost 10 per cent of the entire planet's wine output. Only Germany's wines ignore the French tradition – and look at German wine's current problems (see page 260). The French even produce their own answer to port (Banyuls) and sherry (*vin jaune*).

It has been difficult, however, for France to come to grips with the modern, fiercely competitive, tirelessly iconoclastic and innovative wine world. The problem is that the average French wine producer simply cannot understand any criticism of his (and most are male) wines. He is so imbued with the notion of terroir (see page 62), the belief that his wine can be produced only from his patch of land, in a way enshrined in the all-important AC regulations (see box opposite), and that he is really only a human instrument of the unique expression of that land, that he finds it difficult to understand the New World's unfettered winemakers who see man as the most important, controlling factor in wine production. Complacency has slowed winemaking improvements, but the great change in French wine producers since the last generation is that virtually all of them now have some formal training and understanding of why, as well as how, they do what they do. And virtually all of the young ones now travel to other wine-producing countries as well, which must be a good thing for us all.

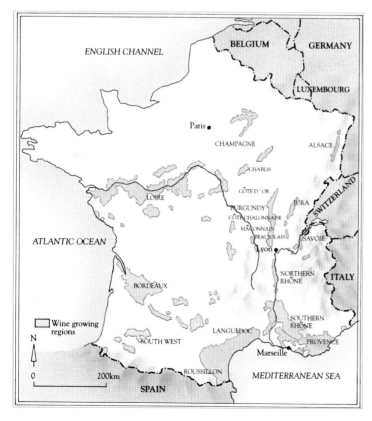

There is a broad difference in style between French wines and New World wines. The French feel that they don't need to woo the drinker with obviously fruity wines designed to be drunk as soon as they are bottled. Instead, they tend to make wines for the medium and long term, in the restrained style of their forebears, so that the average French wine will probably take more effort to appreciate than its New World counterpart but may well repay that effort and will almost certainly last longer.

The French themselves see wine as an important part of their heritage, but are drinking less and less of it. The generation that took a daily litre of rough red for granted is rapidly being replaced by one to whom quality is much more important than quantity. Total wine sales in France are not helped either by the fact that the French very rarely drink wine as an aperitif without food – although they have an unusual fondness for sweet drinks such as port, sauternes and Muscats before meals.

UNDERSTANDING LABELS

AC, Appellation Contrôlée, France's principal and much-imitated quality designation system, devised to protect producers from imitators and to guarantee authenticity to consumers. Well over a third of all French wine and all of its best wine is AC, sometimes called **AOC** or **Appellation d'Origine Contrôlée.** For each appellation strict regulations control the area included, which grape varieties may be planted, how they should be pruned, maximum yields, when the harvest may begin, minimum grape ripeness levels and/or alcoholic strength, and even how the wine should be made. Superior appellations typically fit inside other, less rigorous ones, e.g. Pauillac is an area within the Médoc which itself lies within the general Bordeaux appellation. Appellations are granted by, and their regulations administered by, the Paris-based INAO (Institut National des Appellations d'Origine).

cave, literally cellar or winery and is often used for a co-operative cellar, as in **Cave des Vignerons de...**

Château, French for 'castle' but in a wine context it means a registered wine-producing property whose only building may be a shed or even a corner of a co-operative winery. Most common in Bordeaux.

Clos, enclosing wall, often used in Burgundy for an enclosed vineyard.

Côte(s) de, prefix usually denoting a superior wine. Like **Coteaux** it literally means hillsides.

Cru, literally 'growth' or vineyard site. A **cru classé** is a Médoc or Graves property listed in the most famous wine classification of all. See pages 160–61 for more details.

Domaine, Burgundian name for the accumulated holdings of one grower. Thus a domaine-bottled wine is one bottled by the producer.

éleveur, one who looks after wine between fermentation and bottling.

Grand Cru, a widely used term but in Burgundy it means one of the finest vineyards.

Mis(e) en bouteille par/pour means 'bottled by/for'. France's best wines are almost invariably bottled at the château (*au château*) or domaine. Co-ops are allowed to claim 'mise en bouteille *du* château' for wines from specific vineyards.

négociant, wholesale wine merchant or bottler.

Premier Cru (1er Cru), another vague term but in Burgundy denotes superior vineyards just below Grand Cru status.

récoltant, literally 'harvester', grower.

Supérieur, infrequently used suffix denoting a slightly more alcoholic wine.

VDQS, relatively unusual quality designation for ACs-in-waiting (see page 48).

vigneron, vine-grower.

Villages, suffix usually denoting a superior wine.

Vin de Pays, superior Vin de Table (see pages 48 and 202–4).

Vin de Table, wine at its most basic.

viticulteur, vine-grower.

BORDEAUX

In a nutshell: *Huge quantity of mainly long-lived, medium-bodied, ultra-digestible reds (called claret by the British) with some sweet whites and extremely varied dry whites.*
Main grapes: *Merlot, Cabernet Sauvignon, Cabernet Franc* (RED), *Sémillon, Sauvignon* (WHITE)

Bordeaux is France's most important weapon in the wine war. This large, south western wine region, ruled by the English for 200 years in the Middle Ages, produces more AC wine than any other. About half of all the wine produced in the sprawling Bordeaux region qualifies for its most lowly appellation, simple AC Bordeaux, whose quality varies from vapid red wine to serious, oak-aged, château-bottled liquids made by quality-conscious individuals exasperated by how little money they can get for a wine that qualifies only for the humble generic Bordeaux appellation.

The produce of most of these appellations' finest wine estates, usually called châteaux, is not only quite exceptionally good and long lasting, but also available in much larger quantities than other top wines. It is no wonder that the world has heard of Châteaux Lafite, Mouton-Rothschild, Latour, Margaux and Haut-Brion, the famous five 'first growths', in the top division of the 1855 classification (see page 161).

In many ways Bordeaux still feels like a separate kingdom from the rest of France. Financially secure, very much directed towards the Atlantic and the outside world, the region and its agriculture are dominated by neat, carefully tended vineyards, a significant number of which belong not to locals but to insurance companies, banks or absentee landlords based in Paris, Geneva, Tokyo and elsewhere.

MÉDOC

The Médoc, a flat spur of land on the left bank of the Gironde estuary as it widens out to meet the sea, is Bordeaux's most famous wine district, and the Cabernet Sauvignon vine's homeland. It is also home to most of Bordeaux's famous large estates, most of which have built up their international reputations for the last two centuries. (To put the scale of fine wine production here into perspective, the Médoc, with its neighbour and partner the Graves district, produces almost exactly 100 times as much as all the Grands Crus of Burgundy put together.) The four most famous parishes, or com-

CHARENTE MARITIME
Gironde
CÔTES AND PREMIÈRES CÔTES DE BLAYE
MÉDOC
DORDOGNE
ST-ESTÈPHE
CÔTES DE BOURG
ATLANTIC OCEAN
PAUILLAC
ST-JULIEN
FRONSAC
CANON-FRONSAC
LALANDE DE POMEROL
HAUT-MÉDOC
Blaye
BORDEAUX
LISTRAC
ST-ÉMILION SATELLITES
MOULIS
BORDEAUX CÔTES DE FRANCS
MARGAUX
POMEROL
HAUT-MÉDOC
Libourne
CÔTES DE CASTILLON
GIRONDE
Bordeaux
ST-ÉMILION
PESSAC-LÉOGNAN
ENTRE-DEUX-MERS
GRAVES
PREMIÈRES CÔTES DE BORDEAUX
GRAVES
CADILLAC
GIRONDE Départements
CÉRONS
Wine growing regions
LOUPIAC
Langon
BARSAC
BORDEAUX
N
SAUTERNES
LANDES
STE-CROIX-DU-MONT
0   30km
LOT-ET-GARONNE

munes, of the Médoc, are, heading north from Bordeaux, **Margaux**, **St-Julien**, **Pauillac** and **St-Estèphe**.

The remnants of Château Latour's tower, which overlooks the Gironde estuary.

slightly austere respectively (see page 133 for more details). In practice, in this era of the public

In theory each of these communes produces wines of a distinctive character: silky smooth, perfectly balanced, minerals and cassis, and wine scoreboard of points and praise awarded by an international wine press, all too many producers seem to be making their wines to the same eye-catching and palate-grabbing formula, resulting in deep-coloured, full-bodied, flatteringly oaky wines. Huge quantities of new oak barrels travel up the Médoc each year.

Many are the wine-minded visitors who have navigated their way through the northern suburbs of Bordeaux to worship the world's starriest wine district, only to find an undistinguished plateau sloping imperceptibly towards the grey Gironde estuary, broken only by the odd copse or huddle of houses carrying one of the revered names. True, there are some magnificent railings with some impressively turreted nineteenth-century country houses behind them, but the region has been slow to welcome the visitor who is thirsty for wine knowledge and bottles.

All but the tiniest fraction of wine produced here is sold, via complicated layers of commissions and brokers, to the wholesale merchants who have been based in and around Bordeaux for centuries. Châteaux Prieuré-Lichine in Margaux and Pichon-Longueville in Pauillac were long exceptional in positively welcoming visitors from the D2, the little road that snakes its way up the Médoc (although the locals thought Alexis Lichine was being horribly commercial when he first erected his signs outside Margaux welcoming tourists to the Château).

This is a district with a carefully stratified society. Only a handful of owners actually live there (Anthony Barton of Châteaux Langoa- and Léoville-Barton is an exception). Most estates are run by several ranks of manager, although at last some of the most talented winemaking managers have acquired a certain status. Every now and then the owners descend to entertain wine merchants, wine writers and influential friends and the châteaux are transformed into bustling country houses, their most important rooms being the dining-room and extremely formal salon. (It took me a long time to work out why so few of these large houses seemed to have anywhere to relax in.)

For much of the twentieth century these large wine estates made very little money, but the world economy and a succession of very successful vintages in the 1980s changed all that. During the 1980s the Médoc crawled with architects and builders renovating cellars, vineyards and, often most spectacularly, the château buildings themselves.

But the most obvious stratification was drawn up, doubtless without any realization of quite how influential it was to be, in 1855. Just before Napoleon III's Universal Exhibition in Paris, the organizers asked the Bordeaux merchants to devise a quality ranking of the top wine châteaux. What emerged was a five-division list of 61 **crus classés** which had already established their reputation, together with Château Haut-Brion, the most famous property in the Graves district. Opposite is an up-to-date version, which takes account of the fact that some estates have virtually disappeared, their land having been acquired by other proprietors. Otherwise, there has been no significant change to the classification since 1855 apart from the promotion of Château Mouton-Rothschild from second to first growth in 1973. Baron Philippe de Rothschild, one of the wine world's few marketing geniuses, responsible for the branded wine Mouton Cadet and the growth of château bottling, finally nagged the authorities into it.

Very unusually for a cosmopolitan aristocrat of his period, he had devoted much of the previous four decades to his family's wine estates in the Médoc, and the wine was well worthy of first growth status. But the heavy price premium that a first growth can command over a second (even greater than a second can command over a third and so on) suggests that there is a certain element of self-perpetuation about the 1855 classification. Properties with a higher rank can afford more drainage ditches (vital for quality in this district that was a marsh before the Dutch drained it in the sixteenth century), more new barrels, and more fastidious selection than those whose status, and therefore selling prices, are lower down the scale. Estate owners would claim that their particular land is unique, but many of them would have to admit that there

BORDEAUX

The official Classification of Médoc and Graves of 1855

	Commune	Appellation		Commune	Appellation
FIRST GROWTHS (PREMIERS CRUS)					
Château Lafite-Rothschild	Pauillac	Pauillac	Château Haut-Brion [a]	Pessac	Graves
Château Margaux	Margaux	Margaux	Château Mouton-Rothschild [b]	Pauillac	Pauillac
Château Latour	Pauillac	Pauillac			
SECOND GROWTHS (DEUXIÈMES CRUS)					
Château Rauzan-Ségla*	Margaux	Margaux	Château Brane-Cantenac	Cantenac	Margaux
Château Rauzan-Gassies	Margaux	Margaux	Château Pichon-Longueville (Baron)*	Pauillac	Margaux
Château Léoville-Las-Cases*	St-Julien	St-Julien			
Château Léoville-Poyferré	St-Julien	St-Julien	Château Pichon-Longueville, Comtesse de Lalande*	Pauillac	Pauillac
Château Léoville Barton*	St-Julien	St-Julien			
Château Durfort-Vivens	Margaux	Margaux	Château Ducru-Beaucaillou*	St-Julien	St-Julien
Château Gruaud-Larose*	St-Julien	St-Julien	Château Cos d'Estournel*	St-Estèphe	St-Estèphe
Château Lascombes	Margaux	Margaux	Château Montrose	St-Estèphe	St-Estèphe
THIRD GROWTHS (TROISIÈMES CRUS)					
Château Kirwan	Cantenac	Margaux	Château Cantenac-Brown	Cantenac	Margaux
Château d'Issan	Cantenac	Margaux	Château Palmer*	Cantenac	Margaux
Château Lagrange	St-Julien	St-Julien	Château La Lagune	Ludon	Haut-Médoc
Château Langoa-Barton	St-Julien	St-Julien	Château Desmirail	Margaux	Margaux
Château Giscours	Labarde	Margaux	Château Calon-Ségur	St-Estèphe	St-Estèphe
Château Malescot St-Exupéry	Margaux	Margaux	Château Ferrière	Margaux	Margaux
Château Boyd-Cantenac	Cantenac	Margaux	Château Marquis d'Alesme Becker	Margaux	Margaux
FOURTH GROWTHS (QUATRIÈMES CRUS)					
Château St-Pierre	St-Julien	St-Julien	Château La Tour-Carnet	St-Laurent	Haut-Médoc
Château Talbot	St-Julien	St-Julien	Château Lafon-Rochet	St-Estèphe	St-Estèphe
Château Branaire-Ducru	St-Julien	St-Julien	Château Beychevelle	St-Julien	St-Julien
Château Duhart-Milon	Pauillac	Pauillac	Château Prieuré-Lichine	Cantenac	Margaux
Château Pouget	Cantenac	Margaux	Château Marquis-de-Terme	Margaux	Margaux
FIFTH GROWTHS (CINQUIÈMES CRUS)					
Château Pontet-Canet	Pauillac	Pauillac	Château du Tertre	Arsac	Margaux
Château Batailley	Pauillac	Pauillac	Château Haut-Bages-Libéral	Pauillac	Pauillac
Château Haut-Batailley	Pauillac	Pauillac	Château Pédesclaux	Pauillac	Pauillac
Château Grand-Puy-Lacoste*	Pauillac	Pauillac	Château Belgrave	St-Laurent	Haut-Médoc
Château Grand-Puy-Ducasse	Pauillac	Pauillac	Château de Camensac	St-Laurent	Haut-Médoc
Château Lynch-Bages*	Pauillac	Pauillac	Château Cos-Labory	St-Estèphe	St-Estèphe
Château Lynch-Moussas	Pauillac	Pauillac	Château Clerc-Milon	Pauillac	Pauillac
Château Dauzac	Labarde	Margaux	Château Croizet-Bages	Pauillac	Pauillac
Château d'Armailhac [c]	Pauillac	Pauillac	Château Cantemerle	Macau	Haut-Médoc

[a] This wine, although a Graves (now Pessac-Leognan), was universally recognized and classified as one of the four first growths.
[b] This wine was decreed a first growth in 1973.
[c] Previously Château Mouton-Baron-Philippe, then Château Mouton-Baronne-Philippe.
* Some of the most successful wines (other than first growths) in recent years.

has been a considerable amount of inter-château vineyard exchange since 1855.

There are also some slackers among the châteaux classified in 1855. For example, few would claim that Château Rauzan-Gassies is worthy of second growth status. On the other hand, I have asterisked some properties whose wines are usually superior to their official status.

Just below the 'classed growths', as these châteaux are called, are the so-called 'bourgeois growths' or **crus bourgeois**, making a group of about 60 further wine estates representing some of those who try harder in the Médoc. Between them the crus classés and the crus bourgeois represent about 65 per cent of all the wine produced in the Médoc (which hardly makes any white wine at all).

GRAVES AND PESSAC-LÉOGNAN

Graves is the Médoc's mirror image on the inland side of Bordeaux and the other major 'left bank' appellation. Like the Médoc, much of it is based on grav-elly soils (hence the name of this wine region, which was famous even before the Médoc). Pessac-Léognan is an appellation cre-ated in 1987 to include all of the Graves's most famous châteaux, the greatest of which are actu-ally in the southern suburbs of the city itself: Château Haut-Brion and, once a great rival and now under the same ownership, Château La Mission-Haut-Brion just across the road. As well as making firm, dry wines with the sort of minerally, 'warm bricks' overlay often found in red Graves, these properties also produce a full-

bodied, oak-aged dry white wine that needs plenty of time in bottle (called Laville-Haut-Brion in the case of La Mission's white), which is typical of the Graves region too. Other prop-erties that produce extremely good wine include Domaine de Chevalier and Châteaux Pape-Clé-ment (since 1986), Smith-Haut-Lafitte (since 1990), de Fieuzal, La Louvière, Haut-Bailly and, for white wines, Couhins-Lurton and Clos Floridène. Less glorified properties in the Graves proper, along the left bank of the river Garonne, can provide appetizing reds and some much more interest-ing dry whites (which also age well) than the Bor-deaux norm.

ST-ÉMILION

The Merlot vine reigns here on 'the right bank' (of the Gironde) as it does in the greater Bordeaux region, producing generally warmer, more obviously fruity wines than in Médoc and Graves, most of which mature between three and ten years earlier.

The medieval town of St-Émilion can supply the wine tourist with every-thing the Médoc lacks: pretty countryside round

Château Villemaurine (above) is one of St-Émilion's 70-odd Grands Cru Classés, while Château Ausone (right) is, with Château Cheval Blanc, one of its finest properties, making just 2200 cases a year.

about, cobbled streets, a ruined but cavernous church, cloisters and literally scores of wine shops dedicated, almost too rapaciously, to sell-ing wine by the bottle to visitors. St-Émilion has its own classification system, revised every decade. Only wines described as **Grand Cru Classé** on the label are seriously superior and Châteaux Ausone and Cheval Blanc share the same ranking as a Médoc first growth; the words Grand Cru alone mean little. Other ambitious

wines include Châteaux l'Angélus, l'Arrosée, Canon, La Dominique, Figeac, Tertre-Rotebœuf and newcomer Valandraud.

POMEROL

Like St-Émilion, Pomerol is a region of small wine farms, on an even smaller scale. The most famous Pomerol of all, Château Pétrus, comprises hardly 12 ha (30 acres), and there are other properties such as Châteaux Lafleur and Le Pin whose extremely limited size helps to bolster the prices of their wines. Pomerols are velvety, rich Merlot-dominant wines which can smell almost meaty and can give an enormous amount of pleasure. Bargains from this small appellation are as rare as badly made wines, but the produce of vintages that were much more successful for Merlot than Cabernet (1987 and 1998, for example) are often relatively underpriced because the Cabernet-dominated left bank tends to make the reputation of each vintage in Bordeaux (and to a certain extent in the whole of France).

SAUTERNES AND OTHER SWEET WHITE WINES

In a sense the Bordeaux region's most distinctive (and certainly its least appreciated) wines come from its south east corner in and around Sauternes, the great sweet white bordeaux appellation. Practically every wine region in the world tries to make a fair copy of great red bordeaux, but very, very few have the particular natural conditions that favour the development of noble rot/botrytis (see page 88). Sauternes is unique in being at least theoretically able to produce reasonable quantities of long-lasting, truly noble, full-bodied sweet whites.

Sauternes, including the **Barsac** appellation within it, benefits from autumnal morning mists that form where the cool Ciron flows into the warmer Garonne. Provided nature co-operates by supplying sun to burn off the mist, the botrytis fungus will concentrate fully ripe grapes and

great sweet whites can be made if, and only if, estate owners are prepared to take the risk of leaving the grapes on the vine. Many of these proprietors, particularly those discouraged by the relatively modest selling prices of most sweet wines, simply pick the grapes and add sugar so that, even after fermentation, the wine is sweet, if usually over-sulphured to stop it refermenting. The most famous sweet white wine of all, Château d'Yquem (pronounced 'Ee-kem') can live for well over a century and sells for other-worldly prices but, so demanding is the production process, it is said to be difficult to make even this fabulous property pay.

Other sweet white bordeaux appellations, in roughly descending order of the quantity of wine they produce, are **Ste-Croix-du-Mont**, **Loupiac**, **Cadillac** and **Cérons**, although the appellation **Graves Supérieures** also produces some medium sweet white.

OTHER APPELLATIONS

Perhaps the most significant development in the Bordeaux is the increasing number of seriously dedicated producers in the less glamorous appellations, **Bordeaux, Côtes de Blaye, Côtes de Bourg, Côtes de Castillon, Côtes de Francs, Fronsac** and **Canon Fronsac, Lalande de Pomerol, Premières Côtes de Blaye, Premières Côtes de Bordeaux** and the satellite appellations with St-Émilion in their name for red wines and **Bordeaux, Entre-Deux-Mers,** and **Blaye** for dry whites. Their wines usually fetch a mere fraction of the classed growth prices, but properties such as these offer Bordeaux's best current value: Châteaux de l'Aiguilhe, Belcier, Bertinerie, Bonnet, Carsin, Côte-Monpézat, l'Epéron, Fontenille, de Francs, Le Grand Verdus, Guibon, Haut Rian, Hauts Ste Marie, de Haux, Jonqueyres, du Juge, Lassime, Méaume, Monbadon, Parenchère, Puygueraud, Reynier, Reynon, Roc de Cambes, de Roquefort, de Sours, Suau, Tanesse, Thieuley, La Tour de Mirambeau, Turcaud and Domaines de Cambes, de Courteillac and de la Grave.

BURGUNDY

In a nutshell: Small, dynamic, sometimes infuri-atingly complicated region that delivers paradise in a bottle with increasing frequency.
Grapes: Pinot Noir and some Gamay (RED), Chardonnay and some Aligoté (WHITE)

Burgundy is Bourgogne in French (the source of many a misunderstanding). Although for many people Burgundy/Bourgogne is synony-mous with the heartland of this medieval king-dom, the Côte d'Or (see next page), greater Burgundy (see map on page 156) also encom-passes the Côte Chalonnaise and Mâconnais to the south and the quite distinct subregions of Beaujolais even further south (stretching almost into the suburbs of Lyons) and Chablis, the white wine district a good hour's drive north west of Beaune, Burgundy's wine capital. With its gothic gables and steep, scalloped roofs, the town of Beaune is Burgundy's most obvious tourist attraction, but most wine villages still look remarkably unchanged since the Middle Ages when the Dukes of Burgundy ran the region as a rich, self-governing state.

Unlike France's other famous wine region Bordeaux, Burgundy is still a land of peasant farmers. Today, thanks to the boom in fine wine sales in the late twentieth century, many of them are peasant farmers who eat in three-star restaurants and have a Mercedes in the garage, but their mentality is that of a smallholder.

There could hardly be a greater contrast in social climate between Burgundy and Bordeaux, France's two premier wine regions. While most famous Bordeaux wine estates are large and cen-tred on a grand château inhabited only rarely by their absentee owners, Burgundy's most famous vineyards are in the hands of the men who work them. They may have a peasant's wariness of outsiders, but to people they have come to know and trust they offer the true hand of friendship – and innumerable samplings.

Land that qualifies for one of Burgundy's better appellations is so valuable that it rarely passes out of the family but is generally part of a complex inheritance system which requires all property to be shared between each child.

Until the second half of the twentieth cen-tury Burgundy's vine-growers did just that. They would sell their grapes to the region's powerful merchants, or négociants, who could then as-semble reasonable quantities of wine under each appellation to be sold under the négociant's name. However, the late twentieth-century fashion for demonstrable authenticity changed all this. Demand for domaine-bottled burgundy carrying the stamp of one grower-winemaker-bottler means that the consumer has the choice of the following sorts of wine, all possibly made from the same small vineyard:

1 a négociant-bottled blend of produce from several different growers (récoltants/viticul-teurs/vignerons). This can vary from the cynically dire to the extremely competent as, for example, with Drouhin, Faiveley, Jadot and a host of newer, smaller enterprises.

2 a négociant-bottled wine made exclusively from the négociant's own vineyards. This is an increasingly important phenomenon. Bouchard Père et Fils and Faiveley have particularly significant vineyard holdings of their own.

3 a domaine-bottled wine made by a vine-grower who also happens to be a good wine-maker.

4 a domaine-bottled wine made by a vine-grower who isn't terribly good at making wine.

The chart shows the relative quality of each category:

	dire	average	sublime
1	————————————————————		
2		————————————————	
3			————————————
4	———————————		

CÔTE D'OR

Côte d'Or is usually translated as 'golden slope', an association all too readily made in view of the high prices charged for its wines. But in fact the name of Burgundy's glamorous heartland is an abbreviation of Côte d'Orient or 'eastern slope'. The best vineyards here lie along a narrow band of marl and limestone facing south east to maximize their exposure to the sun. Lower-lying vineyards with more clay drain less well and tend to produce less exciting wine.

The Côte d'Or is divided into the Côte de Beaune in the south, where all great white burgundy and a great deal of very fine red burgundy is made, and the smaller Côte de Nuits (named after Nuits-St-Georges) in the north, which produces Burgundy's most concentrated and longest-living reds. Over the years the villages of the Côte d'Or have tended to append the name of their most famous vineyard to the village name, so that Nuits became Nuits-St-Georges, Aloxe became Aloxe-Corton and both Puligny and Chassagne grabbed the world-famous suffix Montrachet.

There are four levels of appellation among the Côte d'Or's total of more than 60 (some producing only a few thousand bottles a year). The most basic are the **regional** ACs, the most common of which are Bourgogne (often supplementarily labelled Pinot Noir or Chardonnay in a nod to New World practice); Bourgogne Aligoté, a leaner dry white made from Burgundy's second white grape; and its red counterpart Bourgogne Passe-tout-grains in which Pinot's purity is customarily smudged by blending with the Gamay grape of Beaujolais. Wines that are labelled AC Bourgogne can come from less exalted vineyards all over greater Burgundy and should be an easy, approachable expression of Burgundian Pinot Noir and Chardonnay. Too often, however, they are made in the same way as much grander wines (whose concentration can stand long skin contact in the case of reds and high sulphur additions in the case of whites) and their message is the opposite of come-hither.

A distinct notch above these wines are **village** wines (such as those labelled simply Volnay or Meursault), carrying as their appellation the name of

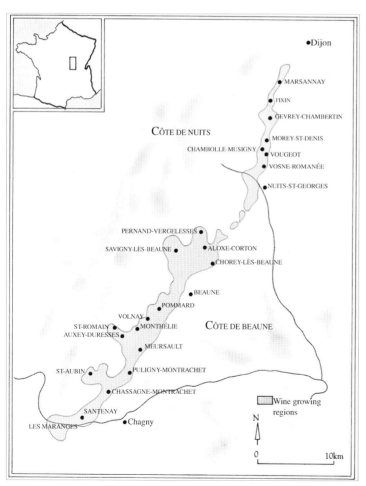

At harvest time the Côte d'Or villages such as Puligny-Montrachet throb with the sound of vineyard tractors.

the commune in which they were made (see map on page 166). They can provide some of Burgundy's most delicious drinking for the first three or four years after a soft vintage but should not usually be kept for much longer than this.

Each village's sites with the potential to make distinctly superior wine (almost invariably those with particularly favourable exposure and good drainage) were classified as **premiers crus** in the last century (Burgundy's answer to the Bordeaux 1855 classification) so that wines made from them inevitably carry a price premium which is sometimes, but not invariably, justified.

The 30 best of these are acknowledged **grands crus** and, in the right hands, make quite sumptuously concentrated wines which can benefit from many years' ageing in bottle. The reds can exhibit Pinot Noir's extraordinary range of textures as well as flavours, while the whites are the most savoury, full-bodied dry whites in the world – a world away from the simplistic appeal of a mass market, varietally labelled Chardonnay. But a high proportion of the wines are disappointments, either because of the weather or poor winemaking.

Most appellations include both red and white wines, even if one colour almost invariably predominates. Red Puligny-Montrachet and white Vougeot, for example, do exist.

There are literally thousands of vine-growers on the Côte d'Or, most of whom nowadays sell some wine of their own, even if they hedge their bets by selling off the rest to the négociants. The average grower owns only 5 ha (12.5 acres), but in nine different appellations (which may be only a few hundred yards apart). Each tiny cellar (usually notably low-tech) harbours scores of different combinations of appellation and vintage, each in minuscule quantity. It is particularly difficult therefore in the Côte d'Or to give comprehensive buying advice. Thanks to deaths and marriages, the precise holdings of each vine-grower can seem to be in a state of continual evolution. In the space available all I can offer is as many as possible of the names whose wines have impressed me over the last few years, but please note that intermarrying is rife in a rural community such as this and many similar but not identical names will be found on bottles from quite distinct domaines. Nothing in Burgundy is simple, and some producers have been known to put slightly different producer names on the same wine for tax reasons.

Some favourite growers:
Reds
Domaine de l'Arlot, Comte Armand, Denis Bachelet, Jean-Marc Boillot, Robert Chevillon, Bruno Clair, Géantet-Pansiot, various Gros, Henri Jayer, Jayer-Gilles, Hubert Lignier, Domaine Leroy, Méo-Camuzet, Ponsot, Domaine de la Romanée-Conti (DRC), Armand Rousseau, Emmanuel Rouget, Tollot-Beaut.

Whites
Jean-Marc Boillot, Louis Carillon, Coche-Dury, Jean-Noël Gagnard, François Jobard, Comtes Lafon, Domaine Leflaive, Bernard Morey, Michel Niellon, Domaine Ramonet.

Some of the most quality-conscious négociants:
Bouchard Père et Fils, Drouhin, Faiveley, Jadot, Dominique Laurent, Olivier Leflaive, Nicolas Potel, Remoissenet, Verget (whites).

Some appellations generally offering better value than most:
Beaune (has no grands crus but some very good wines), Chorey-lès-Beaune, Monthélie, Pernand-Vergelesses, St-Aubin (especially for whites), St-Romain (whites), Santenay and Savigny-lès-Beaune.

Appellations to be wary of:
Wines carrying these particularly well-known names can be absolutely marvellous but bottlers who care more about money than quality often bottle some of Burgundy's worst bargains under them: Meursault, Montrachet, Pommard, Puligny-Montrachet and (Clos) Vougeot. Beware of suspiciously cheap bottles labelled thus from completely unknown producers.

CHABLIS

Burgundy's white wine outpost is one of France's most northern and it is hardly surprising therefore that these all-Chardonnay wines are naturally relatively sinewy, high in acidity and steely rather than luscious. Rather out of fashion, in fact, and a long way from the obvious, richly alcoholic and oaky style of Chardonnay that in the 1980s became so popular with both consumers and wine producers elsewhere. But this is an archetypally refreshing, long-lived style of white wine which very few wine regions, possibly none other than Chablis, can produce.

We Chablis enthusiasts treasure the purity of flavour, the modest dimensions and the rapier-like effect on the palate of the region's better examples, and cannot understand how the word Chablis ever came to be used, particularly in the United States, for sweetened up blends of the most basic white.

For the consumer, Chablis prices are annoyingly inconsistent. This is partly because Chablis is so well known that it tends to be traded as a commodity and is therefore all too subject to pressures quite unrelated to the wine itself. It is also because the volume of Chablis produced can vary considerably from year to year thanks to spring frosts which annually threaten to freeze off a sizeable proportion of the year's crop. Being so far from the equator, and growing almost exclusively the early-budding Chardonnay vine, Chablis has become famous for its anti-frost measures. Small stoves in the vineyard have largely given way to sprinklers that surround the vines with a protective coating of ice.

Chablis comes in four very distinct quality levels. **Petit Chablis** is the principal, often vapid product of the plantings on the outskirts of Chablis proper, undertaken when the Chablis growers found that they were unable to keep up with international demand. Most of the wine produced around the pretty little village of Chablis qualifies for the straightforward Chablis appellation, which can vary considerably in quality (beware of Chablis bottled outside the region) but should usually be drunk young. The region's particularly well-sited vineyards, comprising about a quarter of total Chablis production, are designated **Chablis Premier Cru** and represent some of the district's most reliable buys. The very best vineyards are on the west-facing hill immediately above the village and qualify as **Chablis Grand Cru**. These are the vineyards, particularly Les Clos, that have made Chablis's reputation as offering a remarkable combination of refreshment and longevity. Other Grands Crus include Blanchots, Bougros, Grenouille, Preuses, Valmur and Vaudésir. Some of the best-known Premiers Crus are Fourchaume, Mont de Milieu, Montmains, Vaillons, and Montée de Tonnerre, which in some particularly successful vintages can develop as appetizingly as a Grand Cru Chablis.

Grand Cru and some of the best Premier Cru Chablis can improve in bottle for more than a decade. Indeed its extra acid can make top-quality Chablis a better candidate for ageing than many Côte d'Or whites. But such wines can sometimes smell almost dirty in youth, or if not dirty then at least reminiscent of wet wool or dogs. Wet stones is what I like to smell from young Chablis.

There has been, perhaps inevitably, a trend towards trying to make Chablis in a more luscious, obviously oaky style. This seems a shame to me, but may well be a sign that I and not the Chablis producers am beginning to lose my hold on reality.

Some particularly impressive producers:
La Chablisienne co-operative's top bottlings, Dauvissat, Defaix, Droin, Laroche, Louis Michel, René et Vincent Raveneau.

CÔTE CHALONNAISE

To the immediate south of the grand white wine vineyards of the Côte de Beaune lies the Côte Chalonnaise, named after the town of Châlon-sur-Saône (where in ancient Gaul wine shipped upriver from the south would be offloaded for overland transport northwards). Whereas vines are by far the principal crop of the Côte d'Or, this gentle landscape is much more variably agricultural with the odd vineyard punctuating rolling meadows. The wines, made from Chardonnay or Pinot Noir except for the famous Aligoté of Bouzeron, really do taste like country cousins of those from the Côte d'Or, but their early drinkability makes them extremely useful.

During the 1980s winemaking in the Côte Chalonnaise showed such a high level of consistency that in many cases it made up for the district's lack of top-quality sites and its wines offered the best value in greater Burgundy. Inevitably, however, the market is fast correcting itself and the price of wines from Côte Chalonnaise's four appellations are about the same as those from the Côte d'Or's less well-known villages.

Givry (which is nothing to do with Gevrey-Chambertin, one of the great villages of the Côte d'Or) produces mainly red wine and is an exremely reliable appellation. The grower Joblot makes wines with far more sophistication than is usual and Domaine Thénard is based here.

Mercurey, also predominantly devoted to Pinot Noir, is the district's most important appellation by far. There are several premiers crus vineyards which are capable of making wines with lovely supple fruit. Although the négociant Faiveley is based well to the north in Nuits-St-Georges, its La Framboisière bottling is a reliable reflection of each vintage. Michel Juillot is one of the district's stars.

Montagny, dedicated to Chardonnay, is a name brought to thousands by négociant Louis Latour's long-standing purchasing arrangement with the Buxy co-operative here, one of the most dedicated and innovative in France. The co-op also makes pretty good sparkling wine in the form of Crémant de Bourgogne.

Rully (easy to confuse with Reuilly near Sancerre) is fairly evenly balanced between growing Pinot Noir and Chardonnay. The large merchant André Delorme's Domaine de la Renarde is one of the more prominent labels, as is Antonin Rodet's Château de Rully. Eric de Suremain of Monthélie's also brings some Côte d'Or class to the appellation.

Typical countryside in southern Burgundy where vines alternate with arable farming and other crops.

MÂCONNAIS AND BEAUJOLAIS

The Mâconnais takes its name from the city of Mâcon and constitutes an intermittent sprawl of vineyards south from the Côte Chalonnaise to the northern limit of Beaujolais. In very broad brushstrokes, its whites, typically sold as **Mâcon Blanc** and all made from Chardonnay grapes which can be attractively round and melon-flavoured, tend to be a much better bet than red wines sold as Mâcon, which are often rather coarse ferments of Gamay grapes (since reds made here from Pinot Noir grapes fetch a higher price if sold as AC Bourgogne). **Mâcon-Supérieur**, **Mâcon-Villages** and Mâcon with the name of a village appended are usually a cut above straight Mâcon Blanc and, from winemakers who are as gifted as André Bonhomme, Olivier Merlin and Jean Thévenet, can be just as thrilling as all but the best whites of the Côte d'Or – at a fraction of the price.

Mâcon-Chardonnay, **Mâcon-Lugny** and **Viré-Clessé** are all superior white wines named after their village of origin (Chardonnay is the name of a village in the Mâconnais as well as of the world's most famous grape variety). Lugny has a particularly good co-operative, but the district is a hotbed of ambitious winemaking including some botrytized sweet white. They really do have to try harder here in the south.

The top-quality Mâconnais white wine vineyards are concentrated in the far south east of the district, right up against the northern frontier of Beaujolais. The most notable appellation of all is **Pouilly-Fuissé** which, despite its mouthful of a name, has become so popular that it frequently sells for more than some humbler Côte d'Or appellations, often without justification. Some of the wine, such as that made by Domaine Corsin, Ferret, Château Fuissé and Guffens-Heynen, is extremely good, substantial, sometimes slightly honeyed stuff, but Pouilly-Fuissé is too fashionable a name to offer consistency. **Pouilly-Loché** and **Pouilly-Vinzelles** can also offer some of Pouilly-Fuissé's extra body and are almost indistinguishable from **St-Véran** and the best examples of **Beaujolais Blanc**, a speciality of the north of the Beaujolais district.

Proper, red Beaujolais can be a quite delicious drink – quite unrelated to red burgundy made further north. The only indisputably successful wine made exclusively from Gamay grapes, it is usually light bodied with lots of youthful fruit and relatively high acidity, although more and more ambitious producers are making a denser, more Rhône-like wine. Most Beaujolais should on no account be kept and is good when served lightly chilled. Unfortunately, it is too often souped up and blurred by heavy-handed chaptalization (see page 72), or hurried through its fermentation and brutally stabilized to yield a **Beaujolais Nouveau** or **Beaujolais Primeur**. Most Beaujolais is made by carbonic maceration (see page 78). **Beaujolais-Villages** is usually noticeably better than straight Beaujolais, being made from vineyards closer to the gently rolling, heart-breakingly pretty, granitic hills that form the core of the district.

From these hills comes the Beaujolais élite, wines made to lower yields from one of the **Beaujolais crus**, which manage to combine Beaujolais's appetizing character with greater concentration of fruit and some life expectancy (I have tasted a lively one at 40 years old). These wines are confusing because they rarely carry the B-word on the label. They are **Brouilly**, **Chénas**, **Chiroubles**, **Côte de Brouilly**, **Fleurie**, **Juliénas**, **Moulin-à-Vent**, **Morgon**, **Regnié** and **St-Amour**.

The king of Beaujolais, bottling a wide range of reds and whites, some of them from individual estates, is Georges Dubœuf. Other good smaller enterprises include Jean-Marc Aujoux, Aviron-Potel, Jean-Marc Burgaud, Château des Jacques, Laurent Daumas, Château de Pizay, Clos de la Roilette, Michel Tête, Château Thivin and Domaine du Vissoux.

CHAMPAGNE

Little by little the rest of the world is coming round to the French point of view, that champagne is not just any old fizzy wine, but a place – and a very special place at that. The Champagne region, an hour's drive east of Paris, is one of France's most comfortably confident, devoted to producing one particular luxury product. The Champenois – the inhabitants of Rheims, Épernay and the villages which dot the rolling countryside that looks like, and once was, a continuation of the English South Downs – know that only they can, and sometimes do, produce the world's pre-eminent sparkling wine. It is the combination of being as far north as vines can be grown commercially in France; a high proportion of chalky soils which encourage the roots to burrow as far as a regular but by no means generous supply of water; no shortage of cool, dark, humid cellars; and a head start in the public relations game of establishing champagne as *the* wine of celebration and glamour that makes Champagne unique. This uniqueness has fuelled the Champenois' energetic vendetta against those who use their precious C-word to describe products other than their own. American producers may still call any wine that fizzes 'champagne', but most of the rest of the wine-producing world has been brought to heel by the Champagne lawyers.

VINES AND VINEYARDS

Unexpectedly for a wine that is quintessentially light and white, champagne is made from predominantly black grapes. Less than 30 per cent of Champagne's growing area of neat, low rows of densely planted vines are light-skinned Chardonnay, the white burgundy grape. The red burgundy grape Pinot Noir is planted on about a third of Champagne's infertile vineyard soils, but the most common champagne grape is Pinot Meunier, a fruitier, earlier-maturing rela-

tive of Pinot Noir. Only Pinot Meunier will ripen reliably throughout the region, which is why it is by far the most commonly planted variety in the cooler vineyards of the Marne valley and the outlying Aisne vineyards to the north. Pinot Noir and Chardonnay need particularly well-favoured sites and in general the Chardonnay vine thrives best on the south- and east-facing chalky slopes of the Côte des Blancs south of Épernay, while Pinot Noir grows mainly on the lower slopes of the wooded Montagne de Reims between Rheims and Épernay, as well as being a speciality of the slightly warmer Aube vineyards in the far south of Champagne.

All of the 300 Champagne villages are graded for their grape-growing potential between 80 and 100 per cent, with those 17 earning 100 per cent qualifying as Grands Crus. Of these, Ay, Bouzy and Sillery are some of the best known for black grapes and Avize, Cramant and Le Mesnil for Chardonnay.

White wine can be made from dark-skinned grapes only if they are pressed very gently indeed, and the best juice is generally that which flows first from Champagne's super-delicate wine presses. There are strict limits on how much juice can be squeezed out of a given weight of grapes, but the cheapest champagnes are usually made from the hardest pressed grapes so that they can taste astringent (and, especially when made from grapes grown in the more marginal areas and given a minimum of bottle age, horribly acid).

GROWERS V. HOUSES

Although most non-French champagne drinkers associate champagne with a handful of what are essentially brand names – Bollinger, various Heidsiecks, Moët & Chandon, Mumm, Perrier Jouët, Pol Roger, Veuve Clicquot and so on – in fact 90 per cent of all the raw material for champagne, the grapes themselves, is grown by 15 000 smallholders, whose average vineyard is just 2 ha or 5 acres. Grape prices are higher in Champagne than anywhere else in the world, with a kilo selling in some vintages for more than a greengrocer might charge for hothouse grapes.

This far from the equator, spring frosts and poor weather at flowering threaten each year's crop, with no regard for the state of the champagne market. The fact that Champagne's total harvest can be sufficient to fill nearly 300 million bottles, or may be less than a third of this, adds considerable spice to the relationship between the vine-growers and the wine producers, the houses or 'maisons' of Champagne, including all the well-known names.

Although most growers sell their fruit directly either to a co-operative or to one of the big houses, some of them do produce their own champagne, which is particularly popular on the French market. It varies enormously in quality, some demonstrating cottage industry at its very worst, others representing fine examples of their particular local conditions.

The big houses argue that only by using a wide variety of different base wines, often bought in from all over the region, can a good champagne be produced year in and year out,

DIFFERENT STYLES OF CHAMPAGNE

Non-vintage: The basic emissary of every champagne producer, representing more than 80 per cent of the region's output, based substantially on a single vintage, typically about three years old. Wildly variable in quality.

Vintage: A more expensive blend made exclusively from grapes grown in one specified year, typically released at about six years old but usually reliably superior and capable of ageing for more than a decade.

Prestige, de luxe, or luxury cuvée: The top of the range, often packaged in a fancy bottle, usually vintage dated, almost always exorbitantly priced. The best, such as Bollinger Tradition, Dom Pérignon, Krug and Roederer Cristal, are almost worth it.

Blanc de Blancs: Made exclusively from Chardonnay grapes; good examples can age very well.

Rosé: Variable in both colour and quality and usually made by blending still red and still white wines before the fermentation in bottle. Often fruitier and slightly sweeter than average.

Demi-sec or Rich: Champagnes sweeter than the normal Brut or (slightly less dry) Sec.

and it is certainly true that grower champagnes tend to vary far more from year to year than those of the houses, whose function is to maintain a house style whatever the individual year's conditions. See page 30 for some suggested specific producers.

As well as the famous houses, some extremely successful champagne producers specialize in making 'buyer's own brand', or BOB, champagnes to the individual specifications (and price) of, for example, a supermarket or a hotel chain.

THE ART OF BLENDING

Champagne is quite unlike any other fine wine, apart from sherry and port, in that its existence depends on blending. This is mainly because this far from the equator, the character of each vintage can vary so much, from the lean, hardly ripe grapes of years such as 2001 to years such as 1989, in which hot weather produced particularly ripe base wines unsuitably low in acid.

With the exceptions of Blanc de Blancs and Blanc de Noirs, all champagnes are more or less judicious blends of all three grape varieties, in which Meunier gives youthful exuberance, Pinot Noir gives body, and Chardonnay gives a backbone. Growers' champagnes may not embody geographical blending, but the houses' champagnes (about three in

every four bottles) are made from blends, or **cuvées**, painstakingly assembled from scores and sometimes hundreds of different vineyards. (One or two single vineyard champagnes such as Krug's Clos de Mesnil are aberrant exceptions to the Champenois' dedication to blending.)

This process of blending the base wines into a well-balanced cuvée that will be bottled and encouraged to re-ferment, producing carbon dioxide (see sparkling winemaking on pages

One of the bleakest jobs in the world of wine is pruning during Champagne's harsh winter months. The dead cuttings are traditionally burnt in mobile bonfires.

Veuve Clicquot was such a successful champagne saleswoman that she was able to build a grand, new Château de Boursault for her family in the mid-nineteenth century.

84–6), takes place every winter after the harvest. The tasters' most important job is to assemble the all-important non-vintage blend which must represent the house style and replicate as closely as possible its predecessors (although over the years houses sometimes allow their style to evolve with fashion or availability of grapes). To even out the differences in both quality and quantity between the years, the young wine is typically rounded out with up

175

to 20 per cent of 'reserve wines', still wines kept in store from previous vintages.

There is a school of thought in Champagne that **vintage** champagne (champagne carrying a vintage year and made exclusively from grapes grown in that year) is rather poor form, an ambitious style that tends to cream off the best grapes and diminish the quality of the non-vintage, 'proper' champagne. And the proliferation of luxury, prestige, or de luxe cuvées since Moët's hugely successful Dom Pérignon was launched in 1937, has tended to cream off the finest produce of the top rated villages in the best years.

By spring, all of these blends have been assembled and bottled, along with some yeast and sugar, and stacked horizontally by the thousand in the famous cellars of Champagne.

THE CHARACTER OF CHAMPAGNE

Anyone who has tasted the relatively rare still wines of the Champagne region, sold under the name Coteaux Champenois, will understand the extent to which the champagne-making process can transform the thin, acid, lightweight wines which the region's vineyards produce into noble, creamy, deep-flavoured essences of sophistication. Like base wines for distillation into cognac, the best sorts of base wine for sparkling wine are those that are high in acidity and relatively neutral. Champagne may get its defining bubbles as a by-product of a second fermentation in sealed bottles, and its useful extra degree or two of alcohol as a direct result of the same process, but it, possibly more than any other sparkling wine, owes its nuances of flavour, its savoury definition, to the time the bottles spend simply lying quietly in the dank cellars of Champagne, many of them ancient limestone quarries known as *crayères* (from the same root as 'crayon'). The longer the wine remains in contact with the unappetizing-looking sediment of dead yeast lees which gathers on the under-belly of the bottle, the more character will be

imparted to the final wine, and the fuller and richer it tastes. Research shows that this process has a perceptible effect on the wine after about 18 months' contact, and then an even greater one after about five years. It is a shame therefore that the current legal minimum for ageing non-vintage and vintage champagne on the lees is 12 months and three years respectively, so that the cheapest champagne will hardly have benefited from any flavour development as a result of lees contact. Serious champagne producers, however, allow their non-vintage blends at least two years on lees, and vintage champagnes are generally released after at least six years.

In terms of rounding out champagne's leaner characteristics, bottle ageing is a great substitute for some of the sugar traditionally added just before final bottling (see page 85), called the 'dosage', although champagne's naturally high acidity can bear a great deal of added sugar before any real sweetness can be tasted.

HOW TO DECIPHER A CHAMPAGNE LABEL

1 Look for vintage year. If there is none, the champagne is a non-vintage blend.
2 'Blanc de Blancs' or 'Chardonnay' on the label indicates that only Chardonnay and no black grapes have been used and the wine may be slightly austere. ('Blanc de Noirs' means that only black grapes have been used and the wine may be quite full-bodied.)
3 Look at the two-letter code which accompanies the code number of the producer:
NM négociant-manipulant, one of the big houses/maisons/négociants (see page 30).
RM récoltant-manipulant, a grower who makes his own wine (see page 30).
CM co-opérative de manipulation, one of the co-operatives.
RC récoltant-co-opérateur, grower selling wine made by a co-op.
MA marque d'acheteur, buyer's own brand, usually a made-up label.

Alsace

In a nutshell: Terribly useful, often overlooked, soft, smokey, varietal whites.

Grapes: Riesling, Gewürztraminer, Pinot Blanc, Pinot Gris, Sylvaner, Muscat

Alsace is one of the great, underappreciated treasures of the wine world. This pretty enclave of fairy-tale villages in the lee of the forested Vosges mountains offers a wide range of varietally labelled wines, of which the aromatic whites are much more successful than the light reds. For much of its history Alsace was Elsass and part of Germany. The local surnames and tall green tapered bottles reflect this, along with the dominance of Riesling and the fragrant nature of many of the wines. But unlike in Germany, winemaking philosophy in Alsace is to ferment all of the grape sugar into alcohol, resulting in dry, full-bodied wines (quite different in structure from Germany's lighter, sweeter counterparts). Both deliberately avoid new wood and the second, softening, malolactic fermentation, however, preferring to preserve the direct, fruity aromas of each grape variety.

Alsace is unusual within France in that it has just two appellations, one simply **Alsace** for any wine produced within the region and the other **Alsace Grand Cru** (see page 179), both of which may be followed by the name of a grape variety. The following are the most important wine names, the first four of them being designated 'noble' grape varieties.

Riesling is the most respected grape variety in Alsace, and quite rightly. Alsace Riesling is steely, sometimes tough in youth, and perhaps a little austere for newcomers. It handsomely repays ageing in bottle, however, for up to 10 years in the case of top bottlings such as Trimbach's Clos Ste Hune (although most examples are fine after three or four years). Like all but the very richest Alsace wines (VT and SGN), these wines can make great aperitifs. The late-ripening Riesling vine has to be planted in one of Alsace's most favoured sites, typically in a well-exposed situation in the hillier southern half of the region.

Gewürztraminer – often spelt Gewurztraminer here in France – is the easiest Alsace wine for beginners to enjoy. In fact for many of us, 'Gewürz' (probably the most frequently misspelt wine name of all) is one of the first wine tastes we ever latch on to. It is full-bodied, almost fat, and tastes pleasantly off dry and generally stuns the taste buds into admiring submission – although in very hot years it can topple over into oily flab. The most lightweight, cheapest examples smell gently flowery (often very similar to Muscat) but a really rich, concentrated version can smell of bacon fat, on top of the vaguely lychee-like smell of any Gewürztraminer. This is the white wine to drink with 'red wine food' or, many argue, spicy food.

Pinot Gris, known as Tokay d'Alsace until the Hungarians started to make a fuss about confusion with their sweet white Tokay, can make wonderfully full-bodied-yet-dry wines that go quite happily with such strongly flavoured dishes as venison. These wines are not particularly aromatic, but they taste delightfully smokey and exotic. Pinot Gris makes particularly good late picked (VT) wines (see page 179).

Muscat, or Muscat d'Alsace, is one of the region's most distinctive styles. Usually a blend of Muscat Ottonel and Muscat Blanc à Petits Grains, this unusual wine is delicate, dry, yet smells often overpoweringly grapey and therefore almost sweet. It is not made in huge quantities, and rarely ages particularly well, but can make a delightful aperitif.

Pinot Blanc is Alsace's bread-and-butter variety, and very useful too. Known sometimes as Klevner, the wine is broad and smokey with the distinctive perfume of any Alsace white, but with less definition than a Riesling and much

less body than a Gewürz-
traminer or Pinot Gris. A
similar but distinct variety
called Auxerrois is often
blended with it to be sold
as Pinot Blanc. A Pinot
Blanc from a good pro-
ducer is one of the wine world's bargains.

Sylvaner is much more difficult to appreciate. It can taste quite lean and needs a good site
to ripen fully, even though it does not fetch
particularly high prices, which is why its fortunes are declining in Alsace. Nevertheless, a
Sylvaner from a producer particularly good at

*Riquewihr (seen here from the Grand Cru
Schoenenberg vineyard) is not only
Alsace's picture postcard village, it also
houses the important firms of Hugel,
Dopff au Moulin and Dopff & Irion.*

producing steely Rieslings
(such as Trimbach) can
taste really quite distinguished.

Edelzwicker means
'noble mixture' but is in
fact a blend of any old
varieties, in practice usually the lowly Chasselas
variety, Sylvaner and Pinot Blanc. This easy,
soft blend is also sometimes sold as Gentil.

Pinot Noir is Alsace's contribution to the
world of red wine, except that in all but the
hottest years it is some shade of pink and tastes
very lightweight too. A growing number of pro-

map), is the region's eaux-de-vie, potent colourless spirits distilled from the fruits that grow there. These can smell like essence of raspberry (Framboise) or pear (Poire Williams) and probably need never actually be sipped.

Favourite producers include Beyer, Hugel and Trimbach among the bigger merchants (who buy in substantial quantities of grapes) and Blanck, Marcel Deiss, Kientzler, Kreydenweiss, Muré, Ostertag, Rolly Gassmann, Schlumberger, Schoffitt, the Fallers at Domaine Weinbach and Zind-Humbrecht.

ALSACE LABEL LANGUAGE

(These terms may be applied to wines only from one of the four noble varieties.)

Grand Cru – one of more than 50 individual vineyards granted superior status, amid some controversy, relatively recently. The words Grand Cru are no guarantee of quality as some producers have seen Grand Cru simply as an excuse to charge more rather than an opportunity to make seriously fine wine – although admittedly the maximum permitted yields are lower than the Alsace norm. Many of Alsace's best wines are Grands Crus, however.

Vendange Tardive (VT) – translates directly as Late Harvest, which is indeed what these wines are. Certain minimum ripeness levels have to be met (the best producers generously exceed them) and the grapes may be picked only when official authorization is given. The trouble with Vendange Tardive wines is that they can vary from almost dry (but quite concentrated) to really quite sweet, yet no hint of sweetness level is given on labels. The best of these wines can be aged for many years.

Sélection des Grains Nobles (SGN) signifies a wine made from even riper grapes, often at least partly concentrated by the botrytis fungus (see page 88). These relative rarities are easiest to make in the region's sunniest years, from the obliging Gewürztraminer grape. Their sweetness level can also vary quite considerably, although individual producers will generally ensure that their SGNs are definitely sweeter than their VTs.

ducers make more full-bodied Pinot Noir but most are consoled by the fact that the hordes of German tourists seem quite happy to buy even the palest French 'red' wine.

Crémant d'Alsace is the region's dry sparkling white wine, made like champagne. It can be very refreshing and can age for a few years, but is more notable for its youthful crispness than for great substance.

One of Alsace's great attractions for the gastronomically inclined, other than the wines and the enormous number of Michelin-starred restaurants (so great that Alsace warrants its own specially enlarged box on the Michelin star

LOIRE

In a nutshell: France's most varied, and neglected, wine region. Most wines noticeably crisp.

Grapes (going downriver): Sauvignon Blanc, Cabernet Franc, Gamay, Chenin Blanc, Melon de Bourgogne

Outside northern France, the wines of the Loire, with the exception of Sancerre and Pouilly-Fumé, have been consistently overlooked by modern wine enthusiasts, perhaps because at this northerly limit of commercially viable viticulture the grapes have to struggle to ripen, so the wines' unfashionable hallmark is relatively high acidity. Because long, hot summers are the exception, relatively few of the reds conform to the current expectation of high density, alcohol, tannin and obvious oak ageing, and most of the whites here are also made to the old-fashioned recipe of trapping the fruit in the bottle as early as possible, without exposing them to new wood. It may perhaps seem strange that the wine regions with easiest access to the

best oak in France (the forests of the Nevers, Allier and Tronçais are all in the upper Loire) are not great users of it, but grapes have to be really quite ripe before their fermented juice can take the weight of an oak barrel (see pages 91–3).

Another factor may be the relative complication of wine names and identities here. The same name, Saumur or Anjou for example, may be applied to a range of wines that includes all three colours and a confusing range of grape variety possibilities and sweetness levels.

France's longest, laziest river joins not only some of the most beautiful châteaux and what was once the playground of the French court and is now that of well-heeled Parisians, but also scores of wine districts which can, very roughly, be divided into three zones: the Sauvignon-dominated vineyards of the Upper Loire; the Muscadet region at the mouth of the river (more than 300 miles downstream from Pouilly-sur-Loire and Sancerre); and the vast and varied vineyards in between which produce some great

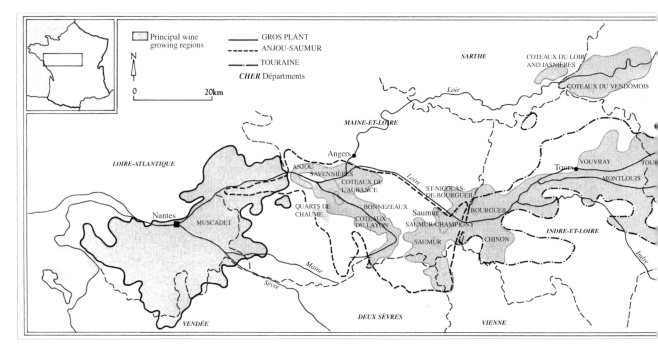

sweet and some useful sparkling white wines as well as a host of still reds, whites and rosés from a host of grape varieties of which Chenin Blanc, Cabernet Franc, Gamay and Sauvignon Blanc are the most important.

UPPER LOIRE

Sancerre and **Pouilly-Fumé** (sometimes called Blanc Fumé de Pouilly) are the Upper Loire's, indeed the Loire's, most famous ambassadors. The two wine districts are separated only by the river, and the hilltop town of Sancerre is just 10 miles north west of the decidedly unspectacular town of Pouilly-sur-Loire. Both of these much-exported wines are made exclusively from Sauvignon Blanc grapes into lean, green, sappy, aromatic palate-sharpeners. Such has been demand for them in the world's restaurants that most of the wines made under either appellation are remarkably similar.

Neatly hedged rows of Sauvignon vines traverse the gentle slopes above the river, vineyards being interspersed with cereal crops and sunflowers, for this is an area of mixed farming. Mechanical harvesting has been the norm for some time and the combination of a damp climate and generous yields can result in almost aggressively aromatic, light bodied, relatively tart wines, reeking of nettles and cats' pee.

Only at the highest quality level is the particular nature of the various terrains in the appellations apparent. Serious restaurants in Sancerre, for example, list their local wines under the names of the appellation's best-favoured communes such as Bué, Ménétréol and Chavignol, where some of France's best *crottins*, or miniature drums of goat's cheese are made.

The region's *enfant terrible* is Didier Dageneau, a gifted and energetic producer of Pouilly-Fumé based in a modest cottage in St-Andelain just north of its grandest building, the Château du Nozet, home farm of the Upper Loire's best-known wine producer, Baron de Ladoucette. Dageneau believes passionately in reducing average yields, in restoring soil texture and quality through an extreme form of organic viticulture, 'biodynamism' (see page 65). He has been in the vanguard of a move towards making local wines concentrated enough to benefit from fermentation and ageing in new oak.

However similar the wines may be, locals argue that the inhabitants of Pouilly and Sancerre are creatures from two different planets, or at least from two different French regions, which amounts to much the same thing: greater Burgundy and Berry respectively. In wine terms the two districts differ because Sancerre produces some light red and rosé appellation contrôlée wine from Pinot Noir grapes, while Pouilly-sur-Loire is the name of a distinctly inferior VDQS wine made from Chasselas, which is a white table grape. Other superior producers include Henri Bourgeois, Lucien Crochet, Gitton, Joseph Mellot, Henry Pellé and Vacheron.

Reuilly, Quincy and **Menetou-Salon** are wine districts to the west of Sancerre producing wines of a very similar style to Sancerre and Pouilly-Fumé but sometimes with more appealing craftsmanship. Their names are so much less well known that the wines have to find a market purely on the basis of their inherent

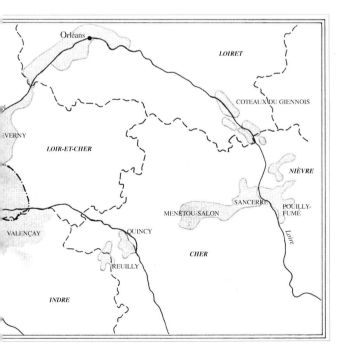

quality. Claude Lafond, Jean-Michel Sorbe and Pierre Clement make reliably good wines.

MIDDLE LOIRE

Wine geography is at its most complicated along the central, westbound stretch of the Loire. Travelling upriver from the Muscadet region, the wine enthusiast is first bamboozled by **Anjou**, the name of the region around the city of Angers, and associated with the often grimly commercial Rosé d'Anjou; the extraordinarily long-lived fine pink Cabernet d'Anjou; the distinctly variable, medium dry, Chenin Blanc-dominated Anjou Blanc; crisp, light reds under the names Anjou Rouge and Anjou-Gamay; and, finest of all when the region is blessed with a hot summer, smooth, silky Cabernet-moulded red wines under the **Anjou-Villages** appellation.

The grape that reaches its highpoint in the Middle Loire is the oft-maligned Chenin Blanc. In cool years it may simply produce a tart and relatively aromatic medium dry white (historically with too much sulphur), but when nature co-operates in producing thoroughly ripe grapes and, ideally, the magic mould noble rot, such appellations as **Coteaux de l'Aubance**, **Coteaux du Layon** and, especially, the particularly well-favoured enclaves, **Chaume**, **Quarts de Chaume** and **Bonnezeaux** within it, can produce great, honeyed, long-living sweet white wines to rival some of the best in the world. Some ultra-sweet

The Château du Nozet, the Ladoucette family's country cottage, is the Loire's most famous wine property, just up the road from the humbler abode of Didier Dageneau, Pouilly-Fumé's wild man.

Sélection de Grains Nobles wines have been made in recent years.

Savennières is Anjou's minuscule but world-famous dry white Chenin Blanc appellation. Nicolas Joly at Coulée de Serrant keeps the famous flame alight and is one of France's most vociferous proponents of biodynamism. The wines are hard to appreciate when young, and the combination of high demand and low production neatly restricts the wines to their greatest enthusiasts.

Current overperformers in Anjou and environs include Domaine de Bablut, Pascal Cailleau, Château de Chamboureau, Châteaux de Fesles, Christian Papin at Domaine de Haute Perche, Claude Papin at Château Pierre-Bise and Vincent Ogereau.

Saumur is the next region upstream and the eponymous town is best known for its usually dry and racy sparkling wines, whose tiny, often persistent bubbles can demonstrate real winemaking skill. All that prevents these wines from finding a wider market is the decidedly un-champagne-like flavours of the Chenin Blanc grape which dominate Saumur Mousseux and the more rigorously made Crémant de Loire, although increasing amounts of Chardonnay used in these traditional-method wines are beginning to 'internationalize' them. Three outposts of Champagne houses perform particularly well here: Bouvet-Ladubay (Taittinger), Gratien & Meyer (Alfred Gratien) and Langlois-Château (Bollinger).

Typical middle Loire valley gable in St-Nicolas de Bourgeuil – Cabernet Franc territory par excellence.

Saumur's other claim to wine fame is Saumur-Champigny, the Loire's most fashionable, and therefore often overpriced, Cabernet Franc-based red. In particularly ripe years these fragrant, silky-textured, gulpable liquids can benefit from careful maturation in small oak barrels. Filliatreau and Foucault are two of the better producers, and superior bottlings can continue to evolve for years in bottle.

The Loire's most famous reds, Chinon, Bourgueil, and St-Nicolas de Bourgueil, are made to the same recipe as Saumur-Champigny, indeed Chinon is virtually an eastern extension of it. Bourgueil can be the beefiest, longest-living Loire red of all, while the lighter St-Nicolas de Bourgueil is even more rarely seen outside its own parish. All three appellations fall within the wine region around the city of Tours, **Touraine**, where the landscape is dotted with wine cellars and even houses carved out of the soft, well-drained limestone known as tuf-feau, to which the region's châteaux owe much.

Gifted producers in these appellations include Daniel Chauveau, Pierre-Jacques Druet, Charles Joguet and Olga and Jean-Marie Raffault.

Touraine is one of France's most confusing wine names. White versions can be made from any or all of four grape varieties – although Sauvignon is the most common and the best examples can rival wines of the Upper Loire. Reds and rosés may be a blend of Gamay (the most common), Cabernet Franc, Cabernet Sauvignon, Cot (Malbec), Pinot Noir, Pinot Meunier, Pinot Gris and two local vine varieties Pineau d'Aunis and Grolleau. An early-bottled Touraine Primeur version rivalling Beaujolais Nouveau is a further confusion. The districts of Amboise, Azay-le-Rideau and Mesland append their name to the Touraine appellation but offer no guarantee of superior quality.

Cheverny and Valençay are two small Touraine satellites which have avoided being subsumed into the appellation Touraine.

Touraine's arguably most distinctive wines are Vouvray and its reflection across the river Montlouis. Like the great sweet wines of Anjou they are made from Chenin Blanc grapes, and vary considerably in quality and even style according to the year's grape sugar level. In great years such as 1947 and 1989, the combination of noble rot, sky-high sugar levels and the naturally high acidity levels of Chenin grown this far from the equator ensure that the deep green-gold versions labelled Moelleux or Liquoreux will last virtually forever. In cool years, however, the grapes may well be better suited to making a crisp base for sparkling wine. And between these two extremes a host of wines labelled Sec (dry) and Demi Sec (medium dry) are made. These can also develop for decades in bottle, and even the Demi Sec versions have enough tang to make them delicious partners for many fish dishes, notably those involving a creamy sauce. Quality-conscious producers include Domaine Delétang, Foreau of Clos Naudin, Fouquet of Domaine des Aubuisières, Gaston Huet of Le Haut Lieu, Prince Poniatowski and Jacky Supligeau.

Parisians should not be allowed a monopoly on all the best wines of the Loire: the stylish sparkling wines and, in riper vintages, the sweeter Chenins and keenly-priced Cabernet-based reds.

MUSCADET REGION

Like Brittany to the immediate north, the Muscadet region at the mouth of the Loire, is quintessentially oceanic. Clouds and sea spray blow in off the Atlantic, untainted by any contact with land for thousands of miles. The relatively light, neutral wine was the creation of the energetic Dutch in the seventeenth century (they encouraged locals to plant the Muscadet grape, the slightly vapid Melon grape of Burgundy) and, as it happens, the terrain round Nantes looks perfectly suited to windmills and tulips.

Muscadet de Sèvre-et-Maine, named after two small rivers which flow to the south and east of Nantes, is by far the most common form of Muscadet. Because the Melon grape is not exactly flavour-packed, many local winemakers leave the fermented wine on the lees, *sur lie*, for several months in order to leech a bit more character (and often an appetizingly light tingle) into the wine (see page 82). When Muscadet was popular as France's white answer to Beaujolais, the term 'sur lie' was far too generously applied but the quality of Muscadet has been increasing steadily. Some ambitious producers – notably Bosset, Guindon, Landron, Marquis de Goulaine, Master de Donatien, Louis Metaireau, and Sauvion – are trying to turn their Muscadets into wines of the 1990s by using oak and dramatically reducing yields, but 95 bottles of Muscadet out of 100 should be drunk as young and casually as possible. Muscadet Côtes de Grandlieu is theoretically a more floral style of wine from the west of the region.

Gros Plant (Nantais) is the region's light, tart white varietal for masochists.

See page 205 for details of the Loire valley's numerous winemaking outposts. The Loire has attracted more than its fair share of VDQSs. Perhaps local pride is particularly strong here.

RHÔNE

In a nutshell: Concentrated, beefy red
wines designed for ageing.
Grapes: Syrah, Grenache (RED), Marsanne,
Roussanne, Viognier (WHITE)

The wide, lazy Rhône links two important
French wine regions (and, in narrower,
swifter form, the vineyards of Savoie, and some
of Switzerland's best). The Northern Rhône
produces small quantities of some very fine wine
indeed, while the much more extensive vineyards of the Southern Rhône produce one of
France's 'commodity' wines, Côtes-du-Rhône,
as well as a host of other wines based on the
Grenache grape.

NORTHERN RHÔNE

It's not difficult to see why vine-growing is relatively uncommon on the steep, wooded banks
of the Rhône south of Lyons. These vineyards,
probably the oldest in France, have had to be
etched into the mountainside on narrow terraces (not unlike port country in the Douro)
and some are so steep that pulley systems have
to be used for grapes and equipment as in
Switzerland. This, furthermore, is countryside
that has now been fully invaded by industry and
is well adapted to other, easier crops such as
fruit trees on the plateaux above the river. To
grow vines in the Northern Rhône's only commercially viable sites, the ones that catch the
sun for long enough to ripen grapes fully, you
have either to inherit an established vineyard
(usually on the right bank) or to be sure of
fetching a high price for the resulting wine.

The great majority of wine made here is
made from the Syrah grape, and the region's
most famous wines are the deep-flavoured, long-
lived reds Hermitage and Côte Rôtie.

The Northern Rhône is also notable
because it is still in the hands of family enter-

prises. The three biggest are Marcel Guigal of
Côte Rôtie, who has been described as the
planet's finest winemaker; Chapoutier where a
new generation is endeavouring to restore ultra-
traditional techniques such as encouraging the
extraction of colour from grape skins by foot
(*pigeage*); and, another Hermitage specialist,
Paul Jaboulet Aîné. They each have their own
vineyards but buy in extensively from the hundreds of smallholders who still cultivate these
physically demanding vineyards. As elsewhere,

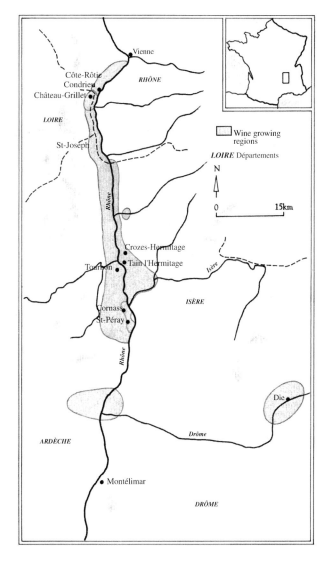

an increasing number of these smallholders are now bottling their own wine and their challenge, along with that of a few ambitious newcomers to the region, has done nothing but good for the overall quality of Rhône wine.

Côte Rôtie is in fact not just one but a series of 'roasted slopes' folded above the little town of Ampuis. Only those facing south or south east on the schists of this right bank of the river are worth the extreme discomfort of cultivating them and, especially, picking their produce. Those to the south are collectively known as the Côte Blonde and the wines they produce supposedly mature rather earlier than those produced on the Côte Brune just to the north, although traditionally the wines from these areas have been blended. (There are vineyards on the flatter land above these slopes but they are entitled only to the generic Côtes-du-Rhône appellation which very much more commonly applies to wines made in the Southern Rhône.)

One man has made a name for himself, and indeed the whole appellation, by flying in the face of Côte Rôtie convention. Marcel Guigal's special bottlings of single-vineyard Côte Rôtie wines La Mouline, La Landonne and La Turque have become the most sought-after bottles in the world, thanks to low yields and their uniquely long maturation in new oak, which makes them massively appealing in youth as well as promising an exciting old age.

Côte Rôtie is stereotypically distinguished from Hermitage by its perfume, which is supposedly due to the possible inclusion of white Viognier grapes (the same as those grown in the neighbouring appellation of Condrieu), but in practice most Côte Rôtie is 100 per cent Syrah. The appellation's vines are trained to help withstand the twin local dangers of wind damage and soil erosion, with pairs of vines staked to meet in a point, making the roasted slopes look as though they are covered in Christmas trees. Some other reliable producers of Côte Rôtie are Barge, Clusel-Roch, Rostaing and Vidal-Fleury (the merchant house for which Marcel Guigal's father once worked as cellarmaster but which now belongs to Guigal).

The amount of Viognier grown in the Northern Rhône is relatively tiny,

Marcel Guigal's pickers (left) are fed in shifts by his wife Bernadette and given much rougher wine than his famous Côte Rôtie to drink. Thirty miles downriver, above the small town of Tain, are the famous Hermitage vineyards (right), overlooking the Rhône river. Perhaps the most famous wine made here, by the large family firm of Paul Jaboulet Aîné, is Hermitage La Chapelle, a reference to the chapel which dominates this vine-covered hill.

and the peachy, full-bodied **Condrieu** it produces could generally be sold three times over by growers such as Cuilleron and Villard, so fashionable has this wine style become. The merchants try to buy as many Condrieu grapes as possible. Guigal's single-vineyard Doriane is setting a new standard, while Delas has a long history of getting Condrieu right. **Château-Grillet** is a 3 ha (5 acre) single-property appellation slightly downriver of Condrieu whose wines are even more dramatically priced.

Hermitage is produced 30 miles downriver on a bald suntrap of a hill on the left bank above the narrow town of Tain, or rather Tain l'Hermitage as it has become known thanks to the fame of Hermitage's densely strapping wines. There was a period in French wine trade history when it was common practice to order red wines that had been *hermitagé*, or had had Hermitage added to them for colour and strength. White Hermitage is also made, from Marsanne and Roussanne grapes. It is unusually full-bodied and can be difficult to appreciate until its bouquet has developed after many years in bottle. Sweet *vin de paille* is a speciality.

In and around Tain and its sister town of Tournon, just across a rickety footbridge over the Rhône, are a bevy of gifted and determined winemakers, not just the large merchant houses of Chapoutier, Paul Jaboulet and Delas but much smaller family domaines such as superstar J. L. Chave. The co-operative Cave de Tain l'Hermitage is also admirably aware of quality.

Most of these producers also make **Crozes-Hermitage**, the area's much, much bigger, less demanding red and white wine appellation on the flatter land around the hill of Hermitage. Red Crozes from one of the area's best merchants or one of the more gifted producers such as Belle, Graillot or Pochon are the Northern Rhône's great wine bargains.

While Crozes-Hermitage regularly represents more than half of all the wine produced in the Northern Rhône, **St-Joseph** (another red and white appellation made from Syrah, Marsanne and Roussanne) can often represent almost one bottle in four. The appellation was, often unwisely, expanded dramatically in the 1970s and 1980s and straggles down the right bank of the river from Condrieu almost as far south as St-Péray. There can be a dramatic difference in concentration and quality between the wines made on difficult terraces just above Tournon and those which gush forth from the much flatter land. It is worth paying St-Joseph's price premium above Crozes only for the likes of Chave, Cuilleron, Émile Florentin, Gripa, Grippat, Jean Marsanne and André Perret.

Even though the Northern Rhône has benefited from an enormous amount of attention in recent years, **Cornas** is still an emerging appellation producing very worthy and, after eight years in bottle, exciting Syrah reds. Clape is the local hero, with Allemand and Robert fast building a reputation too.

The curiosity of the Northern Rhône is **St-Péray**, usually a heavy, sparkling white made from Marsanne and Roussanne grapes which has yet to dazzle outsiders.

SOUTHERN RHÔNE

In a nutshell: Warm, rich reds.
Grapes: Grenache

This is the region of France's most user-friendly wines, and its important source of appellation contrôlée wine after Bordeaux. Côtes-du-Rhône is south east France's warmer, richer, spicier answer to the dry austerity of AC Bordeaux. The wines of the Southern Rhône are France's most alcoholic, with 12.5 per cent being a minimum and 14 per cent by no means uncommon for its most famous appellation, Châteauneuf-du-Pape (and no chaptalization, or extra alcohol from added sugar, is allowed this far south).

Perhaps it is the alcohol that makes these Southern Rhône reds so easy to appreciate. Perhaps it is the openly fruity character of the Grenache grape which dominates here, concentrated by the relatively low yields forced upon it by the stony soils and low rainfall. Perhaps it's because the Southern Rhône is the gateway to Provence, a land of olive trees, cicadas, sunshine and Impressionist summer landscapes.

The wines made in this seductive countryside are, contrarily, best drunk in much cooler climates. They can seem head-thumpingly inappropriate when drunk in the place and season that produces them (although the small proportion of rosés and dry whites made in the Southern Rhône solve this problem – see below).

The Southern Rhône is an important hunting ground for the merchants of the Northern Rhône, and a significant proportion of the wines made here are shipped north in bulk to be sold with a Tain or Tournon address on the label. Co-operative wineries are also extremely important here.

While **Côtes-du-Rhône** can come from a vast area of almost 40 000 ha (100 000 acres) around the southern end of the French Rhône Valley, **Côtes-du-Rhône-Villages** comes from a tightly defined area barely an eighth as big on particularly suitable land north and west of Châteauneuf-du-Pape. Most Côtes-du-Rhône is vinified using the Beaujolais carbonic maceration technique (see page 78) to yield juicy, fruity wines for which life is short. Among the hundreds of Côtes-du-Rhône-Villages producers, however, are many with greater ambitions for their wines, which are made to develop for five and sometimes more years in bottle. With maximum permitted yields a good sixth lower than those allowed for Côtes-du-Rhône, Côtes-du-Rhône-Villages is one of France's best-value appellations, perhaps because promotion prospects are so obvious. Since the appellation was formed in 1966, two of the nearly 20 villages have been granted their own appellations – Gigondas and Vacqueyras – and the other village names encountered on labels and also marked on the map produce some seriously fine, often underpriced wines.

Châteauneuf-du-Pape is the region's most famous and best wine, and all other reds and whites made here seem to use it as their model. Châteauneuf is most famous in wine books as

the appellation in which 13 different grape varieties are permitted. In practice, however, the reds are made predominantly from Grenache, supplemented by Syrah, Mourvèdre and, to a decreasing extent, Cinsaut, while the relatively rare whites are made from a more variable recipe that includes Grenache Blanc, Clairette, Bourboulenc and Roussanne.

Red Châteauneuf is a big, beefy wine with lots of alcohol and extract, with a come-hither, if slightly bludgeoning, approach to the wine drinker. I find this one of France's most reliable appellations, and have had remarkably few disappointments among wines bottled in the signature-embossed, heavy bottle. (In fact if there is a regional fault it is that in some very hot years the wines can be just too alcoholic, and in particularly dry years they can be too tannic – but these faults are so rare among French wines that they are almost refreshing.) The fact that so much Châteauneuf meets a certain minimum standard probably reflects the fact that yields must be kept remarkably low as well as the mandatory selection of only healthy, ripe grapes.

There is considerable variation in how the wines are made, but high-tech methods are rare

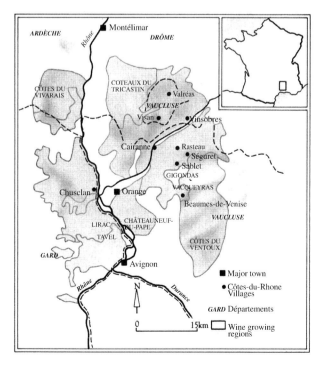

Two faces of the Southern Rhône: (above) the setting summer sun, responsible for so much alcohol, above Châteauneuf-du-Pape; and (right) the dreamy vineyards of Gigondas, whose wines can provide much the same pleasure, often more cheaply.

here among the pines. The stereotypical Châteauneuf vineyard has low bush vines struggling up for sunlight between large boulders (*galets*), illustrated on page 139, whose effect is to continue the warming process well into the night, but in fact many of the best vineyards are on much more conventional ground.

White Châteauneuf obeys far fewer rules. Some of them are still very flabby and unappetizing, while an increasing proportion have enough fruit and acidity (with, always, lots of alcohol) to make truly interesting bottles of wine. Roussanne can be a particularly interesting ingredient.

Châteauneuf has a multitude of good to very good producers, but Beaucastel, Rayas, Vieux Télégraphe, Bosquet des Papes, Clos des Papes and Réserve des Célestins are almost always excellent (and Rayas's second label Pignan and even its Côtes-du-Rhône label Château de Fonsalette are well above average).

Gigondas is another relatively reliable wine made, as a red and full rosé, in the image of Châteauneuf. It costs less and usually tastes rather more rustic, a characteristic which has its own charm these days. Reliable names include Domaine Les Goubert, Domaine St-Gayan and Château du Trignon.

Vacqueyras, the other upgraded Côtes-du-Rhône-Village, is not usually quite so dense, but can be very good value.

With the exception of Châteauneuf, whose regulations are stricter than almost any other's in France, wherever red wine is made in southern France, rosé is too, most of it being drunk locally during the hot summer months. The Grenache and Cinsaut of the Southern Rhône, with their relatively thin skins and open, fruity flavour are particularly suitable for making pink wine. The Southern Rhône's most famous rosé by far is **Tavel**, made on the right bank of the Rhône and a serious, historic wine in its own right. Just as Châteauneuf is France's most positive red, Tavel across the river is its most powerful pink. This is a wine not for gulping in the garden but as a substantial red wine substitute

in hot weather. Chilling is essential. Château d'Aqueria is one of the best-known estates.

Just north of Tavel, **Lirac** produces considerable quantities of rosé very similar to Tavel and full blooded red wine, as well as some full-bodied dry white. Domaine de la Mordorée is one of the best producers.

The Southern Rhône also produces some sweet, relatively alcoholic vin doux naturel (see page 89), most famously **Muscat de Beaumes-de-Venise**. This golden, grapey mix of the juice of the best Muscat vine with alcohol is made in the village of Beaumes-de-Venise, which is one of the designated villages whose red wines are sold as Côtes-du-Rhône-Villages. Another of these villages, **Rasteau**, has its own special appellation for red and oak-aged tawny vin doux naturel which has a much less cosmopolitan taste than Muscat de Beaumes-de-Venise. (Regular red Rasteau is interesting for the amount of Mourvèdre grown there.)

Almost a bridge between the Rhône and Provence is **Côtes du Ventoux**, whose vineyards lie on the slopes of Mont Ventoux, one of the few peaks ever to be covered in snow for the winter in this region. The Grenache-based reds and rosés are usually lighter than most Côtes-du-Rhônes but can be all the more refreshing for it. La Vieille Ferme is a successful brand built on this appellation by the Perrin family of Château de Beaucastel.

Coteaux du Tricastin tastes like a half-way house between Côtes-du-Rhône and Côtes du Ventoux, even though it is in fact effectively a northern enclave within the Côtes-du-Rhône-Villages. Across the Rhône is the rather similar VDQS **Côtes du Vivarais** where Domaine du Belvezet outperforms its neighbours.

And finally, the greater Rhône Valley has its curious eastern outpost, around **Die** on the river Drôme. Hannibal and his alpinist elephants are invoked in the names of the local wines, of which the most famous are sparkling: either dry Crémant de Die made in the image of champagne or the grapier, fuller Clairette de Die. The co-operative is in charge here.

PROVENCE AND CORSICA

In a nutshell: Dry rosés and some firm, spicy reds.
Grapes: Grenache, Cinsaut, Syrah,
Cabernet Sauvignon (RED), Rolle (WHITE)

Although most people firmly associate Provence with holidays rather than with wine, this disparate region's wines are getting better and better. What seems to work particularly well is a conscientiously made, often oak-aged blend of the Cabernet Sauvignon grapes of Bordeaux with the Syrah of the Northern Rhône. What is most obviously made in enormous quantity, however, is light, dry rosé which, if drunk young and well chilled, can seem justification for wine's very existence when sipped on a vine-shaded terrace to the sound of cicadas. (Too much of it, however, seems to be made on the assumption that tourists don't notice what they're drinking.)

The most common appellation of all is the catch-all **Côtes de Provence** stretching right across most of the region. More than six bottles in every 10 carrying the name contain rosé of some sort. Grape varieties also include Carignan, Cinsaut and, a local rarity which can add spice to rosé, Tibouren. Rolle is the region's most distinctive white grape. In this, mainland France's driest, sunniest climate, fungal diseases are not the perennial threat they are elsewhere and the region is particularly well suited to organic viticulture. The area seethes with experimentation but little evidence escapes France.

Coteaux Varois is a new appellation on cooler territory within Côtes de Provence, named after the Var *département*, and harbours some ambitious incomers at estates such as Domaine du Deffends and Château Routas. The other significant appellation is **Coteaux d'Aix-en-Provence**, which is not quite so rosé-dependent. At the western end of this appellation is the very particular **Les Baux de Provence**, vineyards around the haunting rocks which gave their name to bauxite. Domaine de Trevallon is the real star here, but because it refuses to conform to the grape mix specified by the AC laws, it is sold as a Vin de Pays. Good bottles can also be found chez Mas de Gourgonnier as well as the organic Domaine des Terres Blanches.

Provence also has a number of more specific appellations of which the most important is **Bandol**, known principally for its characterful, warmly spicy reds and rosés made predominantly from Mourvèdre. So warm is the climate here right on terraces immediately above the coast, sheltered from the piercing local wind, the *mistral*, that this late-ripening variety can, unusually in France, be relied upon to ripen every year. Domaine Tempier is the best-known producer but there is a remarkably high general standard among Bandol producers.

To France's wine authorities the rapidly improving appellation **Côtes du Lubéron** is part of the greater Rhône Valley, but to estate agents and the millions who have read Peter Mayle the Lubéron *is* Provence – and in viticultural terms it is certainly cooler than either the Southern Rhône or most Provençal vineyards. **Coteaux de Pierrevert** to the immediate north east is even cooler, and sleepier.

In wine books Corsica is traditionally hitched to Provence's wagon, and they share some vine varieties just as they once shared rulers. Few bottles have been exported while the island sorted itself out from the wild and usually unwise vineyard expansion of the 1980s. The Corsican variety Sciacarello is increasingly appreciated, and Sangiovese is grown, as Nielluccio. Vermentino (Rolle) is regarded as the island's own white grape. Much of the island's production is sold as France's most cleverly named Vin de Pays de l'Île de Beauté (Island of Beauty) but its most interesting wines are probably its rare, sweet, strong vins doux naturels, notable among them Muscat du Cap Corse.

SOUTH WEST FRANCE

In a nutshell: Mostly bordeaux-like,
plus some Basque influence.
Grapes: Cabernet, Merlot, Malbec,
Tannat, Negrette, Fer (RED), Sauvignon,
Sémillon, Mauzac, Gros and
Petit Manseng (WHITE)

South west France really means all the wine regions in the south western quarter of the country, with the major exception of the most important one, Bordeaux, and the Cognac region to the immediate north of it, which enjoy separate status. This ragbag of a collection can be roughly divided into those which are effectively continuations of Bordeaux, its vine varieties and its wine styles upriver of the Bordeaux region itself, and those further south and east which have their own distinctive identity. All of them, however, are influenced by the Atlantic rather than the Mediterranean, and tend to have the same sort of build (light- to medium-bodied) as bordeaux.

Into the first, Bordeaux Fringes, category fall Bergerac (and its sub-appellations Montravel, Rosette, Saussignac, Pécharmant and Monbazillac), Buzet, Cahors, Côtes de Duras and Côtes du Marmandais.

Bergerac will continue to have its work cut out to establish a truly independent identity from its big, commercially acute brother just down the Dordogne river. (The town of Bergerac is hardly 30 miles east of Bordeaux's St-Émilion.) Although those sold as Côtes de Bergerac are usually more concentrated, its wines are basically just what the map suggests, country cousins of red and dry white bordeaux, with the sub-appellations rarely seen outside France except for **Monbazillac**. In very sunny years such as 1990, Monbazillac can provide some truly great value sweet whites made in the

LEFT *A wine bar in*
Toulouse. The local herby
red and rosé wine is made
around the town of Fronton
to the immediate north.
RIGHT *The rolling*
countryside of the Tarn-et-
Garonne département.
Any further north is too
cool for widespread
viticulture, although a
small quantity of
Lavilledieu, like light
red bordeaux, is made here.

image of Sauternes but veering towards the slightly more obvious flavours of barley sugar rather than crème brûlée. An increasing number of Monbazillac producers are prepared to wait for botrytis (noble rot – see page 88) to develop in exceptional years, and some of the resulting wines can be bargains. Château La Grarière is the star, Clos d'Yvigne in Saussignac up and coming.

Immediately south of Bergerac is **Côtes de Duras** which, with **Côtes du Marmandais** centred on the town of Marmande, continues to skirt Bordeaux in a clockwise direction. It is history more than geography that excludes these vineyards from the cosy umbrella of the Bordeaux appellation and I would take my hat off to any blind taster who could unerringly distinguish between the Bordeaux, Bergerac, Côtes de Duras and Côtes du Marmandais appellations.

Buzet produces similar wines, but with a little more stuffing and cohesive direction since the region is largely governed by a particularly ambitious local co-operative – one of the French coopers' better customers for many years.

Cahors is quite another matter. In fact many producers of Cahors on the river Lot would be insulted to be categorized as a shadow of Bordeaux since the wines have etched their own very distinct personality – chiefly because the devastating winter frosts of 1956 hit Cahors's vines particularly badly and a dramatic replanting programme was undertaken virtually from scratch. Rather than relying on the standard Bordeaux recipe of varying the proportions of Merlot with the two Cabernets, Cahors depends principally on a variety considered relatively minor in Bordeaux, Malbec (called Auxerrois in Cahors), typically bolstered with more or less Merlot and/or Tannat. (Cabernet Sauvignon would not ripen reliably this far inland.) The result is a plump, full-bodied but often rather coarse country red, although those made from grapes grown on the less fertile plateau land last notably longer than the produce of lower land. Cahors has attracted a

number of well-heeled outsiders, whether from Paris or New York, and is in the throes of redesigning itself as a thoroughly modern wine in its historic image as deep, dark, colouring wine for blending with the vapid stuff produced downriver in Bordeaux. Châteaux de Haute-Serre, Lagrezette, St-Didier-Parnac and Triguedina are trying harder than most.

Almost due east of the city of Bordeaux and yet way up on France's flat, wild interior, the Massif Central, the **Marcillac**, **Entraygues** and **Estaing** appellations cling to existence with scented, peppery distinctive wines which owe much to the local Fer Servadou vine, the sort to send a shiver down the spine of vine-variety sleuths like me.

Gaillac has an identity and history that is indisputably quite distinct from Bordeaux. Vines were almost certainly planted on the rolling farmland around the historic city of Albi long before they were known in the Bordeaux region, and they were long used for strengthening the light reds made downriver. All of which gives the locals a certain inherent superiority, but the truth is that in the modern marketplace, Gaillac has yet to make much of a stir. Such a wide range of grape varieties are planted here, and such a broad variety of wine styles, that Gaillac tends to be a local hero rather than international superstar. The most exciting local red varieties are Duras (no relation to Côtes de Duras) and the Fer of Marcillac, but they are usually blended with Gamay and Syrah (imports from Beaujolais and the Rhône respectively) and sometimes the Cabernets and Merlot of Bordeaux. Mauzac is Gaillac's signature white variety and adds a certain twist of apple peel to its whites which come in all degrees of sweetness and fizziness. The Bordeaux white varieties of Sauvignon, Sémillon and Muscadelle are also widely grown together with local specialities Len de l'El and Ondenc. Is it any wonder that Gaillac's image is confused? The appellation is dominated by two co-operatives, Labastide de Levis and the Cave de Tecou, whose wines are tasting more and more sophisticated, but Robert Plageoloes is the media star of the appellation and makes, among other things, local answers to sauternes, champagne and sherry.

Côtes du Frontonnais is a small but interesting red and rosé appellation just north of Toulouse where the grainy local variety Négrette is preserved, and producers such as Châteaux Bellevue-La-Forêt and Montauriol make thoroughly modern, almost 'international' wines.

But the really characterful wines of the south west come from Gascony (Armagnac country) and Basque country in the far south of the Atlantic hinterland. **Madiran** is that region's most substantial wine, a deep-coloured, barrel-aged masculine red made to last and last, chiefly because of the local Tannat variety (whose name, it is assumed, derives from its mouth-puckering tannin content). There are some exciting winemakers here such as Alain Brumont of Châteaux Bouscassé and Montus, who seem to have mastered getting subtlety and smoothness out of the variety, which is usually blended with Cabernets and a little Fer. Other notable producers include Château d'Aydie and Domaine Laffitte-Teston. Anyone with a serious interest in wine should keep a keen eye on developments in this often underrated, proud Gascon winemaking outpost.

The group of local co-operatives, known collectively as Plaimont, has played an important part in reviving the area's viticultural traditions and is the most important producer of the keenly priced wine **Côtes de St-Mont** as well as of Gascony's real bargain, fruity dry white Vin de Pays made from grapes surplus to the requirements of the Armagnac distillers.

The white wine made, in relatively small quantity, in the Madiran district is **Pacherenc du Vic-Bilh**, which itself is an often slightly paler shadow of the great white of this corner of France,

Jurançon, made in the green foothills of the western Pyrenees around the town of Pau, not far from Lourdes. A palette of local grape varieties is responsible for Pacherenc but green-gold tangy Jurançon depends on its own vine specialities, Gros and Petit Manseng. The small-berried Petit Manseng is the key to making Jurançon Moelleux, which owes its sweetness not to noble rot but to shrivelling, or raisining, on the vine. Jurançon comes dry (Sec) or sweet (Moelleux). Domaine Cauhapé makes some of the best wine (the dry can make a great aperitif) but great bottles have also come from Château Jolys and Charles Hours at Clos Uroulat.

The small appellation of **Tursan** is being revived, with sophisticated oak-aged white wines, and the light wines of **Béarn** (of Béarnaise sauce fame) are also produced in several different parts of this area.

But the real curiosity comes from Basque country, where almost dangerously steep, high vineyards right up in the Pyrenees produce white, pink and light red **Irouléguy**, chiefly from Cabernets and Mansengs. The co-operative makes interesting light but firm wines and Brana is the most dedicated individual producer.

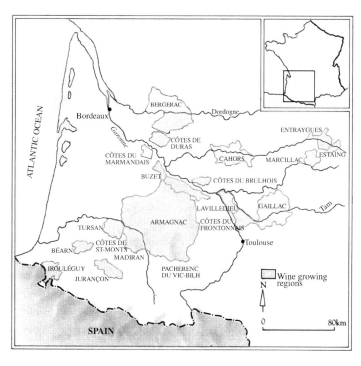

LANGUEDOC

In a nutshell: France's New World wine region, with some improving appellations too.

Grapes: Carignan, Syrah, Grenache, Mourvèdre, Cinsaut (RED), Maccabéo, Grenache Blanc, Bourboulenc, Picpoul, Chardonnay (WHITE)

The Languedoc is my adoptive French home. I see it as Provence without the tourists, without *too* many incomers like me pushing up prices and without, regrettably, the ubiquitous smell of lavender, thyme and pines. It is, however, archetypal mediterranean wine country, with wild landscapes, Spain just over the Pyrenees, and vines stretching in every direction. Those which stretch on the flattest land, notably the vast, arid plains between Narbonne and Montpellier, are chiefly responsible for France's still significant production of basic light red Vin de Table (see page 48) and therefore for much of the European wine lake.

Although the Languedoc was the first French region to be introduced to vine-growing and winemaking by the Romans, its modern reputation as a wine producer has been for quantity at the expense of quality. Once the railways had reached this reliably sunny southern part of France, it was developed as an outdoor factory producing vast quantities of light red to be shipped to the recently industrialized north of the country. The hillside vineyards established by the Romans were rapidly swamped by the sea of much less demanding vineyards established on the wide coastal plain.

So high were yields – often far more than 200 hl/ha (11 ton/acre) – and so ignoble the grape varieties that France came to be dependent on importing robust, deep-coloured red wine from Algeria and then Italy and Spain in order to bolster the produce of the Languedoc. Co-operatives dominate, and still the great majority of growers, peasant smallholders in the main, have no experience at all of winemaking.

By the 1980s the Languedoc was regularly producing 10 per cent of the entire planet's wine output, but as the decade progressed, and French consumption of basic Vin de Table plummeted, it became clear that there was no long-term future for the sort of wine on which the Languedoc rural economy was based.

Today one of Europe's most pressing problems is how to transform the Languedoc from a region of thousands of vignerons producing wine no one wants to drink into a much smaller one in which perhaps hundreds of producers concentrate on the medium- to high-quality wine of which the region is capable.

The hills of the Fitou, Corbières, Minervois and Coteaux du Languedoc appellations are home to some of France's oldest vines, often gnarled stumps of Carignan, which ooze super-concentrated, often super-tannic deep red, suitable for blending with more recent plantings of fashionably Rhônish varieties.

Today the Languedoc is producing two types of wine, among which are some of the best value bottles in the world: not just these appellation wines but members of the rank below, Vin de Pays d'Oc, which has become the region's most important product, and a host of other, more geographically specific Vins de Pays (see pages 202–4), many sold as varietals.

This is red wine country, although small proportions of rosé (particularly from Cinsaut, Syrah and Grenache) and increasingly interesting whites are made (from a cocktail of varieties including Grenache Blanc, Bourboulenc, Maccabéo, Rolle, and Viognier, Marsanne and Roussanne of the Rhône, and the local varieties Picpoul, Terret and Clairette). Tough old Carignan still makes up the backbone of most Languedoc reds, but the proportion of improving varieties' is increasing all the time. These include Grenache, Mourvèdre and, particularly, Syrah. Thanks to the influence of the Southern

Rhône to the east of this enormous sweep of vineyards, Grenache predominates in the east of the Languedoc while Syrah is more important in the west. Mourvèdre is restricted to the warmest sites.

Selling prices have been very low, which has put a natural brake on modernization of the Languedoc's often primitive wineries. Destemmers and oak barrels are still widely seen as luxuries, and the prevailing habit has been to vinify whole bunches of Carignan in a version of Beaujolais's carbonic maceration (see page 78) so as to soften its often rasping tannins. Things are fast becoming more sophisticated, however, and the best wines offer a bordeaux-like structure (although wines, as in Bordeaux, are getting stronger) to support much wilder, more mediterranean flavours – at prices rarely more than AC Bordeaux.

Fitou, unusually for the Languedoc an all-red appellation, is its most southerly, in the arid foothills of the Pyrenees in the south of the Corbières region. Its enormous potential is as yet unrealized, perhaps because the dominant co-operatives, with the exception of the dynamic Cave de Mont-Tauch, have been slow to realize that quality is the key to survival. Château de Nouvelles is one of the few individual producers of any distinction.

Corbières just to the north is, for the moment, a much more exciting appellation, with scores of ambitious, dedicated smallholders determined to persuade the varied, dry, hillsides of the appellation to yield herby, slightly wild red wines of real quality and integrity. The Val d'Orbieu association of co-operatives does a good job and individual properties of note include Châteaux La Baronne, Caraguilhes (organic), Cascadais, Étang de Colombes, Hélène, Lastours, Les Ollieux, Les Palais-Rondolin, Pensées Sauvages, St-Auriol, La Voulte-Gasparets, and Domaines Fontsainte, du Grand Crès and du Révérend. Some of the cheapest bottlings of Corbières (and Minervois), however, taste little better than basic Vin de Table.

Immediately inland of Corbières are the

Vines can seem to stretch forever in the Languedoc.

gentler hills which are responsible for Blanquette de Limoux and Crémant de Limoux, the Languedoc's very serviceable traditional method sparkling wines. The former is made chiefly from the region's Blanquette grape (the Mauzac of Gaillac), the latter includes substantially more Chardonnay and is a less distinctive but probably more sophisticated product. **Limoux** is a promising new appellation for barrel-fermented, still Chardonnays – very cosmopolitan!

Côtes de Malepère and **Cabardès** are twin wine zones south and north of the walled city of Carcassonne which can produce some excellent value, relatively simple reds in which the grapes of south west France (Cabernet, Merlot and Fer) are blended with those of the Languedoc.

Minervois in the north west corner of the Languedoc produces slightly smoother, more refined wines than Corbières, but is otherwise quite similar (and equally dominated by co-operatives with extremely varied degrees of skill). The hills are gentler here but some of the most characterful wines are made high up in the foothills of the Cévennes, notably above the ancient wine village of La Livinière, such as Château de Centeilles and Domaines La Combe

Blanche and Piccinini. Other producers who have produced exceptional wines include Châteaux Fabas, de Gourgazaud, La Grave, Laville-Bertrou, d'Oupia, La Tour Boisé, Ville rambert-Julien, Domaine Ste-Eulalie and Comte Cathare. A small amount of dry rosé and increasingly sophisticated white is also made.

St-Chinian is right up in the dramatically craggy Cévennes foothills and it benefits from the dynamism of the dominant co-operative, whose wines are sold under the Berloup label (whites can also be good). Sandwiched between eastern Minervois and Faugères, it can produce characterful reds which represent a half-way house between Syrah and Grenache influences on the ubiquitous Carignan. Other good producers include Château Coujan and Domaines du Fraisse and des Jougla.

Faugères has a similar profile, with over-performers including Gilbert Alquier and Château de la Liquière. Both St-Chinian and Faugères are effectively regarded as special 'crus' or growths within the wide-ranging **Coteaux du Languedoc** appellation. The region stretches from the strange seaside hill of La Clape on the coast south of Narbonne (particularly good for marine-scented, dry whites based on Bourboulenc) to the high, dependable vineyards of **Pic-St-Loup**. This terrain yields hundreds of interesting Vins de Pays made from a wide range of vine varieties, but properties such as Abbaye de Valmagne, Domaines d'Aupilhac and de l'Hortus, Châteaux de Flaugergues, Pech-Redon, Pech Céleyran and Rouquette-sur-Mer, and Mas Jullien also make AC reds, whites and rosés to show they have not given up France's beloved appellation precepts altogether. Picpoul de Pinet is a special full-bodied white.

Costières de Nîmes is really part of the Southern Rhône, and its wines tend to taste like a blend between a Languedoc and Rhône wine, as one would expect from looking at a map. I have enjoyed wines from Château Grande Cassagne, Grand Plagnol and Paul Blanc.

One reason why I like the Languedoc so much is that it produces the full gamut of wine styles: not just reds, whites and rosés well mannered enough to drink on a hot summer's day, and the fizz of Limoux, but also not a few sweet wines, vins doux naturels made from the Muscat grape. **Muscats** de Frontignan, Lunel, Mireval and, most delicate and tender of all, St-Jean-de-Minervois. These golden syrups tend to be about 16 per cent alcohol, should be served well chilled, but once opened keep for a week in the refrigerator. As in Roussillon, an increasing proportion of the region's pale grapes are made into scented, dry full-bodied white table wines.

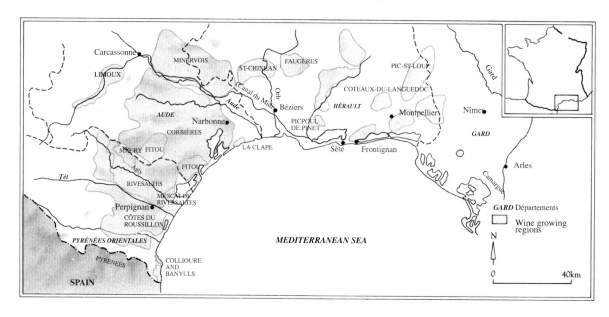

ROUSSILLON

In a nutshell: A tradition of rich dessert wines.
Grapes: Grenache (RED), Muscat,
Grenache Blanc, Maccabéo (WHITE)

Roussillon is often appended to the Languedoc, as in Languedoc-Roussillon, but has a quite distinct character of its own, in landscape, in ethnic roots (Roussillon still regards itself as part of Catalonia across the border in Spain), and in wine styles. Whereas the Languedoc is almost entirely dependent on vine-growing, the farmers in Roussillon's fertile valleys, overlooked by the brooding Pyrenees, can choose between all sorts of fruit. The climate here is almost Spanish, and is particularly suitable for growing cherries, plums, peaches, apricots and nectarines.

Roussillon's wine speciality is a wide variety of vins doux naturels, France's answer to port in which barely fermented sweet grape juice is stabilized by a good dollop of neutral grape spirit (a technique discovered long before the distillation of stronger stuff). See page 89.

Banyuls is the most revered of these, made mainly from almost-raisined dark Grenache grapes grown on rocky, terraced vineyards that tumble into the sea just north of the Spanish border. The vin doux naturel producers employ all sorts of methods to trap their region's sunshine in their wines. Some put the young wine in large glass jars or barrels and leave them out in the hot sunshine to bake (as shown on pages 58–9). Others employ a complicated regime of moving it between barrels of different sizes and ages. Most leave the wine for some time to bake under the rafters during at least one summer. The result is wines which can vary from light red to deep brown, often tasting quite raisiny, sometimes having acquired a nutty, almost rancid taste called 'rancio' by exposure to air and heat. Banyuls Grand Cru wines have to be aged in wood for more than two and a half

years, but producers such as Domaines du Mas Blanc and de la Rectorie may prolong the ageing for many years to produce treacly yet balanced wines which are recommended by many fastidious palates as good partners for chocolate.

Maury is Banyuls's inland cousin and wines made by the likes of Mas Amiel can be almost as fine. Between Banyuls and Maury is a vast area allowed to produce both **Rivesaltes** and **Muscat de Rivesaltes**, which are generally very much less distinguished products, better suited for pouring into halves of melon than for sipping with attention. Muscat de Rivesaltes is produced in enormous quantity, mainly from the less distinguished Muscat of Alexandria vine (unlike Languedoc and Beaumes-de-Venise Muscats). Quality is gradually improving however. A really well-made Rivesaltes could be very fine but most are vague blends of Grenache of various depths of colour aged, not necessarily in very demanding circumstances, for the statutory minimum of just over a year.

The unfortified wines of Roussillon have been improving enormously as evidenced by Casenove, Gauby, Piquemal, Mas Crémat, Mas Segala and the top bottlings of larger merchants Sarda-Malet and Cazes. The **Côtes du Roussillon-Villages** appellations are still struggling to establish their identity and many of the region's most interesting wines are Vins de Pays (see overleaf) or even, in the case of Fernand Vaquer, Vin de Table. Some of the most interesting wines are full-bodied, often oaked whites flavoured with such varieties as Roussanne, Rolle (Vermentino) and Marsanne with Grenache Blanc providing body and Maccabéo providing acidity. Muscat is increasingly made into a grapey, dry, sometimes lightly fizzy white. **Collioure** is the heady, almost fiery red wine made from well ripened Grenache vines in the Banyuls zone. It speaks Spanish rather than French...

VINS DE PAYS

In a nutshell: Some fine value underappreciated by the French.
Grapes: Practically anything but especially the international varieties

Vin de Pays means 'country wine' to the French, but can mean New World with a French accent to outsiders. These are the wines which the French authorities unreservedly allow to be labelled with the grape variety from which they were made.

It is difficult to overestimate the importance of this large and growing category of wines for the future of the French wine trade. The French themselves tend to see any Vin de Pays as distinctly inferior to any AC wine (see page 48) whereas many of their customers abroad see the better Vins de Pays as good-value, user-friendly emissaries from the world's most revered wine producer.

The Vin de Pays category, a product only of the 1970s, is designed to allow greater flexibility, and higher yields, than the AC rules. A much wider range of grape varieties (including the 'international' ones Chardonnay, Cabernet Sauvignon, Sauvignon Blanc, Merlot etc.) is allowed for Vins de Pays, and some producers bottle the produce of vines too young for AC wines as Vins de Pays. The normal maximum permitted yield for a Vin de Pays is 90 hl/ha (5 ton/acre) whereas most ACs are limited to about 50 or 60 hl/ha (3 or 3.5 ton/acre), although the smaller the area designated by the Vin de Pays, the more demanding the rules.

The two systems overlap geographically so that most wine producers have a choice between making an AC wine or Vin de Pays, but the choice tends to be dictated by economics. Few Burgundian producers choose to abandon their valuable appellation wines in favour of making a Vin de Pays de la Côte d'Or. But scores of producers in the Languedoc, for exam-

ple, find it commercially more rewarding to produce a Vin de Pays d'Oc which can also be labelled varietally with a magic name such as Chardonnay or Merlot, or a more geographically specific Vin de Pays, than to make one of the Languedoc appellation wines.

Partly because the appellations of the Languedoc-Roussillon don't command a particularly high price, and partly because so many vineyards lie outside these appellations (having been planted to produce Vin de Table), the great majority of Vins de Pays come from this vast vineyard area. The Languedoc's regional Vin de Pays, called 'd'Oc' after the defining local word for 'Yes', is the single most important Vin de Pays produced, and certainly France's principal varietally labelled wine.

Because the area is so large, individual Vins de Pays d'Oc vary considerably but Chardonnay and Merlot seem to have adapted particularly well to the mediterranean climate here (even though they are relatively recent arrivals). Sauvignon Blanc, Cabernet Sauvignon and Syrah are more variable but can shine, while plantings of Viognier continue to multiply as this variety's fame spreads. Vins de Pays are also a good vehicle for such local vine specialities as Terret, Rolle and Clairette. Oak ageing and rarity (in the case of early Viognier plantings) pushed the price of some Vins de Pays above that of appellation wines.

The most striking example of high-priced Vin de Pays are Mas de Daumas Gassac and Granges des Pères, whose concentrated Languedoc wines are sold simply as Vins de Pays but at almost classed growth bordeaux prices.

This illustrates one of the most common sorts of Vin de Pays, one named after the local *département*, or county. The Aude and Gard are the other two Languedoc départements, while the most common Vins de Pays of Roussillon are 'Catalans' and 'des Côtes Catalans'.

The French authorities have always been most keen to avoid any possibility of confusion between Vins de Pays and any of their precious appellations, so the names of Vins de Pays can sometimes be very difficult for those of us with a less-than-complete grasp of French history and geography.

The table shows some more common Vins de Pays with some geographical guidance as to where they are located (often with reference to the nearest AC) and the likely style of wine.

Vineyards near Cucugnan, ideally suited to producing dense red wine within the Corbières appellation in the Languedoc, but with its very own Vin de Pays which allows more prolific yields and a greater range of grape varieties.

VIN DE PAYS DU/DE LA DE L'/DES/D'	LOCATION	MOST COMMON WINES
Aude	W. Languedoc inc. Minervois, Corbières	Wide range of international and experimental wines
Bouches-du-Rhône	Around Aix-en Provence	Useful varietals
Catalans	Flatter Roussillon	International varieties
Charentais	Cognac country	Very light dry white, surplus to the distillers' needs
Cîté de Carcassonne	Between Cabardès and Côtes de la Malepère	Light reds
Collines Rhodaniennes	Northern Rhône	Lightish Syrah, Marsanne, Viognier
Comtés Rhodaniens	Anywhere in N. Rhône, Beaujolais or Savoie	Light reds
Comté Tolosan	All south west	Bordeaux-like reds
Coteaux de l'Ardèche	Plateau on right bank of the Rhône S. of St Péray	Some interesting Chardonnay and Viognier
Coteaux de Murviel	S. of St-Chinian	Some very good varietals
Coteaux du Quercy	SW of Cahors	Good value country Cahors
Côtes Catalanes	Hillier Roussillon	Deep flavoured reds, dry Muscat
Côtes de Gascogne	Armagnac country	Fresh, fruity dry whites made from Colombard and other brandy grapes
Côtes de Thongue	NE of Béziers	Some fine varietals, esp. Syrah and Chardonnay
Gard	Costières de Nîmes	Country versions of Côtes du Rhône
Gers	Armagnac country	Very similar to Côtes de Gascogne
Hérault	Central Languedoc	Very wide variety
Île de Beauté	Corsica	Light reds, some rosés
Haute-Garonne	Around Toulouse	Some very serious international varietals
Jardin de la France	Loire Valley	Crisp, 'northern' wines of all three colours
Loire-Atlantique	Muscadet country	Occasional Chardonnays of interest
Oc	The whole Languedoc	Very wide variety of grapes and wine-making skill, some excellent value
Principauté d'Orange	N. end of S. Rhône	Some fine varietals
Sables du Golfe du Lion	Sand spit near Sète	Light whites and rosés, from Listel

REST OF FRANCE

Any voyage round France via the main wine regions tends to overlook the eastern ones that are extremely important locally but whose wines rarely make much export impact.

The wines of Savoie tend to taste of the French alps in whose foothills they are made – all crunchy crispness and herby, sappy flavours. My favourite is the curious deep-coloured, racy, slightly bitter red Mondeuse, but there is a wide range of light but fruity, crystal clear whites, of which Roussette is potentially the finest, and some increasingly interesting Pinot Noir. The local fizz, Seyssel, can be a bargain and other names occasionally seen outside France include Crépy, Apremont and Chignin-Bergeron (Bergeron is the Rhône's Roussanne). Superior wines come from Michel Grisard, Château Ripaille and a clutch of producers called Quénard. Even less Bugey escapes its base around Bourg-en-Bresse (the Bresse of chicken fame) but some wines do manage to spread knowledge of the Jura's very particular styles. The seclusion of the Jura in the hills due east of Burgundy has perhaps preserved its traditions of making a sort of sherry, called *vin jaune* (matured under a film of yeast just like sherry; see pages 23–5) and, even rarer, the ultra-sweet *vin de paille* made from grapes dried on straw (see page 89), which is also made in Hermitage. The key names of the appellations here are the extremely varied Arbois and Côtes du Jura together with L'Étoile and Château-Chalon, the latter for *vin jaune* only. Some sparkling wine is also made here.

Even further north in eastern France are the very light, often tart whites and rosés of the Côtes de Toul and Vins de Moselle, the latter being effectively a continuation of the wines produced on the river Moselle in Luxembourg.

The Champagne region produces markedly acid, dry still wines too, mostly in the Coteaux Champenois appellation, which may be white or, in very ripe vintages, lightish red such as the unforgettably named Bouzy Rouge. A local still pink speciality is Rosé des Riceys.

There are also various obscure appellations in the south west such as Côtes du Brulhois, which are very Bordeaux-like, and the weirdly named Vins d'Entraygues et du Fel and Vins d'Estaing, which share characteristics with neighbour Marcillac. The rest of France's AC and VDQS wines mostly fall within the greater Loire basin (which is very great indeed). Sauvignon de St Bris is regarded administratively as part of greater Chablis but the razor-sharp style of this Sauvignon Blanc is pure Loire in taste.

Travelling upstream from the mouth of the Loire, the extremely light whites of the Fief-Vendéens are like Muscadet shadows, while Coteaux d'Ancenis and Vins du Thouarsais are on the fringes of Anjou-Saumur. Haut Poitou is far from the river itself, well south of the Touraine, and produces a wide range of well-made modern wines almost exclusively from a single co-operative. Coteaux du Loir is the confusingly named northern outpost of Touraine with some very fine dry and sweet Jasnières being made from Chenin Blanc grapes – most successfully by Joël Gigou and Aubert de Rycke. Coteaux du Vendômois makes light wines around the town of Vendôme, while Orléans and Gien give their names to the local Vins de l'Orléanais and Coteaux du Giennois on the most significant bend in the river Loire.

Well inside that bend are the Gamay-dominated Châteaumeillant and St-Pourçain-sur-Sioule which make wines from a wide range of grape varieties, with the Loire's hallmark of high acidity and relatively light body. Between St-Pourçain and Lyons are the very similar, gutsy Beaujolais-like wines of Côtes du Forez and Côte Roannaise, as well as the varied but rarely exported wines of the Côtes d'Auvergne.

Coteaux du Lyonnais are Beaujolais-like wines made in the outer reaches of Lyons.

ITALY

Ah, Italy – what a beautiful, hedonistic, disorganized, frustrating country! Italy can provide wine lovers with so many distinctive, unique flavours and styles, bottles full of Italian verve and creativity. It also sluices forth rivers of disgracefully thin, characterless stuff to be sold under its most commercially useful names: Soave, Valpolicella, Lambrusco, Frascati and the like.

Although the key to understanding Italy is to understand that it is a group of regions rather than a single homogeneous country – from the heady, often sweet, ferments of the deep south to the delicate subalpine essences of the north – it is possible to generalize about Italian wine styles to a certain extent. Reds have a certain bitterness that is by no means unpleasant. In fact it is so addictive that I find Italy is the one country I come home from positively determined to continue to drink its wines (rather than, as usual, desperate for a complete change). Italian white wines have in the past been distinguished by their lack of aroma and lack of obvious fruitiness (very unmodern), but this is changing – not least as a result of incoming 'flying wine-makers' (see page 68).

For many of us, this is Italy. A simple shop in Chianti country where no one needs a special licence to sell something as life-enhancing as wine.

UNDERSTANDING LABELS

cantina means literally cellar or winery.
A **Cantina Sociale** is a co-operative winery.
Classico, usually original heartland of a wine zone.
cru is, especially in Piedmont, a specially designated vineyard.
DOC, Denominazione di Origine Controllata, Italy's failed attempt at a system of distinguishing its superior wines fashioned in the image of France's Appellation Contrôlée. Some argue it was imposed too early and too strictly, others that it was too late and not strict enough. The truth is probably that the Italians do not willingly submit to regulation. For the consumer, DOC means precious little, for in many DOCs the allowed yields are often far too high to concentrate quality in the resulting wines.
DOCG, Denominazione di Origine Controllata e Garantita, the super-DOC category wines are reliably among Italy's better bottles.
fattoria, farm (a **podere** is even smaller)
frizzante, lightly sparkling.
IGT, newish category of regional wines between DOC and Vino da Tavola.
Riserva generally denotes prolonged ageing under carefully prescribed conditions.
spumante, sparkling.
Superiore, usually a little higher in alcohol.
tenuta, wine estate or smallholding.
vendemmia, vintage.
Vino da Tavola, Italy's supposedly basic table wine category, designed to be on a par with France's Vin de Table. For some time it also included a significant proportion of Italy's best wines, which don't happen to conform to any DOC regulations, though the new IGT is designed specifically for them.

NORTH WEST ITALY

PIEDMONT

In a nutshell: Italy's most terroiriste *area,
with strong similarities to Burgundy.*
Grapes: *Nebbiolo, Barbera, Dolcetto* (RED),
Moscato, Cortese, Arneis (WHITE)

Of all the places I visited in the preparation for this book, Piedmont won my heart for its sheer *joie de vivre*. And the use of French is not too undiplomatically inappropriate here, for this region is only just over the alps from France and the local dialect is perfectly comprehensible to a French speaker. I have to admit that Piedmont also stole my stomach. I know of no other part of the world where every café and restaurant in the smallest village, no matter how unprepossessing, seems able and willing to serve course after course of stunningly fresh, stylishly but minimally prepared food – the raw meat-based antipasti, the risotti, the tartufi. Tartufi are knobbly white potato-like truffles which are hunted by carefully trained, zealously guarded and occasionally sabotaged dogs – ideally white so that the hunting can take place in the dead of night and everyone can keep their favourite spots a secret ... but I must stop. This is a book about wine.

The scenery is stunning too, however, especially in autumn at the height of the white truffle season when each patch of vines turns a different shade of pink, orange, brown, purple and green. Whenever the fog, or *nebbia*, clears, the tightly folded Langhe hills which expose the Barolo and Barbaresco vineyards (Piedmont's most famous) are dwarfed by the snow-covered alps to the north and west. Most of Piedmont's excitingly varied wine is produced in conditions of enviable beauty and gastronomic luxury to which everyone seems to have access. Do these people pay tax?

Unusually for Italy, Piedmont is a wine region to which grape varieties are the key. Its most famous wines have for decades been dramatically intense, subtly perfumed, alcoholic, long-lived, occasionally unbearably tannic red wines which owe everything to the finicky, local speciality, the late-ripening Nebbiolo vine (supposedly named after the fog). But enormous quantities of much tarter (or crisper), lively Barbera and softly mouth-filling Dolcetto are also grown as well as some local rarities such as strawberry-flavoured Brachetto, curiously sweet and sparkling Freisa, light and tangy Grignolino and unusual Ruchè or Rouchet. (See Section Three for details of how these and other varieties taste.)

Piedmont is also home to a variety of local white grape specialities which to my palate share delicacy, dryness and an aroma that often reminds me of ripe pears. Cortese is the grape of the most respected white, Gavi; the perfumed Arneis has been very fashionable; and Favorita is also grown in the Roero just north of Barolo and Barbaresco country. Erbaluce makes small quantities of sweet white wine but the most prolific white grape of Piedmont is **Moscato** (Muscat), which is responsible for oceans of Asti and various other featherlight, grapey Moscatos, many of which are sparkling, or spumante. For many years it was fashionable to be rather snooty about this style of wine but as usual every action is followed by a reaction. Some of the finest palates in the wine business are now great fans of the best examples of the smartest category, Moscato d'Asti. These wines have the great virtue of being extremely light, often less than six per cent alcohol, refreshingly fizzy and fruitily sweet – which makes them a good choice for serving with dessert after a heavy meal.

Many Piedmontese wines are labelled varietally, as in Nebbiolo delle Langhe, Barbera d'Asti and Dolcetto d'Alba. Monferrato, Diano, Ovada and Acqui are other geographical zones.

One of these wines labelled Nebbiolo can offer some of Piedmont's dark, satanic majesty in a bottle at a fraction of the cost of a great Barolo or Barbaresco, although so can some of the best Barbera. Barbera is grown in great quantity all over the region and for decades was dismissed as the region's light, tart, quaffing wine to be drunk as young as possible. Perhaps the greatest of many revolutions Piedmontese wine has seen in the last decade however is the rehabilitation of Barbera. Nowadays the **Barbera** found outside the region is much more likely to be a serious (for which read 'expensive'), deep-coloured wine designed for medium to long ageing. Taking the lead from the late Giacomo Bologna's prototype oaked Barbera, Bricco dell'Uccellone, hundreds of producers have now made changes to their Barbera production in both vineyard and cellar. The produce of low-yielding Barbera vines matured in small French oak barrels, or barriques, can be a revelation and is also definitively Piedmontese in character. Although the historical essence of Piedmontese wine was as single, 100 per cent varietals, an increasing number of producers now experiment with blends: Nebbiolo blended with Barbera, Merlot, Cabernet or even Syrah.

Piedmont's most friendly wine is **Dolcetto** which should burst with fruit while being impressively deep-coloured and, often, quite alcoholic. Dolcetto is particularly useful for growers because, unlike ultra-fussy, late ripening Nebbiolo, it will ripen on less favoured sites, even north-facing ones. Dolcetto is called that (meaning 'little sweet one') because, being so much lower in acidity than Barbera, it really does taste sweet in comparison. And, unlike most Piedmontese reds, it is designed to be drunk within the first three to five years of its life. Many of the best examples are labelled Dolcetto d'Alba, with Dolcetto di Ovada and Dolcetto di Dogliani also providing some of the best-value choices on Piedmontese wine lists.

More and more producers are beginning to look at the wider world of wine (for reasons I don't entirely understand; if I made wine here I'd be an incorrigible introspect). The result is that many of them have planted little plots of 'international' varieties: Cabernet Sauvignon; some Chardonnay which can be transformed into very elegant wine, thanks to barrel fermentation; some Sauvignon Blanc; and even some Riesling and Viognier. If the Piedmontese are importing grape invaders, it's no wonder the rest of the world is.

It is beyond question, however, that the greatest wines of Piedmont are Barolo and, very slightly lighter and earlier maturing, Barbaresco. These are two of the wine world's pinnacles but, as Aldo Conterno placidly observes, they are not easy to understand and, since they are made in small quantity, that matters little. Certainly, to judge from the fleets of Mercedes and BMWs which arrive from Switzerland and Germany to fill up with some of the world's most expensive wines, there is no shortage of enthusiasm for this wine style.

The Langhe hills around the town of Alba, with their different altitudes and expositions, are Italy's answer to Burgundy's Côte d'Or, and different vineyards can, similarly, produce quite different wines, which is why there has been an increase in single-vineyard bottlings. **Barolo** conventionally known as Italy's 'wine of kings and king of wines', is particularly rich in different wine characters, created by the turn of a hillside, a seam of sandstone or marl. It is majestic in every sense, the most concentrated expression of the Nebbiolo grape which has needed coaxing and a fine autumn to ripen properly. But there are huge and demonstrable differences between different parts of the five small parishes that make up the Barolo DOCG. Wines made from grapes grown in the western villages of La Morra and the village of Barolo itself tend to be a little lighter and more open than those made in Castiglione Falletto, Monforte d'Alba and Serralunga d'Alba to the east and north.

Barbaresco, another DOCG, has more in common with the lighter wines of Barolo, with its rather fewer vineyards planted on generally

Eating al fresco at the famous annual autumn Wine and Food Fair in the town of Asti – now as famous for its concentrated dry reds made from Barbera grapes as for its sweet, grapey fizz.

warmer, lower land which means that both grapes and wines mature slightly earlier – though this can mean waiting only 10 years rather than 20. These wines are not for the impatient, and it is a tribute to the intrinsic excitement of these anachronistic wines that they are held in such high esteem even in this impatient age of the fast forward button. The man who can take considerable credit for this is the most famous inhabitant of Barbaresco, Angelo Gaja, as talented a showman as winemaker. Gaja's were the first internationally-marketed – at sky high prices – single vineyard wines from either Barolo or Barbaresco. Today, there are hundreds of such wines from each area, many carrying the words Sorì or Bricco (local dialect for specific sites) on the label. And Gaja himself has now expanded not just into Barolo but also Montalcino and the Maremma in Tuscany.

Wines here have traditionally, as throughout Italy, been matured in large, old Slovenian oak oval casks, but the importation of French barriques in the 1970s and 1980s caused a stir

and some revision of wine styles, making some of them more open and less distinctive (or, to put it another way, earlier maturing and less cussed). Much has been made in the last two decades of the modernists v. traditionalists debate in the Langhe, but in truth the wines have in general gently evolved so that none of Nebbiolo's extraordinarily haunting resonances, reminiscent of violets, tar, truffles and sometimes roses, is lost, but these relatively expensive wines are approachable after a decade or so in bottle – and sometimes even earlier.

Other factors than imported small French barrels have dragged these wines into the 20th and even 21st century; producers today use a mixture of barriques and larger-sized oak containers. It was only relatively recently that Langhe winemakers graduated from being peasant growers selling grapes or their own distinctly rustic wines to large merchant bottlers to becoming sophisticated winemakers with their own labels. They have now learnt to control fermentations, particularly the temperature of them, so that they extract just the best bits of the grape, not fiercely astringent tannins.

Another reason why the character of Barolo and Barbaresco has changed recently is climatic. Global warming seems to have targeted this part of the world in particular, delivering a consecutive run of great vintages in which even the late-ripening Nebbiolo managed to reach full and glorious maturity – and even occasionally overripeness – throughout the second half of the 1990s and the early years of this century.

Even the colour of the wines seems to have changed. Traditionally Barolo and Barbaresco were not notably deep-coloured and often had an orange tinge at only a few years old. Today the wines are in general much deeper-coloured and more likely to be crimson than orange. This may be partly because of the evolution in wine-making and partly because, like Pinot Noir in Burgundy, the Nebbiolo grape mutates easily and has been adapting itself to local conditions. But there is many a whisper that these deeper colours owe much to a judicious slug of Barbera or even Cabernet or Merlot – even if Barolo and Barbaresco have officially been meant to be 100 per cent Nebbiolo.

There are dozens of inspired producers in these two small wine zones. My favourites include Elio Altare, Ascheri, Clerico, Aldo Conterno, Giacomo Conterno, Conterno-Fantino, (recent vintages of) Fontanafredda, Gaja, Elio Grasso, Marchese di Gresy, Mascarello, Parusso, Pira, Prunotto, Ratti, Bruno Rocca, Sandrone, Vajra, Vietti and Roberto Voerzio.

Another group of slightly earthier, lighter bodied Nebbiolo wines is made in communities around the town of Gattinara in subalpine hills almost due north of Alba where Nebbiolo is known as Spanna: **Gattinara**, **Ghemme**, **Boca**, **Lessona**, **Bramaterra**, **Sizzano**, **Fara** and, right on the border with Valle d'Aosta, **Carema**.

These wines are still likely to have an orange rim but can often provide a much better value Nebbiolo experience than the world-famous greats of the Langhe.

VALLE D'AOSTA

Very little wine leaves this alpine region on the French border but it is fertile hunting ground for lovers of ancient grape varieties, both red and white, a mix from Piedmont, the Rhône, Burgundy and Switzerland as well as some intriguing local specialities which are increasingly valued and understood. Chambave, Morgex, Nus and La Salle are all names found on the labels of these wines, which can often taste, not surprisingly, Swiss.

LOMBARDY

Some of the most extraordinary wines produced on the plains and hills north of Milan are the slightly tough Nebbiolo-based reds of **Valtellina** on vertiginous, south-facing slopes just south of the Swiss border, the innocuous dry white **Lugana** made on the shores of Lake Garda, and **Franciacorta**, an extremely varied but interesting area for serious red, dry white and sparkling wines. The region also produces most of the raw material for Italy's most skilled sparkling winemakers such as Bellavista and the dynamic Ca' del Bosco whose fine, Chardonnay-based Annamaria Clementi bottling is superior to the great majority of champagnes. This is most certainly an area under-represented on export markets.

LIGURIA

The dramatic vineyards of the coast around Genoa produce hardly enough wine for the region's tourists. Cinqueterre and Dolceacqua are the place names most commonly encountered outside the region. Local grape varieties are Ormeasco (the Dolcetto of Piedmont), light red Rossesse, and crisp white Vermentino and Pigato.

NORTH EAST ITALY

This is the land of the Tre Venezie: Veneto, Friuli and Trentino.

VENETO

In a nutshell: Lots of commercial Soave and Valpolicella, centre of dried grape wine production.
Grapes: Corvina, Molinara, Rondinella (RED), Garganega, Trebbiano di Soave, Chardonnay (WHITE)

The Veneto, centred on Verona in the hinterland of Venice, is Italy's wine factory. Here lakes of pale red Valpolicella and Bardolino and watery Soave are drained into bottles by the million for shipment to Italian and Italianate restaurants all around the globe where, one must assume, they are gulped by a thoroughly undiscriminating public. Vineyards that are typically flat and fertile have been allowed to spew forth overgenerous yields of characterless wine which still qualifies as DOC. Soave, Valpolicella and, to a certain extent, Bardolino have been reduced to the same status as Liebfraumilch – wine as a commodity.

The difference, however, is that whereas no one would even try to make truly serious Liebfraumilch, many ambitious winemakers within these three wine zones are making extremely good wines. As their influence, fortunately, increases, the real challenge for the consumer (and the wine retailer) is to distinguish the goodies from the baddies.

One easy (although not infallible – this is Italy, after all) starting-point is to look for wines described as Classico, which are pro-

The Veneto is the world's capital of grape-drying, a process which concentrates the natural grape sugar and results in alcoholic, concentrated wines.

The handsome Villa Allegri near Grez-zana north of Verona, surrounded by vines in the Valpaltena zone of Valpolicella.

duced within the original central zone rather than the current much larger regions cynically expanded to make the most of the names' currency on international markets. **Valpolicella** described as Superiore must be at least 12 per cent alcohol and aged at least a year before bottling (whereas basic Valpolicella may be just 11 per cent alcohol and as much of a rush job as Beaujolais Nouveau). Another indi-cator of quality, it must be said, is a premium price. Valpolicella that is lively crimson rather than sludge pink, and tastes of bitter, juicy cherries rather than just tasting bitter cannot be produced cheaply. Yields must neces-sarily be much lower than on flatter, more easily mechanized vineyards. Reliably superior Valpoli-cella producers include Allegrini, Boscaini, Dal Forno, Masi, Quintarelli, Santi and Tedeschi.

Something has gone wrong with the Valpolicella recipe too. Corvina is by far the most characterful of the three grape varieties from which it may be made, but all-Corvina wines are outlawed by the Valpolicella regulations so that they, like so many good Italian wines, must be sold simply as a Vino da Tavola. The Molinara vine tends to produce thin, acidic wine, while it can be difficult to squeeze much flavour out of Rondinella. (In fact largely because the regulations allow a maximum of only 70 per cent Corvina, the seriously good producer Allegrini withdrew its wines from the Valpolicella DOC, threatening just as much anarchy in the Veneto as has been common in Tuscany.)

The classic way of adding depth and bite to Valpolicella (which should be a refreshing, tangy wine rather than one to age years and years) is to add additional grape skins, ideally those whose sugar content has been concentrated by drying, a technique known as *ripasso* or 'repassed', which increases the final alcohol and phenolic content in wines described as *passito*.

The Veneto's true distinction in the world of wine is that it is the only region where any serious quantity of wine is still made using grapes dried to concentrate their sugar content. This was the only way the Greeks and Romans had of increasing the resulting wines' alcohol content, because distillation and therefore alcoholic spirit was still unknown. Such wines are described as **Recioto**, and may be red or white, dry or sweet. If all the grape sugar is fermented out to alcohol such wines are also described as **Amarone**, or bitter, for Valpolicella grapes dried to yield a wine of perhaps 16 per cent alcohol can certainly taste extremely intense (and should be sipped with care, ideally after a meal like port rather than swigged throughout a meal).

The white wine version, a refreshingly sweet Recioto di Soave, is much less common but it too concentrates the inherent qualities of the local grapes, in this case the appley Garganega. **Soave**, the Veneto's most famous white wine

ambassador, is every bit as unpredictable in quality as Valpolicella, with the added variable that a wider range of grape varieties may be used: not just the local Garganega and Trebbiano di Soave (Trebbianos of various sorts abound in Italy) but also Chardonnay, Pinot Bianco (Pinot Blanc) and the neutral Trebbiano Toscano. Good Soave is straw coloured and has a distinctive flavour reminiscent of almonds and apples.

Anselmi and Pieropan have for years shown that Soave can be so much more than a vapid, aroma-free mouthwash, but the increasing number of other producers now giving them a run for their money includes Bertani, Ca' Rugate, Gini, Inama, Prà and Zenato. There is now sufficient confidence in the green terraces of Soave that producers of this calibre bottle all sorts of different vineyards' produce separately, so much character does each imprint on the wines produced there. Some of the wines have so much flavour and concentration that they can stand up to barrique ageing. Such characterful wines are a world away in quality (and price) from commodity mouthwash called Soave produced in such quantity mainly by the co-operatives that dominate this region.

Bardolino, made on the shores of Lake Garda, is basically a lightweight Valpolicella and good examples from producers of the calibre of Corte Gardoni, Guerrieri Rizzardi and San Pietro can make delicious summer drinking. The rosé version is called Chiaretto and local, pretty Soave-like whites include Lugana (just over the border in Lombardy) and Bianca di Custoza. Gambellara is made just east of Soave and is also difficult to distinguish from it. The varied wines, red and white, made around Vicenza and Padua with their handsome Palladian villas are known as Colli Berici and Colli Euganei respectively. These wines are based on a mixture of local grapes and such international travellers as Merlot, Cabernet and Pinot Bianco (Pinot Blanc). A similar range of grapes is grown around the town of Breganze just north of Vicenza where one hard-working producer,

Maculan, and one local grape, Vespaiolo, have been responsible for putting Breganze on the world's wine map. Vespaiolo is thought to get its name from the wasps attracted to its particularly sweet grapes, which Maculan has proved can make great sweet white wine. Torcolato is made from semi-dried grapes and manages that Italian sweet white wine trick of being very sweet but also very tangy and refreshing.

East of here, across Piave river above the plains stretching towards the lagoons and Venice, is the source of north east Italy's favourite sparkling wine, Prosecco, based on the grape of the same name. Many a traveller has fallen in love with this at Harry's Bar where it was first blended with peach juice to make a Bellini, or at the Locanda Cipriani on the spookily silent island of Torcello where it is served in glass jugs. I have to confess that I am relatively immune to its charms. Even the best examples such as those from Adami, Bisol and Carpeni-Malvolti strike my palate as just slightly too sweet and frothy but it is probably my fault that I expect it to be too much like champagne. Conegliano-Valdobbiadene is the best zone.

Most of the still wines made on this fertile plain go under the name Piave or Lison-Pramaggiore. They tend to be decent, light (though generally uninspiring) Cabernets, Merlots or the local white grape Verduzzo. More interesting (if uncompromisingly dry) are reds from Raboso and Refosco grapes.

FRIULI

In a nutshell: Pure, aromatic varietals.
Grapes: All the universals plus Refosco (RED), Tocai Friulano, Picolit, Ribolla, Verduzzo (WHITE)

Friuli, or Friuli-Venezia Giulia to give this curious north east corner of Italy its full name, is worshipped by many Italian wine lovers. Its popularity illustrates nicely that the 'grass is always greener' rule holds as firmly in the world of wine as elsewhere. Basically, every nation of wine consumers treasures most what it finds most difficult to produce. In Germany, for example, the homeland of light, aromatic whites, it is full-bodied, deep-coloured reds that are in greatest demand. But because Friuli is the only part of Italy in which light, aromatic whites have been produced with ease (thanks largely to the early introduction of refrigerated ways of getting pure, fresh, varietal fruit into a bottle), Italian connoisseurs have been prepared to pay well over the odds for them.

In a way Friuli wines are foreign to Italians. They are a product instead of a hilly no man's land between the Veneto, Slovenia and southern Austria – and they taste like it. This is the land of the varietal, wine made principally to express the fruit of the grape variety specified on the label. All of 17 different varietals are allowed within the scope of Friuli's two most respected DOCs, **Collio (Goriziano)** and **Colli Orientali (del Friuli)** which means Eastern Hills. Of these the most common are Tocai Friulano, Pinot Grigio (Pinot Gris), Sauvignon Blanc, Pinot Bianco (Pinot Blanc), Merlot, Chardonnay and Cabernet Franc/Frank (which most people nowadays believe to be the Carmenère of Chile in fact), but local specialities include Ribolla, Verduzzo and the always expensive Picolit for white wines and the tangy Refosco and rare Schioppettino and promising Pignolo for the red wines of Colli Orientali. In general the best red wines come from the south western corner of the Colli Orientali, most of which is almost alpine, being effectively the foothills of the Dolomites. (Quite) sweet white Picolit is a local golden speciality of the Colli Orientali, once fashionable and still too expensive, made from dried grapes.

Collio is almost indistinguishable from that part of Slovenia just over the hills of Gorizia on its northern border, and there is no shortage of fine, increasingly fruity and interesting white wine made here. Traminer, Malvasia and Riesling Italico (Welschriesling rather than the classic Riesling of Germany which is known in Italy as Riesling Renano) are all grown here.

Now that Italian winemakers south and west of Friuli have also mastered the art of making fresh, fruity white wines, however, their counterparts in Collio (Goriziano) and Colli Orientali (del Fruili) are having to try harder to justify their price premium, typically but not necessarily with greater use of small oak barrels. The standard of winemaking here is generally very high, and yields relatively low, even if the price for this is that the wines can taste remarkably similar.

Some of the producers most revered within Italy are Abbazio di Rosazzo, Borgo Conventi, Borgo del Tiglio, La Castellada, Girolamo Dorigo, Filliputi, Felluga, Gravner, Jermann, Marin, Puiatti, Radikon, Ronchi di Manzano, Ronco del Gnemiz, Schiopetto, Tercic and Villa Russiz, whose wines can continue to develop in bottle for two or three years.

Other important DOC zones such as **Isonzo** (to the south and subject to more warming influence from the Adriatic) and, especially, the prolific **Grave del Friuli** are on flatter land and tend to produce less impressively rapier-like flavours. Nevertheless, producers such as Di Lenardo, Lis Neris, Masut da Rive, Pighin, Pittaro, Vie di Romans and Vistorta show just what can be done with the best sites in this part of the world. Other DOCs produced here include **Aquileia**, **Latisana** and **Carso**.

TRENTINO-ALTO ADIGE

In a nutshell: Alpine vineyards producing
usually lightish varietals.
Grapes: All the universals plus Teroldego,
Schiava, Lagrein (RED), Traminer, local
Muskatellers (WHITE)

The two neighbouring wine regions of Trentino (the lower, more southerly part of the Adige valley around the town of Trento) and the upper (Alto) Adige valley produce Italy's most alpine wines in a region dominated by co-operatives. **Trentino** is the catch-all DOC for a wide range of varietal wines, from smudgy, light,

sweetish red Schiava (Vernatsch in German) to some fine high-altitude, barrel-fermented Chardonnays. Local variety and varietal Marzemino is one of the few wines to be mentioned specifically in any opera, in this case *Don Giovanni*, and often made as a sweet, slightly fizzy pale red. Teroldego, or Teroldego Rotaliano, is a more commonly planted local red named after the Rotaliano plain in the north of Trentino (one of the very few flat stretches of land in the whole Adige valley) that can be, if not overcropped, intensely fruity and deep-coloured. The most serious examples are made by Elisabetta Foradori but there is no shortage of bitter, cheaper examples. The full range of international varietals is produced, generally in rather pale versions. The likes of Pojer & Sandri (who make one of the world's few sought-after Müller-Thurgaus), the aristocratic San Leonardo estate with its Bordeaux blends and the research institute at San

Michele all'Adige prove just what can be achieved in this lower zone due north of the commercial battleground of Verona. The region's potential for top quality sparkling wines has long been demonstrated by Ferrari.

Alto Adige, however, is a more distinctive environment – not just because it is known as the South Tyrol, or Südtirol (German is spoken by many of the older inhabitants here), but also because of the contrast between the warm summers and cold winters of vineyards grafted on to the Dolomite foothills. The region undoubtedly has enormous, but often unrealized potential (although some of its wines might well impress more widely if chaptalization were allowed as in Switzerland to the north). Schiava is quantitatively important but is increasingly being replaced by the other local red speciality Lagrein which has come to be recognized as potentially rather an exciting grape so long as its bitterness is softened by careful winemaking,

often barrique ageing. The dark red version is known as Lagrein Scuro (Dunkel in German) while the pink one is Lagrein Rosato, or Kretzer. Gries just west of the town of Bolzano is a particularly good zone for Lagrein. Alto Adige can rival Friuli for pure, varietal, more internationally familiar flavours from producers such as Castel Schwanburg, Franz Haas, Hofstätter, Alois Lageder, Niedrist, Tieffenbrunner, Elena Walch and Widmann, notably for Gewürztraminer which may have its origins in the village of Tramin (Terlano in Italian).

Co-operatives have long been important here and some of them such as Colterenziore among Italy's most admired.

Distinctly Austrian-looking church in Alto Adige where vines are trained on the famous pergola trentina *strips of well-ventilated vines angled towards the sun.*

TUSCANY

In a nutshell: *Italy's dynamic wine powerhouse.*
Grapes: *Sangiovese, Cabernet Sauvignon (RED),*
Trebbiano, Malvasia, Vernaccia (WHITE)

It may seem logically and geographically absurd to single out Tuscany from the rest of central Italy (see page 224) but it makes perfect sense for wine lovers. The Veneto may be the Italian wine industry's commercial centre, Piedmont may be the source of the country's greatest gastronomic thrills, but in the forever medieval

Some rather upmarket grape pickers having lunch on the terrace at Riecine, one of the most admired estates in Chianti Classico (below). In most years it would be unthinkable to remain exposed to the sunshine for longer than absolutely necessary, but as the autumn deepens, mists can often invade Tuscany's valleys below the many-towered San Gimignano (opposite), famous for its full, dry white Vernaccia.

hills of Tuscany is Italy's greatest concentration of ambitious, dedicated winemakers. Toscana, as it is known in Italian, is the land of the small-holder rather than the co-operative, many of these smallholders having earned their not inconsiderable fortunes elsewhere (as in California's Napa Valley). Since the 1970s they have invaded this beautiful countryside dedicated to olives, pines and vines, which was once dominated by aristocratic, Florentine wine-merchant houses such as Antinori, Frescobaldi and Ruffino.

In the 1960s, when the entire wine world was driven so much more by the need to supply quantity rather than quality, some extremely questionable clones of Sangiovese were planted, producing wines so light they had to be beefed up with undercover additions from the hotter climates of southern Italy and its islands. The Chianti region's researchers' major task more recently has been to identify those clones of Sangiovese which produce the best quality wine, which means that today the great majority of Chianti exported is almost unrecognizable from the pale, tart ferments of old. It is deep-coloured, carefully matured in oak, with ageing potential and flavours intriguingly reminiscent of prunes and chestnuts.

The relentlessly undulating landscape and its temperate climate make it ideal for producing red wines with the same sort of digestible weight (about 12 to 13 per cent alcohol) and ageing potential as red bordeaux. But the wines' flavours are very different from their French counterparts. The Sangiovese vine is king here and the quality of wine it yields depends heavily on the exposure and altitude at which it is planted. (As anyone who has visited Tuscany in the winter knows, it can be inhospitably bleak.)

Greater **Chianti** is Tuscany's, indeed Italy's, most important, if much-divided wine zone. Chianti was for long made from Sangiovese lightened to a greater or lesser extent with the unexceptional white Trebbiano grape and occasionally with white Malvasia and red Canaiolo. Not surprisingly, it comes in all quality levels,

from dire to sublime (the sublime not necessarily costing all that many times more than the dire). A wine labelled simply Chianti is quite likely to be a very basic red sold to meet a price. To discover what the Tuscan hills really have to offer the taste buds it has usually been necessary to seek out a wine labelled with the name of one of the seven superior subzones.

Named respectively after the hills surrounding Arezzo, Florence, Pisa and Siena, **Chianti Colli Aretini**, **Chianti Colli Fiorentini**, **Chianti Colline Pisane** and **Chianti Colli Senesi** are not widely exported. The relatively new **Chianti Montespertoli** is effectively a western extension of the Colli Fiorentini, **Chianti Montalbano** is generally a lightish wine made west of Florence while **Chianti Rufina**, from east of the city, can be both one of the finest and longest lasting, even if it can seem a little light and tart when young. Selvapiana is a prime example. Undoubtedly the most important Chianti zone in terms of quality and durability, however, is **Chianti Classico**, which is the hilly heart of the Chianti zone.

It is fair to say (and this is a generalization which can rarely be made of any other wine zone anywhere) that Chianti Classico is one of the most consistently well-made wines in the world. You may not like the defiantly rural, almost farmyard-like flavours of traditional Sangiovese but an admirably low proportion of all Chianti Classico is carelessly made.

Regulations introduced in 1984 (and with almost farcical disregard for the fact that this was Tuscany's most disastrous vintage in living memory) elevated Chianti Classico to DOCG status (straight Chianti is just a DOC) and insisted on suitably low yields, sensible minimum ageing periods and disqualification of the produce of vines younger than five years old. The rules also formalize what had in reality been happening for some time in recognition of the shortcomings of the Chianti grape variety recipe. Although Sangiovese continues to provide the backbone of Chianti Classico (and the better clones, carefully transformed into wine, can display lovely ripe, pruney nuances), producers may all but ignore the white grape varieties specified in the basic Chianti recipe and may add up to 10 per cent of such immigrants as Merlot, Syrah and Cabernet Sauvignon, all of which have produced some stunning wine in Tuscany. (Some argue that Syrah may in fact be the most successful of the three.) If French grape varieties have been the most notable recent import to Tuscany's vineyards, then small French barrels have had the same dramatic effect in its cellars. Wines were traditionally aged in large old Slovenian oak ovals, but the effect of widespread use of newish, small, French oak barriques has been to concentrate and smooth the flavours of wines matured in them.

The typical Chianti Classico estate produces much more, however, than a straight Chianti Classico red, best suited to early drinking. Most of them also make a Chianti Classico Riserva, aged for longer before bottling, designed to be further aged in bottle, a basic white wine into which their portion of Tuscany's Trebbiano surplus goes, perhaps a barrel-aged Chardonnay or Sauvignon Blanc, usually some olive oil produced from the estate's olive trees, often some sweet, strong, barrel-aged Vin Santo (a sweet, golden, nutty Tuscan speciality made from dried grapes, traditionally Malvasia), and almost invariably a serious, premium red wine based on Cabernet, Merlot or Syrah vines, often blended with each other or with varying proportions of Sangiovese.

Until the introduction of the IGT category (see page 207), these so-called **Supertuscans** qualified only as Vino da Tavola, so their producers dreamt up a plethora of special names for them – just as the house of Antinori did with its prototype Supertuscan Tignanello (a barrique-aged blend of Sangiovese and Cabernet Sauvignon) in the early 1970s. To work out which Supertuscan belongs to which Chianti Classico estate can require considerable sleuthing at the bottom of the wine label.

The most interesting development in the late 1990s and early years of this century has

been the re-evaluation of Chianti Classico Riserva. While imported French grape varieties were a novelty, producers tended to view their Supertuscan blends as their top bottlings. Today, however, most have come to realize that what best expresses the particular character of Chianti is a really serious Sangiovese, made from some of the best quality plants of course. This Sangiovese may well have a small proportion of foreign grapes or such other Tuscan red grapes as Colorino or Canaiolo blended in to it, but it is basically designed to be the finest expression of Sangiovese grown on that particular estate.

In this region, invaded as it is by tourists and well-heeled wannabe country peasants from all over northern Italy, northern Europe and North America, there is no shortage of investment, ambition and expertise (usually in the form of a well-paid, hired-in consultant). Not surprisingly, there are dozens if not hundreds of estates, some of them prefixed by Castello (castle), making good wine. The most common wine fault – indeed one of the few you are likely to encounter here – is over-oaking, a mistake that only the rich can afford.

Some of the better estates include Badia di Coltibuono, Castello di Ama, Castell'in Villa, Fattoria di Felsina, Fonterutoli, Fontodi, Isola e Olena, Fattoria di Montevertine, Il Poggio, Castello di Querceto, Querciabella, Castello di Rampolla, Riecine, San Giusto a Rentennano, San Polo in Rosso, Vicchiomaggio and Castello di Volpaia, but this is far from a complete list. Others with a more recent and sometimes therefore less tired reputation include Brolio (recently revitalized), Cacchiano, Castellare, Collelungo, La Massa, Monsanto, Monte Bernardi, Nittardi, Paneretta, Terrabianca, Valtellina and Villa Cafaggio.

The larger merchants Antinori, Frescobaldi and Ruffino all produce some very fine wines, many of them single vineyard bottlings and, in the case of Antinori, produced from all over central Italy. Indeed one of the most significant trends in modern Italian wine is for producers to spread their wings from their geographical origins. This is not so surprising perhaps with companies as big as Antinori whose tentacles stretch from Prunotto in Piedmont as far south as its extensive vineyard holdings on the heel of Italy, but even such an individualist as Angelo Gaja has outposts from his base in Barbaresco that include a spectacular winery on the Tuscan coast and one of Montalcino's top estates.

Essence of Sangiovese is captured in the southern **Brunello di Montalcino** zone around the town of Montalcino near Siena, Brunello being a super-concentrated local strain of Sangiovese that is solely responsible for this, potentially one of Italy's greatest wines.

South of Chianti and with usefully poor, infertile soils, the almost square Montalcino zone has no trouble ripening the vines' relatively low charge of grapes in its much milder climate. This produces a sort of essence of Sangiovese, capable of ageing for ever and a day. In fact Brunello di Montalcino is not released before it is four years old and rarely drunk for pleasure in its first decade.

If Chianti Classico Riserva is generally best at between four and eight years, Brunello can evolve for a decade or sometimes two. The lighter (and in many ways more useful) wines of the zone are sold as Rosso di Montalcino and, from one of the best producers such as Altesino, Argiano, dei Barbi, Biondi-Santi, Caparzo, Case Basse, Col d'Orcia, Costanti, Lisini, Pacenti, Pieve Santa Restituta, Poggio Antico, Il Poggione, Sesta and Talenti, can be an especially good buy and are drinkable at three to seven years. It is here that Luce, the joint venture between Frescobaldi and Robert Mondavi of California, is based, as well as the major investment by Villa Banfi, a giant exporter whose fortunes were based on shipping an ocean of Lambrusco to the US in the 1980s.

The south west corner of the zone, at its lowest altitudes, tends to produce the most concentrated wines; the highest vineyards just south of sleepy Montalcino itself produce some of the most refined (though refined Brunello may be an oxymoron).

As everywhere in Italian wine, everything is in a state of constant movement towards modernism. A new DOC has been created, San'Antimo, for wines made from international grape varieties within the Montalcino zone. And the use of small new French oak barrels is increasing and threatening to blur Brunello's distinctive character. On the other hand, can one blame producers for trying to satisfy the desires of today's impatient wine drinkers?

Vino Nobile di Montepulciano was elevated to DOCG status at the same time as Brunello but, with the exception of local hero Avignonesi, has been slower to show quite the form and concentration of Brunello – perhaps because of its even warmer climate or because the overall standard of winemaking is lower. It, too, produces a slightly lighter and earlier maturing wine sold as Rosso di Montepulciano. The local strain of Sangiovese is called Prugnolo Gentile and here too minimum oak ageing periods have been reduced, in this case to just one year rather than the two required for Brunello. Some would describe Vino Nobile as a sort of cross between Brunello and Chianti Classico. Poliziano is another name that is more reliable than most.

But perhaps Montepulciano's real gift to the wine drinkers of the world is the superlative quality of its Vin Santo (see page 221).

Tuscany's fourth DOCG is **Carmignano**, a small but interesting zone near Pisa which has embraced Cabernet Sauvignon for years and has therefore been a particularly easy wine for non-Italians to understand. The Capezzana estate dominates production.

Tuscany is essentially red wine country. Various noble and/or well-funded estates have tried to make copies of white burgundy, Loire Sauvignon Blanc and even Condrieu, and there are various nondescript Trebbianos to be drunk strictly within the region itself, but there are few whites worthy of export.

The most interesting Tuscan dry white wine is **Vernaccia di San Gimignano**, made from the powerfully flavoured Vernaccia grape around the wonderful, be-towered hilltop village of San Gimignano (pictured on page 219). The wines can vary from innocuous through firmly fruity to positively oily. Some benefit from oak ageing. Others are overwhelmed by it. Montenidoli and Terruzi & Puthod are two of the most ambitious producers.

All over Tuscany are various small wine zones but the area that seems to have the most serious potential for great winemaking is the Maremma on the western **Tuscan Coast** south of Livorno, particularly but not exclusively around the little village of Bolgheri. A member of the extended Antinori family first showed at the Tenuta San Guido that the area could produce world class Cabernet in the form of Supertuscan Sassicaia. More recently, a younger Antinori has made his name with Ornellaia (mainly Cabernet) and Masseto (mainly Merlot), produced almost next door, and there are now ambitious plantings aplenty along the old Appian Way. These are mostly the hobby wineries of rich men, built with every modern appliance that money can buy and designed to produce wines of the stature and, for better or worse, style of the great wines of Bordeaux.

Antinori has been expanding rapidly here and its Guado al Tasso is surely just the start of a major line of expansion. The Ornellaia estate has been sold to Robert Mondavi of California. Gaja of Barbaresco has fashioned his Ca'Marcanda winery in an area already proven by the likes of Le Macchiole and Grattamarco. Although it is generally agreed that Bolgheri, along with the Médoc and Graves, Napa and Sonoma, Chile's Maipo and the Margaret River in Western Australia provides one of the world's most auspicious areas for ripening subtle, refined Cabernet Sauvignon, Michele Satta has proved that Sangiovese grown here can also be pretty smart.

But perhaps the most exciting thing about this part of the world is that there is still so much land to explore. Tua Rita shows that the Suvereto zone to the immediate south east of

In Tuscany wine is difficult to divorce from the agriturismo *business – the conversion of many buildings on wine estates into holiday accommodation.*

Bolgheri has real potential, and others such as Bellavista of Franciacorta in Lombardy and Foradori of Trentino are buying up suitable land at an extraordinary rate. We will be hearing more of names such as Val di Cornia, Montecucco, Monteregio di Massa Maritima and, already an established winning combination of grape and place, Morellino di Scansano.

It is heartening for thirsty observers such as me to see that even one of the world's oldest wine producers can discover, or perhaps rediscover, new wine regions.

REST OF CENTRAL ITALY

EMILIA-ROMAGNA

The wide plains south of the river Po are the source of a great deal of relatively dreary light red Sangiovese di Romagna (bearing no relation whatever to top quality Chianti Classico) and neutral dry white Trebbiano di Romagna. Interestingly, though, the clonal researches on the Sangiovese vine mentioned on page 220 have revealed that Romagna's Sangiovese can be some of the best, in a concentrated and lively way, provided yields are limited and it is grown on a promising site, such as those of Zerbina and Paradiso. Albana di Romagna is another local

white speciality making some fine sweet wine, along with the pale-skinned Pagedebit grape. This large region is also home to Lambrusco, which in the 1980s was to Italy what Liebfraumilch was to Germany. The larger companies, supplied mainly by a handful of giant co-operatives, have turned Lambrusco into a sweet, low-alcohol, fizzy drink in virtually any colour, which bears little resemblance to wine. Good Lambrusco exists, however, in the form of deep cherry red, lightly fizzy dry wine that can taste perfect with the porcine dishes of Bologna, but is rarely exported. As for Emilia, the northern half of the Emilia-Romagna region, it is domi-

nated by grapes making light, fruity red wines from Barbera and Bonarda which have more in common with the north of Italy.

MARCHE

This extensive region down the Adriatic coast south of Romagna from Rimini to Ancona and beyond is in an exciting stage of evolution and improvement. The most famous wine product of the central eastern coast is Verdicchio, a dry white which can please and increasingly excites. The two best known DOCs for this lemony, potentially

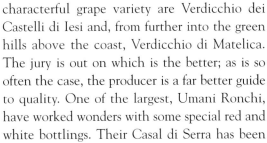

characterful grape variety are Verdicchio dei Castelli di Iesi and, from further into the green hills above the coast, Verdicchio di Matelica. The jury is out on which is the better; as is so often the case, the producer is a far better guide to quality. One of the largest, Umani Ronchi, have worked wonders with some special red and white bottlings. Their Casal di Serra has been one of Italy's most reliably interesting and well-balanced whites for years, just as their oaked Cumaro and San Lorenzo reached new heights for the local red wine, Rosso Conero named after Monte Conero just south of Ancona, when they were first launched. The important grape for Rosso Conero, as for Rosso Piceno produced from a much, much bigger area of southern Marche is Montepulciano (nothing to do with the Tuscan town which produces Vino Nobile from its own strain of Sangiovese). Montepulciano is clearly one of Italy's most useful grapes, producing dark, juicy, well-structured red wines in the right hands which are usually quite incredibly cheap (not a claim you can make about many Italian wines). It is often blended with Sangiovese in this part of the world. Other good producers are Bisci, Fazi Battaglia, Garofoli and Le Terrazze.

UMBRIA

Umbria, effectively a south eastern extension of Tuscany, is potentially the most interesting

Late autumn mists over vines stripped of their foliage in Umbria (left), whose most famous wine is Orvieto (above) – increasingly exciting stuff.

region of this varied collection and has changed the most in the last 10 years.

That international wine drinkers had heard of Umbria was for long largely thanks to just two producers. Lungarotti was for long the dominant producer, with a creditable track record of long-lasting Torgiano wines showing fruit to the end. Antinori also have some highly successful vineyard holdings in Umbria, most notably at Castello della Sala where the finely oaked white Cervara is made, increasingly demonstrating just how good a grape the local Grechetto can be.

Some interesting Pinot Noir is being produced as well as barrel-aged, full-bodied dry whites (and nobly rotten *muffato* sweet wine) from such local grape varieties as Grechetto, sometimes blended with Chardonnay and/or Sauvignon Blanc. But the region's most famous wine by far is Orvieto, a full-bodied Trebbiano-based white which is usually dry but may be slightly sweet or *amabile*. Bigi's and Barberani's is better than most.

But the producer who has put the top wines of Umbria on the map in the last decade or so is Arnaldo Caprai (run by son Marco), whose softening work on the intrinsically tough local grape variety Sagrantino made Italian wine connoisseurs scurry to their maps to locate the little town of Montefalco in the hills north of Spoleto in the southern Apennines. This hard-working textile family has since been rewarded with the compliment of the sincerest form of flattery, and granting of DOCG status to Sagrantino di Montefalco in the early 1990s. These wines positively crackle with life and can last for many years in bottle, however much they display modern winemaking techniques. Sagrantino is often blended with Sangiovese, the most common red grape of Umbria and particularly

Malvasia grapes are picked in a hardly densely-planted vineyard for Frascati in the Castelli Romani.

226

successful in the Colli di Trasimeno, around the classically famous lake of Trasimeno.

The other producer who has made the wine world take notice of Umbria is Riccardo Cotarella who, with his brother Renzo, long-term technical director of the Florentine merchant house Antinori, runs one of Italy's most dynamic wine consultancies from a base on the border of Umbria and Latium (see below). Applying modern winemaking techniques whereby fruit must be super-ripe and barrel treatment ultra-suave, he has turned out a stable of wines which could be criticized for being more international than Italian but could not be reproached for quality or value. He consults to a list of wine producers which extends from the far north of Italy to Sicily but his achievements are particularly notable here on his home ground in Umbria and Latium.

LATIUM

Frascati is to the vineyards that surround Rome in Latium (called Lazio in Italian) what Orvieto is to Umbria. It can sometimes be difficult to distinguish between these two full-bodied dry white wines – which can too often lack discernible characteristics. Castel de Paolis and Tenuta Le Quinte are trying particularly hard.

Riccardo Cotarella has worked some magic on Latium's northern white, usually more memorable for its name, Est!Est!!Est!!!, than its flavour. At the family winery Falesco in the region of production centred on the town of Montefiascone, he has somehow managed to make a wine that seems much more interesting than the official recipe of mainly Trebbiano with a little Malvasia. (Frascati, incidentally, is supposed to be substantially Malvasia – a much more interesting grape than the various Trebbianos that abound in Central Italy – but can often be 100 per cent dull Trebbiano.) His most famous Latium wine internationally however is a particularly luscious 100 per cent Merlot called Montiano which now fetches prices unheard of for a Latium wine in the pre-

Cotarella era. Apart from a little Marino white made just west of Frascati and some Cesanese red in the hills, the Roman region is surprisingly undistinguished in terms of wine.

ABRUZZI AND MOLISE

These wild, hilly, eastern regions on the Adriatic coast of Italy between the Marche and Puglia are arguably Italy's most isolated, and those few who manage to produce exciting wine from the overhead trellises and two grape varieties that dominate production here are to be congratulated.

The two grape varieties officially sanctioned here are the Montepulciano (also planted in the Marche) for red wines and a local Trebbiano, called Trebbiano d'Abruzzo and also known as Bombino Bianco. In general, the red wines here have a great deal more character than the whites, even if most of them are the none-too-demanding, but keenly-priced produce of the local co-operatives.

In the hands of the near-fanatical Eduardo Valentini, however, Montepulciano d'Abruzzo has become a cult wine: deep, dense, brooding and capable of becoming yet more interesting after many years in bottle. His trick is much lower yields than average and extreme selection, sending the great majority of his crop to a co-op and choosing only the very best grapes for the wines carrying his label. If his red is exceptional, his Trebbiano d'Abruzzo stands even higher above the norm, another concentrated essence of subtlety that can be aged for at least as long as a fine white burgundy. Other Abruzzo producers are beginning to present a challenge to his reds.

In Molise, the pace-setter is Di Majo Norante, a family concern that began following organic methods years before they became fashionable (and another of Cotarella's clients). The best wines are made from Montepulciano and the great red and white grapes Aglianico, Fiano, Falanghina and Greco of southern Italy of which we will learn more overleaf.

SOUTHERN ITALY AND ISLANDS

CAMPANIA

In a nutshell: 'Ancient Greek' vine varieties and great potential
Grapes: *Aglianico* (RED),
Fiano, Falanghina, Greco (WHITE)

The vineyards of the region dominated by the city of Naples are in many ways some of Italy's most exciting. Many of them are planted with vines thought to be direct descendants of those brought here by the ancient Greeks. The very name of Aglianico, a red grape of enormous character which is so late-ripening it cannot be grown economically further north, is a corruption of Elleniko, or Greek. And then among white grapes Greco's origins are fairly obvious. Falanghina is thought by some to have been responsible for the brownish wines of long-aged Falernum, arguably the most famous wine in classical literature. Fiano, capable of making nutty white wines which can also be aged, was mentioned by Pliny. All this could be dusty archive stuff were it not for the fact that so many producers are doing their best to make fine modern wines from these ancient grapes, each of which is bursting with character.

The most famous wine based on stern and sturdy Aglianico is Taurasi made in hills directly inland from Naples where it may be picked as late as November. The most famous Taurasi producer is Mastroberardino but they are now being rivalled by the likes of Caggiano, Molettieri, Terredora di Paola and the thoroughly modern Feudi di San Gregorio which has put an international polish on these ancient grape varieties. Perhaps their best-known wine is Serpico, an oaked blend of Aglianico made universally intelligible by blending in a bit of Merlot. They, like others here, also grow the local red grape Piedirosso which is even more

commonly grown in vineyards nearer the coast of Campania.

The modern wine drinker is most likely to meet Fiano grapes in a dry but powerful, age-worthy white labelled Fiano di Avellino after the town on the way to the Taurasi zone from Naples. Feudi di San Gregorio make several single-vineyard bottlings with even more character and some oak ageing. Today's Falernum is the multi-coloured Falerno del Massico made on the coast north of Naples, most successfully by Villa Matilda. But perhaps Campania's most intriguing white wine is Greco di Tufo, made from Greco grapes grown in tufa, a sort of soft, particularly well-drained limestone, just west of Taurasi.

APULIA

In a nutshell: Heady blending wine but improving fast.
Grapes: *Negroamaro, Malvasia Nera, Primitivo, Uva di Troia* (RED)

Puglia is the local name for the region known as Apulia in English which is hugely important in terms of quantity, if not always quality, to the world of wine – and is to be found on an increasing number of wine labels. This region which includes all of the heel of Italy and as far again up the back of the heel along the Adriatic coast produces more wine than Australia, even if only a small proportion of it so far is sold in bottle rather than tanker. Things are changing fast here however.

Until the 1990s, Puglia was a guilty secret, its potent reds and heavy whites shipped quietly north to beef up the less ripe produce of more famous vineyards further north in Italy, to add colour and weight to thin ferments from southern France, and to provide the raw material for manufacturers (there is no other word) of alcoholic drinks such as fizz and vermouth all over northern Europe. If wine producers knew anything about Puglia, they tended to keep quiet about it.

The advent of New World wines however gave a new respectability to wines produced in hot climates, and a new breed of flying winemaker was set to work on the vineyards and vast cellars of Puglia to fashion something reliable and inexpensive for the supermarket buyers of northern Europe. Chardonnay and other international varieties were duly planted and – hey presto – another source of anodyne but predictable bargains emerged. Many of these wines are described on the label as IGT Puglia, or IGT Salento after the peninsula that constitutes the heel of Italy.

There are DOCs in Puglia but few of them have forged any sort of international reputation. In fact only three or four per cent of all Apulian wine is sold as a DOC – most likely Salice Salentino, Copertino, Squinzano or Primitivo di Manduria, all of them strong, sometimes almost porty, reds.

For the moment, Puglia's strong suit is alcohol and flavour and a range of powerful local red grape varieties. Negroamaro, meaning 'black and bitter', is one of the most planted grapes in the region, popular with growers for its sturdy performance in the vineyard, and with wine producers for its depth of colour, flavour and alcohol. It is often blended with the softer, more velvety Malvasia Nera which some think has an even more exciting future in its two strains named after the towns of Lecce and Brindisi. Uva di Troia, another grape whose name suggests Greek origins, is grown in the north of the region. Montepulciano can be found in the very north towards the boundary with Molise.

But the grape of most interest to non-Italians is the early-ripening Primitivo, a speciality of the Gioia del Colle plain just south of Bari and Manduria, the western coast of the heel just south of Taranto. DNA analysis has proved what many had suspected all along, that this vine variety is one and the same as California's

Zinfandel, and is related to the Plavac Mali of Croatia. Some producers have even labelled wines for export Zinfandel.

You can find all sorts of wines coming from this, Italy's New World wine region, where winemakers are writing their own rules, and none of them is fiendishly expensive – yet. There are inexpensive branded varietals which could have been made anywhere; intensely alcoholic ferments that offer perhaps the biggest kick per buck in the world; suspiciously pale, light versions thereof (suggesting grossly high yields or deliberate dilution); and there are some finely crafted, supple, rich reds that really are expressions of the best this very varied region can offer the modern wine drinker. Producers to look out for include Felline, A Mano, Pervini and Promessa.

BASILICATA

Aglianico del Vulture, another Greek grape variety, is this small, deep southern region's claim to wine fame. Its depth of colour and impressive tannin level certainly distinguish it in youth, although it needs many years in bottle to show its best. Leading producers Fratelli D'Angelo show some real mastery of local conditions in their special Canneto bottling and Paternoster make some fine versions of this local strain of the Aglianico grape grown at relatively high altitudes on the slopes of an extinct volcano.

CALABRIA

The vineyards on the toe of Italy are as wild as every other aspect of life there with few exported, or even exportable wines being produced. A curious exception is the extraordinary, classical-tasting, sweet white Greco di Bianco (Bianco being the name of the main town in the production zone). The obvious exception is Ciró, which desultorily produces a deep, intense red. Librandi's Duca San Felice is the best to date, though San Francesco is trying hard.

SARDINIA

In a nutshell: Developing.
Grapes: Cannonau, Carignano (RED),
Vermentino, Nuragus, Torbato (WHITE)

Sardinia is more than an island, it is only just part of Italy. For much of its modern wine-making history it was governed from Spain, and many of its distinctive local grape varieties such as Bovale, Carignano, Cannonau, Monica, Vermentino and possibly Torbato are Spanish in origin. (This is just one of scores of examples of social history being reflected in a country's vineyards.)

The island lies somewhere between Corsica and Sicily, both in terms of geography and wine. Like Corsica (see page 193) it experienced a recent boom and bust in heavily subsidized new vine plantings. Like Sicily it shows signs of real potential and determination to make the most of its own raw ingredients (the Centro Enological Sardo is an active wine research station).

Most of its produce is varietally labelled, some of it is aggressively modern and character-less (the co-operatives ruled without vision until recently). Vermentino is often a creditably light, appetizing white, nowadays made particularly in the north of the island. Nuragus di Cagliari can occasionally be a worthy modern dry white example of one of the island's oldest grape varieties. Carignano di Sulcis from the south shows just how juicy the tough red Carignan can be if exposed to enough warmth, while Cannonau is the local strain of Grenache, or rather Spanish Garnacha. Vernaccia di Oristano is western Sardinia's answer to sherry – interesting but unlikely to be a big commercial hit. Sella & Mosca, owned by Campari, is one of the few notable producers independent of the co-operatives. By far the most sumptuous wines are made by Argiolas, whose Turriga blend of Cannonau and Carignano from ancient vines is sought after all over the world. The Santadi co-op's Terre Brune is also reliably interesting.

SICILY

In a nutshell: In complete transformation and, in parts, very promising.
Grapes: Catarratto, Inzolia (WHITE),
Nero d'Avola, Nerello Mascalese (RED)

Sicily is as fascinating to students of the modern wine world as it is to those of ancient civilizations. This large island, not far from the African coast, regularly produces as much wine as Australia, Chile and Bulgaria put together – yet exports remarkably little under its own flag. Like Apulia, it is a key supplier to northern blenders and, less usefully, a key contributor to the European wine lake. Surprisingly, it grows far more white grapes than red, the local Catarratto being so widely planted that it is second only to Sangiovese in Italy's league table of grape varieties.

Yet there are more signs of dynamic indigenous winemaking here than in any of the southern mainland regions. The island's chief viticultural research station just outside Palermo has been hard at work harnessing the potential of local varieties such as the white Inzolia and red Nero d'Avola and Nerello Mascalese. Inzolia is probably intrinsically more interesting than the widely planted Catarratto but it is the deep-coloured, crisp, cherry-bright Nero d'Avola that is increasingly recognized as Sicily's trump card. It blends well with other local red grapes such as Nerello and Frappato (which tend to be lower in acidity) as well as with an ever-widening roster of international varieties such as Cabernet Sauvignon, Merlot and Syrah. In fact blends of international and Sicilian varieties (Catarratto and Chardonnay, for example) have proved particularly successful for the flying winemakers who have invaded the island, eager to harness the keenly-priced grapes that are grown in such profusion. There has also been considerable progress with cooler and more sophisticated fermentations and, inevitably, the use of small oak barrels.

The island benefited for years from enormous subsidies from Brussels and, thanks to its isolation, none-too-keen overseeing of how they were spent. But today there are signs of real dynamism in both vineyards and cellars as foreign and mainland wine producers eye up the potential on this diverse and historic terrain. The family firm of Planeta in the western interior of the island played an important part here by launching a series of highly-priced, extremely well-made international varietals on the world market. The Planetas have subsequently concentrated most on Sicilian, or at least Italian, grapes such as Nero d'Avola and Fiano from Campania however.

Other particularly quality-conscious producers of unfortified wines from both local and imported grape varieties include Castiglione, Abbazia Sant'Anastasia, the Elorina co-op (specializing in Pachino, historically the finest Nero d'Avola), Donnafugata, Duca di Salaparuta, Regaleali and Calatrasi who have even used their Sicilian winery as a base for making wine from their Tunisian vineyards. Regaleali's heady yet structured red Rosso del Conte, made from Perricone and Nero d'Avola, provided the first signs of Sicily's modern revival as a producer of table wines, thanks to vineyards at an altitude of more than 500 m (1600 ft) – generally the key to producing high-quality table wines on the island.

For years the island's most famous wine was Marsala, made in Sicily's wild west. Made from very ripe white grapes to which heated, or cooked (*cotto*) musts and grape spirit are added before ageing in the hot warehouses of the port of Marsala, the wine is not unlike madeira but tends to be darker brown, sweeter, much less acid and, in most cases, much less admired. Until recently Marsala producers were allowed to reduce the wine to something simply cheap, strong and sickly. The rules have recently been tightened up, however, so that although basic cooking Marsala and the odd eggy syrup designed to put a *zabaglione* taste in a bottle exist, there are some finer wines produced here

Sicily could be said to be a sea of vines, as here in spring countryside in the obscure Alcamo wine region south west of the capital city of Palermo.

– notably by De Bartoli who offers a range of different strengths and sweetness levels.

Sicily's temperatures make it ideal for dessert wine production and the island has a long history of making noble, rich Muscat. Moscato di Pantelleria is still made on an island just off the Tunisian coast but a slightly more subtle, still orange-tinted, powerful sweet wine made off Sicily is Malvasia delle Lipari. Carlo Hauner was single-handedly responsible for the survival of this curious wine, a direct link with ancient civilizations and winemaking techniques on the almost black, volcanic island of Lipari off the north east coast. There are also some admirable attempts to revive serious Moscato.

SPAIN

In a nutshell: *Land of American oak, sherry,
and low-yielding bush vines.*
Grapes: *Tempranillo, Garnacha (Grenache)
(RED), Airén, Viura (Maccabéo),
Verdejo, Albariño (WHITE)*

Spain was for long a viticultural miracle wait-ing to happen, but in the late 1990s things changed. Proud possessor of more land devoted to vines than any other, Spain is only just beginning to capitalize on this resource in any consistent or cohesive way – which is perhaps not surprising. If it had Germany's love of effi-ciency, or France's respect for bureaucracy, Spain might be sending us oceans of judiciously priced wine made expressly for the international market. But Spain is an anarchic jumble of dis-tricts and regions, just as its landscape is an anarchic jumble of staggeringly raw scenery and heartbreakingly awful human constructions,

and has to be treated as such by the wine enthu-siast. There is real treasure to be found by those prepared to dig, however and, as a connoisseur class develops in Spain itself, all manner of ambitious investors are already changing the image of Spanish wine.

A look at the map suggests just how much climatic diversity there is likely to be between Spain's many wine regions, from the soggy vine-yards of Galicia on the north Atlantic coast to the baked Mediterranean south east. Spain's saving grace, viticulturally, is the altitude of her vineyards, many over 650 m (2000 ft). A high proportion of Spanish vineyards therefore manage to produce grapes with good levels of colour and acidity simply because night-time temperatures are relatively low, and grapes do not ripen until the end of a usefully prolonged growing season. And because irrigation has not until recently been officially allowed in Spain (and many areas simply do not have access to sufficient water), vines are typically planted as widely spaced bushes so that yields tend to be very low, ideally resulting in grapes packed full of flavour. Lower altitude vine-yards, notably those of the Levante area on the south-ern Mediterranean coast, tend to produce wines whose main problem is an excess of alcohol and a lack of acidity. The standard Spanish recipe for correcting this imbalance has been to add white grapes or white wine. Spain's wine surplus makes an ideal com-plement to the vapid sort of red that makes up France's wine lake.

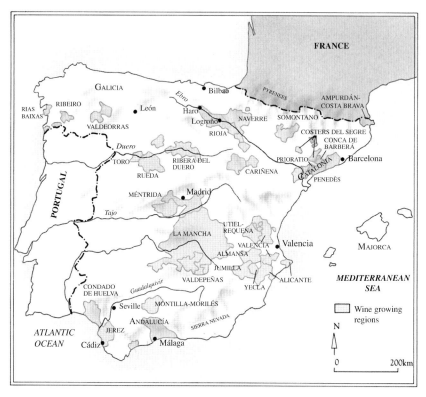

232

Spain also has a handsome array of indigenous grape varieties. Tempranillo produces some of the country's most admired red wines and is planted widely under several aliases. France's Grenache was probably imported as Garnacha, one of Spain's most planted varieties. The Monastrell vine so common in the

Typical landscape in the high Penedès. Vines trained on wires, rather than growing unsupported, are still the exception.

Levante is none other than the fashionable Mourvèdre. Two white grape varieties of undisputable class are Rueda's Verdejo and Galicia's Albariño, the former having been rescued quite recently from obscurity. There are many other possible candidates, with Rioja's Graciano and Galician Godello being obvious examples.

Spain's main wine problems lie not in the vineyard but in the cellar, or rather the cellars of many of the co-operatives that vinify so much of the country's wine and the blending halls of the big bottlers which have dominated the country's wine trade. Only since the early 1980s has a significant number of quality-conscious individual producers emerged, and even today it is extremely rare for wine producers to grow all their own grapes. Almost all of the top names in the top regions depend on local farmers to a greater or lesser degree.

Another common national characteristic is Spain's traditional fondness for American oak. Ever since the colonization of the Americas there has been a lively import trade in American oak, which has been used extensively in Spanish wine cellars for extended maturation of both reds and whites. This often resulted in red wines that were relatively light in colour and marked by a vanillin-sweet overlay, but more recently Spaniards have come to worship more deeply coloured, tannic reds (which has encouraged the spread of Cabernet Sauvignon and Syrah vines imported from France).

THE SMARTEST REGIONS

Wine names likely to be encountered on labels outside Spain are listed here in my own highly subjective and debatable descending order of current prestige. The map on page 232 shows how they relate to each other geographically.

Red wines
Ribera del Duero
Priorato
Rioja
Penedès
Toro
Somontano
Conca de Barberá
Costers del Segre
Toledo
Majorca

White wines
Galicia
Rueda
Somontano
Conca de Barberá
Canary Islands

But in one sense Spain's great gift to the world of wine is not a table wine at all but its incomparable late-fortified wine, a sure-fire appetite-whetter that has been much copied elsewhere, and often downgraded even in its homeland Jerez: sherry (see pages 247–9).

The Spaniards are also extremely enthusiastic consumers of sparkling wine, mostly their own answer to champagne, Cava, almost all of which is made in Penedès in north east Spain. For more details see page 242.

UNDERSTANDING LABELS

blanco, white.
bodega, wine cellar or winery.
clarete, unique light red somewhere between pink and full tinto, now outlawed by EU.
Crianza, the most basic level of wine that has been deliberately aged, usually for at least a year, in small oak barrels. Intermediate quality level between Joven (Sin, or without, Crianza) and a Reserva.
DO, Denominación de Origen, Spain's answer to France's AC. Most of Spain's best wines still qualify for their local DO; Spain is not (quite) as anarchic as Italy.
DOCa (Denominación de Origen Calificada) is a theoretically superior category, to which Rioja was elevated in 1991.
espumoso, sparkling.
Gran Reserva, theoretically top of the range wines, aged for longer than a Reserva.
Joven, literally young, a wine that has not been aged like a Crianza or Reserva.
Reserva, special bottling aged for longer than a Crianza.
rosado, pink wine – quite popular in Spain.
seco, dry.
tinto, deep red (cf. clarete)
vendimia, vintage.
viña, vineyard.
vino, wine.
Vino de la Tierra, Spain's answer to France's Vin de Pays.
Vino de Mesa, table wine (as opposed to DO or Vino de la Tierra).

NORTH WEST SPAIN

In a nutshell: Spain's centre of fine
white wine production.
Grapes: Tempranillo (aka Tinto Fino
or Tinta de Toro), Mencía (RED),
Alboriño and many local specialities (WHITE)

The most important wine region of north west
Spain is Ribera del Duero – see page 237.

First-time visitors to Galicia in far north
west Spain are almost invariably amazed to find
quite how un-'Spanish' it is. The countryside is
green, lush and gentle, sometimes oddly reminiscent of Ireland. Rain-bearing clouds speed in
off the Atlantic, which forces its way into the
mainland along many-fingered estuaries called
rías, bringing an enviably rich variety of fish to
an originally Celtic population.

For years Galicia made slightly fizzy, bone
dry, light dry whites and reds rather similar to
the Vinho Verde made over the border in Portugal (see pages 250–1), which rarely escaped the
fish restaurants of the region itself. But since the
early 1980s Galicia has been increasingly valued
by Spaniards as their one source of fine, often
exotically scented, crisp white wines and the
top white Galician wines, usually made from
the Albariño grape, are some of the most sought
after in Spain.

Rías Baixas, right on the coast to which
Christopher Columbus returned with the news
that it did not represent the end of the world, is
the most famous region in which Albariño
seems to thrive and the locals swear it must be
related to Riesling, so pure is its aroma and surprising its ability to age in bottle. Do Ferreiro,
Lagar de Cervera, Lusco do Miño, Morgadío
and Pazo de Señorans are some of the most
admired producers, and Adegas das Eiras and
Agro de Bazán have pioneered barrel fermentation, which may not be ideal for these delicate
wines.

Ribeiro is slightly further inland and is most

like Portugal's Vinho Verde in that it is
upstream along the same river (the Miño in
Spanish), depends heavily on Treixadura vines,
but also makes substantial quantities of light,
tart, deep-coloured reds made from a special
red-fleshed strain of Garnacha, Garnacha Tintorera, for strictly local consumption – often,
curiously, in white porcelain bowls. Emilio Rojo
and Vilerma make some fine wines here.

Even further inland is **Valdeorras**, whose
best, light dry whites are flavoured by the local
Godello grape, most successfully by the likes
of Guitián, Godeval and Joaquin Rebolledo.
The steep, inhospitable vineyards of nearby
Valdeorras can also produce some quite juicy
reds from the local Mencía grape which has mer-
ited attention from Alvaro Palacios of Priorato.

Rueda is Spain's most promising and most
versatile white wine region, its produce having
rather more body and international appeal than
that of Galicia. On the same high plateau as
Ribera del Duero, Rueda has its own highly successful grape variety, Verdejo, whose crisp nuttiness hints at its previous existence in a
sherry-like wine. It now makes very modern,
aromatic unfortified table wines and the region's
success in this field was much helped by the
importation of Sauvignon Blanc vines by Marqués de Riscal of Rioja in the 1970s. Other individual producers experimenting with serious
techniques such as barrel fermentation include
Belondrade y Lurton, Marqués de Griñon
(whose red wines are produced round Toledo
south of Madrid, in Rioja and also in Ribera del
Duero in a joint venture with Berberana) and
Palacio de Bornos. The region, with its cool climate and good acreage of fashionable Sauvignon
vines has also attracted many a flying winemaker.

One of Spain's most dynamic red wine
regions is **Toro** just west of Rueda. For years it
was regarded simply as a source of rather rustic,

deep-coloured red from the local Tinta de Toro grape, a strain of Tempranillo. But an influx of sophisticated wine producers (including some of Spain's most famous) has changed all this and the region is a hotbed of investment in which we can expect prices to rise. One of the most ambitious newcomers is Vega Sicilia of Ribera del Duero whose winemaker is fashioning extremely

Typical vineyards in the Rías Baixas district of Galicia, in the rain-washed far north of Spain, with vines raised high off the ground on pergolas made of the local granite to keep rot at bay.

grown-up red wine at Alquiriz estate. The wines are chocolate-rich and, in the right hands, can have great sweetness and smoothness. Being down-river of Ribera del Duero, Toro is usefully less prone to spring frosts.

Cigales can make agreeable reds and some rosés while nervy dry whites are made in **Basque** country round Bilbao.

RIBERA DEL DUERO

This barren plateau between Valladolid and Aranda, self-styled roast lamb capital of the world, is currently producing Spain's most admired red wines, much to the amazement of the peasant farmers who have lived on the banks of the Duero river for generations. Downstream and over the Portuguese border their counterparts farm port grapes in what is known as the Douro valley. But whereas port has been famous for three centuries, the wines of the Ribera del Duero region are a relatively recent phenomenon.

Only at the end of the last century did one producer, now called Vega Sicilia, gain some sort of recognition for the intensity of its wines. And it was not until the mid-1980s that another, an agricultural machinist Alejandro Fernández of Bodegas Pesquera, managed to establish the region as a viable source of high-quality, long-lived, concentrated, deep-coloured vibrant, oaked reds with relatively high acidity.

It is the altitude, about 650 m (2000 ft), which keeps nights cool and extends the grape-ripening process until well into October, sometimes November in a particularly cool year. This means that the grapes are harvested with very high levels of colour and flavour. Some vineyards east of Aranda may be as high as 800m, but as the Duero snakes west towards Portugal, it is flanked by successively lower vineyards so that Bodegas Mauro and Abadía de Retuerta, a vast estate revitalized by the Swiss pharmaceutical giant Novartis, both just west of the official boundary of the Ribera del Duero boundary, are significantly warmer than the DO average.

Most of the vines grown are Tempranillo – which is so common here it is often called simply Tinto (red) Fino or Tinto del País – but Cabernet Sauvignon is encroaching and was indeed imported in 1864 at Vega Sicilia so is hardly an upstart. Rot rarely threatens in the crisp dry air of this tableland with its little

L'Ermita chapel in vineyards above Pesquera, whose wine made by Alejandro Fernandez arguably put Ribera del Duero on the international map in the early 1980s.

plateaux and clumps of umbrella pines. Spring frosts, on the other hand, are a perennial danger. This is sweater country; it has nothing whatever in common with Spain's popular mediterranean image. Flocks of long-haired sheep are still driven along the main roads.

A high proportion of the locals have always made some wine for their own consumption. Almost all of those with some to spare used to sell it to the co-operative in Peñafiel in the centre of the region. But since Pesquera became a cult wine in Madrid and the United States, all manner of bodegas have sprouted up, some of them showing the same sort of vibrant potential as Pesquera but many of them clearly staffed by opportunists rather than skilled winemakers. Towards the end of the 1990s, the region sprouted dozens of flashy new bodegas bringing the total to well over 100 (there had been 24 when the DO was created in 1982). Most of these edifices are prominently situated by a main road, several are of mysterious ownership and many without any obvious source of grapes or wine. As in Rioja less than two hours' drive away to the north east, in Ribera del Duero grape-growing is largely in the hands of peasant farmers who can find themselves in a command-ing position in terms of grape prices. (This has led to the same sort of irritating price fluctua-tions as in Rioja.)

It is small wonder therefore that the region's most admired winemakers such as Dane Peter Sisseck of the fabulously priced Dominio de Pingus and the slightly more affordable Hacienda del Monasterio, are extremely reti-cent about where exactly they source their finest grapes. It is generally agreed however that soils here vary enormously, even within a single vineyard. White limestone outcrops, most common north of the river, can be useful in retaining such little rain as falls here in the summer. Rain at vintage time however is a perennial threat and vintages can vary enor-mously in quality (see pages 337–41).

There is little correlation between price and quality within this extremely fashionable DO

but Arzuaga Navarro, Dehesa de los Canónigos, Hermanos Cuadrado, Ismael Arroyo, Monte-baco, Pago de Carraovejas, Perez Pascuas, Sastre, Teófilo Reyes and Valtravieso have all produced some fine wine in their time.

Thanks to a policy of maturing wine in small barrels for years longer than any other producer I know, Vega Sicilia now produces a very individ-ual and necessarily expensive style of Ribera del Duero (now supplemented by the faster matur-ing Alión wines). In 1995, for example, Vega Sicilia launched its finest bottling, Unico, from the 1970 vintage (as well as magnums of its leg-endary 1968). Even the lesser Valbuena bottlings were matured in wood for up to five years. Although troubled by the effects of a noxious wood treatment in the 1990s, Vega Sicilia now clearly has impeccable cellar techniques in both the completely renovated original winery and its newer Alión bodega.

Pesquera's modern style of bottling the wine after just three or four years in cask is more com-monly adopted by the newcomers – for obvious financial reasons, but also probably because the livelier style of the wine finds more favour with modern drinkers. In 1995 Alejandro Fernández released his first bottlings from the high-altitude Roa de Duero vineyards, hewn out of rocks east of Pesquera under the name Condado de Haza.

If Vega Sicilia first brought this mountain region to the notice of the world's wine lovers, it was Alejandro Fernández who spawned today's rash of wannabe wine producers there. It is to his credit that he believes so passionately in the indigenous Tinto Fino grape, foreswear-ing once-fashionable Bordeaux varieties, and has not overcharged for his wines, despite being firmly convinced they are the equal of Château Pétrus and Romanée-Conti.

A young vineyard (of which there are many) in Ribera del Duero on high-altitude tableland with a high chalk content, which is good for drainage and therefore wine quality.

RIOJA

Rioja, in north east Spain, was for long Spain's only high-profile wine region, but it is now in search of a new identity. In the 1980s it lost many friends by overpricing and underperforming (a pattern which shows signs of recurring in Ribera del Duero now that it has taken over the mantle of Spain's most revered red wine region).

Rioja has traditionally been American oak's most expressive ambassador. The wine is made from a blend of Tempranillo and Garnacha (Grenache) grapes aged for a considerable number of years in the sweet, vanilla-scented warmth of small American oak barrels. The result of this prolonged ageing was to allow a high proportion of phenolics (see page 73) to be left behind in the bottom of the barrel, making bottled Rioja a relatively pale, gentle, soft wine reminiscent of strawberries and stewed fruit. It was this flattering, easily appreciated character, and the fact that fully mature examples did not cost very much, that made Rioja the first non-French wine to woo non-Spanish wine drinkers in the late 1970s.

Rioja producers have since been confused by the canny fickleness of modern wine consumers. Unimpressed by a succession of younger and younger, duller and duller, yet dearer and dearer wines, Rioja's old customers became disaffected. Seeing the recent success of Ribera del Duero's much deeper-coloured, more tannic and, often, more alcoholic wines, many producers are trying to ape this style. A number of technically well-made red wines which have no American oak characteristics whatsoever are now made by much more careful, slower fermentation and extraction of colour and flavour from the grapes, followed by shorter ageing, often in French oak barrels.

Some producers are deliberately leaning more heavily on the fuller bodied Garnacha wines produced in Rioja Baja, the region's eastern, Mediterranean-influenced vineyards, when constructing their blends. (Very, very few Riojas are estate bottlings, although Contino and Granja Remelluri provide notable exceptions.) Rioja Alta is in the mountainous far west of the region, so high and Atlantic-dominated that grapes are regularly picked in late October. That part of the region which falls within the province of Alava to the north is known as Rioja Alavesa and can produce some very fine wines on soils that are not too fertile.

Although Tempranillo and Garnacha dominate the vineyards of Rioja, Mazuelo (local name for Carignan) and the much more exciting but rare Graciano are also allowed for red Rioja. Viura, the rather tart Maccabéo of southern France, is the staple ingredient for white Rioja but white Grenache, Garnacha Blanca, sometimes adds ballast, and the small amounts of Malvasia still grown can add real character. Most white Rioja is either a squeaky-clean, cool-fermented thirst-quencher as pioneered by Marqués de Cáceres or a very oaky, often heavy wine such as Viña Tondonia.

Rioja's fortune was made in the late nineteenth century when Bordeaux wine producers, devastated by the twin scourges of mildew and phylloxera, brought their techniques over the Pyrenees. The oldest bodegas therefore tend to be centred on the small town of Haro in Rioja Alta which had good rail links, although Logroño in the centre of the region is its administrative capital. Firms such as La Rioja Alta, CVNE, Lopéz de Heredia, Muga, Marqués de Murrieta and Marqués de Riscal belong to what might be called the Rioja aristocracy, all with long-standing reputations and in many cases a mixture of traditional and more modernist wines to offer. Baron de Chirel from Marqués de Riscal for instance presents quite a different, more concentrated rendition of Rioja to the lighter, sweeter reds dating back to the early

Viña Salceda on the north bank of the river Ebro that winds, with its poplar-lined banks, through the Rioja region. Salceda now belongs to the Chivites of Navarra.

years of the twentieth century and beyond that are stored in the firm's historic cellars in the village of Elciego – now dominated by a futuristic bodega built for the firm by architect Frank Gehry, whose famous Bilbao museum is not that far to the west.

The traditional big names of Rioja are fast being usurped in the international press however by an army of newcomers making seriously deep-coloured, deep-flavoured wines aimed straight at the modern consumer in San Francisco and Singapore more used to New World reds. Some of the most obvious practitioners of this new art are Artadi, Finca Allende, Finca Valpiedra, Marqués de Vargas, Remírez de Ganuza, Roda, Señorío de San Vicente, Sierra Cantabria and Torre de Oña.

For many years, Rioja bodegas did little other than blend and age wine. Not only did they not own vineyards, many of them bought

wine that had been already made by the local farmers or co-operatives. Today the overall and thoroughly healthy trend in the region's most ambitious wine producers (and there are still far too many producers who are not ambitious or do not understand wine quality) is to control the whole process of production as closely as possible. This means that at long last an increasing proportion of Rioja's vineyards, many on terraces high above the poplar-lined River Ebro, are owned by the people who own the labels we see on bottles from the region.

They may still believe firmly in the virtues of blending, and deliberately include wines from all three subregions – Rioja Alta, Rioja Baja and Rioja Alavesa – in their wines. Most will also use a mixture of grapes. Tempranillo still dominates but it is now possible to choose from various Garnacha-dominated wines, a few all-Graciano bottlings and even one or two Mazuelos. There has been a limited amount of Cabernet Sauvignon grown in the region for more than a century, however, and the area devoted to international imported grape varieties, both red and white, is increasing every year, whether officially sanctioned or not.

NORTH EAST SPAIN

NAVARRE

Navarre is effectively a north eastern extension of Rioja, and is centred on the great bullfighting town of Pamplona. Like Rioja it benefited from Bordeaux's misfortunes in the late nineteenth century. Like Rioja its vines tend to be grown by smallholders, many of whom sell their grapes to co-operatives (more dominant in Navarre than in Rioja), while its wines are bottled by one of the larger merchants.

For many years Garnacha was by far the most planted grape variety in the vineyards interspersed with the fruit and vegetable farms for which Navarre is so famous. Once temperature control systems were introduced into Navarre's wineries, Navarre was able to churn out vast quantities of clean, fruity, dry rosado so beloved by the Spaniards, thanks to the light-coloured Grenache's suitability for pink wine production. Chivite's Gran Fuedo is Spain's pink answer to Marqués de Caceres' white Rioja and is available in any self-respecting Spanish restaurant.

The Navarrans realized, however, that it would be unwise to base their future on demand for simple pink wine. Considerably aided by a local government research programme, growers have been encouraged to plant not just Tempranillo (generally regarded by Spaniards as a very much smarter grape than the ubiquitous Garnacha) but a host of glamorous imports from France such as Cabernet Sauvignon, Merlot and Chardonnay.

The results are very respectable if only very rarely outstanding. Without a long tradition of ageing in American oak, Navarre's bodegas have been able to invest in French oak for their French grapes and there is a host of affordable combinations of these and Spanish grape varieties, often oaked, on the market. Guelbenzu and Chivite make some of the finest examples of Navarre wine, including a stunning botrytized Muscat labelled Vendimia Tardía from the latter.

This is more mixed farming country than Rioja, but as in Rioja there is a huge difference between the flatter more southerly vineyards and vineyards in the much more mountainous north where grapes may even occasionally be harvested as late as December.

SOMONTANO

This small region right up in the southern foothills of the Pyrenees is one of Spain's most exciting, even if much of its produce tends to be fashioned in the image of international classics (including red and white burgundy) rather than demonstrating more inherently Spanish qualities. The innovative producer Viñas del Vero nevertheless has a fine, juicily vinified Tempranillo and a surprisingly delicate Gewürztraminer. Enate, another company in private hands, also makes some fine reds and whites from imported grape varieties while the dynamic local co-op, Bodegas Pirineos. nurtures the region's own grapes Moristel and Parraleta. This is another Spanish wine region worthy of international attention.

PENEDÈS

Penedès is the most important wine area in Catalonia, the proudly self-conscious, hard-working region in the north east of Spain. Catalonia has its own language, Catalan, in which the region is known as Catalunya, Priorato is known as Priorat, San Sadurni de Noya as Sant Sadurní d'Anoia and so on. Its most obvious product is sparkling Cava (see opposite) but the region also produces a wide range of still wines of many colours and styles. Although Tempranillo is widely grown here, as throughout northern Spain (and called Ull de Llebre in Catalan), Miguel Torres was responsible for importing French (and German) varieties and techniques in the 1970s and has for long been the region's most famous producer, turning out an increasingly confident array of bottlings of imported and local varieties, typically blended together. After years of experimenting with Cabernet Sauvignon, Merlot, Pinot Noir, Chardonnay, Sauvignon Blanc, Gewürztraminer and Riesling, and a substantial diversion into Chile, he finally produced his best wine, an intensely characterful red called Grans Muralles, from a blend of ancient indigenous vine varieties.

On lower land, closer to the coast, local grape varieties Garnacha, Monastrell and some Cariñena ripen much more easily, and less subtly, to produce round local reds that find a ready home in and around Barcelona. Moscatél and Malvasía are also grown for dessert wines and the hinterland of Tarragona was long famous for its sweet and sticky reds.

In the hills above Tarragona to the west, between this port and the increasingly fashionable Priorato DO, is a particularly fast-developing wine region, the recently created Montsant DO around the town of Falset, gateway to Priorato. Producers to look for here are the extremely well-run local co-op Celler de Capçanes and the privately-owned Joan d'Anguera.

All over Penedès are pockets of vine-growing and (particularly) wine-making ambition. Some of my favourite producers include Can Feixes, Can Ràfols dels Caus, Jané Ventura and Jean León. Even north of Barcelona there are now some interesting producers such as Oliver Conti in the Ampurdàn-Costa Brava zone.

CAVA

Cava is not the name of a Spanish wine region but of a type of wine, Spain's much-loved answer to champagne, a dry white wine made sparkling by the traditional method.

The great majority of Cava is made from grapes grown in Penedès, in one of a handful of giant bodegas based in and around the town of San Sadurni de Noya. Grapes used traditionally were extremely local: Macabeo (the Viura of Rioja), Parellada and the somewhat earthy-tasting Xarel-lo. The result of these varieties and the local relatively warm environment is that Cava, although usually technically very well made with a steady stream of tiny bubbles, often tends to seem aggressively frothy, and to taste oddly rustic and sometimes rather sweet, to those brought up on Chardonnay/Pinot fizz such as champagne. Nowadays Chardonnay and more recently Pinot Noir are grown increasingly and the result is Cava that has begun to taste much more familiar to international palates, even if less distinctively Catalan.

All this may well simply be a question of conditioning and certainly one of the top bottlings from the likes of Codorníu, Freixenet, Joan Raventós, Juvé y Camps, Nadal, Parxet and Moët & Chandon's particularly French-influenced Cavas should do what all the best sparkling wines do: refresh and stimulate.

The Spaniards buy so much Cava that the larger Cava houses Codorníu and Freixenet have managed to finance their own wineries in California (see page 291).

Although the Cava business was established on a commercial scale in Penedès as recently as the 1880s, by José Raventos, founder of the Codorníu dynasty, after a trip to France, it now produces about 130 million bottles of traditional method sparkling wine a year, roughly half as much as France's Champagne district.

CONCA DE BARBERÁ

Conca de Barberá is effectively a western extension of Penedès in which the winter temperatures fall even lower. The area grows many of the grapes used for Cava and is most famous as the home to the Chardonnay responsible for Miguel Torres's highly acclaimed rich, oak-aged Milmanda.

PRIORATO

If potential were measured in financial and human investment, then Priorato (Priorat in Catalan) is Spain's most exciting wine region. On dramatically steep slate terraces like those of Banyuls over the French border, low-yielding ancient Garnacha and Cariñena vines ooze tiny quantities of super-concentrated, tannic, occasionally over-alcoholic wine, sometimes well over 16 per cent.

Until recently Priorato was a relatively unsophisticated product but a recent influx of capital and enthusiasm, spearheaded by René Barbier, originally of the eponymous Penedès winery and subsequently installed at Clos Mogador, resulted in several estates or 'clos' run by ambitious newcomers such as Alvaro Palacios. The best of these wines such as Palacios' L'Ermita and Finca Dofí have already proved to be some of Spain's most thrilling wine sensations. Most of these new producers are adding some Cabernet, Merlot and/or Syrah to provoke yet more layers of flavour in these inky wines. The invasion of this primitive, mountainous hinterland of Tarragona in southern Catalonia

has continued in no uncertain manner with the likes of Miguel Torres literally re-sculpting the land into easy-to-work terraces. The key to Priorato's extraordinarily mineral-laden flavour is the special soil here, a dark brown slate called *llicorella* whose stern substance really does seem to have infused the wine, providing one of the world's most directly taste-able influences of *terroir*.

New producers and labels seem to be emerging by the minute but those who earned their spurs relatively early in the short modern history of this region (which is named after the Carthusian priory whose monks made wine here as early as the twelfth century) include Cims de Porrera, Clos Erasmus, Clos de l'Obac, Mas Martinet and Rotllán Torra.

COSTERS DEL SEGRE

Costers del Segre, in the arid, harsh hinterland around the Catalonian city of Lerida, is almost a one-winery DO. Raimat is an extensive property converted to wine production over several decades by the owner of Codorníu, the giant Cava producer. Tempranillo and the usual gamut of international grape varieties are planted. Its oaked reds made from Bordeaux grape varieties can be extremely winning. There is considerable potential in this disparate zone, however, thanks to some characterful old vines, notably red Garnacha and white Macabeo sold under the Cérvoles label.

OTHER REGIONS

Other DO regions include Alella (for white wine), Campo de Borja (source of some great value, juicy red), Calatayud, Cariñena and the promising Terra Alta to the west of Tarragona and Priorato.

Vineyards near Tarragona in north east Spain where a massive re-evaluation of quality is taking place, thanks to the success of nearby Priorat.

REST OF SPAIN

This vast and important wine production centre is a sleeping giant in the process of being awoken by all sorts of internal and external winemaking influences and preferences. It makes some crisp cheap whites and some heady reds.

LA MANCHA, VALDEPEÑAS AND ENVIRONS

The majority of Spain's vineyards lie on the table-land around the capital Madrid, particularly on the plains of La Mancha to the south east, which provide much of the country's basic Vino da Mesa and raw ingredients for the Brandy de Jerez drunk in such quantities by the Spaniards. Much of this is relatively characterless dry white made from the Airén grape, so common here – and planted at such a low vine density in these extremely arid, non-irrigated vineyards – that its total acreage is greater than that of any other single grape variety in the world. La Mancha itself is Europe's largest single demarcated 'quality' region (i.e. DO), encompassing 160 000 ha (400 000 acres), although little of its wine is seriously superior.

This is inhospitable country, whose name is derived from Manxa or 'parched earth', as it was known by the Moors. In summer it is boiling hot and there is hardly enough rain to sustain a crop. In winter it can be freezing cold for weeks at a time, with frequent frosts. The one advantage of this dry climate is that vine diseases are practically unknown, so no expensive spraying is required. Most of the vines are grown as low bushes. This is minimalist vine-growing.

Since the mid-1980s modern winemaking has gradually invaded La Mancha, and in particular temperature control for fermentations, which have resulted in fresh, crisp, inexpensive, if fairly characterless dry whites.

Such vineyards not planted to Airén tend to be planted with Cencibel, the local name for the ubiquitous Spanish red Tempranillo. This is a speciality of Valdepeñas, a southern enclave within La Mancha which is a source of some delightfully keenly priced, juicy, sometimes carefully aged reds. So dense is the colour of much of the Tempranillo harvested from the low-yielding vines of La Mancha and Valdepeñas that the wines have traditionally been lightened by adding surplus white grapes.

As evidence that even the most workaday wine region can today attract ambitious outside investment, La Mancha now has at least two top quality estates, both of them at altitudes of almost 1000 m (3000 ft). Baronia and Manuel Manzaneque are, perhaps inevitably, introducing international grape varieties and being rewarded with rapturous acclaim in Madrid.

Outside the denominated zone of Mentridá, at the Dominio de Valdepusa near Toledo, previously famous only for the strength of its mainly co-operative-made reds, is the dynamic red winemaking estate of Marqués de Griñon, which is making some of Spain's most respectable Cabernet Sauvignon, promising Syrah and even some interesting Petit Verdot. Clever canopy management techniques for training the vines in such a dry climate have played an important part here.

THE MEDITERRANEAN COAST

The Levante has traditionally produced wine too sweet, sickly and strong to appeal to the serious wine drinker but all this has been changing rapidly as the Monastrell is re-evaluated (largely in the light of its French counterpart Mourvèdre's international stardom). This heavily-planted, sun-drenched stretch of vineyards has already yielded some of the world's best-value reds and we can expect to see many more. Initially what was required was the combination of the Levante's inexpensive, easily-ripened grapes with some imported expertise mindful of the requirements of the international consumer. Today, increasing numbers of local wine producers are cottoning on to and investing in more sophisticated winemaking techniques and equipment. Another key ingredient in the taming of the ultra-ripe Monastrell and Bobal grapes grown here has been planting and blending in other varieties such as Merlot, Syrah and Tempranillo that lighten the overall effect.

Official DOs in the Levante include, roughly north to south, Valencia, Utiel Requena, Manchuela, Almansa, Alicante, Yecla, Jumilla and Bullas. Producers in and around these regions who have already won international recognition include Agapito Rico of Alicante, Balcona of Bullas, Casa Castillo of Jumilla, Laderas de El Seque of Alicante and Solanero of Yecla.

Alicante was long known for tooth-rottingly sweet wines and Enrique Mendoza with Dolç de Mendoza and Gutierrez de la Vega with Casta Diva Cosecha Miel carry on that tradition in a way that even modernists will appreciate – not least for the value they offer.

THE ISLANDS

For years the Balearic Islands and the Canaries were ignored by Spain's growing band of sophis-

ticated wine fanatics. Today a handful of inspired wine producers on **Majorca** is making waves with the quality of their intense, sensitively-oaked reds, often but not always based on the local Manto Negro grape. Anima Negra is one of the most talked-about wines to qualify for the relatively new Plà i Llevant DO.

If rich reds are the keynote of Spain's islands in the Mediterranean, fine-boned whites represent the best of the extremely varied produce of its islands in the Atlantic, the **Canary Islands**. These islands boast no fewer than 10 different DOs, which may smack of an excess of local politicking but, as I say, the wines really are very varied – not just stylistically but qualitatively. One of the best producers is Viñátigo which makes extremely stylish dry whites, including one from the local Marmajuelo grape, as well as a light, sweet but spine-tingling pale Malvasia Classico. Wines like this must have been made since the Middle Ages when merchant fleets brought the Malvasia grape from the Aegean to these islands and, fatefully, Madeira to the south.

The vineyards of Lanzarote in the Canary Islands where vineyards have been dug into black lava flows, with walls to protect them from the wind.

SHERRY

In a nutshell: *The world's
most neglected wine treasure.*
Grape: *Palomino*

Many modern wine drinkers will look at this section and wonder why on earth I think it worthwhile devoting three whole pages to such a dinosaur of a wine as sherry. The answer is plain to anyone who has tried a good quality version. The trouble is that most people have not. They tend to have been put off by the tired, very undistinguished syrupy stuff that lurks in the bottom of sherry bottles and decanters all over the world.

So fine, varied and noble a wine is sherry – and so intriguingly complicated is it to make – that replicating sherry, just like imitating a top quality champagne, is a common daydream for many of the more talented winemakers in the world.

There are two basic styles of proper sherry, neither of which bear any relation to the sweetened-up popular brands. **Fino** sherry and the similar **Manzanilla** are very pale, delicate, prancing, palate-reviving thoroughbreds that are only about 15.5 per cent alcohol, bone dry and tingling with life and zest. These sorts of sherry are as fragile as an unfortified table wine and rapidly lose their appeal if kept in an opened bottle for longer than a few days. They should be drunk well chilled, and their life can be prolonged by keeping them in ever smaller bottles in the refrigerator.

The other major style of sherry is dark, nutty and can thrill the palate with its subtle shadings of mahogany and nuances that are the direct and delicious results of extended ageing in oak. Dry **Amontillado** and, even deeper, Dry **Oloroso** seem tailor-made for staving off winter chills. These names are also given to sweetened, darkened commercial blends of young wines, but the best owe their character more nobly to time, and top quality base wines. Sweet sherry can also delight, but also has to be much older than the heavily advertised **Cream** sherries usually are. (**Pale Cream** is just Cream with the colour taken out.)

The sherry region, the only one that is allowed to use the word sherry in Europe, is one of the hottest fine wine regions in the world, just a short distance from the coast of North Africa in the south of Spain's most southern province, Andalucía. It takes its name from the principal sherry town Jerez (pronounced 'Hereth'), characterized by its brilliant white bodegas, dusty jacaranda-lined avenues and *mañana* culture.

It is just as well that the Jerezanos are not impatient people because the sherry-making process is prolonged. Ordinary sherry-like wine can be made by blending relatively young ingredients, but true, intense, subtle sherry demands decades (and yet, thanks to its current unfashionable status, its price rarely reflects its age).

SHERRY-STYLE WINES OUTSIDE SPAIN

Flor-influenced wines are made in the Jura as vin jaune, *and to an even more limited extent in Gaillac. Most countries sell fortified local wines in various styles labelled as though they were sherry but they can be rather stale, raisiny, distinctly inferior products. Both Australia and South Africa, however, have a sound tradition of producing the full range of sherry styles with some competence. Cyprus has been making cheap sherryish wines for decades, as well as supplying much of the dubious base grape concentrate for UK-reconstituted stuff called British sherry (see page 305), but the winemaking culture is not nearly so demanding here.*

The vineyards are on dazzling, white undulating countryside between Jerez and the two sherry ports of Sanlucar de Barrameda and Puerto de Santa Maria, with the most valued being predominantly chalky and able to dripfeed the vines with what little rain falls each year. Palomino is the light-skinned sherry grape and a certain amount of slightly flabby, full-bodied, dry white table wine is made from it but, as still Coteaux Champenois demonstrates champagne's worth (see page 172), it serves mainly to demonstrate that the Jerez vineyards are designed to produce sherry.

These are some of the world's hottest vineyards and so pressing stations tend to be close by (yet another parallel with Champagne), with base wines transported to the major wineries for transformation into the final product, the first stage of which is to fortify, or add neutral grape spirit to, freshly fermented, clarified wine.

But the making of Fino sherry requires more than the chalky albariza soils of Jerez and the Palomino grape. Fino owes its special tangy character to a strange sort of yeast called *flor*, indigenous to the Jerez region, which grows a bread-like film on the surface of the wine. To give it surface to work on, and to sustain its effect and its protection against oxidation, winemakers fill the barrels, or butts, in which sherry has always been matured only about five-sixths full, and add younger wine at regular intervals so as to give the yeast something new to feed on. Fino style wines matured in the bodegas of Sanlucar rather than in the warmer, drier climate of inland Jerez are called Manzanilla and can taste even tangier. It is easy to persuade oneself that there is a whiff of ozone and salt in these lovely wines, so light they are drunk with the tapas and seafood of the region as though they were table wines.

Flor is very particular, however, and grows only on wines with an alcohol content of around 15.5 per cent. The finest, most elegant base wines are therefore fortified to exactly that strength, whereas more alcohol is added to the rather more full-bodied, perhaps slightly coarser wines that are destined to become darker, nuttier sherries, sometimes sweetened with specially concentrated Pedro Ximénez (PX) grapes.

The constant replenishment of Fino and Manzanilla barrels has led to another unique feature of sherry production that is known rather technically as fractional blending or, in Spanish, the *solera* system. This is the sherry producers' clever way of maintaining a consistent blend year in, year out. With very few exceptions, sherry is not a vintage-dated wine but the blended product of a system whereby a certain proportion of old wine is taken out of a blending stage and replaced by the same amount of younger wine. The more blending stages there are to a system, and the older the system, the more subtle the wine, and in theory at least, every bottle of sherry should contain some fraction, however tiny, of wine as old as the blending system itself – which may in some cases be more than a century. Sherry is surely one of the most undervalued wines made today.

Most of the large sherry producers make small quantities of top quality wines, but the following rules should help pick out the real

SOUTHERN SPAIN'S OTHER SPECIALITIES

*The **Montilla-Moriles** region east of Jerez doesn't benefit from Atlantic cooling and therefore has a less satisfactory relationship with the flor yeast. The result is that Montilla wines are very similar to sherry (in fact Amontillado means 'in the style of Montilla') but lack some of the finesse. Some even looser imitations of sherry are made to the west of Jerez in the region of **Condado de Huelva**. For wine lovers, the busy Costa del Sol town of **Málaga** is associated with a delicious, dark, raisiny, treacly fortified wine of the same name. It can also be paler but no less fascinating, as in Molina Real.*

Jerez: sherry sales would revive if more people visited this beautiful bit of Andalucía.

sherries from the more commercially expedient, sweetened-up blends.

• Most bottles labelled Dry Amontillado and Dry Oloroso are trustworthy.

• Look for Fino and Manzanilla at alcoholic strengths as low as possible. Those at 15.5 per cent will be as the Spaniards drink them, more like table wines than fortified wines.

• Quiz your retailer or waiter about the date of shipment of any Fino or Manzanilla, and avoid any bottle that has obviously been open for more than a few days. These wines do not improve in bottle.

• Sherries labelled Almacenista are from special private stockholders and are usually well worth the price premium for their extra character.

PORTUGAL

*In a nutshell: The home of port,
madeira and a host of increasingly modern,
often bargain, table wines.
Grapes: Rich variety of local specialities
still being researched*

Portugal's advantage in wine terms, its isolation which has kept its inheritance of indigenous vine varieties intact and virtually unaffected by Chardonnay- and Cabernet-mania, is also its disadvantage. The Portuguese have had this strange habit of making wines to suit the palates of other Portuguese rather than making the sort of fruity, juicy-yet-structured wines that appeal to the majority of the world's wine consumers. Until very recently the wines that have been most respected within Portugal are incredibly tough reds that have typically spent rather too long in storage before being bottled, and some slightly tired whites whose unfamiliar flavours may strike some outsiders as slightly rank.

In fact Portugal has some first-class raw materials and is gradually amassing the will and skill with which to transform them into exportable wines. There seems to me to be little correlation, however, between the country's denominated regions (DOCs) and inherent wine quality. Dão is one of the traditionally most respected wine regions, for example, but I have found far more wines capable of giving real pleasure from much more obscure corners of this essentially Atlantic-influenced country (where vines are grown almost everywhere).

Rainfall varies enormously according to proximity to the coast. The Vinho Verde region in the far north west, famous for light, dry whites, for example, is one of the wine world's wettest, while the Douro valley to its immediate south east is one of the driest during the crucial growing season. This extraordinarily arid, harsh valley is responsible for Portugal's second greatest gift to the wine world, port, the sweetest,

strongest, darkest wine known to man and his cranium (see page 256). Its most significant contribution of course is cork, of which it is by far the world's most important source.

Wine production has been largely in the grip of co-operatives which have only slowly been rejuvenating their ideas and techniques. The picture is further confused by the fact that some of the DOCs – Carcavelos for example – reflect Portugal's rich wine exporting history more than modern reality.

The main wine regions follow, roughly from north west to south east.

VINHO VERDE

The verde or 'green' in Vinho Verde (pronounced something like 'Vino verge') refers not to the colour of the wine but to its youth. The red and white Vinho Verde wines produced in this rainwashed region just south of the Minho river which forms the border with Spain are all designed to be drunk when still young and fresh. High acidity and more than a trace of post-fermentation fizz are their hallmark. They bear a very strong resemblance to the Rías Baixas

---

UNDERSTANDING LABELS

adega, winery or cellar.
branco, white.
colheita, vintage.
DOC, Denominação de Origem Controlada, Portugal's equivalent of France's Appellation Contrôlée system, but a less sure guide to the country's most user-friendly wines.
garrafeira, supposedly superior, well-aged wines.
IPR, Indicação de Proveniencia Regulamentada, Portugal's answer to France's VDQS.
quinta, farm or wine estate.
Vinho Regional, like Vin de Pays.

wines made just over the river in Spain's Galicia – indeed the same aristocratic white grape variety, here spelt Alvarinho, is the most admired, and is a speciality of the area around the town of Monção. Other grape varieties that are grown on the typical overhead pergolas that supposedly help fight fungal diseases in this damp Minho region, are Azal, Loureiro, Trajadura, Avesso and Pedernão. A typical white Vinho Verde is a blend of some of these. Some of the more commercial bottlings are deliberately sweetened and slightly carbonated, but the likes of Palacio de Brejoeira, Paço do Teixeiró, Quinta de Alderiz and Quinta do Ermizio bottle a wine that a local would recognize. Some producers in the region are becoming a bit more worldly and producing white wines with more body and even some oak (not necessarily a good thing). Quinta da Covela is a particularly innovative and successful producer of modern wines from this region that don't qualify as Vinho Verde and are therefore labelled as Minho. The locals drink twice as much red Vinho Verde as white but hardly any of this slightly fizzy, very dry, very light red is exported, with good reason.

DOURO

The dramatic Douro valley, for long dedicated almost entirely to port production, has become a significant producer of robust, characterful red table wines with some of the tannins which distinguish vintage port. To some port producers such wines are heresy but to quality-conscious wine drinkers they are intriguingly satisfying, with a concentration of flavour many winemakers elsewhere would kill for. Port producer Ferreira's Barca Velha was the prototype and still commands very high prices, but an exciting range of much cheaper dense crimson table wines is now available. This remote valley well upriver from Oporto is one of the wonders of the wine world. Between viciously cold winters, its summers are so dry (often without a single drop of rain) and the slopes of schist and slate so steep (up to 60 degrees) that few plants can

flourish here. But deep-rooted vines, often on painstakingly constructed terraces, manage to burrow their way through the rock to such water as there is. Yields are naturally low and the grapes naturally very concentrated in colour, tannin and sugars to ferment into alcohol. All of which makes for some exciting red wine.

Some of the most ambitious examples are Dirk Niepoort's bottlings, including his Redoma range (of which there is also, most unusually, a white and a pink), Fojo and Chryseia, a vaguely claret-like variant made for the Symington port family (who produce Graham, Dow, Warre and a host of other ports) by Bruno Prats, once owner of Château Cos d'Estournel in Bordeaux. Other producers of characterful red Douro table wine with a reliable track record include Quinta do Côtto, Quinta do Crasto, Quinta da Gaivosa, Quinta de Leda, Quinta de la Rosa Reserva, Quinta do Vale D. Maria, Quinta do Vale Meão and Quinta do Vallado, but newcomers appear with exciting offerings every year.

DÃO

For many years this large red and white wine region south of the Douro valley was well and truly strangled by old-fashioned winemaking methods, particularly long maceration with bitter stalks and unwisely prolonged ageing before bottling so that most wines tasted hard rather than fruity. Things are slowly changing, however. Producers such as Quinta dos Roques and Quinta da Pellada show that the region can make wines that have a fine core of fruit on the palate with no lack of ageing potential and interest. Both have been experimenting with varietal wines while getting to grips with the essential characteristics of the grapes allowed by the Dão regulations. Touriga Nacional, the most revered port grape, is clearly a star here, as Sogrape's Quinta dos Carvalhais can show, but Spain's Tempranillo (known as Tinta Roriz in northern Portugal) and Jaen can also produce some good wine in the right hands. White Dão has tended to be an even more anachronistic product, even if the Encruzado grape used in most blends can be quite crisp and fragrant. Quinta dos Roques makes some quite fleshy white wine – a far cry from the dried-out white Dão of yesteryear. Dão will surely realize its potential before too long.

BAIRRADA

Unusually for a Portuguese wine zone, this mixed farming region between Dão and the coast is dominated by a single grape, the small, thick-skinned Baga, which would result in relatively tannic wines even if all Bairrada wineries were equipped with destemmers. As it is, many of the all-important co-operatives still make tougher wines than necessary, although it is (just) thinkable that one day the concentrated reds of Bairrada might be as popular outside Portugal as they were in early seventeenth-century London. Luis Pato makes better wines than most. His Vinha Barrosa in particular qualifies as one of the world's most interesting and seriously-made reds although, like many pioneers, he has quarrelled with the local authorities and withdrawn his wines from the official denomination. For the moment, the word Bairrada is not to be found on his labels. Quinta do Poço do Lobo and Quinta de Baixo, both superior producers of Bairrada, have no such qualms.

LEFT *Grapes for Tinta da Anfora being picked in the useful Alentejo region.* OPPOSITE *Typical Portuguese tiles on a house near the Setúbal peninsula.*

Some interesting dry whites and sparkling wines are also being made in Bairrada. The region's light-skinned grape Bical is almost as characterful as the purple Baga, with just as high a degree of acidity, which makes it a good candidate for fizz.

The famous Palace Hotel on the edge of Bairrada bottles its own blends of Buçaco red and white wines bought in Bairrada and Dão which are renowned as some of Portugal's best, but perhaps the region's most famous wine is Sogrape's blended Mateus Rosé which is produced at a giant winery within Bairrada. Mateus's mid-twentieth-century success supposedly owed much to the fact that it was neither sweet nor dry, white nor red, still nor sparkling. The Guedes family who developed Mateus have sensibly been branching out into more distinctive wines, notably those made at their Quinta dos Carvalhais winery in the Dão region, designed to introduce wine drinkers all over the world to some of the flavours and styles Portugal has to offer. Wines made from a larger region encompassing both Dão and Bairrada are labelled Beiras and can be very promising.

COLARES

This tiny DOC is more famous for its exceptional situation, a narrow strip of sand on the windy Atlantic coast not far from Lisbon, than for the quality of its wines. Since phylloxera (see page 96) cannot live in sand, the Ramisco vine responsible for red Colares (yet another tannic, tart Portuguese red) is possibly the only vine variety never to have been grafted on to phylloxera-resistant American vine roots. Here the modern wine drinker's interest in Colares may end. Some full-bodied white Colares is made from Malvasia grapes.

BUCELAS

Bucelas or Bucellas is a name often found on nineteenth-century decanter and bin labels in Britain, showing just how popular this 'Portuguese hock' was then. The wine is a potentially scented dry white based on Arinto grapes. It is made in relatively small quantity but some newish produc-

Portugal is the world's most important supplier of cork. Wine corks are punched out of strips of the bark of cork oaks like this one growing in the Algarve.

Cartaxo and Santarém. Most common Portuguese grapes here are the juicy red Trincadeira Preta and the one variously known as Periquita, Castelão Francês and João de Santarém although this fertile region, recipient of many an EU subsidy, is also one of relatively few Portuguese wine areas to be seriously experimenting with international grape varieties. Monte d'Oiro has had success with its Syrah while Quinta de Pancas' Cabernet Sauvignon Special Selection shows that there is real potential here.

SETÚBAL/PALMELA/ARRÁBIDA

The Setúbal peninsula south of Lisbon and the two wine zones that flank it, Palmela and Arrábida, are the sources of some of Portugal's most exportable and exported table wines. Setúbal or Moscatel de Setúbal (pronounced 'Shtooble') is a noble, historic copper-coloured Muscat to which grape spirit is added before ageing so that it tastes like a cross between a southern French Muscat de Beaumes-de-Venise and a tawny port. Of more general interest, though, is the wide range of dry red and white wines made in Azeitão in Arrábida. José Maria da Fonseca Successores is a family firm which bottles blended table wines such as Periquita and Quinta de Camarate while J. M. da Fonseca Internacional is most famous as the bottler of Lancers, Mateus's big pink rival. Australian Peter Bright has done much to put this wine-making base on the map, notably with the full, dry Muscat João Pires from J. P. Vinhos and some competently-made whites from both Chardonnay and Portugal's own Fernão Pires. Pegos Claros is another dependable producer, of generally dense reds.

ers, notably Quinta da Romeira, are trying hard, perhaps encouraged by the proximity of the capital Lisbon, and its thirsty populace.

RIBATEJO

This large fruit- and vegetable-growing region upstream of Lisbon, whose name means 'the banks of the river Tagus', is Portugal's most important source of basic blending wine (together with the Oeste or Estremadura region between it and the Atlantic). Much of the wine produced here is relatively light, but that can be a blessing relative to some of Portugal's more austere wine styles. Co-operatives rule the roost, but sometimes benevolently, as witness keenly priced reds carrying names such as Almeirim,

ALENTEJO

The warm, dry Alentejo region in the south east is the country's most fashionable source of full-bodied, deep-coloured, accessible table wine. In fact, this is where many a port shipper used to come for a decent, full-bodied red to put on the table before getting down to the serious business of port-drinking. Many of Portugal's cork forests are in this rolling farmland on the Spanish border. The climate is so well-favoured that grapes are routinely picked in August. Whereas northern Portuguese viticulture is dominated by peasant smallholders, this is a land where vines are an unusual sight on its often large estates.

Another Australian, David Baverstock, who tired of making nothing but port in the Douro, is exporting increasingly interesting wines from the large Esporão property. As an Australian, it was natural he should experiment with varietal versions of the Alentejo's grapes: Tempranillo here known as Aragonêz, Trincadeira Preta and Periquita as well as the indigenous pale-skinned grape Roupeiro which usefully retains its acidity. Touriga Nacional has of course been imported along with some Cabernet and Syrah, although this last was for long an unofficial import that had to be labelled Incógnito by its prime exponents Cortes de Cima. Co-operatives such as Borba, Granja, Redondo, Reguengos de Monsaraz and Vidigueira are some of Portugal's most energetic. But there are many exciting individual estates such as Mouchão, Tapada de Coelheiros, Quinta do Mouro and Quinta do Carmo (part-owned by the Rothschilds of Château Lafite), and special bottlings such as Tinta da Anfora. Prices here are not too ridiculous and this is certainly one of the most promising wine regions in the world. Even whites can be interesting. João Portugal Ramos, who consults throughout southern Portugal, has established Marques de Borba as a successful and increasingly delicious brand from Alentejo.

REST OF PORTUGAL

Many other parts of the country apparently have the ability to produce sound wine at a good price – Tras-os-Montes and Beiras to name just two. And now even the Algarve, for long a vinous wilderness, has been put on the map by none other than the crooner Sir Cliff Richard and his Vida Nova red. It is worth noting with Portugal, incidentally, that retailer reputation can often be a sounder clue to quality than producer geography.

Grape pickers in the Alentejo, an increasingly important wine region.

PORT

In a nutshell: *Deep, sweet, strong wine, mostly very consistently made in many different styles.*
Grapes: *Touriga Nacional and many others* (RED)

Although there are wines made outside Portugal to taste like port (see below), there is nowhere in the wine world at all like the Douro valley in northern Portugal, the home of port. The peasant farmers who inhabit this wild, silent valley in which only the vine will grow, rely for their livelihood almost entirely on the port shippers, the un-Portuguese likes of Cockburn, Croft, Dow, Graham, Sandeman, Taylor and Warre, based half a day's drive downstream in Oporto – or rather in lodges on the quayside of Vila Nova de Gaia across the river from it. Ever since the late seventeenth century when British merchants scoured friendly Portugal for goods that would replace heavily taxed items from France, the commercial end of the port wine trade has been in predominantly British hands, which has made for an even more delicate relationship between growers and bottlers than in most wine regions.

The steep, rocky, necessarily terraced vineyards of the Douro were long since mapped according to the concentration of the wine they are able to produce, and grape payments decided accordingly. The best port country is about 75 miles upstream of Oporto, well away from the rainy coast. Some very promising vineyards are not that far downstream of the point at which the Duero of Spain (see page 237) becomes the Douro of Portugal. The land is so inhospitable here, with only a dusting of topsoil, that many a vine sends it roots yards down into deep fissures in the schist, apparently the only possible route to the water necessary for growth.

It has taken the port producers much longer than most to understand, or even just identify the 80-plus vine varieties responsible for their amazingly concentrated, deep-coloured product. But then port, like sherry, champagne and madeira, is essentially a blended wine and many of the greatest ports I have ever tasted were made decades before the term 'varietal' was even coined. Touriga Nacional is generally regarded as the top quality port vine, supplemented with Tinta Barroca, Touriga Francesa, Tinta Cão and Tinta Roriz.

The aim of the port producer is to make a wine that is as deeply coloured and sweet as possible. To preserve the grapes' natural sweetness, spirit is added at quite an early point in the fermentation process to stun the yeasts, which means that colour and tannin must be extracted as fast as possible. The Douro valley is one of the very few wine regions where foot treading is still practised, to the delight of photographers and visitors from tamer wine regions, but machinery usually does the job.

The most ordinary port goes into the shippers' basic blends, sometimes called wood ports

NON-PORTUGUESE PORT-STYLE WINES

Many winemakers in climates as hot at the Douro valley try their hand at making dark, sweet fortified wines in the image of port – notably in Australia, but also in South Africa and California.
Very few producers have any substantial plantings of the port vine varieties however (although this is slowly changing). Any wine labelled Tawny is likely to be the product of long ageing in cask while a Ruby is likely to have been bottled relatively young. Perhaps the wines most like port are Banyuls and Maury made in Roussillon, southern France
(see page 201).

---

as they are not expected to age in bottle (although many of them nowadays are aged in cement or stainless steel rather than barrels). A **ruby** port is a young port bottled after two or three years in bulk. The great majority of port sold today, and certainly all the advertised brands, is this vigorous, juicy stuff. (If it carries the words **late bottled vintage** or **LBV** it will be a ruby from a single year bottled after four to six years' ageing.)

A cheap **tawny** port is ruby's commercial cousin, from lesser vineyards or made lighter and browner by blending in some **white** port, the result of applying port production techniques to the Douro's minority of white grapes. Real **aged tawny** owes its alluring light, shaded, jewel-like tawny colour to extended ageing in wood, for 10, 20, 30 or over 40 years, according to the label. Some of my most hedonistic port-drinking experiences have been with 20-year-old ports, which taste as good served chilled in the heat of a Douro summer as they do next to the fireside in a British winter. This is the style drunk most regularly by the port shippers. Some

MADEIRA

In a nutshell: *Exceptionally long-lived, tangy, fortified wines.*
Grapes: *Tinta Negra Mole, Malvasia, Sercial, Verdelho*

Madeira is a volcanic island in the middle of the Atlantic, a wine, and a miracle. Good quality madeira (which, alas, can cost at least as much as classed growth bordeaux) is the world's longest-living wine. Its high alcohol and natural acidity and the fact that it has been virtually baked during the production process mean that it is indestructible, whether in a wooden cask, maturing under the rafters of a lodge in Funchal or in a bottle at home, however long ago it was opened. Madeira is the only wine that can be kept in a decanter on a sideboard for months without deteriorating. I also reckon that this unique fortified wine also has the strange property of protecting the drinker, well this drinker anyway, from a hangover (cf. port).

The trouble is that most of the madeira produced today is rather ordinary – very good for cooking and adding richness to meat reductions, but hardly fine enough to savour by the thimbleful. This is partly because so many of the noble light-skinned grape varieties Sercial, Verdelho, Bual and Malvasia (for Malmsey) were replaced long ago by the easier to grow, much more prolific but rather coarser dark-skinned Tinta Negra Mole. A shortcut to good quality madeira is to look for one of the four noble varieties on the label.

But madeira's real distinction is that the young wine is subjected to extreme heat, which is where its deep caramel colour should come from.

UNDERSTANDING MADEIRA LABELS

Bual/Boal, rich, dark, sweet madeira that ages well but can be drunk younger than Verdelho and, especially, Sercial. Drink with or after cheese. Lesser imitations made from Tinta Negra Mole are labelled Medium Sweet.
Malmsey, the sweetest, darkest madeira, for drinking after a meal. Lesser versions are labelled Sweet or Rich.
Sercial, the driest style of madeira which can make an extremely fine aperitif but demands many decades of ageing before it reaches its full potential. Lesser versions are labelled Dry.
Single Harvest (Colheita), new category of younger wine from a single year, typically released at about five years old.
Solera, madeira that is the produce of gradual, fractional blending like sherry (see page 247) in an ageing system that began in the year specified. (A madeira labelled Solera 1870 comes from an ageing system established in 1870.)
Verdelho, the second lightest, driest madeira with a delicious tangy nuttiness. Lesser versions are labelled Medium Dry.
Vintage madeira. A madeira labelled, say, 1944 without any mention of the word Solera should contain nothing but wine harvested in 1944.

The Douro valley above Pinhão in summer (left), and in autumn (opposite). Only recently has there been systematic research into the best way to design vineyards in this wild, underpopulated region, which comes alive only during the grape harvest in September.

Such wines, the produce of a single, superior year, generally about every third year, depending on the quality of the wine and state of the market, have to be made from the Douro valley's finest, most concentrated, most tannic produce, to benefit from all those years in bottle (during which they develop a monstrous sediment, known as 'throwing a crust'). Such wines have to be decanted. These wines, called simply by the shipper's name and year, as in Fonseca 1992, represent only about one per cent of the Douro valley's output. Poor man's vintage port is **single quinta vintage** port which is the produce of a single wine farm, typically but not exclusively one owned by a shipper, such as Graham's Quinta dos Malvedos, from a year not 'declared' as a vintage by that shipper. It offers a way of experiencing the style of vintage port without having to pay quite so much or wait quite so long.

Then there are some intermediate styles. **Crusted** port is a blend of different years bottled early in a specified year without filtration so that, like vintage port, it matures in bottle and has a heavy sediment from which it should be decanted (see page 25).

Portuguese port shippers (they do exist and the likes of Ferreira, Nieeport [Dutch in origin] and Quinta do Noval make some superb wines) age a blend of tawny ports from a single vintage for many years in wood to produce **colheita** ports.

All these ports are matured in bulk before bottling rather than being expected to mature, like fine table wine, in the bottle in which you buy them.

The style of port traded in the auction room, however, and talked about most, is **vintage**, a long-lived wine that is relatively easy to produce because it is bottled after two or three years in cask and then left to mature in consumers' own cellars for decade after decade.

GERMANY

In a nutshell: Some of the world's finest, lightest, longest-living whites.
Grapes: Riesling, Riesling-like crossings, Pinots and their derivatives.

The German wine business is in turmoil, thank goodness. Throughout the 1970s and 1980s it prided itself on its equipment and administration – a combination unrivalled elsewhere in the world – but somewhere along the line lost sight of the taste of the wine itself. Today it is, somewhat painfully, rediscovering what makes it so special.

The well-intentioned German Wine Law of 1971 neatly assigned a number to every batch of wine, and allowed all but a tiny minority of them to call themselves 'quality wine', or Qualitätswein, the same rank as France's Appellation

UNDERSTANDING LABELS

German labels are some of the world's most confusing. Quite apart from the usual advice that producer is crucial and vintage year (pages 340–1) can affect quality, look for (1) quality level, (2) grape variety and (3) region.

(1) In ascending order of natural grape ripeness: Tafelwein, Landwein, QbA, Kabinett, Spätlese, Auslese, BA and TBA (see below).

(2) Most German wines are made from single grape varieties, specified on the label. For more details see, in declining order of importance within Germany's vineyards overall, Müller-Thurgau, Riesling, Silvaner, Kerner, Spätburgunder (Pinot Noir), Portugieser, Scheurebe, Bacchus, Faberrebe, Morio-Muskat and so on. Riesling, Scheurebe and Silvaner in Franken tend to be the best bets, although some fine dryish Grauburgunder (Pinot Gris) and Weissburgunder (Pinot Blanc) is also produced.

(3) Labels on all but the most basic German wines should carry the name of one of the wine regions (listed on the following pages), which may be a lot more helpful than the often very complicated name of the wine itself. Like burgundies, German wines tend to be named with a combination of village and vineyard name, although in the case of German a possessive 'er' is usually added to the village name, as in Bernkasteler Schlossberg for the Schlossberg vineyard in the Bernkastel district. The Germans have made life even more difficult for consumers than it was already by giving vast zones called a Grosslage a familiar name so that it is extremely difficult even for a professional like me to remember whether, for example, Badstube is a Grosslage zone or a small, single vineyard or Einzellage. Some of the most famous Grosslagen are Zeller Schwarze Katz, Kröver Nacktarsch, Bernkasteler Badstube, Bernkasteler Kurfürstlay, Piesporter Michelsberg, Klüsserather St Michael, Wiltinger Scharzberg, Niersteiner Gutes Domtal and Oppenheimer Krötenbrunnen – how on earth is the poor wine drinker to distinguish these from the genuine produce of a single site?

Auslese, naturally fully ripe grapes produce what is usually a long-living medium sweet wine, although dry, very alcoholic Auslesen are sometimes made.
Beerenauslese (BA), very sweet rarities usually sold at a very high price.
Deutschertafelwein, the most basic sort of German wine constituting less than five per cent of an average crop. Although see also Tafelwein.
Eiswein, Ice wine, which often fetches more than Beerenauslese. See page 89 for details of how it is made.
Gutsabfüllung, estate bottled.

Contrôlée élite. More disastrously, it ordained that wine quality could be measured with one simple device, the refractometer with which vine-growers check the sugar content of their grapes. To qualify as a higher grade, or Prädikat, of wine (see panel), the grape juice simply had to be sweeter. The result was a steady invasion of German vineyards by vine varieties specially bred to provide super-ripe grapes (which tend to produce wines which taste as bland as giant, prize-winning vegetables). The major casualty was the difficult-to-ripen Riesling vine, Germany's greatest asset.

Yields, for long unregulated (in sharp contrast to France and Italy), grew so that such flavour as grapes could be persuaded to develop in a climate as cool as Germany's was all too often virtually undetectable in a sea of inexpensive, low-alcohol, medium dry white shipped abroad at ludicrous prices and sold as innocuous, but hardly vinous, blends labelled Liebfraumilch, Niersteiner Gutes Domtal, Piesporter Michelsberg, and so on.

Meanwhile, a small band of obstinately quality-minded estates continued to provide evidence of the miracles that can be achieved

---

halbtrocken, half dry, wines which taste medium dry.

Kabinett, the least ripe of the QmP categories. Such wines can make lovely light bodied dryish aperitifs.

Landwein, Germany's answer to France's Vins de Pays. Still embryonic as a serious category but arguably the entire QbA category should be demoted to Landwein status.

Liebfraumilch, strictly a creation for export markets. In practice almost any medium dry, vaguely aromatic blend can qualify as Liebfraumilch, which is traded savagely as a commodity.

Qualitätswein is sometimes used as an abbreviation for QbA.

Qualitätswein bestimmter Anbaugebiet (QbA), Germany's shame. By far the dominant quality (*sic*) category, this includes all Liebfraumilch and the basic Grosslage blends sweetened up with added grape concentrate (Süssreserve). The category also includes, however, some perfectly creditable wines from top producers who decided they needed chaptalization (which is outlawed for QmP wines) to make them balanced.

Qualitätswein mit Prädikat (QmP), the best of Germany, truly its higher-quality wines which qualify for one of the following 'predicates', in ascending order of natural grape ripeness: Kabinett, Spätlese, Auslese, BA and TBA. Much of the meat of German Wine Law is laying down minimum grape ripeness levels (measured by a system called degrees Oechsle) for each combination of predicate, vine variety

and region.

Sekt, sparkling wine, usually made from imported (often Italian) wine rather than the products of German vineyards.

Spätlese means literally 'late harvest'. This category includes many fine, concentrated wines from bone dry (trocken) to medium dry.

Tafelwein, basic table wine which may not even be made entirely from German wine – in fact these 'European blends' are often made up of cheap dry white from Spain or Italy, 'Germanized' by a dollop of a particularly aromatic German wine and sweetened by added grape concentrate.

trocken means 'dry' and any wine so labelled is designed to be drunk with food. It is also likely to be more alcoholic than wine not labelled trocken because the grape sugar has been fermented into alcohol. These wines are particulary popular in Germany and increasingly so abroad.

Trockenbeerenauslese (TBA) (literally 'dried grapes that were late-picked', a reference to the shrivelling effect of botrytis or extreme heat), the sweetest, richest most luscious sort of QmP wine, produced in tiny quantities and usually sold for fabulous prices. Noble rot (Edelfäule) is usually needed to concentrate grape sugars sufficiently to meet the required ripeness levels – although some grape varieties (such as Ortega and Optima) have been specifically bred to ripen spectacularly, if not always sumptuously.

Winzergenossenschaft, Winzerverein, two common names for co-operatives.

in German vineyards, where the relatively cool climate generally provides summers which result in high levels of natural acidity, and cold winters which favour ultra-natural winemaking, relying on long, cool fermentations and minimal wine treatments. The classic wines of Germany may be high in extract (see page 16), thanks to the soils, but relatively low in alcohol. Riesling grown on the steep, slatey banks of the river Mosel is the epitome of traditional German wine: aromatic, delicate, racy, long-lived, and unlike any wine made anywhere else in the world, which is more than can be said for most of the wine made over the border in France.

But since the mid-1980s a healthy air of self-doubt has refreshed the almost infinitely fragmented German winescape (the average vineyard is an acre or two farmed as a weekend income supplement), so that at long last a new generation of wine producers has emerged to join the standard-bearers of the old brigade. Aware of the great progress made in the rest of the world since the inception of the somewhat stultifying German Wine Law, they have been experimenting, even occasionally using new oak barriques when the traditional German wine container was either a neutral large oval barrel or more commonly a stainless steel tank. The best of them know that limiting yields is the first essential step towards producing wines of real interest and flavour.

There has also been a trend towards making much drier wines in Germany than was the norm, so that the average alcoholic strength of German wine has risen (as more of the natural sugar has been fermented into alcohol instead of remaining as sweetness in the wine). This means that those of us who used to regard German wine as incapable of producing a hangover have had a few nasty shocks, but it has resulted in a new palette of wine styles from Germany which are much more at home on the dinner table than their predecessors: relatively full-bodied, positively flavoured racy whites, but always with a backbone of fine acidity which can make them much more refreshing than most Chardonnays, for example.

If Germany's wine drinkers have developed a taste for drier wines, they have nurtured a passion for red wine, encouraging a dramatic increase in plantings of red wine vines, specifically early ripening varieties such as Pinot Noir, known here as Spätburgunder.

The vineyards are green, the river is green and the wines somehow even taste green, here at Cochem in the lower reaches of the Mosel valley.

MOSEL-SAAR-RUWER

The vines which grow on the banks of the Mosel (Moselle in French) and its tributaries Saar and Ruwer constitute Germany's third biggest wine region in terms of area, but its most important in terms of international prestige and dependence on viticulture. No other crop could economically be grown on the land dedicated to the steepest, finest vineyards, and many of the thousands of small-scale vine growers in the region complain that vines are hardly economic at today's low prices.

The large modern bottling plants which have sprouted in this extraordinary, green, essentially rural landscape process so much wine that the Mosel has become Germany's most important source of wine, even if by no means all of it was grown in the Mosel, or even in Germany. The tourist village of Bernkastel is well used to having supertankers thundering through it.

The Upper Mosel valley is uncannily like the English Lake District, with its late Victorian mansions, slate and water everywhere, its permanent residents mainly long-established farmers or caterers to the needs, real and confected, of the region's swarms of tourists.

This picture-postcard, steep-sided valley follows the meandering Mosel river, folding the land into such an irregular concertina that without the sun, visitors can be completely disorientated. Local vine-growers, on the other hand, know that the great Riesling grape can be ripened only on the sunniest south and south west facing sites, steep enough and close enough to the river to benefit from its function as mirror, on porous slate soils which not only drain away the region's frequent surplus rainfall, but also retain daytime heat to act as night storage heaters.

These are the most labour-intensive vineyards in the world, requiring about seven times as many man-hours as, for example, the flat vineyards of the Médoc. In the Mosel it is said that each stake, up which individual vines are trained without restrictive wires in order to allow vineyard workers the flexibility to work the vineyard on the horizontal rather than the more tiring vertical, must be visited at least seven times each year.

Some of the slopes are so steep and so irregular that over the years some vineyard workers have even lost their lives tending these tenacious vines. I know from personal experience that keeping oneself vertical on a slope of even 30 degrees is exhausting, and many vineyards are far steeper than this.

As in Burgundy, where farming inheritance patterns are complicated by the fact that a few metres in one direction can dramatically affect the quality of the wine produced from it, and therefore the land's value, each vine-grower tends to own tiny plots in many different named vineyards. In fact the difference in altitude or exposition can have an even more dramatic effect here in the Mosel than in the Côte d'Or because in some spots the Riesling vine may not stand much chance of ripening at all, and so an earlier ripening but inevitably less glamorous variety may have to be planted instead.

The obliging Müller-Thurgau has been the obvious alternative vine variety here, and has been widely planted on flatter land that never had any hope of matching the Mosel's best sites. In fact its produce is so dull compared with the racy, nervy, tingling, long-lived essence that Mosel Riesling can be, that this inferior Mosel fetches very little money. This, tragically, has had the effect of dampening selling prices for all Mosel wine, even that produced with such care and difficulty from the best sites. Many of the peasant farmers who make up the population of this narrow, isolated valley (regarded as on the fringes of civilization by most Germans) are experiencing real financial hardship as a result of the fragile state of the German wine market.

The silver lining from the consumer's point of view of course is that top quality Mosel is underpriced in terms of the quality on offer for about the same price as a *petit château* bordeaux, for example. In view of the effort that goes into producing wine from the Mosel's steepest, most inaccessible sites, prices are almost ludicrously low – except for the best sweet BA and TBA rarities, which generally sell at highly publicized auctions.

Best value in the Mosel is in Kabinett and Spätlese wines made from the Riesling grape grown in an individual site from the likes of Bischöflichen Weingüter, J. J. Christoffel, Robert Eymael, Friedrich Wilhelm Gymnasium, Fritz Haag, Willi Haag, Reinhold Haardt, von Hövel, Karthäuserhof, von Kesselstatt, Dr Loosen, Milz, Egon Müller, J. J. Prüm, Max. Ferd. Richter, Schloss Saarstein, von Schubert (Maximin Grünhäuser), Selbach-Oster, Wegeler-Deinhard, Dr Weins-Prüm and Zilliken.

The Ruwer and particularly Saar valleys high upstream (just east of the Luxembourg border) produce some of the world's finest low-alcohol wines, many of them reaching barely eight or nine per cent alcohol, yet capable of ageing well and being genuinely interesting to drink thanks to their intensely fruity acidity and mineral-layered extract.

The Middle Mosel, the stretch including Klüsserath, Trittenheim, Piesport, Brauneberg, Bernkastel, Graach, Wehlen, Zeltingen, Ürzig and Erden, produce some of the valley's most complete, longest-lasting wines.

AHR

Germans, and practically no one else, associate this very small northerly wine region with light red, often slightly sweet wines made mainly by co-operatives from Spätburgunder (Pinot Noir) vines. Some more notable exceptions exist.

MITTELRHEIN

This small wine region is well known internationally for one producer, Toni Jost of Bacharach, whose concentrated off-dry Rieslings show just what can be achieved in the famous vineyards of the Rhine Gorge.

NAHE

This is one of Germany's most rewarding wine regions at the moment, with several of the best producers way off the beaten track. The river Nahe flows into the giant Rhine at the western end of the Rheingau, and the vineyards which flank it are therefore well south of their counterparts in the Mosel, but the best wines often manage to combine the raciness of the best Mosel with the substance of the best Rheingau wine – although they can be easier to appreciate in youth than either. Schloss Böckelheim, Bad Kreuznach, Burg Layen and Niederhausen are important wine centres of the Nahe, their surrounding vineyards specializing in zesty Rieslings.

Diel, Dönnhoff, Emrich-Schönleber, Schäfer, Schloss Wallhausen and Staatliches Weinbaudomänen, the state's own wine estate, are all reliable names to look out for.

RHEINGAU

The Rheingau, a south-facing slab of vineyards on gentle slopes leading down to the Rhine, usefully protected from chill winds by Taunus mountains to the immediate north, was for years regarded as Germany's noblest wine region. This was partly because of its long association with aristocratic estates and the famous abbey Kloster Eberbach, which has been a focus for German wine's promotional activity. Grand and ancient castles such as Schloss Johannisberg, Schloss Schönborn and Schloss Vollrads have winemaking reputations which stretch back almost as many centuries as their cellars. As the 1980s wore on, however, it became clear that winemaking conscious life was much more exciting in some other regions (notably Pfalz) than here and that there was a real danger that the Rheingau was coasting on its past reputation. Fortunately, new life is now being breathed into the region by the likes of August and Johannes Eser and, not least, by the Japanese whisky giant Suntory, which seems determined to extract wines of Yquem's reputation and price from its Robert Weil estate. Key wine villages here, in countryside almost devoted to the vine (separating villages devoted to entertaining the human spillage from Rhine cruise boats) include, moving downstream, Hochheim (inspiration of the word 'hock' which nowadays means just any old Rhine wine), Eltville, Hattenheim, Oestrich-Winkel, Geisenheim (famous for its wine research institute), Rüdesheim and Assmannshausen where red Spätburgunder of varying quality is made.

The best Rheingau wines are almost invariably Rieslings with strongly pronounced mineral qualities and rather more body than most Mosels. A significant proportion of Germany's best sweet BA and TBA wines have been made here (the famously deep golden 1959s, and 1971s which are still in their youth) but the Rheingau is the home of the trend towards making drier German wines. The dynamic Bernhard Breuer founded the Charta (pronounced 'Carter') group of top quality wine estates dedicated to styling Rheingau Riesling into medium-bodied, refreshingly crisp, dry wines suitable for the dining table. Twin Romanesque arches embossed on a brown bottle is the Charta group's trademark.

J. B. Becker, Domdechant Werner, the Esers, Knyphausen, Franz Künstler, Langwerth von Simmern and Robert Weil are the region's overachievers, but more should emerge or re-emerge as this somewhat complacent part of winemaking Germany is revitalized. Perhaps it is just too close to the wine-collecting Germans of Frankfurt?

RHEINHESSEN

This varied terrain, much of it rolling farmland across the Rhine from the Rheingau, is Germany's biggest wine region, and one for long used as a source of blending wine (more than half of all Liebfraumilch comes from the Rheinhessen). But it also has its fine wine district, the dramatic Rheinterrasse, vineyards steeply rising from the left bank of the Rhine, of which the

Roter Hang strip with its distinctive red soils just north of Nierstein is one of the most characterful. It must be particularly depressing to be an ambitious, dedicated winemaker here, knowing that most of the world's wine drinkers associate your precious Nierstein with the dreariest, cheapest commercial blends sold as Niersteiner Gutes Domtal, made up of over-produced Müller-Thurgau grown miles away on flat, much less promising land.

The Rheinhessen is famous for the variety of grapes it grows and it specializes in the exotic range of new(ish) crossings such as Ortega and Optima which need conveniently few rays of sunshine in order to ripen their grapes to impressive QmP levels. Some of the most conscientious producers include Gunderloch, Guntrum, Heyl zu Herrnsheim and St Antony.

PFALZ

The old Palatinate or Rheinpfalz is, like Rheinhessen, a very varied wine region but one of great current interest to bargain-hunting drinkers. Because of the region's relatively low land prices, increasing numbers of ambitious young wine producers have been able to make their mark here in some of Germany's warmest vineyards, where in many years natural alcohol levels of more than 13 per cent can easily be reached by those prepared to restrict yields. Old estates such as Bassermann-Jordan, Bürklin-Wolf and von Buhl have been joined by some of Germany's winemaking stars such as Josef Biffar, Kurt Darting, Koehler-Ruprecht, Rainer Lingenfelder, Müller-Catoir and Pfeffingen.

Riesling is just one of the varieties capable of producing intensely flavoured, concentrated, full-bodied wines, from dry to Trockenbeerenauslese. Others include Scheurebe, Rieslaner, Grauburgunder (Pinot Gris) and reds.

BADEN

The most southerly of Germany's wine regions, just across the Rhine from Alsace, has the climate to produce some impressive red wines and some sturdy Grauburgunder and Weissburgunder. By far the most important producer is the Zentralkellerei, or co-op, based in Breisach, which is commendably ambitious. Some very good 'experimental' Pinots, including deep red Spätburgunders, are underappreciated abroad. Dr Heger, Karl Heinz Johner and Wolff-Metternich are notable individual producers.

WÜRTTEMBERG

Most Württemberg wine is consumed locally and is typically slightly rustic, dryish Riesling and light red, sweetish-to-outside-palates wine made from the local Trollinger vine. Fürst zu Hohenlohe-Oehringen makes particularly distinguished wine.

HESSISCHE-BERGSTRASSE

Small and scattered wine region in the state of Hess, producing mainly dry Rieslings, quite like those of Rheingau to the north, for local sale, particularly in Stuttgart.

FRANKEN

Franken is German for Franconia, the most easterly of the many wine regions based on the Rhine or its tributaries, producing earthy, dry white wines that are quite different from the German norm, but which tend to be expensive because of local demand. Because winters can be so severe here, frost is a real danger every year and the size of the harvest varies enormously. For the consumer, Franken wines are distinguished by the flat green flask, or Bocksbeutel, in which they are sold (a shape impossible to fit into a

wine rack). Silvaner is *the* Franken vine but, like Riesling, it needs to be planted in the very best sites to have a chance of ripening fully. Rieslaner, the local crossing of Silvaner with Riesling, can produce some impressive late harvest wines too. Würzburg is the capital of the region and Würzburger Stein is one of the most famous vineyards. Bürgerspital, Castell, Juliusspital and Wirsching are some of the top German producers.

EAST GERMANY

East Germany's two main centres of wine production Saale-Unstrut and Sachsen (Saxony), almost on the Polish border, are still in the process of being reconstructed. It is likely to be many years yet before their light, dry produce is widely exported.

Assmannshausen, a red wine enclave at the western end of the Rheingau.

AUSTRIA

In a nutshell: Great dry Rieslings and
reliably botrytized sweet wines.
Grapes: Grüner Veltliner, Welschriesling,
Riesling, Müller-Thurgau (WHITE), Zweigelt,
Portugieser, Blaufränkisch (RED)

Austrian wine is possibly the best kept secret
in the wine world – partly because the
Austrians themselves are such dedicated, and
well-heeled, wine enthusiasts that they are not
keen to let the rest of the world know just what
exceptional liquids lurk behind their easily misunderstood wine labels.

It will be many decades before Austrian
winemakers are allowed to forget that in 1985
some Austrian wine merchants tried to give
extra body to certain wines by adding a harmless but illegal substance, most unfortunately
also an ingredient in antifreeze. As a result of
this national disgrace, Austria now probably has
the world's strictest wine regulations, and its
wine producers (most of whom were entirely
unimplicated in the scandal) are making some
of the world's purest, highest-quality white
wines, which range from dry and piercing to
sweet and racy.

LOWER AUSTRIA

The north eastern corner of the country (which
is known in German as Niederösterreich) is
where most Austrian wine is produced. The
Wachau is a beautiful stretch of crags above the
Danube, upstream of Vienna, and is probably
the Riesling grape's most consistent showcase.
(The Mosel and Rheingau in Germany have
similar potential, but much of it is unrealized at
the moment.) On terraced vineyards Riesling
and Austria's own signature grape variety, the
crackling white Grüner Veltliner, provide long-
ripened grapes which small, family concerns
(such as Alzinger, the Pichlers, Prager, Knoll,

Jamek, and Hirtzberger) transform by punctilious winemaking into powerful yet fragrant,
fine, dry whites that are all too rarely seen outside Austria. Its most concentrated wines are
called Smaragd. Federspiel is one category
lower. There is also some experimentation with
producing BA and TBA wines, but dry Rieslings
are the Wachau's strength.

Kremstal, centred on the ancient town of
Krems and **Kamptal**, whose chief wine town is
Langenlois, are to the Wachau's immediate east
and produce wines of almost as much finesse but
which tend to cost rather less. Bründlmayer is
one the best producers.

Donauland and **Carnuntum** encompass a
great sweep of varied vineyards round the east
of Vienna, and are home to the most famous of
Austria's many wine abbeys, including the
research institute and winery Klosterneuburg.

Thermenregion is the new, post-1985 name
for the district responsible for the plump, fiery
whites of Gumpoldskirchen.

The **Weinviertel**, or 'wine quarter', is the
extensive, fertile, Danube plain stretching
north from Vienna to the Czech border, which
produces most of Austria's everyday wine, its
sparkling Sekt and some interesting red wine
too. Müller-Thurgau and Welschriesling are the
common grapes here. Eiswein is possible.

VIENNA

Austria has the only capital city in the world in
which wine-growing, as well as wine drinking, is
seriously important. Vienna has some fine vineyards in its suburbs, as well as the unique
Heurige tradition, whereby the city's vintners
are allowed to sell their wine straight from the
fermentation vat, in their own taverns, most
famously in the suburb of Grinzing. Franz Mayer
(whose son-in-law is an ebullient Australian)
and Wieninger are two of the best producers.

BURGENLAND

This flat, quintessentially Middle European region is almost as Hungarian in spirit and landscape as it is Austrian, and produces almost all of Austria's great sweet white wines and most of the best red.

Neusiedlersee is the most important sweet white wine district, named after the large, shallow lake that dominates it (although so flat is the landscape that visitors have to climb towers to see the lake beyond the reeds). This large body of water is partly responsible for reliable, annual 'noble rot' infections (see page 88) that shrivel the grapes, concentrating the sweetness, and making wines rich enough to qualify as Beerenauslesen and Trockenbeerenauslesen, rivals to great Sauternes. The fact that many of the best vineyards are surrounded by land designated as a bird sanctuary makes life particularly difficult for growers such as Alois Kracher, Nittnaus, Stiegelmar, Umathum and Willi Opitz, who grow an unusually wide variety of grapes that includes Weissburgunder (Pinot Blanc), Traminer, Scheurebe, Chardonnay and Welschriesling, which performs particularly well here.

Neusiedlersee-Hügelland is on the western lakeshore and produces wines that are similar to Neusiedlersee. The historic local speciality is Ausbruch wines made in the postcard-pretty village of Rust. Ernst Triebaumer and Heidi Schröck are widely admired.

Mittelburgenland is celebrated as Austria's red wine district, where hot summers help to ripen such grapes as the lively central European Blaufränkisch, Pinot Noir, Cabernet Sauvignon and Austrian specialities Zweigelt and the Pinot-like St Laurent. Producers such as Gesellmann and Igler have shown that, now that they have mastered malolactic fermentation, Austrian winemakers are capable of producing ambitious, deep-coloured, well-structured red wines too.

Südburgenland is best known for lightish red Blaufränkisch.

STYRIA

Styria, or Steiermark in German, is the mountainous south east of the country, producing relatively little but often extremely exciting varietals – notably aromatic Sauvignon Blanc and some variable Chardonnay often labelled Morillon. The wines are less characteristically Austrian than close relatives of those piercing grape essences made in neighbouring Slovenia, or even Friuli in north east Italy. It is officially divided into south, south east, and west (Süd-, Süd-Ost-, and Weststeiermark respectively). The most important of these in terms of quantity is Südsteiermark (southern Styria) where on relatively high-altitude vineyards round Liebnitz, producers such as Alois Gross, Reinhold Polz, Sattlerhof and, particularly, Tement make pure, mainly white varietals.

UNDERSTANDING LABELS

Ausbruch, traditional sweet wine speciality of Rust, usually deeply coloured and with more than a hint of Tokay character (see page 272).

Auslese, late picked, lightly sweet wines.

Beerenauslese (BA), very sweet wines, often with noble rot, with more weight and usually less acid than their German counterparts and should therefore be drunk sooner.

extratrocken, bone dry.

halbtrocken, medium dry.

Kabinett, light, dryish crisp wines with real character.

Landwein, superior to Tafelwein.

lieblich, medium sweet.

Qualitätswein, quality wine.

Spätlese, between Kabinett and Auslese in quality and character.

süss, sweet.

Tafelwein, basic table wine, rarely exported and sold only in larger bottle sizes.

trocken, dry.

Trockenbeerenauslese (TBA) – nobly rotten grapes produce some truly fine wines almost every year in Burgenland. Austrian TBA is less expensive than German.

SWITZERLAND

In a nutshell: Fragrant whites and some surprisingly concentrated reds from three very different cultures.
Grapes: *Chasselas, Sylvaner* (WHITE), *Gamay, Blauburgunder (Pinot Noir), Merlot* (RED)

Most non-Swiss people dismiss Swiss wine as slightly heavy, nondescript liquids called Fendant and Dôle, sold far too expensively in mountain restaurants. It is true that Swiss wine, like Swiss anything, is expensive. It is a direct reflection of the Swiss cost of living, and its reputation has not been helped by the fact that the bigger Swiss wine merchants have been allowed too free a hand with blending imported wines. (Because Switzerland is not a member of the European Union, it is not answerable to European wine law, although it tightened up its wine laws considerably over the last few years.)

But all over Switzerland are passionately obsessive winemakers who each year are making better and better wines, many of them red, in such small quantities that they go straight into the cellars of the connoisseurs of Geneva, Zurich and Vaduz (Liechtenstein is close to one of the best wine regions) and are rarely mentioned in the international wine press.

The Swiss have been careful to preserve their agricultural heritage, which means not only the preservation of the clanking cowbell, Heidi tradition, but the preservation of some of the world's prettiest and most inconvenient vineyards – the great majority of which are in the western, French-speaking part of the country.

Swiss wines taste quite unlike those of Germany and Austria, for example, because Swiss winemakers routinely encourage the second, softening malolactic fermentation (see page 72) so the wines seem much less obviously acid. They also increase most of their wines' final alcohol content quite considerably by adding sugar to the fermentation vat (a practice that is familiar to any Frenchman as chaptalization) and so most Swiss wines are much less tart and thin than the country's high altitude and relatively continental climate might suggest.

FRENCH SWITZERLAND

The main grape variety here by far is Chasselas, which is also sometimes sold as a table grape. The sunny, south-facing slopes of the **Valais** in the upper Rhône valley south east of Lake Geneva produce more Swiss wine than any other region. So dry and warm are summers here that some vineyards, many of them so steep they need to be worked with pulleys, may need irrigation from time to time. Local vine variety specialities in some of the highest vineyards include Petit Arvine, Humagne and Amigne and some serious late harvest sweet wines are made, sometimes from raisined, or *flétri*, grapes. Further down the valley some concentrated whites from Fendant (Chasselas), Johannisberg (Sylvaner), Ermitage (Marsanne), Malvoisie (Pinot Gris) are made, as well as some deep, red Syrahs which would impress many winemakers in Tain l'Hermitage, miles further down the river Rhône in France. Much of the Pinot Noir and Gamay grown in Valais is blended to be sold as Dôle, Switzerland's answer to Burgundy's Bourgogne-Passe-tout-grains (see page 166). The best producers include Josef-Marie Chanton, Marie-Thérèse Chappaz, Urbain Germanier, Didier Joris and Simon Maye.

The canton of **Vaud**, on the northern shore of Lake Geneva, is also an important Swiss wine region, and houses many of the larger merchants. Aigle, La Côte, Lavaux, Dézaley, Chablais and Yvorne are the main Vaud wine regions and are dominated by Chasselas. Salvagnin is Vaud's version of Dôle, although it usually displays even less Pinot Noir influence.

Densely planted vines, almost certainly Chasselas, in vineyards above Sion in French-speaking Switzerland, where every square metre is made to pay its way.

Some Chardonnay and Pinot Gris is also grown here on vineyards which slope gently towards the lake, benefiting from its reflected, grape-ripening light. Some of the most respected winemakers are Jean-Michel-Conne and Henri Cruchon.

There is also a wide range of vine varieties grown around the city of **Geneva** itself. Gamay is particularly easy to sell. In **Neuchâtel**, pale pink Œil de Perdrix (partridge's eye) is a popular local invention.

GERMAN SWITZERLAND

The wines of eastern Switzerland are quite different. Pinot Noir, or Blauburgunder, is particularly popular and is made in a wide range of styles from slightly sweet and juicy through seriously Burgundian to a strong, sweet version made from dried grapes in the **Graubünden** region, a hotbed of experimentation. Müller-Thurgau dominates white wine production, and indeed the largest wine region **Schaffhausen** is effectively a southern extension of Germany's Baden region. Baumann, Gantenbein, Kesselring and Schwarzenach are some of the most promising performers.

ITALIAN SWITZERLAND

The **Ticino** is yet another quite distinct wine-making zone in Switzerland (with an unusual tradition of still cultivating hybrids – see page 97). Much of its produce is light Merlot designed to satisfy the Swiss thirst for wine of any quality so long as it's red.

Some top quality, oak-aged Merlot del Ticino and other international reds are made, however, from low-yielding vines grown in particularly well-favoured sites – even if few of them escape the clutches of the Swiss themselves. Daniel Huber, Adriano Kaufmann and Werner Stucky are some of the most cosmopolitan winemakers.

CENTRAL & EASTERN EUROPE

HUNGARY

In a nutshell: Some fiery whites and some good value, plus a historic sweet relic.
Grapes: Furmint, Hárslevelű, Leányka and many more (WHITE), Kadarka plus the usual international mix (RED)

Like all wine-producing countries in eastern Europe (and there are many), Hungary is busy trying to restructure its wine business in the wake of the collapse of the Soviet bloc. Until 1989 wine was viewed as simply a commodity like grain or potatoes to be supplied, according to long-term economic plans, to Hungarians and, particularly, Russians. The state monopoly handled all wine sales and distribution and, although much of the vineyard land remained in private hands, many vines were planted in unsuitable areas. Quantity was the priority. Quality was regarded as subversive.

Today, Hungary's vine-growers and wine-makers are trying to grapple with a completely new system which offers them no security and no very obvious market. The Russian one has evaporated, the domestic market is shrinking, and export markets have never been so competitive. All things considered, Hungarian wine is doing quite well, in the British market at least.

Of all the eastern European wine producers, Hungary has been most comprehensively invaded by the so-called 'flying winemakers', technically clued-up wine producers who spend just enough time in the wine region to make the cleanest, fruitiest, most 'international' wine out of that harvest's grapes. This has resulted in a bevy of inexpensive, well-made, if not breath-stoppingly characterful varietals from Hungary – notably Chardonnay, Sauvignon Blanc, Pinot Noir, Cabernet and Merlot, which are increas-ingly joined by the likes of Hárslevelű, Irsai Oliver, Furmint and Leányka among whites and Kadarka, Kékfrankos and Kékoporto among reds.

If Hungarian whites can be said to share a characteristic it is that the whites are relatively full-bodied and have a certain Magyar fire or spice. Reds are less distinctive. The best exported tend to be merely clean, frank and fruity, although locals swear by the more characterful offerings of the likes of Josef Bach. Young Kékfrankos can be particularly juicy and appetizing, while some vintages (Hungary's weather can vary considerably from year to year) yield some fine Pinot Noir fruit.

If many Hungarian vineyards are under-achievers, many Hungarian wineries are severely underfunded, since the production system moved into private hands. Most of the newer equipment has been provided by western invest-ment, often with only one intermediary between a British supermarket shelf and the imported tank press.

The country's legacy of native vine varieties is distinctive, rich and diverse, encompassing light-skinned grapes such as Furmint, Hárslevelű, Irsai Oliver, Juhfark, Kéknyelű, various Muscats, Sárfehér and the rarities Ezerjó and Juhfark. Olaszrizling is the Welschriesling of Austria, Szürkebarát is the Hungarian name for France's Pinot Gris, Tramini is Traminer, Leányka is Romania's grapey Feteasca, while Királeányka is Fetească Regală.

Kadarka is Hungary's signature red grape variety, although it has been a casualty as growers have increasingly planted the internationally better-known varieties Cabernet, Merlot and Pinot Noir. Some of the best Kadarka is grown in Szekszárd, although it is also cultivated in Kiskun, Hajos-Vaskút, Csongrád and Villány-

Siklos. Kékfrankos (sometimes called Nagyburgundi) is Austria's Blaufränkisch and Kékoporto is Germany's Portugieser. All of these are found on labels of wines exported from Hungary, some in considerable quantity.

Quite apart from the difficulty of pronouncing and spelling most of them, it will surely be some time before wine drinkers outside Hungary come to demand Hungarian wine by the names of the regions. It is also far too early in Hungary's reconstruction to make long-term generalizations about the aptitude of various regions for different varieties and wine styles. The country is still being plundered by outside investors and the success of the resulting wines can often reflect the level of investment more than the natural potential.

It seems unlikely, for instance, that **Sopron**, which is effectively a continuation of Austria's Neusiedlersee sweet wine region, will be producing wines to match Austria's most sought-after half-bottles in the foreseeable future. It is best known for dry reds today. **Somló's** wines tend to aromatic whites, while the town of Mór and nearby **Etyek** are establishing a reputation for exportable varietals of both colours.

On the shores of **Lake Balaton** are many important and increasingly modernized vineyards, with **Badacsony** on the westernmost part of the northern shore and **Balatonfüred-Csopak** at the north eastern end.

Three wine regions on the right bank of the Danube (Duna) in the south of the country are **Szekszárd**, **Villány-Siklós** and the **Mecsek** hills centred on the town of Pécs, once famous for its Olaszrizling. Many fine, concentrated red wines are made here and the historic Italian firm of Antinori conferred international respectability on Szekszárd by launching a joint venture with its co-operative to produce wines under the Bátaapáti Estate label.

Just across the Danube from here is Hungary's famous **Great Plain**, or **Alfold**, a flat, sandy expanse populated largely by gypsies and horses. Vines joined them in quantity soon after phylloxera invaded the country (phylloxera

cannot thrive in sand). This is the source of Hungary's bulk of basic blending wine, although it has three designated areas which can produce some good value international varietals, **Hajós**, **Kiskun** and **Csongrád**.

The rest of Hungary's vineyards are in the north west of the country. In the **Mátra Foothills (Mátraalja)**, vines are protected from cold winds by the Northern Massif, and the Chardonnay and Sauvignon Blanc of Gyöngyös Estate were some of the first 'new wave' Hungarian wines to be exported.

To the east is the historic town of **Eger** whose most famous wine, Egri Bikavér was sold for years on export markets as red, sometimes powerful but often not, Bull's Blood. Today the Egervin Vineyard Company, the old monopoly revitalized by a $10 million injection of capital, is trying to forge a new, controlled, recognizable identity for Bull's Blood.

But Hungary's most famous wine by far is made in the north east corner of the country in a strange region known as **Tokaj-Hegyalja** (which historically extended over the border into Slovakia – except that the Czechs exchanged the right to use the name Tokay for a large beer contract). Tokaji, the wine named after the town of Tokaj (and often called Tokay outside Hungary), was in its time the world's greatest sweet white wine, made from nobly rotten grapes as early as 1650, according to local history – long before botrytized wines were recorded in Sauternes and the Rheingau, the birthplace of such wines in Germany. The main ingredients are Hárslevelű and, especially, Furmint, with some Muscat grapes. The local conditions around the 28 Tokaj-Hegyalja villages in this very protected corner of middle Europe are such that in a good year the best are affected by noble rot, here called *aszú*, and can reach exceptional sugar levels. (As in Sauternes, a confluence of rivers encourages morning mists.) They range from dry to quite extraordinarily sweet, with the following descriptions: Szamorodni (in which there is no selective picking of grapes affected by noble rot), dry or sweetened; then Aszú 3, 4, 5 or 6 puttonyos, a puttonyo being the traditional hod of sweet grape paste (made from pulverized botrytized grapes) added per barrel (big enough to hold 7 puttonyos) of wine made from unaffected grapes before a slow second fermentation. Aszú Essencia is made only from the produce of the best years and the best vineyards, while Essence or Tokaji Nectar is very rare grape sugar essence made from the tiny amount of free-run juice from the botrytized grapes that are used to make Aszú paste. Because its sugar content is so high, yeasts can work only at a snail's pace and these wines continue to ferment in cask for many a year. These were the sorts of wine which made Tokay's reputation as elixir of life and love. The final ingredient in Tokay's extraordinary character is that it has traditionally been aged rather like sherry, under a film of local yeast, in barrels partly filled, in strange underground caverns lined with mould like black felt and signalled only by the low doorways hollowed out of the region's small hills. Of all Hungarian wine regions this one has attracted most attention from outside investors who include no fewer than three French insurance companies (AXA own Disznókó), and a consortium, the Royal Tokay Wine Company, involving the British wine writer Hugh Johnson. Many wines made since 1992 have much less characterful, 'cleaner', more Sauternes-like and less Hungarian flavours than their predecessors, which were effectively thrown into a communal blending vat by the state monopoly. All of them are bottled in a distinctive half-litre clear glass flask.

BULGARIA

In a nutshell: *Cheap international varietals.*
Grapes: *Cabernet Sauvignon, Mavrud, Melnik* (RED), *Rkatsiteli, Aligoté, Chardonnay* (WHITE)

With much less promising raw materials than Hungary, but a similar commercial climate, Bulgaria managed a minor economic miracle in the 1970s and 1980s. Lacking a domestic wine market

of any size, and an exciting range of indigenous varieties, what was then the Bulgarian state wine monopoly successfully sold most of its basic wine to the Soviet Union and systematically planted the varieties it somehow knew it could sell, in vast quantities, to the British market: Cabernet Sauvignon, Merlot, Pinot Noir, Chardonnay, Sauvignon Blanc, Traminer and Riesling.

Of these, the full-throttle, somewhat rustic but recognizable blackcurrant-flavoured Bulgarian Cabernet Sauvignon was then by far the most successful, to such an extent that Bulgaria became the UK's fifth most important supplier of wine (after France, Germany, Italy and Spain) in 1988. California winemaking expertise was extended to Bulgaria, provided the country granted the cola market to PepsiCo. In the mid-1980s the state-controlled Bulgarian wine industry, bolstered by huge and regular orders from the Soviet Union, seemed in good shape.

But by 1989, even before the collapse of the Soviet bloc and with it Bulgarian wine's most important market, Bulgaria's vineyards were in considerable disarray. Gorbachev's anti-alcohol measures were immediately reflected in neglected vineyards left to grow wild, or at most to produce poor quality wine. Total wine production in 1990 was only a quarter as much as in 1985, despite buoyant sales in Britain.

The Bulgarian wine industry is slowly trying to reconstruct itself in the entirely new economic climate into which it has been propelled so rapidly. Winemaking discipline, hygiene and equipment are still more important factors in determining whether a Bulgarian wine is likely

Racking wine in the strange, mould-lined cellars responsible for the rich, golden, but extremely variable wines of the Tokaj region in Hungary. Winemaking standards slipped considerably towards the end of the Soviet regime, but are currently being revived by a host of outside investors.

to suit a western palate than the natural conditions of where the grapes were grown. Many of the older wineries such as Assenovgrad in the south were built, Soviet style, effectively as bottling and distribution centres close to cities rather than vineyards (although Assenovgrad has produced a run of excitingly rich, age-worthy Mavrud). Wineries such as Russe and Suhindol close to the Romanian border to the north, Preslav and Burgas in the Black Sea hinterland in the east and Sliven in the Balkan foothills have been relatively successfully modernized. Other wineries which regularly supply western markets include Suhindol and Svischtov in the north, Khan Krum and Varna in the east, and Stambovolo in the south.

I have yet to taste a seriously exciting white Bulgarian wine – most are very pale renditions of the variety specified, both 'international' and the local grapey Misket, Aligoté and Rkatsiteli imported from Russia, and Fetiaska (sic) imported from Romania. As I write, however, there is doubtless a stunning barrel-fermented Chardonnay just waiting to be bottled... Bulgarian reds, on the other hand can be great value. I have detected a certain inadvisable love affair with oak chips and am not entirely convinced by some Bulgarian wineries' determination to make soft, plummy, light, fruity blends of such varieties as Merlot and Pinot Noir, Merlot and Gamza (the Bulgarian name for Hungary's Kadarka), and Merlot and Pamid (Bulgaria's least exciting native red grape), but there is undoubtedly some well-made, absurdly inexpensive Cabernet Sauvignon, Mavrud and Melnik, the impressive speciality of the eponymous town near the Greek border.

ROMANIA

In a nutshell: Seriously underdeveloped.
Grapes: *Feteascas, Welschriesling, Tămaîioasă* (WHITE), *Cabernet Sauvignon* (RED)

Romania has great potential for varied and high-quality wine production, but it is unlikely to be fully realized for many years. The country has a greater area of vineyard than any other in eastern Europe (other than the ex-Soviet Union), and the sweet white wines of Cotnari in the north east were as famous as Tokaj and Constantia in their day.

Romania is also, unlike Hungary and Bulgaria, a wine-drinking country. It lies on the same latitude as France, even if its climate is more dramatically continental (although winters tend to be much less harsh on the Black Sea coast in the east).

Romania boasts that it has considerably more Cabernet Sauvignon planted than Bulgaria (which has had such success with exporting the variety) but the chief grape varieties are the indigenous white Feteasca and a twentieth-century crossing Fetească Regală. They yield aromatic wines which vary enormously in sweetness level and quality. Welschriesling (the variety behind Banat Riesling from the far west of the country), Aligoté and Merlot are other important varieties, although there are also considerable acreages of Sauvignon Blanc, Pinot Gris, Rkatsiteli, Muscat Ottonel, Traminer and the native Romanian Grasă and Tămaîioasă which were responsible for Cotnari.

The atmospheric, wooded hills of Transylvania in the middle of the country are the source of many, potentially haunting white wines, notably in the **Tîrnave** (or **Tarnave**) region. Other geographical names to have escaped the country on the mere 15 per cent of wine production that is exported include **Murfatlar** on the coast, which has a certain reputation for sweet wines (a Romanian speciality) and **Dealul Mare** on the Carpathian foothills north of Bucharest, which can turn out some superior red wines, including some rather soupy but very inexpensive Pinot Noir-like wine.

For the moment, however, Romania's wine producers suffer like all Romanians from the chronic shortages of materials and equipment that are considered commonplace in the west, notably bottling equipment and refrigeration to control fermentation temperatures.

MOLDOVA

In a nutshell: Right climate, lots of vines.
Grapes: International mix

The independent state of Moldova is so far the only member of the CIS to have established any sort of reputation as a wine producer abroad. Sandwiched between Romania and the Ukraine, both geographically and ethnically, it has its own very strong, if troubled, wine identity. An extraordinary 10 per cent of this gently rolling country, with ideal natural conditions for wine production, is taken up with vineyard – much of it planted with export-friendly varieties such as Cabernet Sauvignon, Chardonnay, Sauvignon Blanc and Pinot Noir. Immediately after independence in 1989 the country's wine industry attracted considerable interest from outside investors. Even Penfolds, the giant Australian wine producers, not to mention a fleet of flying winemakers, got in on the act.

There is nothing wrong with Moldova's natural gifts as a wine producer, but those involved with trying to export bottled wine from the country still bear scars marked 'no decent corks', 'transport strike' and the like. This is an area to watch.

CONFEDERATION OF INDEPENDENT STATES

Within the old Soviet Union (now known as the Confederation of Independent States), the states surrounding the Caspian Sea all produce considerable quantities of wine, notably Georgia which has an extremely vibrant wine culture. Azerbaijan, Kazakhstan and Uzbekistan's wines could seem raisiny, unsophisticated stuff if they were ever exposed to western palates.

The Ukraine, and in particular the Crimean peninsula, has clearly excellent potential – as witness the Massandra central winery bottlings of rich dessert wines sold by Sotheby's in the late 1980s. Rkatsiteli and Saperavi are two fine indigenous Georgian white and red varieties

respectively. There is clearly great potential here, as French giant Pernod-Ricard who have invested directly clearly realize.

CZECH REPUBLIC AND SLOVAKIA

Wines here tend to be white, light and crackling, often lacking the dead hand of co-operative wineries and post-fermentation sweetening that blurs much of the eastern European wine picture. Some exciting Riesling Grüner Veltliner and Pinot Blanc has escaped. Slovakia is the major producer, with the **Nitra** region in the south exporting with particular enthusiasm.

SLOVENIA

This is the most westernized wine producer of all, making some extremely fine, pure, lively, mostly white varietals in two zones, respectively in the extreme west and east of the country. The western wines are made in the image of the best of Friuli just over the border in north east Italy, while there are some similarities between the eastern wines and their near neighbours in Austria's Styria. Welschriesling, often called Laskirizling here, was a staple for many years, exported in often murkily sweetened-up form under the Lutomer label in the days before the Germans managed to ban calling this unrelated central European vine variety 'Riesling'.

EX-YUGOSLAVIA

Some hints of the potential here escape this troubled region which has traditionally supplied Germany with vast quantities of cheap, slightly sweet red wine. Croatia may eventually yield up some secrets about its vine varieties and their relation to various Italian and Greek names. Fruska Gora in Vojvodina can produce some very pretty white varietals with a middle European accent. Vranac is a deep and respectable red from Montenegro in the south with real potential for ageing.

MEDITERRANEAN COUNTRIES

In very general terms, the wines produced close to the eastern and southern shores of the Mediterrean tend to be full-bodied, relatively alcoholic, and most successful when either red and concentrated or sweet but, as ever, there are exceptions.

GREECE

Largely unobserved by the rest of the world, Greece has been modernizing her wine industry rapidly. There is no shortage of the sorts of ambitious, pig-headed wine producers with international tasting experience who are keen to prove that Greece, too, belongs to the dynamic greater world of wine.

This is particularly thrilling in view of the fact that the Greek wine industry is so ancient and seems determined to avoid the Chardonnay-and-Cabernet-only trap in its modern incarnation. It is quite possible that some of the vine varieties grown today are the same as those experienced by participants in classical symposia (much more hedonistic gatherings than their modern namesakes) and Dionysian revels. (One common and widely spread vine at least owes its name to its Greek origins: Malvasia is a corruption of the name of the Greek port of Monemvasia, through which many ancient sweet Malvasias passed in the Middle Ages.)

Many Greek varieties are extinct or nearly so but the aromatic white Malagousia has been rescued, as has Lagorthi, and Crete's Vilana. Assyrtiko, Roditis and Savatiano are widely planted varieties for white wines and Agiorgitiko, Mavrodaphne, Xynomavro and, to a lesser extent, Limnio are some of the better-known dark-skinned grapes.

Modern Greek wine is very much more than retsina, the aggressively pine resin-flavoured, full-bodied white of blessed taverna memory. North-facing slopes are increasingly valued for their moderating effect on the high summer temperatures in Greece, just as, for the same reason, high-altitude vineyard sites are being replanted. Wineries such as Tsantalis' new extension at Aghios Pavlos, Kourtakis at Ritsona and Boutari's outpost on Santorini are some of the world's most modern and best equipped. Greece now has small, well-funded, quality-at-all-costs winemaking establishments such as Gentilini on the almost Adriatic island of Cephalonia, Ktima Mercouri near Olympia, Ktima Hatzimichalis near Parnassus, and Strofilia not far from Athens (with a useful, eponymous high-quality wine bar in the city itself). The country's first modern, family-owned winery was Domaine Carras, established in Chaldiki in the late 1960s by shipowner John Carras.

The vinescape is changing rapidly, but some of the most interesting wines to reach export markets are the scented dry whites made from Robola grapes on Cephalonia and Gaia's tinglingly nervy Thalassitis, made from ancient Assyrtiko vines struggling for survival on the black, volcanic island of Santorini. Among wines that attest to Greece's ability to make well-balanced but truly interesting reds too are firm and oak-aged Naoussa made from Xynomavro in the far north, intensely perfumed Agiorgitiko grown at Nemea on the east coast of the Peloponnese, and some interesting experimentation between Thessalonika and the Turkish border to the east. The wines that are probably closest to those made in ancient Greece and those that were shipped around Europe by the Venetians and Genoese are the

Greek café culture prefers spirits to wine.

country's host of sweet wines such as Muscats of Samos, Lemnos and Patras, which also produces some gloriously mellow wood-aged Mavrodaphne. There is undoubtedly, however, more to come – especially as this renaissance in winemaking coincides with a dramatic fall in wine consumption in Greece.

TURKEY

Turkey's vineyards are most famous for producing dried fruit but some modern (that is to say, cool-fermented) wine is also made. Buzbağ, produced by the powerful state monopoly which controls about 20 wineries, is the memorable name of one of the best-distributed brands of rather rustic red. Sarafin near the battlegrounds of Gallipoli is the country's first 'boutique winery' producing – what else? – barrel-aged Cabernet Sauvignon. There are white wines, but they are clearly much more difficult to get right in this meteorological and social climate. Turks themselves generally prefer raki, their aniseed-flavoured spirit, to their wines, which are largely consumed by tourists.

Nevertheless, there are vineyards in many very different parts of Turkey. In the distinctly European soils and climate west of Istanbul, the countryside, and wines, could be extremely similar to those of eastern Greece and southern Bulgaria, although there has generally been serious under-investment in modernizing wineries in Turkey. The vineyards on the Aegean coast around Izmir produce some of Turkey's best whites, some of them sweet and almost as classical as the remains and tourist sites in this part of the world. The vines planted in Anatolia in the eastern interior of Turkey have to cope with extremely cold winters and very dry summers. With their ancient grape varieties and proximity to the Euphrates, they may hold many clues about the origins of viticulture itself. Perhaps it could be said that Turkish wine for the moment is more of interest to historians than modernists – but there is no lack of potential.

CYPRUS

The island's most exciting vine product is Commandaria, a historic dark, raisiny dessert wine which could be very good indeed. For a long time Cyprus concentrated too heavily on very ordinary bulk wine, grape concentrate and pretend sherries to have a particularly bright medium-term future. (See page 336.) But President Gorbachev's attempt to sober up his nation

and the fall of communism had the indirect effect of waking up the Cypriot wine industry from its long slumber. The docile Soviet market, for long a repository for the sort of very cheap, very ordinary wine exported in bulk by the island's dominant large producers, disappeared. Today, companies like Etko and Keo are making increasingly sophisticated Cabernet Sauvignon and Grenache table wines, and there is greater understanding of the need to process grapes as close to the vineyard as possible rather than trucking them through the midday sun to the coast where the big traditional wineries are. Grapes are also being picked earlier in order to retain their fruitiness. (When I last visited Cyprus, admittedly in the 1980s, I soon learned to order the youngest possible vintage available in the hope that it would have just a little freshness, even though the Cypriots themselves seemed to revere age and oxidation.)

LEBANON

The latitudes of the Lebanon on the eastern Mediterranean coast may seem too low for high-quality wine production, but the Bekaa Valley on an inland plateau as high as England's tallest mountains eases the temperatures considerably and can yield some very exciting red wines. Chateau Musar is the label best known outside the Lebanon and its bordeaux-like structure (filled out with much headier Cabernet Sauvignon and Cinsaut fruit than the Médoc is ever likely to produce) was inspired by a visit to the Bartons of St-Julien. Whites tend to flab (although Musar's Serge Hochar is working on his) but some respectable dry rosés are also made by producers such as Kefraya and Ksara. These last two are giving Chateau Musar some increasingly stiff competition. Chateau Kefraya's oaked Bordeaux blended red is more than respectable and Ksara's dry rosé goes perfectly with the fresh vegetables and powerful flavours of Lebanese *mezze*. A prominent declaration of intent is Massaya, a serious red wine enterprise backed by top quality St Emilion and Châteauneuf expertise.

ISRAEL

A quiet revolution has been taking place in the cellars and vineyards of Israel, where demand for local wine is unfortunately so enthusiastic that the wines seem unreasonably expensive if they manage to reach export markets. For some time the Golan Heights winery's Yarden wines were the unchallenged leaders of Israel's modern wine offering, but there is now an increasing number of others, from vineyards being planted in several different regions. Castel makes some fine copies of red bordeaux and white burgundy in the Judean Hills. Dalton manages a very creditable Sauvignon Blanc from fruit grown in Upper Galilee where Margalit produces a terrific Merlot. And all over the country some well balanced, ripe Cabernet Sauvignon is grown.

For many outsiders, sweet red kiddush wine represents all Israel has to offer the wine drinker, but this is an outmoded view. Indeed, many of the new boutique offerings are not even kosher, and are aimed at the country's most modern restaurants.

MOROCCO

In the 1950s North Africa was one of the most important sources of wine for European consumption, when French blending vats depended heavily on the deep, heady reds produced in colonial Algeria. Today, wine production along the North African coast is plummeting as the influence of Islam increases, but Morocco still makes some interesting wines and has the potential to produce more. The state still has a heavy hand in wine production, which is geared to tourists and export to couscous cafés all over France. Some characterful dry pink wines sold as Vin Gris and some rich, strong Muscat dessert wines are made, but a number of incomers, notably but not exclusively the French giant Castel, are busy modernizing vineyards and wineries to exciting effect. Meknès is a key area of production.

USA

It is not generally appreciated that the USA regularly makes more wine than any country other than France, Italy or Spain. Its annual output is, for example, well over twice as much as Australia's. All but the Midwestern states produce some wine, but the output of each of these diverse wine regions (most of them young) varies enormously in both quantity and style – as one might expect of such a vast country.

California, with its ideal mediterranean climate, produces nine out of every 10 bottles of American wine. Washington and New York state are the only other two states to produce wine in any significant quantity (although rainy Oregon has earned quite a reputation for quality).

When Europeans colonized the North American continent one of their first botanical discoveries was its rich diversity of indigenous vines. Botanists have identified more than 20 different species of vine native to north eastern America. At the time the early settlers hardly appreciated just how different these American vines were to the European vine species *Vitis vinifera* (see pages 96–9). They soon tried to make wine from native American grapes but found their flavours and textures off-puttingly unfamiliar. As early as 1619 they were trying out imported cuttings of European vines in eastern states, and for nearly three centuries remained mystified at how poorly these vines adapted to life on the other side of the Atlantic. (What ungrafted European vines lacked, of course, was the native American vines' resistance to native American vine pests and diseases such as mildew and phylloxera.)

To this day north eastern states in general and upper New York state (like Ontario in Canada) in particular continue the tradition of making wine from the native *Vitis labrusca* species, hybrids of native American vines (American hybrids) and hybrids of American and European vines (French hybrids). The most popular variety is Concord but others include Baco, Catawba, Maréchal Foch, Seyval Blanc and Vidal. In the south east of the United States musky wine is still made from the slithery juice of the Scuppernong vine.

Improved communications have brought increasing internationalization, however, and the proportion of American wine made from well-known, easy-to-sell vinifera varieties such as Cabernet and Sauvignon Blanc continues to increase, even in areas which were traditionally the stronghold of all-American wine made from all-American vines and hybrids that are particularly suited to the local conditions.

Many of the smaller, so-called 'boutique' wineries which have sprouted in relatively new wine colonies such as Maryland, Connecticut and New Mexico have been founded with tourist visitors and owner lifestyle considerations in mind rather than to grasp an unmissable viticultural opportunity.

So varied is the terrain, the climate and the varietal heritage of the United States that few generalizations can be made. But one national wine phenomenon is the AVA, or American Viticultural Area, an embryonic American answer to the controlled appellations of Europe which concerns only the specified area's geographical, and sometimes distinctly questionable, boundaries.

The great majority of American wines are named after the grape variety from which they are principally made. A 'fighting varietal' is one which commands less than the premium (verging on excessive) prices demanded for the wines about which most noise is made. 'Jug wines' are the American equivalent of European 'table wines'. Blush wines (rosés by another name) have been particularly popular, often called by a dark-skinned grape variety prefixed by the word White (as in the hugely popular White Zinfandel).

CALIFORNIA

In a nutshell: Some very fine wine indeed, but relatively few bargains.
Grapes: Chardonnay, Sauvignon Blanc (WHITE), Zinfandel, Cabernet Sauvignon and some surprisingly successful Pinot Noir (RED)

Of all the wine regions in the world, California is the most fun to visit. The climate is benign. The people could not be more welcoming (in stark contrast to Bordeaux and Burgundy, the wineries of Northern California seem to operate for, rather than despite, tourists). The food is fantastic; you can eat superbly, and be served wine knowledgeably (by the glass or bottle), in hundreds of sensibly priced restaurants. In most California wine regions the gentle, golden landscape is well protected against the construction industry's baser instincts. Life is easy; man has devised ways of overcoming all natural discomforts. To a California wine producer, lifestyle can be what it is all about. Rather like Tuscany, California's wine districts have been systematically invaded by those who have made a packet elsewhere, determined to squander it on their very own winery. People whose business empires were built on counting every paperclip, suddenly seem to abandon parsimony at the beautifully designed door of their own winery, happily consigning millions to smart architects, fashionable consultant winemakers, chic label designers and French coopers.

The California wine business is easily misunderstood from the outside, however. It seems blindingly obvious in the most famous wine regions of Napa and Sonoma that winery proprietors here live a charmed life, enjoying a standard of living unknown among wine producers since the Golden Age of the Médoc estates in Bordeaux. They live in lovingly restored Victorian mansions or villas specially commissioned from famous architects. They have not only swimming pools and poolhouses, but also their own stables, art galleries and concert halls. They play croquet at the country club and dance to jazz at the regular charity auctions.

This glossy façade is often coupled with the fact that hardly any California wine bargains are seen outside the USA, and interpreted as gross overcharging or misplaced priorities in the California world of wine – especially as virtually every other wine-producing nation seems desperate to export at whatever price. What such criticisms overlook, however, is the size of the American population. California does not need to export in the way that Australia, Chile and many Europeans do. Although California's acreage of the famous international grape varieties increased just as rapidly as Australia's and Chile's in the 1990s (after a period of shortage, exacerbated by the phylloxera crisis in northern California – see panel on page 287). The reaction on the part of some growers, particularly in the less glamorous regions, has been to switch to another crop entirely. There is keen competition on international markets for cheap Chardonnay and Cabernet in particular. By the early years of this century, only the giant Gallo of Modesto and Sonoma – the biggest wine company in the world, marketeer and merchandiser extraordinaire and family-owned to boot – had made any really significant inroads into export markets.

Which is a great shame as, at the top end of the quality scale, California is all but unbeatable. Because Californians have not carved out a solid base of non-American consumers introduced via less expensive bottles, many of the world's wine drinkers are unaware of the sheer exciting glamour of the state's finest wines which, thanks to local demand and not a little competitive pride, are often overpriced. Indeed, even those of us who are already convinced of California's achievements can find it difficult to keep up with the latest developments unless we live in the state itself – so small are some of the quantities involved, and so fast-changing the roster of winery and winemaking names.

This lack of permanence is one of California wine's distinguishing marks. Even if few New World wine regions experienced such a dramatic boom as California did in the 1880s (when wine from what was by then established as America's 'wine state' was admired around the world), almost all of them have at least experienced fairly constant evolution. California's wine history is a series of jerky stops and starts, with phylloxera pulling the plug on the performance of the nineteenth century, and total national Prohibition stopping play altogether between 1918 and 1933.

It was not until the late 1960s that a serious, ambitious, premium California wine industry began to emerge (the construction of the Robert Mondavi winery in Oakville, Napa, still one of

the most recognizable landmarks of California wine, is generally agreed to have marked the start of this new era). Throughout the 1970s and 1980s California wine country, particularly the Napa Valley and to a lesser extent Sonoma, was invaded by those who had made a fortune in a more conventional business but were determined to exchange it for the good life.

With one or two notable exceptions, the California wine industry is the friendliest, least competitive, most open in the world. Which means that when a new idea or scheme appeals to one of these new wine producers, it tends to spread like wildfire throughout the industry. Trends have, furthermore, been accentuated by protectionist wholesaling and retailing systems and a very concentrated, critical national wine press (famous for awarding points out of 100 to individ-

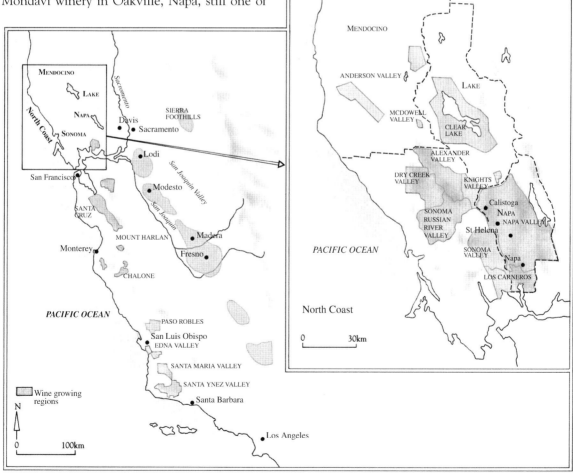

The Napa Valley, with its wealth of local talent, perhaps the most photographed wine region in the world. The milk cartons used to protect the young vines are clearly visible, and can be seen all over the valley as it struggles to reconstitute itself in the face of the damage caused by phylloxera (see page 287).

ual bottles). Points awarded by either the *Wine Spectator* magazine or the critic Robert Parker have been used so widely and unquestioningly both to buy and sell wine that there are now consultancies offering a template of the sort of wines that attract high scores and ways and means of achieving them. The critics tend to award high points, for example, to Cabernets and Zinfandels that are very deep-coloured, very ripe, with high alcohol and perceptible but ripe tannins (the sort of wines that stand out in a big comparative tasting – though not necessarily the ones that are most rewarding to drink with food). Because of this, winemakers all over California have been seeking riper and riper grapes, and growers have been pushed to extend the 'hang time' of grapes on the vine. It is by no means unknown for such grapes to be picked with a potential alcohol content of 17 per cent or more. Some of them have been bottled and labelled as is. Others are routinely diluted to bring them back to a more digestible level of alcohol – a process known euphemistically as 'humidification'. Similarly, a few high-profile winemakers enjoyed enormous acclaim for their equally enormous Chardonnays, laden with sweetness, alcohol, extract and oak. You can imagine the effect of this on the state's Chardonnays, of which there are thousands, remarkably difficult to tell apart.

The result of this is that a wine-producing development, which in any other part of the world might be a just-perceptible eddy, can in California easily become a tidal wave. The enormity of the phylloxera problem is one example of this, but so is the dominance of Chardonnay and Cabernet Sauvignon, and the strong similarities in the style of many of them.

One obvious brake on progress in California, although this began to change in the 1990s, has been the emphasis on winemaker at the expense of vine-grower. As in most New World regions, the functions of grape-growing and winemaking are generally quite distinct, with cash-conscious farmers supplying more urbane characters, who tend to have cleaner hands, with the necessary

raw material. The heat of a California summer has also helped to keep the state's vineyards the domain of the Mexican workforce rather than its new generation of wine producers. At long last, however, the California wine industry acknowledges that the best winemakers are those who know their product from the roots up.

The good news, however, is that California growers have been encouraged to widen the range of good quality grape varieties grown. (There was always a soft underbelly of workhorse varieties such as French Colombard and Chenin Blanc for cheap whites and Carignane (sic) and undervalued Grenache for light reds.) The general wine-drinking public – and possibly winemakers – at long last tired of oceans of bland Chardonnay and Sauvignon Blanc (considerably fatter and less herbaceous in California than in the cooler climes of the Loire or New Zealand) has increasingly been allowed to flourish. Throughout the 1990s Rhône varieties both red and white became increasingly fashionable. This led to widespread planting of Syrah, a re-evaluation of Grenache and the grape Italian immigrants called Mataro (which turned out to be trendy Mourvèdre), Viognier (which reaches incredible alcohol levels here), Roussanne and Marsanne. A subsequent but shorter-lived Cal-Ital fad led to enthusiasm for Pinot Gris (renamed Pinot Grigio), Sangiovese, Barbera and the like. And, as explained below, Pinot Noir emerged as rather a star in some of the state's cooler corners – in some cases having initially been planted to supply the sparkling wine industry which took off with a whizz in the 1980s, attracting enormous investment from Champagne and Catalonia, but had rather fizzled out by the end of the century.

Although midsummer afternoon temperatures in most California vineyards are blistering, in the best sites they are mitigated by a unique climatological phenomenon which delays ripening so that interesting flavours and structure can develop, and this is the main reason why California can produce any serious wine at all.

The **Central Valley**, the baking hot, flat sprawl of vineyards between Sacramento in the north and Bakersfield in the south, is indirectly responsible for this phenomenon, and for an amazing three-quarters of all the wine produced in the state (as well as providing the world's biggest supply of raisins).

If Napa and Sonoma are the Bordeaux and Burgundy of California in terms of attracting all the attention and high prices, then the Central Valley is its Languedoc-Roussillon which really does the work – except that while the Languedoc is now almost fashionable, there seems to be no such danger for the Central Valley.

The far northern end of the Valley around the state capital is, strictly speaking, the Sacramento Valley where Lodi and Clarksburg, not far from the Sacramento Delta, can produce some much more distinctive Zinfandel and Chenin Blanc respectively than further south. But most of the vineyards are well south of here in the San Joaquin Valley, with a third of the annual crush being supplied by the vineyards of Madera and, to a lesser extent, Fresno counties. High-yielding French Colombard (the local name for Colombard) and Chenin Blanc produce vast quantities of medium dry white for jug wine, but Zinfandel is an important red wine grape and Quady has shown that there is potential for quite serious dessert wine and port and

THE PHYLLOXERA SAGA

Never has California wine optimism been so tested as in the late 1980s when it was found that the rootstock onto which practically all Napa and Sonoma vines had been grafted, AXR-1, was not in fact phylloxera-resistant after all (see page 97). This meant that, at a cost of billions of dollars, the great majority of California's most celebrated vineyards had to be replanted, to be converted from luxuriant fields of dollar-generating vines to bare land punctuated only by old milk cartons protecting the tiny young vines inside them. The University of California at Davis, supposedly the fount of all wine industry knowledge, had counselled AXR-1, admitting its phylloxera resistance was low but condoning the popular wisdom that this was more than outweighed by the high yields it generated. Privately there has been much recrimination. Publicly, the California wine industry enthused about this great opportunity to plant the right varieties in the right place according to the right training method with less embarrassingly luxuriant leaf and riper fruit than of old. The fatal vine disease, Pierce's disease, was the next big threat to some of the world's most beautiful vineyards.

madeira styles, next time they swing into fashion.

The unremittingly high temperatures in the Central Valley encourage the cold wall of fog that hangs over the Pacific for much of July and August to be sucked into the narrower valleys between the coast and the Central Valley, depending on how much land mass is in the way. The marine expanse of the San Pablo Bay north of San Francisco in particular encourages morning fog to cool down the Carneros region on its northern rim, and the southern ends of the Napa Valley and Sonoma's wine districts too. In fact, in Northern California it is an almost invariable rule that the further north you travel, the warmer it gets.

In the state's wine showcase, the **Napa Valley**, for instance, the land round the Trefethen winery in the far south is quite significantly cooler than Calistoga at the northern end of the valley. 'The Valley', as it is known by its residents, is fiercely protected by ordinances designed to keep its agricultural base. As recently as the early 1970s this narrow 20-mile stretch of valley floor was planted with crops as unglamorous as walnut and plum trees. Today, Highway 29, which bisects the valley, is lined with spruce, folksy, kitsch and slick wineries, each apparently frantic to attract any visitor to its tasting room and

ABOVE *Mustard in flower in the spring near Rutherford in the Napa Valley. Such cover crops
are increasingly planted to improve the texture of the soil and cut down on excess leafiness in the vines.*
OPPOSITE *Cabernet Sauvignon vines in Knights Valley show the summer face of
northern California – luxuriant, irrigated vines beneath the parched hillsides.*

winery tour. The middle reaches of the valley floor, around Oakville and Rutherford, have established an entirely justified reputation for their intensely coloured and flavoured Cabernet Sauvignon which, now that winemakers have been weaned off the habit of adding acid automatically (the 'tannin is good so lots of tannin is very good' theory fell out of favour earlier), regularly exhibit a layer of richness most Bordeaux wine producers only dream of. Many of the most consistent vineyards lie on higher ground at the foot of the low mountains which flank the valley floor.

All over the state hillside sites, with their excellent drainage and low fertility, are being cleared and planted by those who can afford it and circumnavigate the conservation laws. These may well prove even more exciting sources of wine quality.

Most wineries buy in grapes from such a wide variety of sources, many of them outside the valley (although any wine labelled Napa Valley must contain 85 per cent of grapes grown in it), that there is little correlation between winery location and the style of wine it produces. The Napa Valley has, however, proved a source of great Cabernet Sauvignon. Some of its most famous Cabernets are made in such tiny quantities that they have achieved cult status, being eked out by the single bottle sometimes only to those lucky enough to be on the mailing list for such names as Screaming Eagle, Harlan Estate, Araujo, Grace Family, Cask 29 and Bryant Family. These wines regularly fetch completely crazy prices at the charity auctions which are a feature of the American way of wine.

Such has been the reliance of winemakers on new oak for fermenting white wines and maturing wines of both colours that the Valley houses several highly successful cooperages. There is such a concentration of ambition and high achievement in the Valley that it seems invidious to name names, but labels with an established track record for top quality include Beringer's top bottlings, Caymus Special Selec-

tion, Chateau Montelena, Cuvaison, Dalla Valle, Dunn, Grace Family, Heitz Martha's Vineyard, Hess Collection, Robert Mondavi Reserve, Newton, Niebaum Coppola, Joseph Phelps', Stag's Leap Wine Cellars, Shafer, Silver Oak, Stony Hill, and two joint ventures with Bordeaux luminaries Dominus and the luxuriously priced Opus One.

For years **Sonoma** could not help nursing a grudge about the publicity attracted by Napa Valley, its neighbour just over the Mayacamas mountains to the east, but the stunning quality of so many of its wines, exhibiting the sort of district/varietal patterns that comfort wine classicists, has given Sonoma new pride and status. The easiest generalization was that Napa made the Cabernet and Sonoma the Chardonnay, but there is much more to the varied wine districts of Sonoma than this. Simi has done much to raise the profile of the Alexander Valley around Geyserville in the north, which seems to be able to produce a well-balanced example of virtually every varietal. Chalk Hill to the immediate south makes fine Chardonnay while Dry Creek Valley to the west enjoys a well-deserved reputation for sleek Zinfandel and aromatic Sauvignon Blanc. Dry Creek Vineyards is the Sauvignon Blanc specialist while Lytton Springs, Nalle, Ravenswood and several Ridge bottlings have established Dry Creek's reputation for Zinfandel. Thanks to a gap in the coastal range, the Russian River Valley south of this is even foggier and can therefore produce wonderful examples from such delicate varieties as Gewürztraminer and Pinot Noir (as Williams Selyem and Rochioli have proved). Increasingly, ambitious producers are heading west towards the cool Sonoma Coast for more convincingly Burgundian weather and the results are extremely promising. Producers such as Ferrari-Carano, Chalk Hill, De Loach, Flowers, Kistler, Matanzas Creek, Marcassin, Peter Michael and Sonoma-Cutrer show just what can be done with Sonoma Chardonnay – depth as well as gloss. Top quality sparkling wine is also made here by Iron Horse and J. Sonoma has also been chosen by Gallo as the focus of its range of finer Estate wines.

South of Sonoma and Napa, and straddling both counties, is **Los Carneros**, whose reliable wind and fog quotient keeps it cool enough to be the most important source of sparkling wine grapes in the state (even if most of them are trucked out to be vinified further north). Taittinger have built a replica of a champagne manor house in Domaine Carneros, while the Spanish colossi of sparkling wine have established Codorníu and Freixenet's Gloria Ferrer. Saintsbury and Acacia make extremely thoroughbred still Pinot Noir and Chardonnay and Fred Cline is busy making a little enclave of Rhône varieties at the south western end of Carneros. Several individual vineyards have become important enough here to feature on the labels of the winemakers

Autumnal vines in Field Stone Winery near Healdsburg in Sonoma, northern California's 'other' important wine region, where many fine wines are produced.

to whom they sell the grapes. Hudson, Hyde and Winery Lake are some of the most obvious examples, but there are many many more.

California's 'Rhône Rangers' (those, led by Randall Grahm of Bonny Doon, who have fallen in love with the likes of Syrah, Mourvèdre and Grenache) scour the state looking for low-yielding old plantings of these last two varieties, spurned for many years. Cline's grandfather's plantings in **Contra Costa** county just east of San Francisco have been an important source while newer plantings of Syrah, Viognier, Roussanne and Marsanne, such as those of Jade Mountain and McDowell Vineyards, mature.

To the north of Napa and Sonoma are **Mendocino** and **Lake** counties, rather hotter and much less sophisticated. Fetzer are busy extending their empire of organically farmed vineyards – and indeed California's extremely low rainfall means that much of the state could be farmed without recourse to chemical sprays. Even Gallo, the California wine giant based at the world's largest winery in Modesto in the Central Valley, have adopted 'organic' techniques (at the same time as zooming upmarket, notably on their Sonoma Estate). Roederer Estate makes some fine sparkling wines in the cooler reaches of Anderson Valley, which fall in Mendocino county, while Navarro make some of California's most consistent dry and late harvest Riesling and Gewürztraminer.

In the **Sierra Foothills**, the old gold mining counties El Dorado, Amador and Calaveras still have thick-stemmed vines, mainly Zinfandel, which date from the last century. Since being rediscovered these far eastern vineyards have produced Zinfandel in all forms, from porty to pink (White) as well as a wider range of varietals than is common in Napa and Sonoma.

High on a ridge above Silicon Valley, south of San Francisco in the **Santa Cruz Mountains**, is Ridge Vineyards, established as a weekend hobby as long ago as 1962 and one of the state's standard-bearers for Zinfandel and Cabernet quality for decades.

A little further south is **Monterey** county,

where valley floor vineyards have struggled to eliminate grassy and vegetal flavours from their wines but there are exciting, idiosyncratic outposts in the mountains to the east, such as Chalone and, on a limestone outcrop technically in San Benito county, Calera. Both of these make some creditable Pinot Noir.

Perhaps the most exciting developments for California wine have taken place south of here where plantings have been so enthusiastic that the casual visitor driving from Monterey to Santa Barbara might be tempted to think this is now one long vineyard. While anything planted north of San Francisco is called North Coast, this is the vast region known as **Central Coast**. Right through San Luis Obispo and Santa Barbara counties are areas which, thanks to incursions of the fog layer, can extend the grape-growing season to produce grapes with interesting flavours and, often, a vaguely Burgundian nuance. This is particularly true in the Santa Maria Valley north west of Santa Barbara where producers such as Au Bon Climat show just what can be done with the produce of the extensive Bien Nacido vineyard. In the Arroyo Grande a little bit north, Talley and Laetitia show just how well the Burgundian varieties Pinot and Chardonnay can perform here too, while Alban even further north in Edna Valley is one of California's finest producers of Rhôneish wines, red and white. Santa Ynez Valley is the largest wine district in this stretch, with Sanford boasting a serious track record for fine Pinot Noir.

Most of these producers tend to cherry-pick the many different grape varieties that seem to thrive in various corners of the extensive Central Coast region, wherever they may be based. The Central Coast has also become an important source of grapes for some of the most famous names of the Napa Valley, Robert Mondavi and Beringer in particular. But the wine bug is so virulent throughout California that there are even ambitious wine producers crazy enough to be planting vines within some of Los Angeles' most sought-after arondissements.

WASHINGTON

In a nutshell: Bright, fruity, pure, crisp, well-made varietals.
Grapes: Merlot, Cabernet (RED), Chardonnay (WHITE)

Washington state, in the far Pacific Northwest, is the USA's second most important producer of wine made from European vinifera vines (New York is still primarily a producer of wines with less mainstream names and flavours).

Most of the vineyards are far from the capital Seattle in the underpopulated Columbia Valley in the west of the state, in the rain shadow of the Cascade Mountains and in severe need of irrigation. Plantings therefore tend to be limited to the reach of river water and to slopes which protect vines from the area's harsh winters, cold enough every few years to kill a significant proportion of vines. The Yakima Valley is the chief, very dry wine zone, but the Walla Walla Valley south east on the Oregon border has slightly higher rainfall and looks promising. It is relatively early days for growers to discover the special characteristics of specific vineyards in this desert-like region, but the Horse Heaven Hills, Canoe Ridge (also the name of the Chalone group's Walla Walla winery), Red Mountain and the Wahluke Slope just north of the so-called Tri-Cities (the contiguous Richland, Pasco and Kennewick conurbations) have already been identified as superior, tilting the vineyards south towards the sun and offering some protection against the Arctic effect in winter.

Some vines have also been planted in the completely different, relatively wet, mild climate of western Washington, however, with the result that some very Oregonian Pinot Noir has emerged from just north of Portland as well as some Müller-Thurgau and other aromatic whites grown in the distinctly marginal Puget Sound off Seattle.

Topping up barrels at Columbia Crest winery, a sister – but quite separate – operation to the dominant Chateau Ste Michelle.

A high but decreasing proportion of eastern Washington wine is vinified or at least aged in the Seattle area, miles from the Columbia Valley vineyards. The Washington wine business is dominated by one large company, Stimson Lane, whose labels such as Chateau Ste Michelle, Domaine Ste Michelle, Columbia Crest and Snoqualmie are to be found on half of all Washington wine produced and on an even higher proportion of the wine that leaves the state. This is not generally boutique, lifestyle wine country (unlike Oregon to the immediate south) but there is an increasing number of extremely dedicated individual producers – not least because the dominant Seattle manufacturer, Boeing, has a wine club which has encouraged several members to take the plunge from being amateur consumers to professional producers. Leonetti and Woodward Canyon, both based in Walla Walla, were the first to establish national reputations for their extremely impressive, concentrated Cabernet-dominated reds. Others who produce outstanding wines in this style include Col Solare (a joint venture between Chateau Ste Michelle and Antinori of Italy), DeLille's Chaleur Estate bottling, Dunham Cellars, Quilceda Creek and Trey Marie. Winemakers here tend to use American oak as well as French, and there are many refugees from more precious California wineries to the south – though little close contact with the neighbouring Oregon wine industry.

Merlot and Cabernet Franc have shown themselves even more at home in the hot, dry summers of western Washington than Cabernet Sauvignon, which can be stringy and austere thanks to its late ripening and the Washington winter's early arrival. In fact Washington had demonstrable success with Merlot long before it became fashionable in California (it is a natural habit to compare everything in Pacific North-

west wine with the dominant state to the south). The wines are generally supple, attractively fruity but with good, crisp natural grape acidity, often preserved by cool September nights.

Andrew Will is Washington's master of Merlot, though most producers turn out something creditable. Cabernet Franc comes into its own in one of Washington's many severe winters, being much hardier than Merlot.

The vineyards of Washington state are also showing great promise for Syrah. Columbia Winery's bottling from the Red Willow vineyard showed the way and now the state even has Rhône specialists such as Cayuse, Glen Fiona and McCrea.

But Washington is probably more distinguished from its competitors as a producer of fine white wines, of all degrees of sweetness. Chardonnay is now, perhaps inevitably, the most planted variety and winemakers generally show good craftsmanship with it. Semillon can also be distinctively attractive, with some plumpness but Sauvignon-like aromas. L'Ecole No 41 of Walla Walla has kept the faith with this particular variety, making an impressive, full-bodied, oaked wine with layers of lemon and fig from it. But the aromatic varieties Riesling and, to a lesser extent, Gewürztraminer can also be deliciously pure here. Washington appears to be one of the few wine regions of the world to take Riesling relatively seriously, and even styled itself a Riesling specialist – before Chardonnay-mania overtook the local population. None other than the talented Ernie Loosen of Germany's Mosel valley has been responsible for making some great Riesling under the Chateau Ste Michelle label, so taken was he by the quality of the Riesling fruit here. Eroica is a relatively inexpensive, off-dry bottling available in good quantity which just might re-ignite American enthusiasm for this grape. But Loosen has also made small quantities of an extraordinary Single Berry Select, a botrytized sweet wine that brooks not a murmur of dissent about the potential for Riesling in the Pacific Northwest.

Cabernet Sauvignon vines on Mercer Ranch in eastern Washington, one of the state's oldest and now called Champoux.

OREGON

In a nutshell: *Pinot Noir.*
Grapes: *Pinot Noir and Pinot Gris*

Oregon produces quite a small amount of wine but an awful lot of noise. Which is not at all to say that the state's wine industry is overrun by brash publicists – rather the reverse. The typical Oregon wine operation consists of relatively neat, high-trained vines round a few old wooden shacks manned by a highly educated loner who revels in the contrasts between his wine region and California.

The most obvious difference is the climate, which in most of Oregon is distinctly cool and cloudy, especially in the Willamette (pronounced with the emphasis on the 'a') Valley just south of Portland where most of the wineries are clustered. Much is made locally of the fact that Oregon shares the 45th parallel with Bordeaux – although Burgundy would have been more convenient, given the determination with which Oregon wine producers have pursued the Holy Grail of Pinot Noir. This supposedly fickle grape is the state's most planted by far, representing more than half of all vines. Pinot Gris, Chardonnay then a Riesling follow. Oregon has no such thing as cheap, bulk wine of indeterminate pedigree.

The other wine areas include the drier Umpqua Valley and the much hotter Rogue Valley almost on the California border (though many miles from any California vineyards), as well as a few vineyards which are effectively extensions of Washington state wine regions. (The Seven Hills vineyard, for example, which is in inland Oregon, is actually part of Washington's official Walla Walla AVA.) The southern part of the state, the Umpqua and Rogue Valleys are also warm enough to ripen even Cabernet vines consistently, although producers such as Abacela suggest that Tempranillo may have a future here.

Basically, the further north you go in Oregon's coastal vineyards just one mountain range in from the foggy coast, the more open it is to ocean influence, the cooler the vineyards and the more delicate the wines. But only a little further south, in the heart of the Willamette Valley, summer drought can be a problem, strangely enough. Rain at the wrong time is Oregon's lament.

The perennial challenge for most Oregon wine producers is to persuade their grapes to ripen fully on the vine before the autumn rains arrive, bringing rot and spoiling the colour and flavours of the delicate Pinot Noir grape especially. So variable are the vintages here that the grape harvest may take place at any time from early September to November.

Wineries tend to be small family affairs (although Montinore Vineyards, and the even newer King Estate in the south of the Willamette Valley, are exceptions). Winemaking equipment has therefore tended to be fairly homespun, with steel-lined open fruit boxes commonly used as fermentation vats for example. Perhaps the most carefully designed winery, however, is Domaine Drouhin, the first American outpost of a Burgundian merchant and, quite rightly, a source of great local pride.

There is more evidence of Oregon's appeal to outsiders in Argyle, a sparkling winemaking venture spearheaded by Brian Croser of Petaluma, arguably Australia's most influential winemaker, and Beaux Frères, a small but successful Pinot Noir producer owned by American wine critic Robert Parker and his brother-in-law.

Long-serving members of the Oregon wine community (and it is very much a community rather than an industry) include Adelsheim, Bethel Heights, The Eyrie Vineyards, Knudsen Erath, Ponzi, Sokol Blosser and Tualatin. Cristom is a noteworthy newcomer which makes a particularly fine Viognier as well as

The famous Red Hills of Dundee in Yamhill County, Oregon's most important concentration of vineyards, with Mount Hood 65 miles to the east.

Pinots of distinction. Other superior producers include Archery Summit (owned by a refugee from the Napa Valley), BrickHouse (which is somehow managing to produce concentrated and interesting wines using organic viticulture), Chehalem, Lemelson, Panther Creek, WillaKenzie and Ken Wright Cellars. All these and more are involved in a uniquely friendly annual winefest known as the International Pinot Noir Celebration at McMinnville in Yamhill county, just south of the Red Hills of Dundee, Oregon's most famous wine terroir.

Success tends to be measured in terms of Pinot Noir, and Oregon Pinot tends to be delightfully true, not too heavy and convincingly variable in character according to the autumn weather. For many years Oregon growers depended on Swiss and California clones of Pinot Noir which tended to produce wines that were respectively either too facile or too jammy. The big leap forward was taken in the late 1990s when more recently planted Burgundian clones (known here as Dijon clones) came onstream, resulting in more depth of flavour, some savoury notes and better structure for the long term. But Oregon Pinot Gris has long shown real distinction (which is more than can be said for most Oregon Chardonnay – although the new clones are already demonstrating their superior flavour and structure), as do some Rieslings and Gewürztraminers.

There have been experiments with using Oregon oak for wine maturation and it seems unlikely that the idiosyncratic inhabitants of this characterful wine region will stop their quest for ever greater wine quality.

REST OF NORTH AMERICA

NEW YORK

New York state is one of America's most important wine producing states with four quite different wine regions. Most important in terms of quantity of wine produced (as opposed to grape juice or table grapes) is the **Finger Lakes** region in the west of the state. The slopes of these deep lakes are sufficiently steep to keep cold air moving in winter while vines bud too late in spring for frost to be a serious threat. The Cayuga Lake is warm enough to ripen European vinifera vines, but most of the wine is produced from earlier ripening hybrid or American vines of which red Concord is the most common example. Nevertheless some extremely fine dry Riesling is produced in the Finger Lakes (even if this is not the most fashionable wine on the American market) and in warmer years some appetizing dry red wines emerge too. Superior producers include Dr K Frank, Heron Hill, Chateau Lafayette, Lamoureaux Landing, Macari and Hermann J Wiemer. The vineyards surrounding **Lake Erie** produce mainly grape juice, Concord jelly and table grapes, while those of the **Hudson River** due north of Manhattan are notable for their continuous existence over 300 years. Most of the wine, made from European, American and hybrid vines, is sold locally although Millbrook, under the same ownership as California's famous Williams Selyem and specializing in the relatively obscure white grape Tocai Friulano, has a national presence and even manages to penetrate the odd restaurant in Europhile Manhattan.

The most exciting wine region is only just in New York state, the easternmost tip of **Long Island** where the climate, thanks to the ocean which surrounds it, is mild enough to allow vinifera vines to flourish in all vineyards. Cabernet Franc, Chardonnay and Merlot do particularly well here and have a finesse, natural acidity and delicacy that distinguishes them from most other American wines. The North Fork of the island, potato country, is the predominant wine region and high achievers include Bedell, Gristina, Jamesport, Lenz, Macari, Palmer, Peconic Bay, Pellegrini and Pindar.

OTHER AMERICAN STATES

Although wineries have sprouted all over the United States (even in Hawaii), one of the states which has taken a predictably large-scale stake in the burgeoning American wine industry is **Texas**, where wine styles are still emerging but are sufficiently encouraging for Bordeaux wine merchants of substance, Cordier, to have invested heavily in the high plains of Trans Pecos in the west of the state.

But Pennsylvania, Ohio, Virginia and Missouri all have more wineries than Texas. **Missouri** was the centre of the American wine industry in the nineteenth century, growing vast quantities of hybrids, particularly the distinctly superior Norton red grape, as well as vast quantities of Concord grapes for jelly. Its only rival historically was **Ohio**, first famous for sparkling Catawba developed by a Frenchman. **Michigan** and **Wisconsin** can produce some fine Icewine and Riesling, although as in other states wineries often ship in grapes from elsewhere.

In terms of wine quality **Virginia** has one of the most interesting modern wine industries, producing a host of well-made, rather French-tasting Cabernets and Chardonnays. The wine business of **Pennsylvania** is perhaps more motivated by tourism opportunities and summer humidity can be a problem for thin-skinned grapes such as Pinot Noir, though an increasing proportion of well-made Cabernets and Chardonnays are emerging here too.

CANADA

Canadians are extremely proud of their wine industry (or rather their wine industries – 2,500 miles divide those of **Ontario** in the east and **British Columbia** in the west), and quite rightly.

Canada's most famous wine, and the style most frequently exported, is Icewine, surely the most delicious product of her freezing cold winters. These sweet but refreshingly crisp light wines are made by painstakingly pressing grapes frozen on the vine. Unlike the Germans, Canadians have been sure of making these wines every year, so harsh is the Canadian winter. Ontario produces the lion's share of this treasured wine style, made usually from either Riesling or the hybrid Vidal (which has no 'foxy' characteristics and can taste very pure and refreshing for its first two or three years in bottle). Icewine is so important to Canadian wine that Chardonnay, Cabernet Franc and even sparkling Icewines are made.

Many of the vineyards in Ontario, which grows most of Canada's vines, are still planted with Concord and American and French hybrids to maximize the chances of ripening grapes before winter sets in, but the proportion of European varieties has been increasing considerably. This is not just because the planet seems to be warming up, but because growers are ever more quality-conscious on the Niagara Peninsula just west of the Niagara Falls between the Lakes Ontario and Erie where viticulture is most concentrated. Here, as in New York's Finger Lakes region, vine growers benefit from the so-called 'lake effect' where these large bodies of water delay the onset of spring, protecting young buds from frost damage, and prolong the warmth of summer (which can be quite hot here), allowing grapes to reach full ripeness before temperatures plunge. Niagara's many ambitious wine producers are particularly keen to show the world they can ripen even Cabernets here – though Cabernet Franc is generally a safer bet than Cabernet Sauvignon, and some added Merlot flesh usually helps fill in the mid palate, as Henry of Pelham demonstrate eloquently. Some producers, particularly the trailblazer Inniskillin, are betting more heavily on Pinot Noir. Chardonnays are of course made in profusion, with one producer, Deborah Paskus, even managing an almost Montrachet-like weight.

But as in the Finger Lakes region not too far south over the border, the variety that seems most at home in these conditions is Riesling, which can make some very fine dry wines here as well as the famous Icewine which has a vivacity and clarity, if not longevity, rare in German Eiswein.

Although vinifera vines enjoy hugely more cachet with consumers, some fine wines are made from hybrids in Ontario – particularly Malivoire's Old Vines Foch.

Conditions in British Columbia are quite different, even if the long winter is also the main enemy, in this case also fought with a lake, the deep finger of Lake Okanagan three hours' drive inland from Vancouver. The Okanagan Valley is very dry – irrigation is as essential here as in Washington state's wine country to the south – but the cool nights that follow each hot summer day are good at fixing acidity and bright flavours. The result is some very clearly defined white wines and some very determined red wine-making with perhaps the most interesting and distinctive wines so far being made from various Pinots and Sauvignon Blanc. New producers are emerging by the minute here, in a wine region that already has more than half as much vineyard as the state of Oregon, but some of my favourites include Blue Mountain, Burrowing Owl and Paradise Ranch.

A little wine is also produced in **Quebec** and **Nova Scotia**.

CHILE

In a nutshell: Predictable, reliable, inexpensive reds.
Grapes: Cabernet Sauvignon, Carmenère, Merlot (RED)

The Old World envies Chile for its low costs, lack of vine pests and diseases and its dependably dry, warm summers. Much of the New World, and Australia in particular, envies its plentiful and regular supply of water from the melted snows of the Andes. Few winemakers, however, would envy the wine cultural vacuum in which their Chilean counterparts worked.

Chile's golden age was the end of the nineteenth century, when the rest of the wine world had been crippled by downy mildew and phylloxera (see page 96) but this isolated wine producer could supply almost limitless quantities of healthy, deep-coloured wine, made from familiar vinifera vines that had been imported into Chile earlier in the nineteenth century. The world's most prosperous wine industry was then owned by just 10 Chilean families, many of them still in control today. For the next 100 years there were very few changes in the vineyards and cellars of Chile but the return of democracy fuelled extraordinary economic growth throughout Chile in the early 1990s, including a real determination to drag the Chilean wine industry into the modern world.

The vast old *rauli* (evergreen beech) vats have been replaced by oak barriques imported from the US and France. Refrigeration has been installed both for fermentation and maturation.

LEFT *The produce of these vineyards is used for Chile's national drink, pisco, a deliciously aromatic grape spirit.*

ABOVE *Sorting grapes for quality at Concha y Toro. This is a recent innovation in Chile.*

The lazy, hazardous technique of irrigation by simply flooding a vineyard and hoping the water will drain down specially dug channels and water each vine equally is gradually being replaced by the use of drip irrigation systems which administer set amounts of water to individual plants. New wine regions are being sought out which may be more difficult to work than the traditional areas in the hot Central Valley but should yield more interesting wine.

Thousands of acres of vines in the hotter

When Santa Rita, one of Chile's largest producers, bought 7000 new barrels to replace their rauli vats in 1988, it was seen as a milestone not just for the company but for the Chilean wine industry in general.

regions to the north of Santiago are dedicated to Chile's thriving fruit industry and, in the case of some specific aromatic varieties, to the local spirit pisco. Pisco sours are the great revelation for many visitors to Chile.

Until recently few Chileans were interested in wine. This may have been frustrating for Chile's small élite of dedicated native viticulturists and winemakers, but it has done nothing to stop an influx of foreigners attracted by Chile's growing reputation for making good to very good wine. A number of prominent Frenchmen have invested in the Chilean wine business, not least the Rothschilds of Château Lafite (Los Vascos), the owner of Cos d'Estournel of St-Estèphe and the winemaker at Château Margaux (Paul Bruno) – as well as Miguel Torres of Catalonia who was, famously, the first to import small oak barrels into Chile.

Chile's brake on progress, apart from a historic lack of investment, has been the gap between grape-growers and wine producers. Until very recently almost all grapes were grown on large ranches by gentlemen farmers who knew very little about wine and cared even less. By not having to use phylloxera-resistant rootstocks, Chileans were denied this tool for controlling excessively vigorous vines and some soil pests. By the mid-1990s, however, most exporting wineries (of which there were still only about 35) were planting heavily in order to be more self-sufficient in terms of fruit supply. Grape-growers, who benefited considerably during the Chilean wine boom of the very early 1990s, are expected to switch to other fruit crops, although some are building their own wineries.

This new extended control of production should curtail excessive yields, achieved by over-enthusiastic irrigation, should introduce trellis systems designed to maximize quality, and should result in a wider spread of vine varieties matched more carefully to the sites on which they are grown. However, detailed mapping of viticultural potential is still in short supply in Chile.

Apart from the very basic local variety Pais, grown mainly in the unirrigated south for cheap wine sold predominantly in cartons to Chileans, Chile's most important red wine variety by far is Cabernet Sauvignon, which produces particularly exuberant, lush wines here, even if most of them in the pre-barrique age lacked the structure to develop in bottle. Merlot always looked promising, and now that Chileans have discovered that a vast proportion of it is actually an old Bordeaux variety Carmenère, they are busy trying to establish a separate identity for the two varieties – Carmenère tending to be a bit more herbaceous. Young plantings of Pinot Noir have resulted in some surprisingly juicy, pure flavours from the likes of Cono Sur and Valdivieso, while Canepa has been trying its hand with Zinfandel. Meanwhile some wine producers dream of fine Syrah and Sangiovese.

Most of Chile's 'Sauvignon' is in fact Sauvignon Vert, which can produce crisp, aromatic wines, but newer plantings are exclusively Sauvignon Blanc and can be very lively if the site is cool enough. Semillon is extremely widespread (often mixed in the vineyard with Sauvignon) and therefore thoroughly scorned – although there have been some experiments with sweet wines and barrel-aged examples. Chardonnay was planted at a lick and for the moment the style is simply a reflection of winemaker and New World fashion (barrel ferments, malolactic fermentation and so on), although prices are low enough to make this lack of distinction perfectly acceptable. Gewürztraminer can work in cooler, newer areas and the range of white wine varieties will doubtless widen.

The vineyards dedicated to wine production stretch down the Central Valley south from the **Aconcagua** Valley (where Errazuriz has its base) and its fashionable new subregion **Casablanca**, sufficiently cooled by the Pacific that it can be seriously prone to spring frosts. Casablanca's piercing (real) Sauvignon Blanc is particularly distinctive – although the Chardonnay mania which prevailed when most of the new plantings went in, at the end of the 1980s, ensured domination of this particular variety. The western end is cooler than the inland section.

The Chilean wine industry has been keen to promote its own embryonic controlled appellation system, and its chosen geographical areas are the valleys which run from east to west, following rivers from the Andes to the sea. It is particularly difficult to generalize about the three main wine valleys Maipo, Rapel and Maule, however, partly because there is such variation between the valley floor and the increasing number of vineyards planted on higher ground.

Maipo is the most famous Chilean wine region, at least partly because it is so close to Santiago, Chile's capital and centre of wealth. Some famous vineyards such as those of Cousiño Macul are right up against the Andes just south of the city itself. Here wines tend to be fragrant and more elegant than those from central Maipo around Pirque and Buin, where the industry giants Concha y Toro and Santa Rita have their respective main wineries (though each follows the Chilean pattern of buying grapes from all over the Central Valley). Both companies have been developing separate subsidiaries, but such is the extent of their vineyard holdings that Concha y Toro can, for example, claim to be the world's most important grower of Cabernet Sauvignon. There has been some experimentation with growing vines on the west side of the Coastal Range, but it is much more expensive to ensure water supplies here (boreholes have to be drilled instead of just opening sluice gates).

For all the focus of the appellation system, the differences between the east and west of the Central Valley are every bit as telling as those between the north and south. On the eastern edge of the valley, the nights are much cooler than on the valley floor thanks to cold air from the Andes, so that mornings are coolest and acid and colour in the grapes grown here are particularly marked, but frost can be a very real problem. The western edge, on the other hand, is cooled in the afternoon by regular sea breezes whose extent varies with the precise shape of the Coastal Range nearby. A vineyard's distance from the rivers can also affect how usefully cool and damp the soil is.

The wider, wetter **Rapel** Valley south of Maipo has an even less distinct viticultural identity, although Colchagua, which can also boast a great concentration of premium red grapes, is more marked by the ocean's influence. Soils here tend to be fertile alluvial deposits and vines can sprout leaves rather than ripe fruit to

a worrying degree. Fog-cooled Chimbarongo in the Colchagua Valley and Cachapoal to its immediate north are addresses occasionally found on wine labels.

The new appellation system separates **Curicó** (including Lontué) from **Maule**, although few wine professionals could describe the difference in the wines. Curicó has vast tracts of land planted with high-yielding vines and yet there are individual mesoclimates (see page 62) obviously capable of producing distinctly superior wine. San Pedro is one of the biggest wineries to be based near Curicó and has hired French flying winemaker Jacques Lurton to squeeze maximum fruit character out of its vines. The large California outfit Kendall Jackson has been experimenting in Talca in the south of Maule (which, despite the latitude, is generally hotter than Rapel). Parts of Maule with clay soils can be good for fruity Merlot, even at high yields.

Itata and **Bío-bío** comprise the southern region south of Maule and are generally regarded as fit only to produce Pais for boxes, but Concha y Toro is experimenting on a family ranch in Mulchén and there has been French interest in this cooler southern region too. Frost can wipe out crops here, as can fungal vine diseases which are a threat in such a relatively humid climate (unlike further north).

Most wineries are careful to bottle their best produce as Reserve wines. Of the big four companies Concha y Toro, Santa Rita, San Pedro and Santa Carolina, most own several wineries and many different vineyards, although it is also the norm to buy in grapes from a wide range of growers. Some truly magnificent wines are now emerging from Chile in the mould of Concha y Toro's (and Mouton-Rothschild's) Almaviva, Casa Lapostolle's Clos Apalta, Errazuriz's Don Maximiano, Ignacio Recabarren's Domus Aurea and Montes' Folly. And there are signs that the number of seriously interesting mid-priced wines being exported from Chile is increasing dramatically too.

The potential for organic wine production in Chile is vast but is only slowly being realized.

ARGENTINA

Chile dominates South American wine exports but Argentina makes almost five times as much wine, and (like the USA) regularly produces more wine than any country other than France, Italy and Spain.

Only in the 1990s, however, was business confidence in Argentina sufficient to justify the investment needed to drag its wineries into the twentieth century, and exports on a serious scale are a fraction of what they could be. The distinguishing feature of Argentine wine was for a long time the extraordinarily high yields from overhead trellises called *parral* with reliably sun-ripened grapes literally pumped full of melted Andean snow via irrigation channels constructed in the nineteenth century. Since the late 1980s vines have begun to be planted in cooler areas deliberately to prolong the ripening process, and trained carefully on wires for maximum quality of the resulting fruit. No wine producing country in the world made more progress in the closing years of the twentieth century (viticulturally and

oenologically, if not necessarily financially).

The main Argentine wine region, **Mendoza**, is tucked up against the Andes and a long way from the capital Buenos Aires but less than an hour's spectacular flight over the Andes from Santiago, the capital of Chile and its wine industry. Mendoza is a vast and extremely varied region, with the key to seriously high quality this close to the equator being altitude. In fact several of the best producers such as Catena and Terrazas de los Andes (a subsidiary of Moët & Chandon) specify precise vineyard altitudes on their labels. The higher the vineyard, the cooler the nights, which has a beneficial effect on acidity and colour, and the greater the effect of radiation on achieving precise wine flavours. Because of this there has been a land grab on suitable slopes of the Andean foothills, with parts of Tupungato and La Consulta in the Valle de Uco in particular a patchwork of embryonic vineyards planted by investors from all over the world at altitudes of up to 1600 m (4800 ft). Everyone seems to be trying to plant

higher than his neighbour, with the result that some very fine Chardonnay and Pinot Noir (Salentein's in particular) have already been produced, but presumably Nature will eventually impose some limit at which vines are reliably free of frost damage.

Malbec was for years Argentina's most planted red wine grape and was therefore regarded by Argentines as distinctly infra dig (especially in relation to Cabernet Sauvignon), but to many outsiders it seems the perfect grape for Argentina's relatively warm climate, producing rich, intensely fruity yet ageworthy wines which can be far more impressive than any Malbec-based Cahors from south west France. After a period during which Malbec was ruthlessly pulled out to make way for more fashionable varieties, Argentine wine exporters now realize that Malbec represents their unique point of difference (much envied by their competitors across the Andes) and due effort is put into making velvety, welcoming wines from the particular strain of Malbec that has evolved here.

Since so much Malbec was ripped out, the red grape known as Bonarda in Argentina – which may not be identical to any of Italy's

Bonardas – has become the most planted (and therefore least regarded by Argentines). This image too is undergoing refurbishment, however, with an increasing proportion of Bonarda vines being coaxed to produce lower yields of more flavourful, inexpensive, juicy wine for early drinking.

Cabernet Sauvignon clearly has no problem ripening here, but Argentina's strength is the wide range of grape varieties already planted in her extensive vineyards, thanks to successive waves of immigration from Italy, Spain and France. Tempranillo, Syrah, Pinot Gris/Grigio and Tocai Friulano are all capable of making fine wine in the right hands in Argentina. Sangiovese, Zinfandel, Barbera and Nebbiolo wait in the wings.

Mendoza can make fine wine at high altitudes and good value wine in the better managed vineyards lower down. Luján de Cuyo, once regarded as relatively high altitude, is one of the most favoured districts of Mendoza for full-bodied reds and even has its own appellation. Throughout much of Mendoza, summer hail is the major threat and sophisticated netting against this ruinous but regular phenomenon is as common a feature of vineyards here as irrigation channels and a view of the Andes in the distance.

Dr Nicolas Catena's stable of brands and names is an obvious star in Mendoza (his joint venture with Lafite, a red wine called Caro, has set a new standard for Argentina), but other reliable producers include La Anita, Luigi Bosca, Cassone, Dolium, Fabre Montmayou, Los Hormigas, Nieto y Senetiner, Salentein, Terrazas de los Andes, Viniterra and the giant Peñaflor's Iscay blend of their own winemaking guru's Malbec with Michel Rolland of Pomerol's Merlot.

The enterprise for long known as Chandon,

Argentina's largest producer Peñaflor is particularly proud of these high-altitude vineyards at Tupungato, overlooked by the snowy Andes.

which has now spawned the more export-orientated Terrazas bodega, makes enormous quantities of cuve close sparkling wine (see pages 85–6) from Chenin Blanc and other early-picked white grapes for the Argentine market (which has been so effectively trained to worship all things French that domestic wine brand names include Pont l'Évêque and Carcassonne).

The second most important wine region in terms of quantity is **San Juan** immediately north of Mendoza, but it is even hotter and is generally better suited to Argentina's rather coarse vine specialities Criolla and Cereza. These pink-skinned grapes are used for grape concentrate and the deep-coloured, often slightly sweet white that is sold at rock bottom prices, often in cardboard cartons, within Argentina. Some producers are actively developing San Juan's cooler sites, however, and may well establish a fine wine reputation for the region too.

Well south of Mendoza in the romantically named Patagonia on the **Rio Negro** is another extremely promising area for viticulture. The climate is much cooler here, the wines tend to be more elegant, and firms such as Humberto Canale with its French-trained winemaker (far from uncommon in Argentina) show just what can be achieved.

The only other area of obvious interest to export markets is the high-altitude vineyards around Cafayate in the province of **Salta** in the far north of the country. The local vine speciality here is a form of Torrontes which can yield crisp, flavourful, very aromatic dry whites – absolutely the last thing most wine drinkers would expect from Argentina. Michel Rolland of Pomerol has been a consultant to Etchart here for some years and, with members of the original Etchart family, is establishing Yacochuya as a boutique producer of serious red wine (as well as investing, like everyone else, in the high altitude vineyards of Mendoza).

The highest vineyards are in Salta, well to the north of here, at altitudes of well over 2000 m (6000 ft), making them the highest in the world.

In the fashionable Uco Valley, Salentein,
one of the most ambitious and newest bodegas
in Mendoza, is also one of the highest, yet
is dwarfed by the Andes.

REST OF LATIN AMERICA

Latin America was the first continent to be systematically colonized by the European vine, taken there by the Spanish conquistadores in the sixteenth century. (Winemaking was introduced first to Mexico, but Peru, then Chile and Argentina followed soon afterwards.) It is curious therefore that a sophisticated wine culture has been so slow to germinate in Latin America. Mexicans, despite playing such a crucial role in one of the world's most important wine industries in California, are still in general much more interested in beer and brandy than wine.

The following are Latin America's wine-producing countries other than Chile and Argentina (see pages 300–6), in decreasing order of how much wine they produce.

BRAZIL

Brazil is by quite a margin South America's third producer of wine after Argentina and Chile, though it lags behind Uruguay in terms of the sophistication and export potential of its produce. Because of its hot, steamy climate, hybrids with their greater resistance to fungal diseases are widely planted – especially in the southern Rio Grande do Sul region. But vinifera is planted on the sandy soils in the Campanha region on the country's southern border with Uruguay which hold out some promise of wines more serious than the sweet fizzes sold on the mass market. Much of the country is tropical, so vines regularly produce more than one crop per year and need particularly careful nurturing to produce fruit of any quality. International varietals are starting to emerge from the better wine producers.

URUGUAY

Uruguay is South America's fourth most important wine producer and, thanks to a substantial immigration from the Basque country in south west France in the nineteenth century, is one of the world's centres of Tannat vine-growing. Blends of this with other French varieties (and a Semillon-Chardonnay white blend) were first exported to British supermarkets in the mid 1990s. The wines are full-bodied and promising, and there is every sign that Tannat produces more voluptuous and approachable wines here in its South American home than it does in its homeland in south west France – just like Argentina's Malbec in fact. Pisano is one of the best producers of Tannat, particularly its RPF bottling, but Los Cerros de San Juan is doing particularly interesting things with Tempranillo and Chardonnay as well as its own version of Tannat grown on especially stony ground.

Uruguay's rolling green hills produce nothing like the quantity of Argentina's wine regions but quality will surely attract international interest soon.

MEXICO

Unlike Canada, Mexico's problem is a surfeit of heat, which can hustle grapes to ripeness before they have developed much flavour. For this reason, top quality vineyards tend to be in the far north of the country, in **Baja California**, or at high altitudes further south. Mexico was making about as much wine as Uruguay at the turn of the century and an increasing proportion of it is of serious interest to wine drinkers abroad. Vino de Piedra makes an extremely intense Tempranillo while Château Camou's Cabernet Sauvignon, Monte Xanic's Merlot and L A Cetto's Nebbiolo and Petite Sirah are exceptional for Mexico. There is real excitement and ambition in the burgeoning boutique wineries of the Guadalupe Valley and Ensenada.

Peru and **Bolivia** also make small quantities of wine, but hardly any is exported – so far.

AUSTRALIA

In a nutshell: *Export-driven industry making waves and fruit-driven wines, all over the world.*
Grapes: *Shiraz, Cabernet Sauvignon* (RED), *Chardonnay, Semillon, Riesling* (WHITE)

For some years now Australians have seen themselves as at the cutting edge of the New World of wine, and now more and more non-Australians do too as the country has dramatically increased the extent to which it exports both its wines and winemakers (see page 68).

Their wine industry is not fundamentally distinguished by history (Australia was one of the vine's later conquests), and certainly not by geography (Australian wine producers are congenital truckers of grapes and blenders of wines), but by its philosophy. 'Can do' perhaps best sums up the Australian attitude to wine production.

The wine regions of Australia constitute different departments in one huge wine factory, any one of which may be called upon to deliver a spare part as and when required. Part of the explanation for this lies in the division between wine-making and grape-growing as commercial activities – a division even more marked than in California. The typical Australian wine producer buys in most of his grapes and, thanks to the refrigerated transport systems needed in a country as big and as hot as this, may well buy them from several hundred, or even thousand, miles away.

This pragmatism continues through the business of grape processing, as an Australian would call what the French might call vinification. If the winery hasn't enough fermentation tanks, the fruit or juice will simply be stored at low temperatures until there is enough space for the winemaker's carefully controlled fermentation. If the typical French winemaker sees nature as the driving force and the typical American sees it as a demon to be tamed, their Australian counterparts see themselves as simple processors of farm output.

This is underlined by the status of the formal wine training the vast majority of them undergo, at centres variously called Roseworthy, Wagga Wagga and Adelaide, which have enjoyed the status of agricultural colleges. The Australian Wine Research Institute of Adelaide

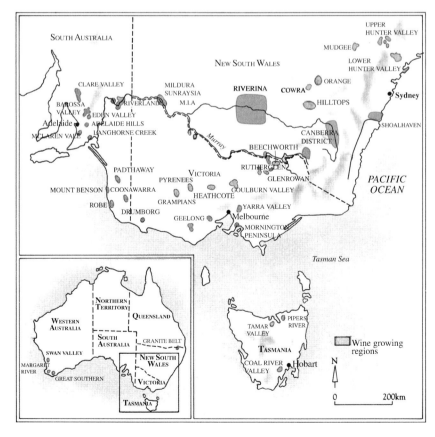

is one of the most admired centres of wine academe in the world and the graduates who use the results of its intensely industry-linked work are taught a healthy respect for science, technology and for what man can achieve when given a free hand.

Australians revel in their lack of the sort of restrictions which dictate what and how a traditional European vine-grower must grow. They can establish a vineyard anywhere they like (although the availability of water is usually an important determining factor) and indeed the current distribution of vineyards old and new suggests there are undiscovered pockets of suitable vineyard land all over the southern quarter of this vast country.

A few higher tracts of Queensland such as the Granite Belt notwithstanding, viticulture is a southern Australian phenomenon. Most of Australia's vines grow where summers are cool enough to allow some flavour to build up in the grapes before they are so embarrassingly high in sugar that they must be picked lest acids plummet to uncorrectable levels. (Most Australian wines will have some acidification, acid deliberately added – see page 72.)

Nearly half of all vines grow in the state of South Australia, a third in the state of Victoria and most of the rest in New South Wales (although Western Australia has an enviable reputation for the quality of its wines). Australian wine is conventionally divided by these state boundaries (across which strict quarantines may apply such as those designed to keep the phylloxera louse crossing from Victoria into South Australia) but there is a more fundamental divide than this.

A high proportion of Australia's vines are farmed, intensively, on the green oases of the heavily irrigated vineyards of the parched, dusty interior. These districts, known variously as Riverina, the Riverlands, the Murray River, the M.I.A. (Murrumbidgee Irrigation Area), Sunraysia, Mildura, Griffith and Renmark, straddle the boundaries between the three most important wine-producing states. Here, vast tracts of internationally familiar and highly exportable varieties have been planted on land reclaimed from the desert so that Australia has recourse to some of the world's most efficiently farmed high-yielding vines (even if salt levels in the soil are starting to present a problem). These less distinguished grapes can make useful bulk filler for the wine boxes, or 'casks' as they are known, that have made up the bottom end of the Australian wine market since the 1970s, but considerable acreages of the irrigated areas are also devoted to filling bottles labelled with the brands on which the Australian wine industry is based. Australians are adept at transforming this fairly humdrum raw material into a palatable and completely dependable drink, often with the help of oak chips.

But the reputation of Australian wine depends on much more exciting fruit produced in one of the country's more distinguished wine regions (even if that fruit is often blended between regions so that its provenance can often be difficult to determine from the wine label). Britons, who fell so deeply in love with Australian wine in the early 1990s that exports tripled between 1989 and 1994, became used to seeing on labels the catch-all appellation 'South Eastern Australia' (which conveniently encompasses all wine regions except the relatively limited ones of Western Australia, including the irrigated areas).

These regions are examined in detail below, but the importance of trucking should not be underestimated. The typical large winery is probably based in South Australia, often in the Barossa, but will buy in grapes from as far afield as Coonawarra or the irrigated interior and possibly even the Hunter Valley in New South Wales. (Conversely, it was long a source of persistent irritation to South Australians that they provided so much fruit to bolster the reputations of wineries based in New South Wales.) The Australian wine industry is dominated by four companies, of which the giant is Southcorp Wines, owning not just Penfolds, but Rosemount, Lindemans, Seppelts, Seaview, Wynns, Tulloch, Tollana and a host of others. Their greatest rival perhaps is the French-owned Orlando-Wyndham, whose brand Jacob's Creek has been Australia's most marked export success. The other monoliths are BRL Hardy and Beringer Blass, both of which are busy diversifying overseas and have already formed alliances with American companies.

Australians are not short of energy or sunshine but they are short of water and, in most wine regions, labour. California can at least rely on a substantial Mexican workforce, but the Australian wine industry is thoroughly mechanized, and hand-picking is now relatively rare. Many vineyards are deliberately picked by machine at night in the relentless battle against heat at harvest time. The campaign tends to continue with deliberate chilling of grapes and must. (Water consumption can be as high in the cellar as in the vineyard.) Oxygen is seen as the other great enemy and protective winemaking has been the norm.

Australians have been avid users of Ameri-can oak, for ageing whites as well as reds, and the wines' flavours can be so full and exuberant that they stand up well. South Australia has some fine coopers of American and French oak. One technique developed in Australian winer-ies is to move red wines off the grape skins into small barrels before fermentation is complete. It is much more difficult in most of France, where a post-fermentation maceration is often needed to extract enough colour from the skins, but many Australian reds from warmer areas are softened and bolstered by this technique. The aim of most Australian winemakers is to exhibit the flavour of the fruit from which the wine was made rather than the characteristics of the place (usually places) where it was grown. Hence the phrase 'fruit-driven' for such wines.

One final particularly Australian phenome-non is the wine show, effectively an agricultural exhibition held annually in the state capitals, in which panels of carefully chosen, extremely professional judges award medals and trophies to wines entered from all over the country. It is all taken extremely seriously.

Ultra-ripe grapes being harvested (left) in the Hunter Valley in New South Wales (right), which has historically benefited from its proximity to Sydney.

SOUTH AUSTRALIA

South Australia produces well over half of the raw material for Australia's wine industry, and most of the large wine companies, many of the small, and all of the official wine trade organizations have their headquarters in the Wine State, whose capital is Adelaide, a city founded on wine. Wine areas are spread over a wide climatic range and are listed here more or less in order from hottest to coolest.

RIVERLAND

This is Australia's most quantitatively important wine region by far, the efficiently irrigated, high-yielding vineyards way up the Murray River towards Victoria's own irrigated wineland. Around townships such as Waikerie, Loxton, Berri and Renmark grape-growing to keep pace with the growth of Australian wine exports is in full swing, thanks to government encouragement. Vineyards here can easily supply drinkable Cabernet, Shiraz and Chardonnay at rock bottom prices, ideally suited to oak chips if not to prolonged contemplation and discussion of its nuances. The planting frenzy around the turn of the century, fuelled by tax breaks offered for viticultural investment, was so heavily influenced by the much-vaunted red wine boom that in some vintages there was, much to everyone's surprise, a shortage of Chardonnay in Australia. Planting and drinking have forever been cyclical, though by no means always in phase.

ADELAIDE PLAINS

Two or three wineries persist on the hot flats north of the city, of which Primo Estate can produce some hand-crafted specialities, some of them from local fruit. Primo's Joseph, a rich, dark red made from dried Cabernet and Merlot grapes, certainly capitalizes on the region's natural characteristics.

BAROSSA

After a long period in the wilderness, the Barossa Valley is now recognized as Australia's quintessential wine region. There are many obvious physical similarities with California's Napa Valley – heavily laden vines growing on a fertile valley floor bounded by hills that are brown throughout the summer, an hour's drive north of a major city, desperately trying to stave off urban development and retain the valley's viticultural character. There is even an old railway running parallel to the valley's major north–south highway in both Napa and the Barossa. But whereas the Napa Valley's wine industry, with its art galleries and music festivals, is substantially founded on well-heeled emigrés from the professions or big business, the Barossa Valley is founded on an extraordinary social group, about 500 families of Prussian descent who emigrated here in the 1840s to escape discrimination and establish a modest, hard-working, Lutheran farming community. They continue these traditions to this day. Tanunda has its Wursthaus and its Kegelbahn. Maranenga has its own brass band, headquartered a conveniently short march from the Gnadenfrei church. The settlers tried all manner of crops but vines were a particular success here and, thanks to the dogged work ethic of the 'Barossa Deutsch', a high proportion of the valley is still devoted to vines, some of them exceptionally old. Many of these grape-growers (most of whom sell grapes rather than vinify) still speak German among themselves. The dusty, unpaved roads that criss-cross the valley are hung with grape-growers' signs, with hardly a non-German name among them.

In the 1970s and early 1980s the Barossa Valley was regarded as distinctly inferior to the new 'cool climate' regions which the Australian wine industry was developing. Thus, the giant wineries of Tanunda, Nuriootpa and Rowland Flat (many by now owned by multinational corporations) were proud to sell bottles with the words Coonawarra or Padthaway on the label, but tended to keep quiet about the fruit they bought on their own doorstep in the Barossa.

A new wave of smaller, local wineries, typically started up in the 1980s by escapees from the big companies (Peter Lehmann, St Hallett's, Rockford, Charles Melton, Grant Burge and others), signalled a resurgence of pride in the Barossa Valley, particularly in the big, bold style of Shiraz, often laden with spice and chocolate flavours, that is the valley's signature.

Sheep and Shiraz vines near Krondorf in the Barossa Valley – what could be more Australian? The contrast between the green vines and the surrounding landscape shows how vital irrigation is.

Dry-farmed (non-irrigated) old vineyards on the cooler west side of the valley are the most treasured and provide tiny quantities of deeply-concentrated fruit for Australia's most famous wine, Penfolds Grange, as well as for an increasing range of top quality concentrated bottlings such as Peter Lehmann's Stonewell, Rockford Basket Press and St Hallett's Old Block, the old guard which has since been followed by a wave of newer labels, some of them better known to American wine enthusiasts than Australian retailers. Three Rivers, Torbrek and Greenock Creek are all examples of this genre which combines tiny quantities with sky-high alcohol and price.

There is now increasing interest, as elsewhere, in the other Rhône varieties Grenache and Mourvèdre (which for years, as Mataro, was scorned). Barossa has its own particular pink-skinned strain of Semillon which can yield exceptionally big, fat, golden wine. Barossa Chardonnay is another big, bold statement and can respond well, like Barossa reds, to American oak. Some of Australia's finest coopers are long-established family companies based in the Barossa.

The Barossa Valley is so hot and dry that most wines need to be routinely acidified, and some producers also add tannin – substituting for the long, tannin-gathering maceration traditional in cooler places like Bordeaux a smoothing process of the wine, whereby the young wine is run off the skins and into barrels before it has finished fermentation.

Not surprisingly, the Barossa is particularly well suited to making fortified wines. Cellars there were once well-stocked with wines made in the image of sherry and, perhaps more successful, port.

SOUTHERN VALES

The growing suburbs of Adelaide are stretching remorselessly further south into what was once wine country so that only the most financially secure vineyards, or those too far from the city centre to be of current interest to the developers, survive. Yet (or perhaps therefore) the winemakers of **McLaren Vale**, south of the city, are a determined, friendly lot who realize that they have much to offer the Australian wine industry. The wines made here have a particularly winning combination of open fruit and glossy texture.

The local mesoclimates vary enormously according to altitude and exposure to cooling sea breezes. Some of the most promising wineries and vineyards occupy ridges with quite amazing views of the blue Gulf St Vincent, which is the starting point for most of Australia's wine exports. Notable achievers among wineries in this tight-knit community include d'Arenberg, Chapel Hill, Coriole, Fox Creek, Geoff Merrill, Noon, Tatachilla, Wirra Wirra and the much bigger Thomas Hardy, whose traditional Tintara winery can turn out some masterpieces. Chardonnays, Cabernets and Shiraz can all dazzle.

Langhorne Creek is a separate and slightly cooler wine region on Lake Alexandrina to the south east, supplying considerable and useful blending material to the bigger companies. But an increasing number of fine individual producers have been emerging from this region, which floods every year, such as Bleasdale (an old timer) and Brothers in Arms.

CLARE VALLEY

This is effectively a northern but considerably cooler extension of Barossa and one of the few wine regions of the world in which the great German grape Riesling comes into its own. Australian Rieslings are – not surprisingly in view of the climate – not at all like the German archetypes. Usually called Rhine Rieslings, or just 'Rhine', they have much more body, a bit less acid (although winemakers tend to

Cloud over McLaren Vale in South Australia, which is more often swathed in sunshine.

compensate for nature's deficiencies in this respect), and a host of different flavours (see Section Three) but are none the worse for that. Like all Rieslings, they age well. Clare Rieslings tend to reach 12 to 13 per cent alcohol and to show strong lime or some form of citrus flavours. With five or 10 years in bottle they can become distinctly toasty and some can even survive 20 or more years in bottle. Leo Buring was the great label here. Today much of the fruit is bottled south of the region itself – indeed it is not too great an exaggeration to say that most serious South Australian wine producers bottle an Eden Valley Riesling or Clare Valley Riesling. But dependable producers include Tim Adams, Jim Barry, Jeffrey Grosset, Knappstein Wines, Leasingham, Lengs & Cooter, Mitchell, Mount Horrocks, Petaluma and Pikes Polish Hill, some of whom occasionally manage to make sweet botrytized examples.

This relatively warm region, including **Watervale** in the south, also makes some fine and often extraordinarily ripe Cabernet, as well as some distinguished Cabernet Franc and even Malbec.

LIMESTONE COAST

Coonawarra was Australia's first widely recognized top quality wine region – and it even had its very own grape variety, Cabernet Sauvignon, to prove it. Coonawarra Cabernet can be a glorious thing, with all the structure, intensity and mineral overtones of a classed growth red bordeaux. The key to this flat, visually completely undistinguished mile-wide stretch of vineyards in the far south eastern corner of South Australia is its famous terra rossa, red loam or clay over a limestone base to ensure that quality precursor, good drainage. When the terra rossa peters out, so do the vines, and the wine industry is still doing its best to convert all available land to vines. Razing houses means the elimination of what was already a sparse work-force, and Coonawarra is probably the most mechanized fine wine region in the world.

Some commentators argue that yields are too high, and certainly in cooler vintages some wines can lack sufficient concentration for their austere frame, but there are always wines such as Bowen, Hollick, Parker Estate, Penfolds, Penley Estate, Petaluma's red and Wynns to renew wine lovers' faith in Coonawarra Cabernet. Shiraz and Chardonnay can also prove their worth and Katnook and Wynns have a winning way with Sauvignon Blanc and Riesling respectively.

But the focus of attention in this part of the wine world has rather shifted from Coonawarra with its endless border disputes to the emerging new wine districts here, so numerous as to earn the entire region a name, Limestone Coast.

Padthaway made its name soon after Coonawarra but was such a one-company (Seppelt) wonder that too few operators have had a vested interest in putting the name on the label. Slightly warmer and even more remote than Coonawarra, Padthaway's strong point is white wine, especially Chardonnay, with a fine streak of natural acidity and good, round fruit. Lindemans is now the prime producer, but much of the fruit is vinified outside the region. And the increasing proportion of vines that are grown without over-watering show that they can produce really exciting wines, possibly usefully bigger-boned than many of Coonawarra's.

Just north of Coonawarra is the very similar district known as **Wrattonbully** where there has been an equal temptation to irrigate too enthusiastically for quality. Once the name has been established with consumers, though, local pride will curb this tendency.

Other suitable land in this cool corner of Australia's Wine State is also being prospected at a keen rate. Bordertown near the Victorian border can deliver useful Chardonnay. Mount Gambier south of Coonawarra has shown it may well be simply too cool to ripen grapes reliably every year. Elgin on the west coast has been planted to a certain extent, but the most promising new regions are **Robe** and **Mount Benson**, also on the west coast but a little further north and therefore more reliable. As has so often been the case with new Australian wine regions, the large companies take a major punt on one. Robe is the Southcorp bet, administered from its base in Coonawarra. Mount Benson (sometimes called Cape Jaffa – so many new wine regions start off with more than one name) has been invaded by incomers from as far afield as the Rhône Valley (Chapoutier) and Belgium (the vast Kreglinger winery with local wine producer Ralph Fowler as initial consultant). Wines here, made on usefully poor soils and cooled by sea breezes, can be much fruitier and approachable than Coonawarra's. This is certainly a region to watch, though many bottlers are using the all-encompassing appellation **Limestone Coast** so as to keep their blending options open. This is Australia, after all.

EDEN VALLEY

Higher and cooler than Clare, the more disparate Eden Valley to the east of Barossa is Australia's other Riesling region. Narrow roads curve through the gum trees, past old homesteads on the way to vineyards as high as Adam Wynn's Mountadam (which makes excellent Chardonnay and Pinot Noir and is now run by the Cloudy Bay/Cape Mentelle team) and the neighbouring Penfolds' Riesling plantations. Road signs warn motorists of kangaroos, and parrots skitter through the trees. Rieslings here tend to be slightly lower in alcohol than Clare Valley's, less obviously fruity, and exhibit more floral than citrus characters – although they do become toasty with age. Winemakers many miles away, such as the talented Pam Dunsford of Chapel Hill and many of the Barossa wineries, regularly plunder Eden Valley vineyards for their Riesling bottlings. The family company Yalumba have important holdings here, not least their Heggies Vineyard Riesling (dry and sweet) and some of Australia's best Viognier.

The Henschke family are the wine aristocrats of the Eden Valley and have red wine vineyards of such distinction (such as the famous ancient Hill of Grace planting of Shiraz)

that they regularly make some of Australia's finest red wines from their base near Keyneton high above the Barossa Valley. Indeed Henschke Hill of Grace and Penfolds Grange (two very different wines in terms of style, with grace a particularly apt word for the former) have virtually created the Australian fine wine secondary market between them, fetching extraordinary prices in the saleroom and in more private wine sales and exchanges between Australian collectors.

ADELAIDE HILLS

The Eden Valley shades south into the Adelaide Hills, where an increasing number of ambitious wine producers punctuate the leafy suburbs in the hills to the east of the city with expensive but promising vineyards. Almost all the vineyards were planted in the 1980s or 1990s, in some of Australia's coolest wine country. Acid is rarely added here, and malolactic fermentation is encouraged in most wines to soften the naturally high grape acids. This makes it an unusually good producer, especially by Australian standards, of sparkling wines (Croser at Piccadilly) and Sauvignon Blanc (particularly round Lenswood). Chardonnays can have exceptional depth and ageing ability and Merlots have already proved themselves.

Brian Croser of Petaluma has been the most influential winemaker by far (and this region is about craft rather than industry), but fine wines are to be had under the Ashton Hills, Chain of Ponds, Henschke, Lenswood, Nepenthe, Shaw & Smith and Geoff Weaver labels. Using Adelaide Hills fruit, Shaw & Smith were Australia's first consistent producers of genuinely appetizing, internationally recognized Sauvignon Blanc. Today Adelaide Hills Sauvignon Blanc is seen as one of Australia's classic combinations of grape and place, although new plantings in hilly countryside to the south and east between here and McLaren Vale suggest a bright future for a wide range of varieties, including some fine reds.

VICTORIA

Wine was extremely important to the state of Victoria in the nineteenth century (fuelled by the gold rush), but phylloxera struck and many of its scattered vineyards were abandoned. In the twenty-first century Victoria is enjoying a fascinating and extremely varied renaissance as a wine producer. Even today, the Victorian wine map is more disjointed than that of any other Australian state, although the great bulk of its production comes from the **Mildura/Sunraysia** vineyards irrigated by the Murray River – not that far upriver of South Australia's Riverland (which produces twice as much wine). Victoria can boast Australia's biggest winery, however, Lindeman's base at Karadoc in Mildura, which manages to produce its Bin 65 branded Chardonnay to an admirably high standard for such enormous volumes.

The real interest of Victoria to the fine wine drinker, however, are vineyards old, new and rediscovered further south (the southern half of the state is the coolest part of mainland Australia). Much of the rest of the Victorian wine map is dotted with isolated single wineries such as Seppelt at Drumborg on the far western coast and loners such as Delatite and Balgownie, one of the relatively few survivors of what was once the important wine (and gold) region of Bendigo. These were all included in a large amorphous region known as Central Victorian Mountain Country by those charged with trying to draw up Australia's official wine map. Victorians tend to produce fine, concentrated, characterful wine in cooler conditions than most other Australians.

The cloudy **Yarra Valley** just north east of Melbourne has been making top quality wine for a century and has earned itself a reputation for delicate to bumptious (depending on vineyard location) Pinot Noir such as De Bortoli, Coldstream Hills, Diamond Valley, Mount Mary, Tarrawarra and others. Excellent sparkling wine has been made at Domaine Chandon (Green Point has been the export label) and the historic Yeringberg estate makes a thoroughly complex Cabernet. The admirably idiosyncratic Yarra Yering estate somehow manages to make much more concentrated wines than most of its neighbours, of which the inventively named Dry Red No 1 and Dry Red No 2 are auction room classics.

On the other side of Melbourne and not much further away, and cooled by Port Philip Bay, is **Geelong**, which has also shown an aptitude for Pinot Noir in various Bannockburn bottlings now supplemented by the winemaker's own label By Farr (including some interesting Viognier), Provenance, Scotchman's Hill and Shadowfax (whose Geelong Chardonnay has been particularly successful).

In fact there are isolated vine plantings all along the coast here. Crawford River sculpt a particularly fine dry Riesling.

Melbourne can boast a third wine region within easy striking distance, on the **Mornington Pensinsula** due south across the Port Philip Bay from Geelong. A tight-knit group of small estates such as Dromana Estate, Main Ridge and Stoniers are working hard here to promote the reputation of this promising cool-climate wine region, which managed to demonstrate a real affinity with Pinot Noir and Chardonnay. T'Gallant has had enormous success with both a Pinot Gris and a (drier) Pinot Grigio. Further east is the extensive, but still relatively unexplored Gippsland region where the brightest star in the firmament by far is the defiantly funky Pinot Noir producer Bass Phillip, but we can doubtless expect others.

Within much easier striking distance of Melbourne is **Sunbury** to the north of the suburbs where Craiglee has been making exceptionally ageworthy, terroir-driven Shiraz for decades.

In the **Macedon Ranges**, varied but higher

country to the north, Virgin Hills has been making some of Australia's most cussed reds for decades with Hanging Rock and Knight Granite Hills, while **Heathcote** even further into the interior has developed real glamour as a wine address – thanks largely to the reds, especially Shiraz, of producers such as Heathcote the wine producer, Jasper Hill, Mount Ida and Wild Duck Creek.

In this state, even the smallest cluster of wineries constitutes a wine region. Great Western (now officially known as **Grampians**) was made famous by Seppelt, who have a Champagne-like honeycomb of sparkling wine cellars there, but Best's and, especially, Mount Langhi Giran make great still wines (notably peppery Shiraz and taut Riesling) nearby. The high **Pyrenees** to the north east can boast Taltarni and Dalwhinnie's best bottles as evidence of their potential.

Over in the east of the state, the **Goulburn Valley** is rather warmer and houses two of Victoria's most commercially notable wineries, Mitchelton (which is part of the Petaluma empire) and the historic Chateau Tahbilk. Both make a wide range of varietals but particularly rich Marsanne is a local speciality.

Further east still are the **King Valley,** where Brown Brothers of Milawa are based, drawing their fruit from vineyards at increasingly high altitudes, and, next door and even higher, the so-called **Alpine Valleys**. In the clear air of this subalpine countryside are a number of growers experimenting with a range of particularly adventurous grape varieties – especially Italian grapes which can perform surprisingly well here, as Pizzini and Gapsted have proved.

North of here on slightly lower land is **Beechworth**, a small but growing wine region named after a particularly pretty town and based on the fame of one wine made here, Giaconda's

unusually un-Australian (a cross between Burgundian and Sonoma) Chardonnay. Others drawn to the flame here include Sorrenberg and Castagna.

But Victoria's glory – indeed one of Australia's great gifts to the wine world – is North East Victoria, comprising the historic wine regions of **Glenrowan** and, especially, **Rutherglen** on the border with New South Wales, source of a unique style of rich fortified wines, Liqueur Muscat (from a dark-skinned version of the best Muscat vine) and Liqueur Tokay (in fact Muscadelle). Ultra-ripe grapes are picked, part fermented, the wine is fortified (as in port production) and the result is matured (ideally) for decades in small oak barrels in baking hot sheds so that the wines are like ultra-syrupy, grapey Banyuls with a touch of madeira. Bailey's are prime producers in Glenrowan, although they are rivalled by Chambers, Morris and Stanton & Killeen of Rutherglen. A new, more precise labelling system has been devised whereby a Rare Muscat is nowadays the only sure guarantee of finding the ethereal beauty of a seriously long-aged elixir of the Australian interior.

Typical Australian scene. Lindeman's Karadoc winery in the irrigated interior of Victoria is the country's biggest winery, churning out unbelievable quantities of Bin 65 Chardonnay.

NEW SOUTH WALES

The New South Wales wine map has been substantially redrawn since the good old days when the Australian wine industry was ruled from the Hunter Valley conveniently close to Sydney – and when the average Australian was introduced to wine via Lindemans Chablis (in fact Semillon) and McWilliam's Hermitage (Shiraz). But the focus of the Australian wine business shifted well away from the Hunter decades ago and the really interesting developments in the New South Wales wine business have been taking place on higher, cooler ground in a large arc around Sydney (see map on page 308), which can in parts offer some of the most marginal vine-growing conditions in the country.

Today that cloudy, humid and often swelteringly hot area is known as the **Lower Hunter** and is as much about tourism as about vine-growing. As well as myriad restaurants, motels and hotels, it houses such traditional high achievers as Brokenwood, Lake's Folly, McWilliam's, Rothbury Estate and Tyrrells (who have the distinction of having produced Australia's first commercial Chardonnay – as recently as 1971). But there are now dozens if not scores of newer, smaller wine enterprises in the Lower Hunter, often the dream of a well-heeled city dweller (in the Napa Valley mode). This is virtually all due to the big city's proximity rather than the Lower Hunter's climate which can be extremely frustrating for vine growers. Indeed many grapes and much wine is trucked into the region.

Notwithstanding that, the Hunter's best, certainly most original, wine is its full-bodied dry Semillon (picked slightly underripe, traditionally minimizing the risk of harvest rain) which, after many years in bottle, can become a most extraordinarily entrancing liquid, smelling of burnt toast and tasting of limes. Today a high proportion of Hunter Semillon is picked much

riper, given the same sort of oak treatment as a Chardonnay and peaks much earlier, if less distinctively. For decades the Hunter has also shown that it can produce great, luscious, long-living Shiraz, once famous for smelling of sweaty saddles. Some of the greatest Australian wines I have ever tasted have been Hunter Shirazes made in the 1950s and 1960s – before the Australian wine industry went all corporate and (temporarily) Francophile. Today Margan and Tower Estate are exporting some fine wine from the Lower Hunter (not all of it made from Hunter grapes) but most wineries depend on the healthy cellar door market.

A good hour's drive to the north from the Lower Hunter is the newer **Upper Hunter**, where the vine already occupies half as much land as in the historic Lower Hunter. The Upper Hunter's great advantage is markedly lower rainfall and therefore less risk of vine disease, although both areas can be dogged by rain in the crucial pre-harvest weeks.

This was Rosemount's original base, and although it buys in fruit from all over the country, its most revered wine continues to be the increasingly sophisticated Chardonnay from the nearby Roxburgh vineyard.

It is significant, however, that Rosemount's winemaker planted his own vines in a much cooler area than the Upper Hunter, south west of Mudgee in **Orange**, where lower temperatures are resulting in some much finer Chardonnays – albeit on a very small scale. On the higher slopes of the extinct volcano Mount Canobolas, Cabernet, Merlot and even some Pinot Noir and Sauvignon Blanc can achieve crystalline purity of fruit and refreshing (though rarely tart) acid levels. One particularly large, investment-driven company invaded this small area long after idiosyncratic pioneers Bloodwood, but Brangayne, a typical family business which switched from orchards to vineyards, is also making some very fine wine. This is just one of many new, cooler wine regions being developed in the state.

To the south is **Hilltops**, otherwise known for its chief town Young, where the climate is so cool that its Shiraz tastes much more Rhône-like (black pepper) than Australian (rich and spicy). There are few wineries here yet but many a winery plunders its vineyards.

One of the most intriguing wine regions is that called **Canberra District** even further south. Dedicated pioneers such as the Kirk family at Clonakilla (famous for its Shiraz/Viognier blend) have been growing vines here for many years but the results were for long a local secret. In fact most of the 'Canberra District' vineyards are outside Canberra itself in hills of New South Wales that surround the nation's capital – although BRL Hardy have invested heavily in a winery-cum-tourist destination within the capital's boundaries. On particularly high ground producers like Lark Hill can make a truly fine Pinot Noir, while others prove that this can be Riesling country.

Other nascent, memorably-named cool wine regions include **Tumbarumba** and, on the coast south of Sydney, **Shoalhaven**.

Much longer established is **Cowra**, even further south (due west of Sydney in fact), which has for years been growing thoroughly hedonistic, golden Chardonnay surprisingly capable of ageing. Cowra has long supplied ingredients for blends, especially Chardonnay blends, to bottlers all over South East Australia.

The source of the cuttings for Tyrrell's, Australia's first, Chardonnay was **Mudgee**, one of Australia's most self-sufficient and well-established wine regions on the dry (but still hot) side of the Great Dividing Range. Mudgee has had its very own controlled appellation system for some time and boasts wineries as successful as Huntington Estate, Montrose and Australia's first organic wine estate, Botobolar. Wines here tend to be full-blooded Chardonnays and Cabernets.

But, like South Australia and Victoria, New South Wales has its giant wine factory, this one

Signs at Broke Road crossroads, Hunter Valley – increasingly a playground for Sydneysiders.

dependent not on the Murray river but on the Murrumbidgee, once called the Murrumbidgee Irrigation Area (M.I.A.), now officially known as **Riverina** and particularly famous for the town of Griffith. This is Australia's second most important wine region, after South Australia's Riverland, and has at least a seriously fine, distinctive wine to call its own. Semillon is Murrumbidgee's most important variety by far, although Shiraz is still important. Griffith is distinguished by its small production of often stunningly good botrytized sweet Semillons. De Bortoli (Noble One) and McWilliam's are notable producers but the area is well and truly cherry-picked by out-of-state wineries, too.

There are isolated vineyards and wineries all over Australia's most populated state, none more isolated, indeed idiosyncratic, than Cassegrain way up the coast at Port Macquarie which has been experimenting with hybrids in this damp region.

WESTERN AUSTRALIA

'WA', as this state is invariably known, may grow only a few per cent of the country's grapes, but it produces a very significant proportion of the country's best wine. Although all of the state's vines are grown in the south westernmost corner of this vast state, the most promising wine regions are those on the far south western tip, which are so new that there is still some disagreement about exactly what some of them should be called.

The most established wine region in south western WA is **Margaret River** (whose history dates all the way back to the 1960s), which is as close to paradise as I have been on my wine travels. Three hours' drive south of Perth is a virtually unpopulated surfer's paradise on a coast lined with gentle eucalyptus forests full of wild parrots and the odd kangaroo. Around the small settlement of Margaret River is a cluster of more than 60 wine estates making some of Australia's best-built Cabernets, some exceptionally long-living Chardonnay, a full but refreshing blend of Semillon and Sauvignon Blanc (a local speciality) and the odd successful Zinfandel. Producers such as Cape Mentelle (birthplace of New Zealand's Cloudy Bay), Cullens, Gralyn, Leeuwin Estate, Moss Wood, Pierro and Vasse Felix make an indecent proportion of Australia's most refined wines.

Perhaps partly because Leeuwin's is one of Australia's most successful Chardonnays, Cullens' one of its (few) subtle Cabernet-Merlot blends and Moss Wood one of its longest-living Cabernet Sauvignons, all of them with a track record of exporting, the name Margaret River is known throughout the world – in a way that no other Western Australian region is. Because of this, it was unlikely to remain a sleepy little wine outpost.

Winery labour may still be hard to come by when the surf is up but there is now a number of large-scale operations, not all of them drawing their fruit from the heartland originally developed in the 1960s. Locals are having to struggle to protect their reputation. One ploy has been to emphasize the difference between the various subregions: Willyabrup, where most of the original estates are concentrated (especially good land for Cabernet); slightly cooler Wallcliffe, where Leeuwin, Cape Mentelle and Voyager Estate are to the south; Karridale, where Southcorp's Devil's Lair is even further south, and vineyards way down on the coast near Augusta such as Suckfizzle's can yield some interesting flavours; the warmer Yallingup in the north and the controversially fertile soils of Jindong, or Carbunup, well inland. All in all, Margaret River is in a state of considerable transition from cosy backwater to a typical Australian wine region important enough to have its own internal tensions between the small and the corporate.

If Margaret River has a climatological problem it is that its winters are sometimes too warm for the vines to have a good winter rest. It is not surprising therefore that there is considerable interest in vineyards and potential vineyard sites south of here where influences are more likely to come from the Antarctic than the Indian Ocean. In the northwest corner of a large wine region now officially known as Great Southern, in the Frankland River subregion, the Westfield vineyard, planted in 1967, has supplied some superlative red grapes for wines that would romp away with top national honours for years – particularly for Houghton's top Jack Mann bottling. It was already clear that this was a part of Australia with real potential.

More recently one or two large investors, Ferngrove in particular, have moved in and planted substantial tracts of land close to where Alkoomi had already established a reputation for Sauvignon Blanc, as Frankland Estate has for Riesling and Cabernet Franc. Further east in Mount Barker, Goundrey has been attempting

to apply big company policies to Western Australia, while Plantagenet acquired a reputation
for fine estate Cabernet many years ago.

Between Margaret River and Great Southern is equally feverish planting in Manjimup
and the slightly cooler Pemberton which might
just prove the spot for fine Pinot Noir.

The greater volume of Western Australian
wine is made to the north, however, in generally hotter vineyards close to Perth. The **Swan
Valley**, conveniently close to the state's only
population centre, was the traditional source of
supply, with Houghton (a subsidiary of South
Australia's Hardys) being the dominant producer. Australians buy more of the full-bodied
aromatic, tangy dry white they used to call

*Kangaroos at sunset in Margaret River.
They are a recognized vineyard pest in Australia,
although fences have to be awfully high to
offer adequate protection to young vines.*

Houghton's White Burgundy (sold more dis-
creetly in Europe as HWB) than any other
white. Moondah Brook also demonstrates the
quality of varieties such as Chenin Blanc and
Verdelho in WA's older vineyards.

Today, vineyards are being planted intermit-
tently all down the long coastal stretch south
from Perth almost to Margaret River and producers such as Capel Vale show that there is
much to look forward to.

TASMANIA

Wine production on Tasmania has always been small, but its potential may be on the point of being realized. Some extremely fine Pinot Noirs and Rieslings are already available on our shelves. The proudly self-conscious island of Tasmania south of the state of Victoria is Australia's coolest, most distinctive wine region with a varied climate and terrain quite unlike anywhere on the mainland. A spate of new plantings in the early 1990s had brought the total number of vine-growers to almost 100 by the end of the century, of whom hardly more than 20 make wine, and each of them only on a small scale.

Tasmanians are particularly fond of their own edible and drinkable produce and only about a quarter of the wine produced from their vineyards escapes from the island itself.

The oldest wine producer of note is Moorilla Estate in the south (established in 1958), but among the continually changing roster of hopeful vine-growers who have followed them there is still considerable disagreement about exactly which one of the island's varied wine districts, which tend to be clustered around Launceston in the north and Hobart in the south, is most suitable for viticulture.

Vineyards here benefit from many hours of summer sunlight, but average temperatures tend to be much lower than mainland Australia and in some years flowering and the harvest itself can be prejudiced by bad weather. Some Tasmanian winemakers argue that they should be excluded from the Australian national constraints on chaptalization, adding sugar during fermentation to make up for a lack of natural, sun-ripened grape sugar, so cool are some summers this far south.

Most of the wines are obviously the produce of a cool climate, with their naturally high acidity, relatively subtle flavours and, often, good balance of clean fruit flavour – a build more German than New Zealand. The chief grape varieties planted have been Riesling, Chardonnay, Pinot Noir and Cabernet Sauvignon, and the well-made examples, which constitute by far the majority, tend to age particularly gracefully.

Aromatic, dry whites predominate but many producers, among them Piper's Brook in the wet and windy north east of the island, Freycinet (known as Wineglass Bay abroad) on the east coast and Domaine A in the warmish Coal River Valley north of Hobart, are making ambitiously styled, relatively concentrated reds. Tasmania is yet another place where Pinot Noir may flourish (see New Zealand, Oregon, California, Chile). Other promising producers include Stefano Lubiana and a clutch of new ones in the Huon Valley, which has had exceptional success in the shows that are so important in the Australian wine industry.

Over the years there has been considerable input from foreign, notably Swiss, investors but the island's Chardonnay and Pinot Noir fruit has attracted attention from sparkling wine producers on the mainland. Domaine Chandon in the Yarra Valley has been using Tasmanian grapes for its sparkling wines for some years now.

The small, isolated nature of the Tasmanian wine industry has enabled it to set up its own controlled appellation system for 100 per cent Tasmanian wines, of which it is especially proud.

OTHER WINE REGIONS

Queensland has more land devoted to vines than Tasmania but usually produces considerably less wine, thanks largely to its low annual rainfall. Almost all vineyards are on the Granite Belt where high altitude compensates to a certain extent for low latitude.

Even the arid interior of the **Northern Territory** can boast one winery, at Alice Springs, of interest chiefly to visitors to Ayers Rock.

NEW ZEALAND

In a nutshell: New World wines with crisp
fruity acids.
Grapes: Chardonnay but most famously
Sauvignon Blanc (WHITE)
Pinot Noir (RED)

The New Zealand wine industry, which produces a small fraction of one per cent of the
world's wine, has a real problem. Like the country
itself, it is so small and vulnerable that navi-
gating a safe course across the treacherous
waters of the international wine market can be
extremely difficult. One strong economic wind
and a pronounced list to starboard can threaten
to capsize the craft altogether.

In 1986, fearing over-production, the government encouraged growers to pull out a quarter
of the country's vines. Just seven years later
(thanks to short vintages, and damage done by
the phylloxera louse) there was such a desperate
shortage of grapes that there simply wasn't
enough wine to mount a serious export effort.

The results of fast and furious plantings in
the mid-1990s have helped, however, to introduce more and more wine drinkers to the unique
character of wines from these Pacific islands
three hours' flying time south east of Australia.

New Zealand wines combine the well-
preserved pure fruit flavours of New World
winemaking with the natural grape acidity associated with northern Europe. This crispness,
sometimes piercing and a characteristic of New
Zealand reds as well as whites, is a feature
markedly lacking in the great majority of New
World wines, including most of those still made
in Australia, which is why a number of Australian producers buy wine and even grapes
from New Zealand (especially Sauvignon Blanc
and ingredients for sparkling wine blends).
There is even a theory that the holes in the
ozone layer that are most common in this part
of the world encourage vines to defend themselves, creating particularly strong flavours in
the resultant wines.

Vines in Europe tend to be planted on poor
soils, so yields are low and the grapes can ripen
fairly well despite the high acidity, but New
Zealand's soils can be very fertile, so New
Zealanders have had to devise ways of manipulating their vines, stripping leaves, and making
every ray of sunshine contribute towards the
ripening process. (New Zealand is the home of
'canopy management' – see page 64.) New
Zealand wine producers are allowed to make
an unusually wide range of adjustments to the
basic wine recipe: irrigation, chaptalization,
acidification and deacidification (see How
Wine is Made, in Section Two) are all sanctioned in recognition of the country's extremely
varied climate.

Those wine drinkers outside New Zealand
who have experienced New Zealand wines
(most of them British or American) tend to
regard the country's distinctively fruity way
with the razor-sharp Sauvignon Blanc as the
country's hallmark wine, but in fact this aromatic variety is less widely planted than
Chardonnay which dominates the country's
wine production (Müller-Thurgau used to,
dating back to an era when most advice came
from Germany).

The most significant development in recent
years, however, has been the surge in plantings
of Pinot Noir, now New Zealand's third most
popular grape. Indeed Kiwis have fallen in love
with their domestic answers to red burgundy.
Pinot Noir is planted and made with some
degree of success in all but the hottest, most
northerly New Zealand wine regions. But if a
region is too warm to ripen Pinot Noir sufficiently slowly, it is probably quite good at
ripening the red grapes of Bordeaux and there
is increasing respect both inside New Zealand
and overseas for the country's best Cabernets and

Merlots – even if such styles are available from many more alternative sources than good quality Pinot Noir.

The country's three biggest wine regions by far are Marlborough, Gisborne and Hawkes Bay. Here hundreds of farmers produce grapes, typically just one of several agricultural activities, for one of the country's big two bottlers: Montana/Corbans, which controls an extraordinary 60 per cent of production, and the privately-owned Villa Maria/Vidal/Esk Valley group, which manages an admirable level of quality at the top end.

Two major developments over the past few years have been the establishment of wineries much, much closer to the vineyards that supply them, which has had a thoroughly beneficial effect on quality, and a sharp increase in the number of what New Zealanders call 'lifestyle wineries'. These are smallish young enterprises owned and run by perhaps just one couple seeking a more bucolic way of life than their previous (usually urban) existence. The amount of foreign capital flowing into the New Zealand wine industry is impressive.

MARLBOROUGH

The wide, flat, vine-covered expanse of the Wairau Valley and the mountains around it are now New Zealand's most photographed wine region (see over), but in 1973 the entire South Island was *terra incognita* to the country's wine industry. The Marlborough region at the island's north eastern tip was created by the Montana winery, which bought up sheep-farming land almost by stealth, gambling on its assessment of the region's potential to produce wines that would be as attractive to consumers as to accountants.

Marlborough Sauvignon Blanc seduced the imaginations and palates of thousands of wine drinkers outside New Zealand in the mid-1980s when the first releases of Cloudy Bay trickled on to the British, American and Australian markets. At that stage Cloudy Bay was just a clever name, label and concept dreamt up by

Western Australian winemaker David Hohnen of Cape Mentelle, but the distinctively lush tropical flavours he and winemaker Kevin Judd coaxed from this sometimes austere variety were sufficient to put Marlborough Sauvignon on the international wine map. Other winemakers such as Hunter's established an early reputation for their Sauvignon and Chardonnay too, while the recent increases in grape prices have encouraged all manner of investors, gamblers and local farmers to chance their arm at vine-growing. Although many of them sell their grapes to the bigger companies, scores of them sell wine under their own label, either made by themselves or at the contract winery, which at one stage transformed the country's wine industry by processing South Island grapes for the large companies based in the North Island (or Australia). Australians have long realized that Marlborough can produce vast quantities of this popular wine style that most Australian vineyards are too hot for.

Marlborough Chardonnays can be attractively lean and refreshing – the ripest of them benefiting imperceptibly from some barrel fermentation and maturation, the lightest making an increasing contribution to some fine traditional method sparkling wines. There is also talk here, as elsewhere in the world, of a Riesling renaissance, although the most exciting examples to date have been intensely refreshing sweet wines made in years when the botrytis mould (see page 88) develops. But Marlborough winemakers' great current preoccupation is Pinot Noir. The variety has been grown here for some time, producing light, tart base wines for sparkling wine blends, but ambitious producers are fired with enthusiasm to show the world that Marlborough can make fine, still, flavourful Pinot Noir too. Just south of the Wairau Valley's particularly poor, stony soils, over a range of low hills, is the Awatere Valley, which is notably warmer and can ripen Bordeaux red grapes most years. Vavasour is the star performer here while my favourite producers in the Wairau heart of Marlborough include Cloudy Bay, Fromm, Isabel Estate and Villa Maria.

REST OF THE SOUTH ISLAND

Nelson just west of Marlborough is drier and warmer and the wines taste like it. Neudorf and Greenhough prove that small can be beautiful.

Canterbury, the vast but far-from-intensively-planted wine region south of Marlborough in the hinterland of Christchurch (more English than England), can produce some fine examples of most of the varieties grown in New Zealand. The Pinot Noirs of Mountford and Pegasus Bay come especially to mind. Giesen has a long history of beguiling Pinots of various colours and Riesling.

Otago, or Central Otago, sometimes just 'Central', is one of New Zealand's smaller wine regions but probably its most exciting. In the south of the South Island in skiing and bungee jumping country, the north-facing shores of its lakes provide some stunning vineyard land (and not a few photo opportunities too). Vines have to be planted on slopes to minimize frost danger and maximize reflection and radiation. Otago has already produced some seriously fine Pinot Noir, Pinot Gris and Riesling from the likes of Felton Road, Gibbston Valley, Mount Difficulty and Quartz Reef, with the roster of impressive producers lengthening each year. So widely planted is Pinot Noir here that Central Otago is more dependent on a single grape variety than any other New Zealand wine region.

GISBORNE

The North Island's self-styled Chardonnay garden provides creamy, rather tropical fruit-flavoured grapes, mainly as raw material for the larger producers. It has also produced the country's best Gewürztraminer (notably from the idiosyncratic Matawhero), which can be very good indeed in some years. The estate bottler of most note is The Millton Estate which preached the gospel of biodynamism (see page 65) years before Burgundy's top producers had even heard of it. Millton is also a believer in Chenin Blanc, in as many degrees of sweetness as in Vouvray.

HAWKES BAY

South of Gisborne in much drier country on the east coast of the North Island, Hawkes Bay is New Zealand's most varied and possibly most promising wine region. Parts of it are quite warm and well drained enough to produce fine, concentrated Cabernet/Merlot red wines following on the coat tails of the region's standard-bearer Te Mata estate, established by John Buck, right-hand man to the head of an important British brewery-owned wine merchant in the mid-1960s. C. J. Pask's and Ngatarawa's reputations were built on rather later vintages. More recent stars include Kingsley Estate, Matariki and Unison. Esk Valley, Vidal and Montana's showcase Church Road winery all do their very best here. The most spectacular new winery here is Craggy Range, a massive investment by an Australian businessman.

One particular area is so proud of its well-drained stony soil that it has evolved New Zealand's first (unofficially) delimited appellation, the Gimblett Gravels. Malbec can do well here, along with Merlot and Cabernet, and

Lake Hayes in Central Otago, New Zealand – wine's new hot spot for Pinot Noir.

The vast Brancott estate in Marlborough, which is owned by New Zealand's largest wine company, Montana. Their size keeps their Sauvignon Blanc inexpensive.

Stonecroft has been flying the flag for top quality Syrah (definitely not Shiraz) for years. But Hawkes Bay also produces particularly luscious, ripe Chardonnay in even greater quantity.

REST OF THE NORTH ISLAND

Martinborough, occasionally called the Wairarapa, is one of my favourite wine regions in the world. Not that this rather flat land over the hills and into the rainshadow east of Wellington in the far south of the North Island provides New Zealand's most stunning scenery. But it does provide some of its most consistent Pinot Noir. Producers such as Dry River, Ata Rangi and Martinborough showed how much potential there was in this region for age-worthy, complex Pinot Noir. Stonecutter, Te Kairanga and Voss Estate are carrying on the tradition.

Northland is the official name for the

extensive and varied wine region on the North Island's northern spike. The most interesting wines so far have emerged from tiny **Waiheke Island,** a short ferry ride from the city of Auckland, where Stonyridge is not short of rivals also trying to prove the island's supremacy over Hawkes Bay at producing fine copies of red bordeaux.

Traditionally most of the wine companies had their base in the suburbs of **Auckland**.

Most of them have been moving closer to the large vineyard regions further south and further from the subtropical climate here that can dog vintage time with rain and rot, although Kumeu River manages to make some of New Zealand's finest Chardonnay here. After a few years in bottle, the wine can be a very passable imitation of white burgundy. Kumen River is one of the many New Zealand wine producers to embrace screwcaps, even for reds.

SOUTH AFRICA

In a nutshell: Mainly whites, some bargains and increasingly convincing answers to international styles.
Grapes: Chenin Blanc (WHITE), Pinotage, Syrah (RED) and the usual international mix

One of the exciting things about the wine business is the reliable way in which it mirrors social and political change. The mixed races of the South African population patiently lining up in the hot sun to vote together for the very first time may well be the most moving image we ever see in our lifetimes. As soon as Nelson Mandela was voted in to power and apartheid reliably a thing of the past, wine lovers the world over had to revise the habits of a lifetime and begin to take a positive interest in once-reviled exports from South Africa, of which wine, with its labelling for all to see, is the most obvious.

For South African wine producers the transformations of 1994 heralded an era of potential prosperity, with previously forbidden export markets opened up almost overnight, but also the new challenge of seeing their wines exposed to international competition. One result of South Africa's prolonged isolation was that wine consumers, commentators and producers there seemed almost unhealthily obsessed by the detailed results of comparative tastings.

Thanks to the country's surplus of clean, well-made, bargain-basement dry white (and to systematic export subsidies), South Africa has seen her wine exports grow rapidly. By the mid-1990s South African wines were enjoying the indulgent and optimistic aura which made all things South African glow even if this was, inevitably, only a temporary phenomenon. But the fact that South Africa's wine country is the most dramatically beautiful in the world has surely done little to harm the fortunes of its produce abroad.

One significant development has been the slow transfer of land and opportunity to the Cape's black and coloured majority. Several worker empowerment schemes are now making, marketing and successfully exporting wines made from the produce of their own vineyards. There has been a notable improvement in farm workers' housing and conditions, and education in oenology and viticulture is no longer exclusively a white man's preserve.

Within South Africa's vineyards and cellars themselves, producers have shown how rapidly they can absorb and adapt new techniques and fashions in wine styles. They have progressed as far in the last few years as many others did in the 1980s and 1990s combined. The current objectives are to continue to maximize the quality of their raw material – most obviously systematically replacing the vines whose output has been seriously affected by viruses, but also continuing to understand better which clones are best suited to local conditions (and getting them through national plant quarantines).

Wine has been made on the Cape of Good Hope since the mid-seventeenth century, which means that South Africa has a much longer, unbroken history of winemaking than either Australia or California. Even today the influence of the Cape Dutch, the original settlers, is strong, as witness the scalloped white gables of many a winery and Afrikaans names whose pronunciation many potential wine importers find quite unfathomable.

Only this southern limit of the country (and continent), lapped by the Indian Ocean but cooled to a varied extent by winds off the Atlantic and currents from the Antarctic, is seriously suitable for vine-growing. The climate of the wine regions is in very general terms slightly hotter than California's best known valleys (few coastal fogs here) but not as hot as much of Australia, and ever cooler areas are being sought, found and planted.

Most table wines are labelled varietally (not so the Cape's sizeable production of dessert wines, made in the image of European classics such as sometimes raisiny but steadily improving 'port' and some often oily counterparts to sherry).

The chief grape variety (almost invariably called 'cultivar' in South Africa) by far is Chenin Blanc, which is yet to produce anything as sweet and sour as a luscious Vouvray on the Cape (although Ken Forrester and David Trafford are trying hard), but which can easily be persuaded to produce large volumes of clean, refreshing dry and medium dry white. Other important white wine varieties include Colombar(d) (a significant ingredient in South Africa's cheap dry whites), 'Cape Riesling' (Crouchen), Clairette, Semillon, Ugni Blanc, Riesling, various Muscats and, of course, Chardonnay and Sauvignon Blanc. It has taken South African nurseries time to offer any seriously good Chardonnay cuttings, which may help to explain South Africa's unusually prolonged fondness for Chardonnay blends (notably but not exclusively with Sauvignon Blanc). An increasing proportion of top quality Burgundian clones of Chardonnay are now planted, however, and South Africa Chardonnays made with a gentle hand and sophisticated French oak ageing can represent some of the wine world's great bargains. Sauvignon Blanc, on the other hand, has been planted here for a century and can make some wonderfully self-confident, fruity wines – as well as some very inexpensive, less concentrated ones.

Less than 25 per cent of the country's vineyard is planted with red wine grapes, of which the national speciality is a 1920s Cape crossing of Pinot Noir and Cinsaut called Pinotage. Pinotage is deep in colour and has lots of spicy fruit if made well, although if not fermented carefully it can have a rather chemical, off-putting smell. In the 1980s, it was rather despised as being local and therefore not foreign and glamorous, but as national pride was regained, so was local pride in this lively, aromatic red varietal, South Africa's answer to California's Zinfandel and Australia's Shiraz.

In fact the big success story of recent times among red grapes has been South Africa's own Shiraz, or Syrah as more Francophile producers such as the stylish Boekenhoutskloof call it. Plantings increased sixfold in the 1990s so that it became the country's second most planted dark-skinned grape just behind Pinotage. The variety is made in all sorts of styles but the predominant influence seems to be Australian rather than French, with American oak used more widely than French. It tends to be planted in warmer areas, although it can easily reach uncomfortable levels of ripeness.

Prior to Syrah/Shiraz's ascendancy Cabernet Sauvignon was regarded as the aristocrat of the Cape's vineyards, but it needs careful treatment in the cellar in order to yield a deep-coloured, well-balanced, seriously long-lived wine. Tannins, and in virus-affected vines green, unripe flavours, can be obtrusive. Merlot is increasingly made as a varietal as well as being used to blend with Cabernet. Some increasingly interesting Zinfandel, Mourvèdre and even old-vine Carignan is made by innovators such as Charles Back of Fairview. There are quite substantial plantings of Ruby Cabernet but this is mainly used to bolster inexpensive blends. The word 'blend' is an emotive if mysterious one on the Cape. There is a recognized red wine style known as a Cape blend (as opposed to a wine labelled varietally), but as one who was drafted in to help judge a national competition between them all, I can testify to the fact that there is no agreement as to what exactly should constitute a Cape blend. Pinot Noir is grown only in the coolest spots with any success and even here growers were for long hampered by a lack of Burgundian (as opposed to Swiss) clones. The Cape's port-making heritage has also resulted in significant plantings of port vines such as Tinta Barroca (usually spelt Barocca here) which are often made into substantial dry reds.

It would be a shame if, in their rush to

prove that they too can produce answers to Bordeaux and Burgundy, Cape winemakers ignored the country's potential for creating strapping, stable dry reds.

The South African wine business has a curious structure, with the 100-odd quality-minded, usually small-scale wine producers vastly outflanked by producers of bulk wine, wine for distilling, grape concentrate and, especially, grape juice. Co-operatives are very important, processing about 85 per cent of each year's grape harvest (although only about a quarter of those grapes ends up as wine). It is only very recently indeed that the individual wine estates have even been allowed to buy in grapes, although a separate name must be used for the wine they produce – quite a contrast with most New World wine-producing countries!

THE MAIN WINE REGIONS

Constantia, on the southern outskirts of Cape Town, is the Cape's oldest wine area and one of its coolest. Its sweet white wines were once as famous in Europe as those of Hungary's Tokay. The Klein Constantia winery has revived this style with a 'Vin de Constance' Muscat, although it and Buitenverwachting also make a fine range of dry whites and Bordeaux-style reds. This is clearly excellent terrain, cooled by currents from the south pole via False Bay, for Sauvignon Blanc, as relatively new wineries such as Steenberg have proved. If there were any market for proper Riesling in South Africa (the name has been ruined because the very ordinary Crouchen is usually labelled Cape Riesling) this would almost certainly be the best place to grow it, as Buitenverwachting has proved.

The university town of **Stellenbosch** is regarded as the South African wine industry's spiritual home. The natural conditions of the district vary enormously but most vineyards benefit from the cooling influence of the Atlantic in summer. This is where the country's greatest concentration of dedicated individual estates is to be found, with a traditional reputation for reds but

some increasingly exciting whites too. South African wine law recognizes regions composed of different districts, which are in turn divided into a number of distinctive sub-districts, called 'wards'. Within the wine district of Stellenbosch, where the amounts of rain, sun and heat are pretty perfect for vine-growing, at least five distinct wards have already been identified. One of the best-known is **Devon Valley**, a charmed little enclave with a fine track record in sophisticated reds, while the slopes of the **Simonsberg** mountain are distinguished by being cooler and better-drained than the Stellenbosch norm. Historically, some of the most successful producers in Stellenbosch have been Blaauwklippen, Delheim, Grangehurst, Kanonkop, Meerlust, Mulderbosch, Neethlingshof, Overgaauw, Rustenberg, Rust-en-Vrede, Thelema, Vriesenhof and Warwick Estate but there are now dozens more.

The district of **Paarl** produces even more wine than Stellenbosch and is the headquarters of the powerful KWV organization which for many years controlled the industry's output with stifling regulation and blanket support but is now a free-standing exporter. Much fortified wine is made here, including some reasonably convincing flor 'sherries' (see pages 247–9). The large producer Nederburg pioneered botrytized Chenin Blanc here. Glen Carlou makes fine Chardonnay, Villiera is multi-talented, Veenwouden has a great reputation for its reds, while Fairview is by a stretch South Africa's most innovative and sensibly priced producer. All of them prove there is more to Paarl than heavy fortified wines.

Franschhoek (meaning 'French corner', a reference to early Huguenot settlers) is a particularly favoured ward in the east of the region and boasts wineries such as Boekenhoutskloof, Boschendal, (Clos) Cabrière, Dieu Donné and L'Ormarins/La Motte. Franschhoek's speciality is vibrant white wines but some fine reds (and some fine dining) can be found there too. The ward of **Wellington** is also in the greater Paarl district and, being to the north of Paarl, is

The differing altitudes and expositions of vineyards at Klein Constantia, some of South Africa's coolest, show just how important it is to match vine variety to specific site.

noticeably hotter than Franschhoek and is best for big, bold reds.

Even further inland than Paarl is the district of **Worcester**, the Cape's answer to California's Central Valley. Hot, dry and fertile, the region's vineyards (20 per cent of the national total) need extensive irrigation and produce vast quantities of grapes, raw materials for brandy, inexpensive dry whites, some rich fortified wines and the full range of 'vine products' other than wine. A local speciality is a richly grapey and distinctly sticky fortified Muscat, often labelled Muscadel, which is usually based on Muscat of Alexandria, known as Hanepoot in South Africa.

South east of Worcester, with a similar dry climate but soils more suited to vine-growing (the limestone has encouraged the odd stud farm), is **Robertson**, a notable white wine-producing region with some interesting co-operative wines as well as estates such as De Wetshof making waves with Chardonnay.

To the east stretches the increasingly hot and arid **Little Karoo** where vines, mainly for

South African vineyard
exuberance (above) over
a grape industry which
can offer the most stunning
landscapes in the world, such
as the Boschendal Cape
Dutch manor house
in Franschhoek (right).

bulk produce, tend to be planted close to rivers for irrigation. This semi-desert has its similarities with the Douro Valley in northern Portugal and the wine producers of Calitzdorp in particular have made a virtue of this, producing South Africa's best ripostes to port whose quality can be really quite exciting.

Potentially more interesting for table wine production are the extensive winelands north of Cape Town which can benefit from sea breezes blowing inland off the west coast. **Tulbagh, Piketberg** and **Swartland** are adjoining wine regions west and north of Worcester, which are at low latitudes but enjoy some influence from the Atlantic. Swartland was for years associated with heavy reds but all three regions now produce some thoroughly exportable, and exported, crisp dry whites at low prices, chiefly but not exclusively through the co-ops. Within the Swartland district, for example, **Groenenkloof** ward near the coast is an enclave so cool that it makes some of South Africa's raciest Sauvignon Blancs, and **Riebeekberg** is another ward that shows exciting potential. This west coast, so far not particularly densely planted with vines, is being scouted at quite a rate by quality-conscious wine producers who have coaxed some particularly exciting Pinotage from it.

Olifants River is the northern, Atlantic-influenced extension of this part of the Cape, transforming the waters of the Olifants River into bulk and distilling wine and some crisp dry whites such as those exported, with surprising success, under the Goiya Kgeisje and other labels by the Vredendal co-operative, South Africa's largest winery.

But some of the country's most elegant wines are produced on the southern, Indian Ocean coast where an increasing number of wine estates are chancing their arm in some of the whole continent's coolest spots. If the west coast of the Cape benefits from Atlantic breezes, it is Antarctic currents that cool the south coast so efficiently that it is one of the most promising areas for Pinot Noir in the New World. The ward of **Walker Bay**, the official

name for the vineyards in the hinterland of the atmospheric little seaside town of Hermanus, was the first to prove that viticulture could succeed here. The pioneer was Hamilton Russell, which has fine and increasingly burgundian Pinot and Chardonnay to its credit, but Bouchard Finlayson soon proved this was no isolated feat. Several other exciting enterprises have since established themselves here on this southern coast. Another exciting ward in the **Overberg** district is **Elgin**, once apple-growing country which, as so often, has proved to be ideal for vines too. Sauvignon Blanc and some Chardonnays from Elgin have been very fine, particularly those from Neil Ellis. Even newer, and further east along this southern coast, are **Elim,** which was initially planted with Bordeaux varieties both red and white, and **Mossel Bay**.

If a South African wine is labelled **Coastal Region**, it can come from anywhere within a wide sweep round Cape Town, starting with Swartland in the west, taking in Tulbagh, Constantia to the south and all of Paarl and Stellenbosch. The generic name for most of the most basic wine is **Western Cape**, which does much the same job in South Africa as the term Southeastern Australia does in Australia.

UNDERSTANDING LABELS

estate, this word usually appears on wines bottled on the farm on which all the grapes were grown, a relative rarity in South Africa.
Méthode Cap Classique, South Africa's own term for the traditional champagne method of making wine sparkle.
Noble Late Harvest, sweet wine made from botrytized grapes.
Premier Grand Cru, dry, light, usually blended white, a misleading term occasionally used within South Africa.
Wine of Origin, South Africa's answer to France's AC system, authenticating the grape variety specified on the label, the vintage and the wine's provenance.

OTHER COUNTRIES

Much to the surprise of the rest of the world, **China** is now among the world's 20 most important wine-producing countries, and is certainly by far the most significant producer in Asia after Australia. Its burgeoning wine industry is aimed not just at tourists but also at its increasingly affluent and westernized middle class.

The best red wine I have tasted with a Chinese label was a Lau Lan Cabernet Sauvignon grown in the Turpan Depression in the far west of China is what is effectively an extension of Kazakhstan. Most Chinese vineyards, however, are on the eastern coast where large foreign companies have been actively encouraged to plant western grape varieties as well as local specialities such as Long Yan. Welschriesling is particularly widely planted, although Huadong Chardonnay from the eastern Shandong province which produces about half of all Chinese wine is probably the finest white wine the country produces.

The much smaller wine industry of **Japan** is, as one might expect, commercially more sophisticated, with a great variety of companies engaged in both producing and importing wine. Vines have to battle against all sorts of natural hazards in Japan, including very acid soils and, in the far north, perilously cold winters.

India on the other hand has been exporting some rather sophisticated wine, sparkling white made to a recipe as close to that of champagne as is practicable in such very different circumstances, often sold under the name Omar Khayyam. Much of the rest of India's wine is made sweet and strong for the local market and suffers from typical hot climate faults – a lack of acidity and an excess of alcohol – but Grover Cabernet Sauvignon and Sula Sauvignon Blanc are worthy of anyone's attention.

English wine (the term rather curiously used officially for wine made from grapes grown in both England and Wales) is not a joke, although the average Briton treats it as such. In fact the British are the only nation to assume automatically, and usually ignorantly, that their own wines are necessarily the worst in the world.

About 1500 ha (2500 acres) of southern England and Wales' best-exposed land (sheltered, south-facing slopes) is planted with vines, which would be a complete waste of time at these latitudes were it not for the moderating influence of the Gulf Stream. Wine has been produced in the British Isles for centuries but the modern English wine industry dates only from the 1950s.

The industry today is much more professional and most wine is made by qualified winemakers who usually have experience of cellars in other countries. Because of England's cool climate, only early-ripening vine varieties stand a chance of reliably producing a crop. The most planted varieties are therefore Müller-Thurgau and the hybrid Seyval Blanc. The German crossing Reichensteiner is also quite widely planted but there is an enormous variety of white and some red otherwise. (The few red wines are generally made from red-fleshed grapes or are ripened in special plastic tunnels.)

Almost all grape musts have to rely on added sugar to produce wines with a decent alcoholic strength (see chaptalization on pages 72–3) and the natural grape acidity is usually notable. Such wines can make excellent bases for sparkling wines and there have been some truly refreshing dry whites which can even stand up to some barrel ageing.

British wine is a very different animal, made from reconstituted grape concentrate imported from whichever region can offer the best price (Cyprus has been a common source). These have tended to be very cheap sherry- and port-style wines, strengthened with added alcohol, but the proportion of wine made in the image of table wine is increasing.

VINTAGE GUIDE

Italicized type denotes difficult years; normal type describes average years; and **bold type** is used for exceptional years.

FRANCE

BORDEAUX

Red

2002 Smallish crop dogged by an uneven flowering and a grey, humid summer which meant uneven ripeness in far-from-uniformly healthy grapes. Growers concentrate on the rescue effect of pretty fine weather from September 9.

2001 Very varied quality demanded a gentle hand in the cellar. Some very good wines, others tart or tough.

2000 **Nature's benevolence coincided with the commercial imperative to have a good vintage in this numerically exceptional year. Great consistency and balance.**

1999 Good potential created almost exclusively by three weeks of sunshine from late August was diluted by rain at harvest time. Fairly early maturing wines with better potential on the left bank.

1998 A very hot August was followed by rain during harvest and most of the best wines, some of them very promising, are on the right bank.

1997 Initially overpriced, relatively light wines for pleasant early drinking.

1996 **Some very great, very classical wines that will repay keeping.**

1995 **Hot, dry summer resulted in ripe wines that have been easy to enjoy even in youth. Generous crop levels, best in Pomerol and Pauillac.**

1994 The best year since 1990 but September rains made the wines less charming than their two successors.

1990 **A second scorching year in a row. Very ripe, velvety, concentrated wines at all levels, many outstanding. Sumptuous. A star.**

1989 **A hot summer and huge crop of rich, opulent wines already drinking well.**

1988 Overshadowed by 1989 and 1990. 'Classic' style i.e. firm and a bit austere.

1986 Dense, brooding and extremely slow to show their class.

1985 **Uniformly lovely, fragrant wines especially from the right bank but many need drinking soon.**

1983 Good but less concentrated than 1982, so need drinking. For once, Margaux excelled.

1982 **Legendary year, horribly expensive but very concentrated and so delicious.**

Dry white

2002 **Small crop of concentrated, fragrant wines.**

2001 **The low temperatures of September helped maintain freshness and produced well-etched, fruity flavours with good acidity.**

2000 Summer was if anything too hot to produce nervy wines and most of these were best drunk young, although there are one or two great wines at the top of the tree.

1999 **Some attractive, aromatic Sauvignon Blanc was harvested but the Sémillon fruit was often dilute.**

1998 **Attractive wines with no shortage of ripeness.**

Sweet white

2002 Vineyards near the rivers were blessed with botrytis. Small crop.

2001 **The rain that spoilt the reds made wonderful botrytised whites.**

2000 Some pretty, bumptious wines for relatively short-term drinking but there was too much rain for botrytis.

1999 Those producers who used only the very rich, botrytised grapes picked first produced some exciting wines but quality is extremely variable as later-picked grapes suffered somewhat.

1998 Very ripe with some botrytis. Variable.

1997 **Highly successful with real concentration; some wines approachable quite young.**

1996 **Fine core of acidity; a vintage that may last longer than its two successors.**

1995 Best Sauternes vintage since 1990 with rapid development of noble rot. Grapes picked by early October.

1994 *Grey rot in September, so choose the châteaux that could afford to be fussy.*

1991 After the April frosts a tiny crop was eventually harvested; not bad.

1990 **Massive, rich wines that presently seem a shade less complex than 1989 and 1988.**

1989 **Huge, almost corpulent wines that are dramatic and exciting.**

1988 **Of the fabulous trio of vintages this shows most botrytis and elegance and may, like so many '88s, live longest.**

1986 **A very strong year, plenty of botrytis and beautifully balanced.**

BURGUNDY

Red

2002 Good vintage. Summer was not especially hot, though it was reasonably dry. Sugar levels were boosted in September but some grapes were adversely affected by scattered rains then. Sugar levels were quite respectable in the end and most wines showed their charms at an early stage.

2001 Wet summer with some heat spikes. As for red Bordeaux from this vintage, a gentle hand was needed in the cellar to retain delicacy and not emphasize the already notable tannins. Quite varied quality. Wines from low-yielding grapes will provide exciting long-term drinking but others are gawky. August hail in Volnay.

2000 *A difficult vintage for growers with rain and rot during harvest. Rather soft, easy wines that were more successful in the Côte de Nuits than in much of the Côte de Beaune. Useful early drinking.*

1999 **Exceptional quality and quantity. Powerful, charming and well balanced with great concentration and colour – particularly in the Côte de Beaune. The Côte de Nuits was hampered by a little more rain. Tannins and pigments achieved sumptuous ripeness. A vintage to drink young or old.**

1998 Excellent colour, well-ripened skins in August. Pretty good but sometimes a bit stolid.

1997 A very mixed bag but the best are charming for relatively early drinking.

1996 **High acidity but good concentration are the hallmarks. For keeping.**

1995 **Reduced crop of fine wines for the long term.**

1994 *A year to highlight Burgundy's infamy for variability as too many let yields balloon after the rains. Nuits better than Beaune.*

1993 **Very pretty, fruity wines from healthy, well-coloured grapes. An insider's vintage.**

1992 Rain at the wrong time again. Soft, tender wines to drink young.

1991 **Grapes had ripened before it rained and some wines from the Côte de Nuits are excellent.**

1990 **A great success: rich and fragrant. The top vineyards are majestic.**

1989 **Nearly up to 1990, if not as intense. The best are charming now.**

White

2002 Good quality and quantity.

2001 Erratic weather produced some rot but also some surprisingly good white wines, if not for the long term, as well as some rather thin, disappointing ones. A variable vintage that rewarded those who limited yields. Devastating hail in parts of the Côte Chalonnaise.

2000 **Extremely ripe, sometimes too ripe, healthy grapes with fairly good acidity that were able to charm even in their youth. Especially good for Chablis and the Mâconnais.**

1999 Large crop ripened by fine weather in late August and early September. Generally slightly crisper than the 2000s and the best may last longer - if they are allowed to.

1998 *Everything went wrong: frost, hail, powdery mildew. Respectable, considering.*

1997 Charming wines for early drinking, especially from southern Burgundy.

1996 **A great year for long keeping with backbone and high acidity. Classic Chablis.**

1995 **Very small crop producing wines with real concentration.**

1992 **Balanced, complete; best from the Côte d'Or rather than Chablis.**

ALSACE

2002 Fine weather at flowering followed an exceptionally cold winter so crop-thinning was necessary for high quality. The summer was much better than in most of France but rain in early October threatened the health of some grapes.

2001 Flowering was extended by low temperatures. Late autumn warmth made up somewhat for a coolish summer and wet September which robbed the region of a great vintage.

2000 **An exceptional vintage in every sense with a very early flowering and a very favourable growing season. A little rot of all sorts developed at the end of August and rains in October were sometimes heavy but good quantities of excellent wines, including late harvest styles, were produced.**

1999 *Rain plagued the growing season and brought rot and mildew. Fine weather began in mid-August and continued for a month so that careful vignerons looked forward to good quality but hopes were dashed by yet more rain.*

1998 Early harvest of very ripe grapes; some botrytis.

1997 **Relatively early-ripening harvest of wines possibly up to the standard of 1959 or 1947 in some vineyards with many late-picked bottlings.**

1996 Good healthy ripeness produced a crop of fine, vigorous wines including some late harvest examples.

1995 Varied year in which those who picked low-yielding vineyards well after the rains made great Rieslings, some very ripe. Rot threatened everyday wines. Slightly reduced crop.

1990 A great year; some wines are still youthful.

NORTH RHÔNE

2002 *Poor weather at flowering dramatically reduced the potential crop and paved the way for a thoroughly horrid summer resulting in rotten, unripe grapes. Some growers declassified a large proportion of them although the odd late-picked bottling may surprise. Good white wines though.*

2001 **One of the most successful regions in France in 2001. Almost as good as 1999 if more elegant and less concentrated than 2000. Very respectable levels of ripeness and good acidity and ripe tannins to support them.**

2000 Good to very good if overshadowed by its predecessor. August was hot with heavy rain on August 21.

September enjoyed exceptionally fine weather allowing a particularly prolonged harvest. Both red and white wines are very charming.

1999 Exceptional quality. A sunny harvest saw good quantities of healthy grapes – a cause for real celebration in the northern Rhône. Quality is at least as good as 1998 (some compare it with 1947) and the quantity was much higher.

1998 Notably dry summer with some stress of vines.

1997 Early harvest producing early-maturing, flattering wines with relatively low acidity.

1996 Sturdy, slightly tough wines with notable acidity. Needs time.

1995 Very promising vintage made from healthy grapes.

1991 A very good vintage, superb in Côte Rôtie: fragrant, forward and charming.

1990 The heatwave slowed ripening. Côte Rôtie suffered but Hermitage is a star for monster wines.

1989 A drought year, irregular in Cornas, otherwise rich and opulent.

1988 Unfairly overshadowed by 1989 and 1990, with majestic Côte Rôties for long ageing.

SOUTH RHÔNE

2002 Some terrible flood damage just before harvest although the best producers will doubtless surprise us.

2001 Variable vintage although hopes were high after a very hot, dry summer. An unusually prolonged mistral at the end of August resulted in thick-skinned berries and accentuated tannins. Later harvesting resulted in better-balanced wines – especially in higher-yielding vineyards – but acid levels are dangerously low in some cases.

2000 Conditions were excellent until quite heavy rains arrived on September 19. The results, especially from those who picked early and fast, are plump, approachable wines capable of giving great pleasure even if they will not be the longest-lasting.

1999 Rather more challenging vintage than 2000 for growers and wines with less obvious richness than 1998 for wine drinkers. Heavy rains plagued the harvest and quality is distinctly variable.

1998 Very exciting, concentrated wines with excellent balance and colour.

1997 Rather muddy flavours from well-ripened grapes.

1996 Cooler, wetter summer than usual resulting in wines less concentrated than usual.

1995 Very good colour and really ripe, concentrated reds for the long term. Some producers claim it is better than 1990.

1990 Exceptionally sumptuous, powerful and heady wines with low acidity, already at their peak.

1989 Fabulously concentrated with perhaps more backbone than 1990.

LANGUEDOC-ROUSSILLON

2002 Extremely variable. An unusually grey summer ended with disastrous floods in the Gard *département* in the far east of the region although many growers in the hills were confident of making good wine.

2001 Summer was so hot and dry that some vines shut down and stopped ripening. Rain in September was a relief for those who picked after it although the wines picked too early may be uncomfortably tough. White wines are particularly concentrated.

2000 Devastating floods in November 1999 damaged some vineyards, as did storms in June and July but the summer was warm and dry (though not excessively so) and was followed by a prolonged harvest with some very good quality wine. Lovely, round, supple wines with ripe tannins.

1999 An exceptionally dry winter was followed by heavy rainfall, and some hail in Roussillon at the end of April. Wines are respectable but not as exciting as the vintages immediately before and after.

1998 A superb if reduced crop (much reduced in the case of Chardonnay) of ultra-ripe, concentrated reds with soft tannins and well-balanced whites.

ITALY

PIEDMONT

2002 Piedmont's run of great vintages was finally broken with disastrous hail in parts of Barolo, rot, unripeness and unusually cool weather. The thin-skinned Barbera suffered most in this small vintage.

2001 Excellent quality (and quantity) from an early vintage slightly more in the voluptuous mould of 1999 and 1997 than particularly long term. No shortage of ripeness or structure, but an occasional shortage of acidity.

2000 Great quality, partly thanks to a prolonged heatwave from mid-August to mid-September. Dolcettos were relatively simple but both Barbera and, especially, Nebbiolo were exceptional with excellent acidity as well as ripeness and great definition of flavour. For the long term.

1999 Very good quality yet again for Nebbiolo-based wines, and Dolcetto which was much more successful than the later-ripening Barbera. Voluptuous Barolo and Barbaresco recalls 1997.

1998 Some producers claim this exceptionally hot vintage was superior to 1997. More structure than 1997. Not for the very long term though.

1997 Extremely ripe vintage resulted in great Barbera but Nebbiolos can sometimes lack freshness.

1996 Superb Barolo and Barbaresco for the long term.

1995 Hail-reduced crop of deep-coloured wines made from grapes which benefited from a sunny autumn. Irregular quality.

1994 Sugar and acid levels reasonable despite prolonged September rains.

1993 Nebbiolo and Barbera didn't really ripen before it rained.

1992 A large harvest, generally low on weight and power, declassified by several reputable producers of Barolo and Barbaresco.

1991 A smallish crop of light to mid-weight early-drinking wines.

1990 With colossal power and big aromas these are very exciting, but need time.

1989 A superb healthy crop. Top Barolos are thrilling and will need keeping even longer than the 1990s.

TUSCANY

2002 Exceptionally wet summer resulted in rotten grapes, many of which failed to reach full ripeness. A real annus horribilis.

2001 Smallish crop thanks to April frosts. June and July were dry but August and especially September were quite wet with rain threatening vine health as harvest time approached.

2000 Easy, ripe wines from a very hot, dry vintage which, unless vineyards were extremely well-managed, resulted in wines with a certain hollowness, though no shortage of alcohol.

1999 Quite exceptionally good quality. A vintage not unlike 1997 but with arguably more finesse.

1998 Irregular vintage after exceptionally hot, dry summer which stressed many vines. Some fine wines resulted.

1997 Quite exceptionally successful vintage in terms of quality, if not quantity. Very hot.

1996 Irregular year. Soft, fragrant, early-maturing wines.

1995 Very late harvest saved by an unusually warm, dry October, although acids were unusually high.

1994 The first dry (if cool) harvest since 1990, producing ripe, well-structured wines.

1993 Survived the rains better than Piedmont, concentration held up, but some picked unripe fruit.

SPAIN

RIOJA & RIBERA DEL DUERO

2002 Exceptionally cold winter and spring was followed by nasty wet weather during summer – disastrous for both quality and quantity. Rain persisted even during harvest. Truly a severe test for both regions.

2001 Smaller-than-usual crop because of spring frosts but distinctly superior quality accentuated in some cases by further deliberate crop thinning.

2000 Record crop levels and extremely variable quality with exceptionally high summer temperatures and in many cases a lack of concentration. Some very good wines from Ribera del Duero though.

1999 April frost in Rioja delayed ripening of grapes that suffered thanks to summer rains. Better quality in Ribera del Duero however although harvest rain reduced acidity. Good quality although not quite as good as 1998.

1998 Despite spring frosts, yields were too high to ripen some grapes sufficiently in Ribera del Duero. Quantity was also Rioja's strong suit.

1997 Rain delayed harvest of early-maturing wines. Much better to the east in Penedès.

1996 Particularly successful in Ribera del Duero where ripe, relatively friendly wines were made.

1995 Another frost-shrunk crop in Ribera del Duero. Rioja's bodegas, on the other hand, were swollen by an enormous harvest of ripe, healthy grapes.

1994 Very fine wines throughout northern Spain. Reservas already exceptional, although the crop was small after spring frosts and summer drought.

PORTUGAL

PORT

2002 The usual very dry summer was followed by an unusually wet September which compromised both the health and ripeness of those grapes that were picked. A most unusual harvest and extremely unlikely to produce vintage port.

2001 Exceptionally wet winter but conditions were favourable throughout the rest of the summer. Useful quantity with good not great quality.

2000 Produced particularly luscious, ripe vintage ports.

1999 Hopes were washed away by continuous rain in September.

1997 Early flowering was followed by a cool wet spring and summer. More structured than 1994.

1994 Textbook year for opulent vintage port, fetching prices way in excess of older vintages.

1992 Among top shippers, declared only by Taylor and Fonseca who made superb wines.

1991 Great potential, very rich with considerable structure. A long-term vintage.

1985 A flattering year but one that looked worryingly irregular in the late 1990s.

1983 Good, brisk and sometimes exceptional. Widely declared and often successful in the lesser names.

1982 Declared by only a few houses, these are supple and for early drinking.

1980 Reliable, medium-weight year that has gained in reputation over the years.

1977 Destined to be legendary, these have monstrous weight and power. Similar to 1970.

1970 Superb, big, full and deep. Now ready, will last very many years.

GERMANY

NB. 1991 and 2000 are the only vintages that could be described as anything less than extremely good quality between 1988 and 2002 for Germany's serious estates.

2002 German growers were in general much happier than

their French counterparts throughout the summer but many were finally caught out by rain before harvest in October which meant that few wines above Auslese quality will result.

2001 **A very great, long-term vintage with remarkable levels of both grape ripeness and acidity. A high proportion of top Prädikat wines were made.**

2000 *Very difficult vintage. Early optimism was finally dashed by September rains which severely compromised the health of the grapes. In many cases the earliest-picked grapes were the best because they were the least affected by rot. Early-picked Spätburgunders were relatively unscathed.*

1999 Everything was going so well ... until the rains which began on September 20 and continued throughout the harvest. Careful selection was needed and in some cases yields were too high for real quality. Acids were generally low but some delicious wines for relatively early drinking were made by the best producers.

1998 **Despite a wet harvest and erratic growing conditions, the grapes seem to have produced vibrant, appealing wines with a particularly significant proportion of Eiswein.**

1997 **Smallish crop but very intense, clearly delineated wines with some very sweet, late-picked bottlings.**

1996 **Bright, fresh wines made in reduced quantities from 1995 and ripened by an Indian summer.**

1995 **An unusually warm summer was followed by a cold, wet late August and September, but the late, great Riesling showed its stuff in the Mosel.**

1994 **Horribly variable, but Riesling showed its class with fine quality from the good estates.**

1993 **A nerve-racking year. Rain hit the early harvests but patient growers picked grapes with welcome botrytis.**

1992 Not bad, particularly in the Rhine. Estates had to control yields to overcome dilution and maintain balance.

1991 Ripe, crisp, even slightly austere wines, just the stuff for Kabinetts.

USA

N. CALIFORNIA

2002 Summer started cool and continued very dry, growers had to bite their nails through September waiting for anything like ideal ripeness. A very difficult vintage.

2001 A respite for growers plagued by unusual conditions in both 2000 and 2002 with most varieties ripening evenly when expected.

2000 Long, late, 'European' vintage thanks to an unusually cool, wet summer. There were very real concerns that Cabernet Sauvignon would ever ripen in some vineyards. A particularly good year for Pinot Noir and Chardonnay.

1999 **Very late, dry, cool growing season which depended crucially on ripeness being boosted by a late September heatwave.**

1998 Exceptionally late cliffhanger of a vintage with extremely varied quality. A warm October saved the day after one of the longest springs on record. The mirror image of 1997. More austere winter than usual.

1997 **Very heavy crops in an early vintage which ripened every variety more or less concurrently, although there was some grey rot.**

1996 Attractive, relatively small vintage without the concentration of its predecessor in many cases.

1995 **Yet another region in which a warm, dry autumn and late harvest saved the day after a difficult growing season. Reds, especially Zinfandels, may be even better than 1991.**

1994 **Generally compared to 1991; the slow ripening benefited the reds especially.**

1993 Erratic growing conditions reduced eventual yields. A mixed bag but some attractive wines.

1992 Plenty of good reds and whites though most of the latter are now way over the top.

1991 **A long growing season reflected in unusually fragrant, complex reds although some whites suffered.**

1990 **A modest-sized crop producing many very successful wines.**

AUSTRALIA

SOUTH AUSTRALIA

2002 **Poor weather at flowering reduced yields considerably and was followed by an unusually cool summer and a late harvest. Inland irrigated regions benefited most obviously from this prolonged growing season.**

2001 A vintage that rewarded the quality-conscious. Very hot, dry weather was broken by rain just before harvest in March.

2000 *Very challenging vintage conditions which included poor flowering, hail, exceptional heat in summer and rain during harvest. There were problems with colour stability. Small crop.*

1999 The record crop was more the result of increased plantings than any natural phenomenon. Several years of drought conditions continued. A cooler year than 1998.

1998 **Record crop from an early, frantic vintage despite drought conditions. Some fine reds.**

1997 **Vintage saved by a hot April with some extremely successful Shiraz made, eventually, for the long term.**

1996 **A big vintage at last, with sugars boosted by a late burst of heat. Very successful reds.**

1995 Inconveniently small crop but some good Shiraz and Rieslings, especially in Clare where quantities were better than elsewhere.

1994 Exceptionally dry but not too hot: the resulting wines are deep and structured, especially from Barossa.

WHERE TO BUY WINE

There are basically four ways to buy wine in modern Britain, only one of which bears any relation to the traditional way: buying from an individual wine merchant. We are extremely lucky in this country to have scores of extremely highly qualified, often innovative wine merchants – some of them centuries old, others much younger, sometimes part-time, operations with very low overheads.

The most common way to buy wine nowadays, however, is from a large retail group, either the powerful supermarkets or one of a shrinking number of specialist chains. They rarely offer quite the same degree of service (advice is usually limited to back labels and 'shelf talkers' rather than the more human sort available from traditional merchants) but below £5 a bottle their prices cannot be bettered, so great are the quantities in which they buy. On the other hand, with fine wines available in very limited quantities, a traditional merchant with long-term trading links or a hard-working, well-informed individual is likely to be the better bet.

Wine is also sold by mail order, either by a mail order wine specialist or by the traditional merchants or, increasingly, by the supermarkets and specialist chains.

And then, as more and more Brits are discovering, it is now possible to import wine from mainland Europe, where excise duty levels are a fraction of Britain's. Few European supermarkets are as serious about their wine buying as their British counterparts so a generic, apparently cheap Muscadet bought in a French supermarket, for example, may turn out to be not such a bargain after all. Best to head for growers' champagne or château-bottled claret from reliable producers and vintages, which French supermarkets often use as loss leaders – or for the increasing number of French branches of UK retailers.

These are some of the British wine retailers I most admire, plus comments on the 'multiples':

SUPERMARKETS

Asda, hard-working buying team and keen prices.

Booths, first-rate, family-owned, try-harder northern company.

Marks & Spencer, rarely the cheapest but surprisingly good at inexpensive wines.

Morrisons, northern-based group which tries to offer all wines in all branches.

Sainsbury's, trying to fight back with some smart wines.

Somerfield, trying hard.

Tesco, very wide range in big stores.

Waitrose, decidedly serious, upmarket range. The best of the 'multiples'.

SPECIALIST CHAINS

Majestic, warehouses with interesting selection. Twelve-bottle minimum order.

Nicolas, British extension of the dominant French chain of wine shops. A very different range from most.

Oddbins, the new face of British connoisseurship. Iconoclastic. Truly excellent Fine Wine shops. Now a sister company to Nicolas.

Thresher/Bottoms Up/Wine Rack/Victoria Wine, giant off-licence group operating at many different levels.

Unwins, family-owned chain which has lost its way somewhat.

WINE MERCHANTS

(M) means mail order only; may be a minimum order of 12 mixed bottles.

Adnams, Southwold, Suffolk 01502 727222
Stunning list, real flair.

John Armit(M), London W11 020 7908 0600
Dozens only but very smart wines.

Australian Wine Club(M), Hounslow, Mddx. 0800 856 2004
Australian cherry pickers. Good stuff.

Averys of Bristol, 0117 921 4146
Once a family firm, now a mail order specialist.

H&H Bancroft(M), Cambridge 0870 444 1700
Characterful, hand-picked domaines.

Bennetts Fine Wines, Chipping Campden, Glos. 01386 840392
Admirably interesting selection.

Berry Bros & Rudd, London SW1 020 7396 9600 and Basingstoke 01256 323566
Historic London premises, wide range of classics being revitalized. One of the first into online, and airport, retailing.

Bibendum(M), London NW1 020 7916 7706
Very open-minded and on-the-ball. All the classics too.

Butlers Wine Cellar, Brighton 01273 698724
Good at odd bottles of rarities.

D Byrne, Clitheroe, Lancs. 01200 423152
One hundred and twenty year-old family company with very wide range and great prices.

Corney & Barrow, London EC1 etc. 020 7539 3200
The City wine merchant, and the Queen's.

Domaine Direct(M), London N1 020 7837 1142
Great for Burgundy's top domaines.

Ben Ellis, Brockham, Surrey 01737 842160
Hand-picked range; case sales only.

Farr Vintners(M), London SW1 020 7821 2000
The fine and rare wine specialist.

Fortnum & Mason of London, SW1 020 7734 8040
Fine range and helpful service, at a price.

Four Walls Wine Company(M), Chilgrove, Sussex 01243 535360
Some great old bottles carefully nurtured.

Gauntleys of Nottingham, 0115 911 0555
Enthusiastic, especially about Rhône.

Great Gaddesden Wines(M), Harpenden, Herts. 01582 760606
Wonderfully comprehensive list.

Great Northern Wine Company, Ripon, N. Yorks. 01765 606767
Interesting range and good service.

Great Western Wines, Bath 01225 322800
Friendly local wine merchant.

Peter Green, Edinburgh 0131 229 5925
Wide range and good tastings for wine (and whisky) lovers. Quite traditional.

Handford-Holland Park, London W11 020 7221 9614
Good service and admirably personal selection.

Haynes Hanson & Clark, London SW1
020 7259 0102
Especially good at Burgundy.

Justerini & Brooks, London SW1 020 7493 8721 and Edinburgh 0131 226 4202
Very pukka; Burgundy and Rhône a speciality.

Lay & Wheeler, Colchester, Essex 01206 764446
Probably the best service in the country. Wide range.

Laytons/Jeroboams, London W1 etc. 020 7629 7916
Not cheap; best at France and Italy.

Lea & Sandeman, London SW10 etc. 020 7244 0522,
Lively scourers of France and Italy. First rate.

O W Loeb(M), London SE1 020 7928 7750
Classic wine merchant particularly strong on Burgundy and the Rhône.

Morris & Verdin(M), London SE1 020 7921 5300
Excellent at Burgundy and California.

James Nicholson, Crossgar, N. Ireland 01396 830028
Very fine list.

Nickolls & Perks, Stourbridge, Worcs. 01384 394518
Extremely fine, and a good website too.

Nobody Inn(M), Doddiscombsleigh, Devon 01647 252394
Idiosyncratic business run by a wine nut.

Philglas & Swiggot, London SW11 020 7924 4494
Originally a jokey Oz outfit but now much, much more.

Raeburn Fine Wine, Edinburgh 0131 332 5166
Fastidious buying from all over the world.

Reid Wines(M), Hallatrow, Bristol 01761 452645
Great list, specializing in the old and odd.

La Réserve, London SW3 etc. 020 7589 2020
Fine wines of Chelsea. Quality is all.

Howard Ripley, London SW18 020 8877 3065
Topnotch Burgundy and German specialist.

Roberson, London W14 020 7371 2121
Big, user-friendly wine store.

Selfridges, London W1 020 7629 1234
Very wide range, particularly strong on champagne.

Tanners, Shrewsbury 01743 232400
Well-run yeoman chain with real dynamism and not greedy pricing.

T&W Wines, Thetford, Norfolk 01842 765646
Best at the best.

Uncorked, London EC2 020 7638 5998
Extremely sharp fine wine specialist in the City.

Valvona & Crolla, Edinburgh 0131 556 6066
Great Italian specialist. Great café too.

La Vigneronne, London SW7 020 7589 6113
Tiny shop, wide range of real character and great tastings.

Vin du Van (M), Appledore, Kent 01233 758727
Entertainingly idiosyncratic Australian specialist.

Vintage Roots(M), Reading 0800 980 4992
Organic wine specialist.

Wimbledon Wine Cellar, London SW19 and W4
020 8540 9979
Very personal indeed.

The Winery, London W9 020 7286 6475
Good on fine finds.

The Wine Society(M; membership fee £40),
Stevenage, Herts. 01438 741177
Great labels, good wines and members can store their own wine here too.

The Wine Treasury(M), London SW8 020 7793 9999
Dozens of appetizing exclusivities; US a speciality.

Peter Wylie(M), Cullompton, Devon 01884 277555
Specialist in the very old and very rare.

Yapp Bros(M), Mere, Wilts. 01747 860423
Experienced Rhône and Loire specialist.

Noel Young, Trumpington, Cambs. 01223 844744
Great wines, specially Austrians and Australians.

How to Find out More

Wine courses

Wine and Spirit Education Trust, 1 Queen Street Place, London EC4 1QS 020 7236 3551
Official, carefully structured wine trade courses, including tastings, at all levels leading, eventually, towards the Master of Wine examination.

Winewise, 107 Culford Road, London N1 4HZ 020 7254 9734
Informal courses for keen amateurs at several levels led by a first-rate wine teacher, Michael Schuster.

Christie's Wine Courses, 63 Old Brompton Road, London SW7 3JS 020 7581 3933
Very smart wines, variable lectures on, mainly, the classic regions.

Further reading

Magazines/newsletters

Decanter, 2–6 Fulham Broadway, London SW6 1AA 020 7610 3929

International Wine Cellar, PO Box 20021, Cherokee Station, New York, New York 10021

La Revue du Vin de France, B450, F60732 Ste-Généviève, France

The Vine, 76 Woodstock Road, London W14 1EQ 020 8995 8962

Wine, 6–8 Underwood Street, London N1 7JQ 020 7549 2572

The Wine Advocate, PO Box 311, Monkton, Maryland 21111, USA 001 410 329 6477

Wine Spectator, 387 Park Avenue South, New York, New York 10016, USA 001 212 684 4424

Annual buyer's guides

Le Classement des Meilleurs Vins de France, Bettane & Desseauve, La Revue du Vin de France
Le Guide Hachette des Vins, Paris
James Halliday's Australia and New Zealand Wine Companion
Hugh Johnson's Pocket Wine Book, Mitchell Beazley
Italian Wines, Slow Food Editore
John Platter's South African Wine Guide, Hermanus, South Africa
Which? Wine Guide, Consumers Association and Penguin

General

Hugh Johnson and Jancis Robinson, *World Atlas of Wine* (5th edn), Mitchell Beazley 2001
Jancis Robinson (ed), *The Oxford Companion to Wine* (2nd edn), OUP 1999
Tom Stevenson, *The New Sotheby's Wine Encyclopedia*, Dorling Kindersley 1997

Specific fine and rare wines

Michael Broadbent, *Michael Broadbent's Vintage Wine*, Little, Brown/Websters 2002

Specific regions

France
Hubrecht Duijker, *The Bordeaux Atlas*, Segrave Foulkes 1997
Jacqueline Friedrich, *A Wine and Food Guide to the Loire*, Mitchell Beazley 1997
Anthony Hanson, *Burgundy* (2nd edn), Faber 1995
Andrew Jefford, *The New France*, Mitchell Beazley 2001
John Livingstone-Learmonth, *The Wines of the Rhône* (3rd edn), Faber 1992
Remington Norman, *Rhône Renaissance*, Mitchell Beazley 1995
Remington Norman, *The Great Domaines of Burgundy* (2nd edn), Kyle Cathie 1996
Robert M Parker Jr, *Bordeaux* (3rd edn), Simon & Schuster 1998
Robert M Parker Jr, *Wines of the Rhône Valley* (2nd edn), Simon & Schuster 1997

Elsewhere
Stephen Brook, *The Wines of California*, Faber 1999
Bruce Cass (ed), *The Oxford Companion to the Wines of North America*, OUP 2000
Lisa Shara Hall, *Wines of the Pacific Northwest*, Mitchell Beazley 2001
James Halliday, *Wine Atlas of Australia and New Zealand*, HarperCollins 1998

A good read

Gerald Asher, *On Wine*, Norman and Hobhouse 1983
Simon Loftus, *Anatomy of the Wine Trade*, Sidgwick & Jackson 1985
Simon Loftus, *A Pike in the Basement*, Flamingo/Fontana 1989
Kermit Lynch, *Adventures on the Wine Route*, Bodley Head 1989
Jancis Robinson, *Confessions of a Wine Lover*, Penguin/Viking 1997

Superior wine websites

www.burghound.com
www.erobertparker.com
www.jancisrobinson.com
www.marksquires.com
www.superplonk.com
www.wineaccess.com
www.wineanorak.com
www.wineloverspage.com
www.wine-pages.com
www.winespectator.com

PICTURE CREDITS

The publisher thanks the photographers and organizations for their kind permission to reproduce the following photographs in this book.

2 Bilderberg/Klaus Bassemeyer; 3 Cephas/Mick Rock; 6 left Jerry Alexander; 6 right Cephas/Mick Rock; 7 Simon McBride; 10–1 Cephas Picture Library/Steven Morris; 14–5 Clay Perry; 19 Cephas Picture Library/Wine Magazine; 21 Matt Prince; 22–7 Paul Bricknell; 31 Cephas Picture Library/Mick Rock; 35 Jerry Alexander; 39 Véron/Skinner; 42 Peter Anderson; 43–7 Paul Bricknell; 55 Guy Bouchet; 58–9 Cephas Picture Library/Mick Rock; 63 Anthony Blake Photo Library/Gerrit Buntrock; 66 Scope/Jean–Luc Barde; 70–5 Cephas Picture Library/Mick Rock; 78 Amphora Design; 79 above Amphora Design; 79 below Michael Busselle; 82 above Cephas Picture Library/Andy Christodolo; 82 below Amphora Design; 83 above Jerry Alexander; 83 below Anthony Blake Photo Library/Gerrit Buntrock; 86 Cephas Picture Library/Mick Rock; 87 Jerry Alexander; 90 above Cephas Picture Library/Mick Rock; 90 below left Alastair Miller; 90 below right Jerry Alexander; 91 Angela Muir; 94–5 Cephas Picture Library/Mick Rock; 98 Jerry Alexander; 99 Richard McConnell; 102 Robert Harding Picture Library/Explorer; 103 Patrick Eagar; 106 Scope/Jean–Luc Barde; 107 Cephas Picture Library/Mick Rock; 110 Scope/Jacques Guillard; 110–1 Cephas Picture Library/Mick Rock; 114–5 Anthony Blake Photo Library/Gerritt Buntrock; 115 Patrcik Eagar; 118 Scope/Jacques Guillard; 119 Patrick Eagar; 122 Cephas Picture Library/Mick Rock; 122–3 Cephas Picture Library/Mick Rock; 126 Jan Traylen/Patrick Eagar; 127 Cephas Picture Library/Mick Rock; 128 Simon McBride; 131 Cephas Picture Library/Mick Rock; 134 above Explorer/N Thibaut; 134 below Cephas Picture Library/Ted Stefanski, 134–8 Cephas Picture Library/Mick Rock; 139–42 Patrick Eagar; 143–7 Cephas Picture Library/Mick Rock; 150 above Cephas Picture Library/Mick Rock; 150 below Patrick Eagar; 151 Cephas Picture Library/Mick Rock; 154–5 Cephas Picture Library/R&K Muschenetz; 159–63 Véron/Skinner; 167–70 Cephas Picture Library/Mick Rock; 174 above André Martin; 174 below Serge Chirol; 175 Alastair Miller; 178 Agence Top/Marie–José Jarry/Jean–François Tripelon; 178–82 Cephas Picture Library/Mick Rock; 183 Richard McConnell; 186 Alastair Miller; 187 Scope/Jean–Daniel Sudres; 190 Scope/Jacques Guillard; 190–1 Images Photoeque/Carcanague; 194 Scope/Jean–Luc Barde; 195 André Martin; 199 Scope/Daniel Faure; 203 Cephas Picture Library/Mick Rock; 207 Agence Top/Pascal Chevallier; 210 Robert Harding/Mike Newton; 212 Anthony Blake Photo Library/Maureen Ashley; 213 Joe Cornish; 216–7 Patrick Eagar; 218 Simon McBride; 219 Joe Cornish; 223 ABPL/John Sims; 224–5 Simon McBride; 226–31 Robert Harding/Mike Newton; 233–41 Cephas Picture Library/Mick Rock; 244 Robert Harding/Michael Busselle; 246 Robert Harding/Robert Frerck/Odyssey/Chicago; 249 Agence Top/Robert Tixador; 252 Cephas Picture Library/Mick Rock; 253 Robert O'Dea; 254 Patrick Eagar; 255 Cephas Picture Library/Mick Rock; 258 Jerome Darblay; 259 Scope/Jacques Guillard; 263 Michael Busselle; 267 Cephas Picture Library/Nigel Blythe; 271–5 Cephas Picture Library/Mick Rock; 279 Bilderberg/Hans Madej; 284–5 Agence Top/G Sioen; 288 Cephas Picture Library/Ted Stefan; 289 Jerry Alexander; 291 Cephas Picture Library/R&K Muschenetz; 293 Robert Harding/Jeff Greenberg/MR; 294–7 Cephas Picture Library/Mick Rock; 300 left South American Pictures/Sue Mann; 300 right Marcelo Montacino; 301 Cephas Picture Library/Rick England; 304–5 Cephas Picture Library/Andy Christodolo; 306 Patrick Eagar; 310 Bilderberg/Eberhard Grames; 311 Zefa; 313–5 Patrick Eagar; 319 Cephas Picture Library/Mick Rock; 321 Patrick Eagar; 323 Cephas Picture Library/Kevin Judd; 327 Image State; 328–9 Cephas Picture Library/Rick England; 333 Cephas Picture Library/Juan Espi; 334 left VISA/A Lorgnier; 334 right Cephas Picture Library/Alain Proust.

INDEX